Herbert S Skeats

A History of the Free Churches of England

from AD 1688 - AD 1851. Second Edition

Herbert S Skeats

A History of the Free Churches of England
from AD 1688 - AD 1851. Second Edition

ISBN/EAN: 9783337166120

Printed in Europe, USA, Canada, Australia, Japan

Cover: Foto ©ninafisch / pixelio.de

More available books at **www.hansebooks.com**

A HISTORY

OF THE

FREE CHURCHES

OF ENGLAND,

FROM

A.D. 1688—A.D. 1851.

BY

HERBERT S. SKEATS.

𝔖𝔢𝔠𝔬𝔫𝔡 𝔈𝔡𝔦𝔱𝔦𝔬𝔫.

LONDON:
ARTHUR MIALL, PUBLISHER,
18, Bouverie Street, E.C.

1869.

PREFACE TO THE FIRST EDITION.

When I resolved upon writing this History I had two purposes in view. I wished to give some information to the members of the various Free Churches of certain details in the ecclesiastical life of England, to which, in my judgment, a sufficiently prominent importance had not hitherto been assigned, and I wished to convey, to persons who stood outside the pale of every Free Church, a correct impression of the part which English Dissent has played in the history of England. With regard to the latter subject, there has seemed, to me, to be a great ignorance in most political circles. I think that England could never have been a country of which Englishmen of the present day could be proud but for the existence and action of Dissent. I think that the best—and those that are universally acknowledged to be the best—features in its political and social constitution, and in its mental as well as its religious life, can be traced to the direct or indirect influence of the principles of Dissent upon the course of legislation. I shall be satisfied to have written this work if I shall have excited or increased a disposition to study this subject as it should be studied by English public writers and English statesmen.

With regard to the separate Free Churches, I have endeavoured neither to exaggerate nor to diminish the facts of their history. I could have little reason for doing so, for I attach comparatively small importance to any of the distinctions which separate the Free Churches from each other. The history of the last forty years is intentionally given with less detail than is that of the previous period. It cannot well be written until more of its lines are completed.

Having completed my labour, I now feel that

> "The field was spacious I designed to sow,
> With oxen far unfit to draw the plough."

Herbert S. Skeats.

London, December, 1867.

PREFACE TO THE SECOND EDITION.

It is naturally a source of gratification to me that a Second Edition of this work should be called for. I have revised the text, but have found it to be impossible, within the time allotted to me, to add to it. My thanks are due to several correspondents who have suggested verbal alterations.

London, April, 1869.   H. S. S.

CONTENTS.

CHAPTER I.

INTRODUCTORY.

REVIEW of Ecclesiastical history from Reformation to Revolution, 2.—Changes in government, doctrine, and ceremonies of Church of England during that period, 2.—Henry VIII. "Supreme Head" of the Church, 3.—The Six Articles, 5.—Persecution of dissentients, 6. —Edward VI. and the First Book of Common Prayer, 7.—Revised, and use of enforced by second Act of Uniformity, 8.—John Hooper, afterwards Bishop of Gloucester, asserts the spirituality of Christ's kingdom, 8.—Further reformation of the Church arrested after Edward's reign, 12.—Queen Elizabeth "Supreme Governor" of the Church, 13.—Third Act of Uniformity, 14, rigidly enforced by Parker, 14.—Thomas Cartwright, leader of the Puritans, 15, opposed by Whitgift, 15.—Character of the Puritan struggle, 16.—The first "silenced" conventicle at Wandsworth, 1572, 21.—Early churches of Baptists, Independents, and Brownists, 22.—Baptists, the "proto Evangelists" of the voluntary principle, 24.—Barrowe, Greenwood, and Penry, 26.—Committed to the gallows, 27.—Hooker, his "Ecclesiastical polity," 29.—Whitgift's "Lambeth Articles," 31.—Calvinistic and Arminian Controversy, 32.—Banishment of Brownists and Anabaptists to the Continent by Queen Elizabeth, and consequent formation of Independent Churches in Holland, 33.—James I.'s new translation of Scriptures, and framing of Canons by Hampton Court Conference Convocation, 37.—James's treatment of Puritans, and exiled Brownists and Anabaptists. Second migration of the latter to Holland; among them John Robinson, Brewster, Smyth and Helwys, 39.—Dissensions among these, causing divisions of Pædo-Baptists, and Anti-Pædo-Baptists, 41.—Smyth and Helwys and the Baptists on the limits of civil authority, 41.—Robinson's church in Leyden, 42; Henry Jacob's church in London, the first in that period (A.D. 1616), 45.—Discussions raised by the Puritans; Selden's tithes; Bound's obligations of the Sabbath. The Book of Sports, 45—48.—Particular

Baptists, 48.—Growth of the sects, 49.—Progress of Free Christianity after death of Charles I., 51.—The Westminster Assembly, 52.—Comprehension of Independents refused by Presbyterians, 53.—The proposal resisted by a few Independents, 52—44.—Liberty of Conscience saved by the Parliamentary Army; "Pride's Purge," 56.—Religious liberty enjoyed under the Commonwealth; Triers; improvement in character of the clergy, 57.—Views on toleration; Cromwell and Milton in advance of the clergy, 60—62.—The religious leaders of this period men of learning, 63.—Popular errors as to manners of the Puritans of the Commonwealth, 63—66.—Religious zeal among the Baptists; Vavasour Powell; William Kiffin, 66.—Independents the founders of the "Society for the Propagation of the Gospel," 67.—Rise of the Quakers; Fox, 67—70; persecuted during the Protectorate, chiefly by Presbyterians and Independents, 70.—Charles II.; the Savoy Conference, 72.—Ejectment of two thousand clergymen (1662), and rapid increase of Nonconformists, 74.—Legislative enactments to check their influence, 75.—Their sufferings; savage persecution of the Quakers, 75—77.—Attempts at comprehension, 78—80.—James II., 80.—Penn unjustly accused of servility, 81—83.—The Seven Bishops and the "Declaration;" Dissenters sympathize with them, 83, 85.—With James II. ended the despotic rule of the Church of England, 85.

CHAPTER II.

THE REVOLUTION TO THE COMPREHENSION BILL. A.D. 1688-89.

DEATH of eminent Nonconformists previous to 1688-89.—Feeling of Bishops towards Dissenters, 90.—Condition and numerical strength of Dissent at this period, 91.—Character of Nonconformist preaching, 93; patronized by eminent persons, 94, 95.—Academies of learning for Dissenting ministers, 96.—Comparative piety of clergy and Nonconformists, 97.—Declaration of the Prince of Orange concerning toleration, 98; his reception by the clergy and Dissenters, 99—103.—Twelve bishops out of fourteen vote against his taking the Crown, 105; William's religious views an obstacle to his friendly reception by the bishops and clergy, 105—108.—Debate on Coronation Oath, 109.—Oath of Supremacy and Allegiance and Corporation Act, 110, 111.—The nonjuring bishops and clergy, 112; their position analogous to that of Anglo-Catholics of recent times, 114.—Proposal to introduce a clause abolishing the sacramental Tests into the Bill of Settlement defeated, 116.—This decision affected by Whig votes; the Whig families now the rulers of the nation, 118—121.—Bishop Burnet, 122; his views on toleration and comprehension, 123.—

Tillotson, Tenison, and Stillingfleet, and their feelings towards Nonconformists, 124, 125.—Religious liberty supported by the highest intellectual power in House of Commons, 125.—Dissenters themselves mainly indifferent to Test and Corporation Acts, because they expected a comprehension scheme, 127.—Toleration Act passed, 128.—Howe on Toleration, 129.—Provisions of Toleration Act, 130.—The Quakers dissatisfied with it, and thenceforth denounced all compulsory exactions, 132.—John Locke also dissatisfied with it, 132; his "Letters on Toleration" strike at the root of all State Churches, 134—138.—A Bill for "Comprehension" introduced into the House of Lords by Earl of Nottingham, 140; nomination of a commission, 144; proposed alteration in services, &c., 146; prorogued and dissolved without result, 147.—Different opinions on the failure of the scheme, 148—150.

CHAPTER III.

THE COMPREHENSION BILL TO THE SCHISM BILL, A.D. 1689—1741.

NUMERICAL strength of Dissent, 151.—The Quakers; Fox, Barclay, Penn, Whitehead, 151—153.—The Baptists; Kiffin, Knollys, Keach, Gifford, 154; Assembly of Baptist Churches, 157; their resolutions as to maintenance of and preparation for the ministry, 158—160.—General Baptists; Russel and Caffin; Assembly of and Confession of Faith; declaration against civil establishments, 161—164; declension, as a denomination during William's reign, 164.—The Independents; Mead, Chauncey, and Lobb, 167—168.—The Presbyterians, Baxter, Bates, Howe, Annesley, Sylvester, Dr. Williams, and others, 169—172.—Proposals for union of Congregationalists and Presbyterians, 172; terms or "Heads of Agreement" framed by Committee, 172—174.—Laymen not consulted, 174.—The new union imperilled and virtually dissolved by the Rothwell and Antinomian Controversies, 175—180.—Presbyterians charged with Socinianism, 183.—Act passed, prohibiting the publication of Socinian opinions, 185.—De Foe on the sin of occasional conformity, 188.—Howe's reply. 190.—Discussion on the rights of Convocation between Binkes, Wake, Atterbury, Burnet, and others, 191—194.—Convocation summoned in 1701, 193.—Disputes of Upper and Lower House, 194, 195; in abeyance after the death of William, 196.—The High Church sympathies of Queen Anne, and her contemptuous treatment of Dissenters, 198.—Accession of Godolphin and Marlborough to power, 199.—Sacheverell and Samuel Wesley stir up a war against Dissent, 200—202.—Replied to by Palmer, Owen, and De Foe, 203—205.—De Foe's "Shortest Way with Dissenters," 206—210; his prosecution and punishment, 211; forsaken and reproached by Dissenters, 211.—Conference between Lords and Commons on occasional Conformity, 215; the Bill of the Commons against "Occasional Conformity" rejected by Lords, and ultimately dropped, 217.—Similar fate of a second Bill; this result chiefly owing to influence of Tenison and Burnet, 220.—The controversy transferred to the people, 221.—De Foe's denunciation of the conformity of Dissenters, 222.—A further attempt and failure to pass the Bill, 224.—Controversy on Church and Dissent; publication of a "Collection of Cases," 226.—Hoadly and Calamy, 227—229.—Calamy's character, position, and writings, 229—230.—Dr. Drake raises the "Church in danger" cry, 231; his "memorial" burned in public, 233.—Resolution of the Lords and Commons on the "Church in Danger" question, 235, 236.—Proposals for legislative union with Scotland, 237; resisted by clergy; encouraged by Dissenters; passed, 238.—Sacheverell's sermon and impeachment, 240; his popularity, 242; condemned to three years' suspension, 243; triumphant progress through the country, 244.—Diminishing influence and isolation of Dissenters about this time, 248.—The Presbyterians and their clergy, 249, 250; Matthew Henry, 251; Lady Hewley's Charity, 251.—The Congregationalists, 252.—Isaac Watts, 252—254; his hymns eagerly used, 254; the link between Puritanism and Methodism, 257.—Neal, Burgess, Bradbury, Clarke, Earle, and Jollie, 259—260.—The Baptists; Stennett, Pigott, Collins, Gale, Mitchel, Crossly, 262; position of the denomination, 263.—The Quakers; their sufferings for church-rates; the founders of home missionary enterprise, 263, 264.—All the sects unaggressive in relation to their civil and political position, 264.—Queen Anne's Bounty, 266.—Occasional Conformity Act again introduced and passed, 267.—Viscount Bolingbroke introduced a Schism Bill, to curtail the power of Dissenters, 269; passed and received royal assent, 273; death of Anne before it became law, 274.—Accession of George I., 274.—Withdrawal of De Foe from political labours, 275, 276.

CHAPTER IV.

FROM THE SCHISM ACT TO THE ORGANIZATION OF DISSENTING DEPUTIES. A.D. 1714—1732.

POPULAR outbreak against Dissenters, and the Government of George I., 277—279.—Neal's Census of the Free Churches in 1715, 180; analyzed and results, 282.—Agitation for religious liberty, 284. The King favourable to it, 285.—Bill for strengthening the Protestant interest, 286—288; carried, 288.—Test and Corporation Act unrepealed, 290.—Bishop Hoadly's sermon on the Nature of the Kingdom or Church of Christ, or the Bangorian Controversy, 291—293. — Condemned by Convocation, 294.—Growth of Unitarianism, 295—298.—Dr. Samuel Clarke, 297.—Thomas Emlyn, 299; fined for advocating Unitarian views, 300.—Unitarianism among Nonconformists, 302.—Peirce, 302; charged with Heresy; The Exeter disputes, 303—305.—The Salters' Hall Controversy, 306.—Subscribing and non-subscribing ministers, 307.—Spread of Unitarianism, 310.—Unitarians a distinct body, 311.—Abandonment of creeds, 313.—Intensity of faith supplanted by breadth, 315.—Agitation of Quakers for substituting affirmations for oaths, 315.—Bill introduced and passed, 316—318.—Origin of the English "Regium Donum," 319; a bribe to Dissenting ministers, 319; its demoralizing effects, 321.—Fund for relief of widows of Baptist ministers, 322.—Thomas and John Hollis, 323.—The Deistical Controversy, 326.—Blount, Shaftesbury, Collins, Woolston, and Tindal, 325—327.—Liberal views and conciliatory temper of defenders of revealed religion, 328.— Lardner, Sherlock, and others, 329—332.—Dr. James Foster, 331.— Warburton's "Divine Legation," and Butler's "Analogy," 332.— Deterioration of spiritual life the result of controversy, 332.—Decline of Dissent, 335.—Philip Doddridge, 336; defends Dissenting cause, 337.—Proposed renewed agitation on Test and Corporation Acts, and formation of Dissenting deputies, 339.

CHAPTER V.

FROM THE ORGANIZATION OF THE DISSENTING DEPUTIES TO THE ESTABLISHMENT OF METHODISM. A.D. 1732—1744.

TEST BILL introduced and lost, 341.—Better success of the Quakers in reference to tithes, 341.—Defeated in the House of Lords, and mortification of Walpole, 343.—Renewed efforts of the Deputies, 345.—Their success and vigour owing largely to Dr. Benjamin Avery, their chairman, 346.—Mr. Baskerville, and occasional conformity among the Baptists, 347.—John Wesley, 348; nurtured as a Churchman, 349; goes to Oxford, 351; holy life there of himself, 349; and his brother Charles, 351.—George Whitefield, 351; joins Wesley's "Holy Club," 352.—Wesley and the Moravians, 353.—Whitefield's preaching, and the opposition of clergy, 355.—Churches closed against him, 356.—Field preaching in the West of England, and intense religious fervour, 357.—Visits America, 359.—Wesley and revivals, 360.—Wesley determined by lot and Bibliomancy to join Whitefield in Bristol, 351.—Methodist societies established, 363.—

Separation of Whitefield and Wesley, 365.—Friendship soon renewed, 366.—Whitefield again in England, and great revival of religion, 367.—Persecution and danger, 368.—Continued labours and persecution of the Wesleys, 369—371.—Establishment of Classes, and rise of lay preachers, 372.—Maxwell and Nelson, 373.—Organization of Methodism, 374.—Wesley denies that he is a Dissenter, 375.—Defines his difference of doctrine from the Church of England, 376—379.—Causes of opposition to Methodism, 376—380.—Attitude of Dissenters, 381.—Causes of success of Methodism; Whitefield's personal character and qualifications, 383—384.—Wesley, the real leader of the new movement, 385.—The Wesleys and Whitefield compared, 386.—Religious liberalism of early Methodists, 388.—Methodism and the aristocracy, and the Countess of Huntingdon, 388.—Countess of Huntingdon; her character; founds Cheshunt and Trevecca Colleges, 390.—Revival of religious life the source of political freedom, 391.

CHAPTER VI.

THE REVIVAL OF RELIGION IN WALES.

THE History of religion in Wales as in Ireland one of oppression, 393.—Penry's description of the clergy, 393.—Rev. Rees Pritchard and Thomas Charles on the same, 394.—Wroth and Cradock, godly clergymen, 395.—Pritchard, the Welsh Watts, 396.—Cradock's labours, 397.—The aforesaid clergymen, the forerunners of Welsh Dissent; the causes of their success, 398—399.—Griffith Jones, 400; the originator of education in Wales; statistics of education, 400—401.—Howel Harris, the Wesley of Wales, 401.—Dissenting denominations in Wales, 402.—Vile treatment of Howel Harris, 404; his attachment to the Church of England, 405.—Daniel Rowlands; his extraordinary qualifications, 406—407.—Growth of Welsh Methodism, 408—410.

CHAPTER VII.

FROM THE ESTABLISHMENT OF METHODISM TO THE SECOND AGITATION FOR THE REPEAL OF THE TEST AND CORPORATION ACTS. A.D. 1744—1793.

DR. WATTS on the advantages and responsibilities of Dissenters, 412; on the question of Civil Establishments of religion, 413.—The first formal statement and defence of Anti-State Church principles by a Congregationalist minister, 414.—Doddridge's views on the same,

415.—The State Church principle defended by Churchmen on new grounds.—Warburton's treatise, 417.—Examination of Warburton's theory, 418.—Rev. John White's "Letters," assailing Watts's work; Micaiah Towgood's reply, 419.—The latter, a standard work; its character examined, 419—421.—Towgood's death, 411.—Loyalty of Dissenters in the rebellion of 1745, 422—423.—Death of Watts, 424.—Character of his writings and labours, 425.—Intervention of George II. for liberty of conscience to Doddridge, 426.—Writings, labours, and death of Doddridge, 427—429.—Robert Grosvenor cited before Court of Queen's Bench for refusing to qualify for Sheriff, 429.—This and other similar cases defended by the Committee of Deputies, 430.—Decision of the Lords given by Lord Mansfield, 431.—Lord Mansfield on religious liberty, 433.—Firmness of Mr. Evans, 433.—George III., 434.—Characterized, 434—435.—Prominent Clergy of this period: Bishops Butler, Warburton, Lowth, and Secker, and Archdeacon Blackburne, 435—437.—Blackburne writes against the Church, 487.—The Methodist clergy, founders of the Evangelical party: Fletcher, Venn, Grimshaw, Berridge, 439.—The relations of the Methodists to the Established Church considered in Conference, 440.—Wesley's views on the same, his hostility to the Baptists, 441.—The Congregationalists: Drs. Gibbons, Fleming, Guise, Stafford, Savage, Jennings, 442—443.—Joseph Hart, Longford, Palmer, 444.—Names of eminent country ministers, Orton and others, 444.—The Baptists; scholarship of Dr. Gill, 445.—Thomas Crosby, the first historian of the Baptists, 446.—Samuel Stennett, Dr. Gifford, 447.—Robert Robinson and his works, 447, 448.—Daniel Taylor, William Thompson, and others, and the New General Baptist Association, 448—449.—Unitarian Presbyterians, Lardner, Priestly, Richard Price, 450.—Dr. Kippis and his literary labours, 451.—Dr. Ferneaux, Dr. Chandler, their literary and public labours, 451—453. Dr. Amory, 453.—The Sandemanians and Swedenborgians, 451.—Clerical subscription, 454.—Clerical subscription led by Blackburne and Lindsey, 454.—Meredith's motion in the House of Commons, 455.—Opposed by Edmund Burke, 456.—Able speech of Sir George Saville, 456.—Bill rejected, 456.—Agitation for Dissenters relief from subscription defeated, 459.—Memorable speech of Earl of Chatham, 460.—Continued agitation and appeal to the people, 461.—Robert Robinson's defence of principles of religious liberty, 462.—Joshua Toulmin, 461.—A modified bill carried, 465.—The Arminian Controversy, 466.—Toplady, 467.—Unscrupulous in controversy, 469.—The American War for Independence, 469.—Sympathy of Dissenters with the Colonists, 471.—Agitation led by Priestly and Price, 471—473.—Testimony of Benjamin Franklin, 474.—Wesley and the clergy side with the Government, 475.—Fletcher's defence of Wesley's conduct

477.—Revival of religion, 479.—John Howard, 479.—Robert Raikes, and the origin of Sunday Schools, 479.—Hannah More's schools, 481.—Slave Trade agitation led chiefly by the Quakers, 483.—Fox, Granville Sharpe, Clarkson, Sansom, and others, 484.—Joined by other denominations, including bishops and Churchmen, 485.—Renewed agitation of dissenting deputies on Test and Corporation Acts, 486; Pitt and Fox in the Debate, 488.—Motion rejected, 489.—Continued agitation amongst the people, 490—493.—Again brought before Parliament by Mr. Beaufoy, 494.—Again rejected, 494.—Redoubled efforts of committee of deputies, 494.—Fox's remarkable speech, 495; opposed by Pitt and others, 496.—Motion defeated, 497.— Causes of that defeat, 497—499.—The French Revolution, and the English Revolutionary Society, and the Dissenters, 499—501.—Formation of an association in defence of the Church, 502.—Birmingham Riots, attacks on Priestley, and sympathy of Dissenters, 502—505.— Priestley goes to America, 505.—General hostility of Churchmen to Dissenters, and cessation of agitation, 506.

CHAPTER VIII.

FROM THE SECOND AGITATION FOR THE REPEAL OF THE TEST AND CORPORATION LAWS, TO THEIR REPEAL.
A.D. 1792—1828.

ORIGIN of the Baptist Missionary Society: Carey, Fuller, Marshman, and Ward, 509.—Ultra-Calvinistic View of the Baptists, 509.— London Missionary Society formed of various denominations, 511.— David Bogue, Haweis, and others, 512.—Becomes a Congregationalist Society in consequence of formation of Church Missionary Society, and Wesleyan Society, 513.—Opposition of Bishop Horsley, 513—515. —Formation of the British and Foreign Bible Society, 516.—Fierce clerical opposition, favoured by Duke of Kent, 517.—Chief opponents: Dr. Herbert Marsh, Dr. Wordsworth, Maltby, and others, 519.— Joseph Lancaster, and the British and Foreign School Society, 521.—Opposition of the bishops and clergy, *note*, testimony of the *Edinburgh Review*, 523.—Mrs. Trimmer and Dr. Bell, 524—525.— Counter scheme of National School Society, 526.—Reasons for opposition of the clergy to education in the character of the clergy, 527.—Increase of Dissenters, 527.—Leading ministers, 530.—Toulmin's "History of Dissent," 531.—Leading Congregationalists: Bogue, Palmer, Burder, Collyer, William Bull, Thomas Toller, 533 —535.—John Clayton, sen., 535—536.—The Baptists: Booth, Rippon, Ryland, Fawcett, James Hinton, Joseph Kinghorn, 536

—539.—Robert Hall, characterized, 537—541.—John Foster, characterized, 541—543.—Secession of Methodists and establishment of Methodist New Connexion, 544.—Leading Methodist preachers after Wesley's death, 545.—Thomas Charles, and the second generation of the Methodists in Wales, 546.—Called "Exhorters," 548.— Morris, Charles and Richard, leading preachers in South Wales, 549.—Unaggressive character of Dissent at this period, 550—552. Its tone strengthened by William Graham, John Foster, and others, 553.—Roused from comparative apathy by Lord Sidmouth's proposed religious census, 555.—Organized opposition of Dissenters in this movement, 556.—Raffles, Pye Smith, Matthew Wilks and others, 556.—Lord Sidmouth's bill defeated, 558.—Formation of Protestant Society for Protection of Religious Liberty led by John Wilks, 558.—Its success in removing religious disabilities, 560—562.—Augmentation of Church livings and Church building commission, 563— 565.—Opposition of Dissenters to Brougham's Education Bill, 566.— The Protestant Society supported by Duke of Sussex, Lord Holland, Sir James Mackintosh, and Lord John Russell, 567.—Test and Corporation agitation, 568—570.—Vigorously prosecuted, 570.—Bill for their repeal introduced by Lord John Russell, 571.—Carried in the House of Commons, 575.—Lord Holland's bill in the Lords, 576; passed and receives Royal Assent, 577.—Friendly attitude of Churchmen during this struggle, 578—580.

CHAPTER IX.

FROM THE REPEAL OF THE TEST AND CORPORATION ACTS TO THE CENSUS OF RELIGIOUS WORSHIP.
A.D. 1828—1851.

CATHOLIC Emancipation promoted by Protestant Dissenters, 582.— Movements to re-establish Free Church principles; Ecclesiastical Knowledge Society, 582—584.—Reform Agitation, 585.—Rev. Andrew Marshall and the Voluntaries of Scotland, 588.—Voluntary Church Associations established, 589.—Organization of Congregational Union, 590; Affirmation of the spiritual character of Christian Church, 591.—Dr. Baldwin Brown's resolutions, 591.—Rev. T. Binney's estimate of the influence of the Church of England, 592.—Church-rate contests and Parliamentary bills, 593.—Convention of Dissenters, attended by John Angell James, Dr. Baldwin Brown, Josiah Conder, John Howard Hinton, and others, 594.—Registration and Marriage Acts passed, 596.—Church Rate Abolition Society, 596.—Introduction and defeat of Church Rate Abolition Bills, 598.—Church Reform,

599—601.—Anti-Slavery Movement, divides the interest of Dissenters 601.—Divisions of Dissenters, 602.—Religious Freedom Society, 603. —Failure of the same, 604.—Evangelical Voluntary Church Association, failure of the same, 605.—Establishment of the *Nonconformist* newspaper by Mr. Edward Miall, 604. Dissenters roused by Sir James Graham's Factory Bill, 606—608. Formation of an Anti-State Church Association urged by the *Nonconformist*, 608. First Conference held; discouraged by Dissenters, 609.—British Anti-State Church Association formed, 611.—The Wolverhampton and Lady Hewley's charities before Parliament, 613.—Effect of their decision upon Unitarians, 615.—The Regium Donum and the Anti-State Church Association, 617.—The Maynooth Bill, 618.—Diverse action in regard to it of Evangelical Churchmen, and Evangelical Dissenters, 620.—The support of Dissenters given to Free Trade, 621.— Division among Methodists, 622.—Result of the Religious Census of 1851, 623.

A HISTORY

OF THE

FREE CHURCHES OF ENGLAND.

CHAPTER I.

INTRODUCTORY.

THE struggles of English Nonconformists up to the time of the Revolution have been so often and so ably described, that it may seem to be unnecessary to add one more page to that painful yet honourable history. No Englishman can look back upon that history without shame, but no Nonconformist can look back upon it without pride. The conduct of the State and the conduct of the Church of that period are now uniformly condemned both by Statesmen and by Churchmen; and if it is necessary, for the purposes of this History, that I should pass it in review, I wish it to be understood that I hold neither the State nor the Church of the present day responsible for acts then committed. It might seem superfluous, if not absurd, to make this remark, were it not the case that, when the facts of those times are revived, they are often treated as though the present historical descendants of the old ecclesiastical parties were, in some manner, accountable for them. No person of common sense dreams of taunting the ministry of Queen Victoria with the acts of the ministry of Charles the Second; but many persons, who are possessed of strong common sense in other matters, esteem it to be a natural thing to taunt the Established Church of the present day with the acts of the Established Church of three hundred years ago. And so, on the other side, men in whom high literary culture and ordinary common sense are often combined, seem to imagine that they have turned the flank of their opponents' position if they have proved that the Independents of the Commonwealth were persecutors, and that they not only had no objection to tithes and Church-rates, but that they held firmly by the theory of a State-established religion. In so far as I may find occasion to repeat the history of religious persecution I shall do it with no such purposes as these. Men may be responsible, in no small degree, for the character and the acts of their descendants, but cannot be held responsible for the character or the acts of their forefathers.

In reviewing the ecclesiastical history of England, from the Reformation to the Revolution, the changes in government, doctrine, and service which the Established Church successively underwent naturally claim the first attention. What is most remarkable in connection with these changes is the comparative readiness with which the more important were received, and the strenuous opposition by which the less important were, after a time, encountered. When Henry the Eighth founded a new Church* in England, he met, excepting from those

---

* I use this expression advisedly, and I imagine that none but eager controversialists will dispute its accuracy. "The existence of the Church of England," says the present Bishop of St. Asaph, "as a distinct body, and her final separation from Rome, may be dated from the period of the divorce." Short's "History of Ch. of England," p. 102.

who adhered to their fidelity to the Romish communion, no opposition to his claim to be the "supreme head" of that Church. The explanation of this fact is natural enough, although it has not been recognized by the historians of that period. The doctrine of the regal supremacy in ecclesiastical matters had been familiar to Englishmen for many generations. It had been successfully maintained, up to a certain point, by the greatest of the Plantagenet kings, and had been ably vindicated by Wycliffe, one of whose cardinal "heresies" consisted in the denial of the supremacy of the Pope.* All that Henry did was to apply and extend a doctrine that had long been filtering through the minds both of the aristocracy and of the commonalty. Hence the otherwise inexplicable circumstance that his assumption of unlimited supremacy excited only what may be described as a professional opposition. Most of the bishops voted against the Act† vesting the sole ecclesiastical prerogative in the Crown; but only Gardiner resisted the exercise of the utmost stretch of that prerogative, when the King suspended all the bishops from the exercise of their episcopal authority, and, of his own sovereign will, afterwards restored it to them. The gallows and the stake made short work of those of the inferior clergy who resisted the new law; and long before the death of Henry, his spiritual headship was effectually established. In that age, indeed, there seemed to be no alternative between the supremacy of the Pope and the supremacy of the King. The minds of the best of men, as is the case with some, even in

---

* Vaughan's "Wycliffe," p. 211.
† 25 Henry VIII., cap. 21.

these days, were so warped by the influence of ancient ecclesiastical precedents, that none dreamed of an ultimate appeal to Holy Scripture. St. Paul, if he were consulted, was to be interpreted by Augustine, St. John by Jerome, and St. Peter by the Popes; and to the interpreters, as a matter of course, was given the principal authority. A Church of Christ, independent, as such, of human control, and existing apart from state-craft, was an idea almost impossible to that age.* If entertained at all, it could only have been by men as humble in life as in spirit, such as afterwards rose to assert the spiritual character of the kingdom of Christ upon earth.

It was not more difficult to compel obedience to the theological doctrines of the new Church, for they differed but little from those of Rome. The King himself undertook to settle what the people should believe, and, with this view, drew up a set of articles of religion. These articles, while they enjoined the belief of the "whole Bible" and the three Creeds, also declared that Baptism was necessary to salvation, that the opinions of all "Anabaptists" were detestable heresies, and that Auricular Confession and Priestly Absolution were commendable. The doctrine of Transubstantiation was set forth without reserve, as also was the doctrine of Purgatory, and Prayers to the Saints were commended. On the other hand, the doctrine of Justification by Faith

---

* Cardinal Pole came near to the right doctrine in his reply to Tunstal. "Those authors," he says, "who write in defence of the King's supremacy, proceed upon this false ground, that the Church and State are one society. Now this is a capital mistake, for these two bodies are instituted for different ends, and governed by independent authorities." Cited in Collier, vol. ii., p. 137.

was acknowledged. The decision of the dignitaries of the Church on these points was what the decision of State functionaries customarily is. Expressed in vernacular English, it was—" We believe whatsoever we are commanded to believe." The new articles might have secured a much wider acceptance than it befel them to receive but for a step altogether fatal to many of their doctrines, and almost equally fatal to the doctrine of the Royal supremacy. The King not only authorized a translation of the Bible into English, but ordered a copy of it to be set up in each of the Churches. This act, however, was soon felt to be, what it undoubtedly was, a political blunder, and, after seven years, was substantially recalled.

Before furnishing his subjects with such a weapon of almighty power against the system which he had determined to establish, the King issued the "Injunctions." He, who was the slave of his own lusts, enjoined the clergy to exhort the people to "keep God's commandments," and to give themselves to the " study of the Scriptures, and a good life." In the "Institution of a Christian Man," the bishops laid down, at greater length, the creed of the Reformed Church, which was further vindicated in the " Necessary Doctrine." Having thus explained and apparently demonstrated the absolute truth of the new theological system, it only remained to enforce it. Some denied the corporal presence, and were accordingly sent to Smithfield. In order to strengthen his power, the King allowed his Parliament to assume the functions of a Convocation, and debate for eleven days the doctrines of the Christian religion. This debate issued in the adoption of the law of the " Six

Articles," which set forth, in the strongest language, the presence of the natural body and blood of Christ in the Sacrament of the Lord's Supper, sanctioned Communion in one kind only, denied the right of Marriage to the priesthood, enforced vows of Chastity, allowed Private Masses, and declared Auricular Confession to be both expedient and necessary. The most fearful penalties were attached to any opposition to these doctrines. The least was loss of goods; the greatest, burning at the stake, which was the punishment for denying the first of the Articles. The law was now let loose against both Protestant and Catholics, but with peculiar vengeance against the former. The English State and Church have generally made a distinction in their treatment of the two classes of Dissenters. There is, to this day, an hereditary tenderness of feeling in the Church towards the members of the Roman Catholic communion, and an hereditary antipathy towards Protestant Dissent. Separation from Rome is looked at with mournful regret; separation from Protestant Dissent with holy pride. Nor has the State been wholly destitute of similar partiality. From the reign of Henry the Eighth down to the thirtieth year of the reign of Queen Victoria, the government of the day has almost invariably relaxed offensive or insulting laws against Roman Catholics before it has relaxed similar laws against Protestant Dissenters. In the reign of Queen Victoria this feeling is exhibited by ministers of the Crown fighting the battle of the Roman Catholics, and leaving Protestant Dissenters to fight theirs' as best they can; in the reign of Henry the Eighth it took a grosser form. Catholics were only hanged, Protestants were burned; Fisher was sent to the gallows, Anne Askew to the stake. And so the new Church was founded. The work begun by one royal profligate was, a hundred and thirty years later, fittingly finished by another. Henry the Eighth's natural successor in ecclesiastical politics is Charles the Second. The two great pillars of the English political Church are the author of the first " Act of Supremacy," and the author of the last " Act of Uniformity."

No change took place in the ceremonies of the Church in the reign of Henry. A Commission had been appointed in 1540 to examine into them, but no action was taken upon its proceedings. The Services in use were of several kinds, and varied according to ancient custom. York had its custom distinct from Exeter, and Hereford and Lincoln from Bangor and Sarum. The first step in the direction of uniformity was made in the second year of Edward the Sixth, when an Order of Communion was published. The word " Mass " was now dropped, and the cup was restored to the laity. In the same year appeared the first book of Common Prayer, which was adopted by Parliament, and ordered to be used, without having been submitted to Convocation. It was compiled, with a few important alterations, from the old Missals. The compilers had, however, left some questions open, and there was doubt as to what was meant in certain portions. The book, therefore, was ordered to be revised. On this revision the German Reformers exercised some influence, which appears in the omission, in the second book, of Prayers for the Dead, and the doctrine of Transubstantiation, and in the adoption of simpler ecclesiastical vestments— the second rubric forbidding the use of any vestments excepting the rochet and the surplice.* For the second time Convocation was not consulted, and the new order of worship was published without having been submitted to its decision. Those who, in later days, have expatiated on the claims of this body seem to have forgotten history. In the settlement of the Protestant religion in England it was altogether ignored by the State. The use of the second book was enforced by a second Act of Uniformity. The State having, in two years, changed its opinions, required all the people to do the same.

The greater simplicity of the second Service-book was probably, in some measure, due to the bold position assumed by the first Nonconformist, John Hooper, Bishop of Gloucester. History, while it has done justice to the character and the abilities of this eminent man, has not done similar justice to his opinions. He appears on its pages as a conscientious opponent of all ecclesiastical ceremonies and habits that are not expressly warranted by Scripture, as a sufferer for his opinions on this subject, and as a martyr for the Protestant religion; but he was more than this. All Protestants and Puritans have been accustomed to hold his name in reverence, but it belongs in a more especial manner to the English Nonconformists of the nineteenth century. It was his voice which first publicly proclaimed the principles of religious freedom. He stood alone amongst the English Protestants of his age in denying the right of the State to interfere with religion. While the young King, acting under the advice of his council, was submitting to Parliament Acts of Uniformity, and compel-

---

* See Cardwell's " Two Prayer Books of Edward VI. compared."

ling assent to new Articles of Religion,* Hooper was publicly denying the right of any king to interfere in the government of the Church. "Touching," he says, "the superior powers of the earth, it is not unknown to all them that hath read and marked the Scripture that it appertaineth nothing unto their office to make any law to govern the conscience of their subjects in religion."† "Christ's Kingdom," he adds, "is a spiritual one. In this neither Pope nor King may govern. Christ alone is the governor of his Church, and the only lawgiver." He told the people, in words proclaimed to thousands at Paul's Cross and throughout various parts of the kingdom, that their consciences were bound only by the Word of God, and that they might, with it, judge "bishop, doctor, preacher, and curate." "The laws of the civil magistrate," he elsewhere says, "are not to be admitted in the Church."‡ Preaching before the King, he called for the restoration of the primitive Church, and demanded the abolition of all vestments, crosses, and altars. It is a wonder that such a man should have been asked to accept a bishopric; but, next to Latimer, he was the greatest and most popular preacher of his day; and his zeal not only for the Reformation, but for a further reformation, knew no bounds. And the King liked him. Hooper was a man peculiarly calculated to fascinate such an open, frank, and tender nature as that of Edward. He was one of the few ecclesiastics of his age who was more than an ecclesiastic. He had a

---

* The forty-two Articles of Religion of this reign, which are substantially the same as those now in force, were issued without consulting either Parliament or Convocation. Burnet, vol. iii., p. 210.

† "A Declaration of the Ten Commandments." Early Writings, p. 280.

‡ "A Declaration concerning Christ and his Offices." Ib., p. 82.

generous human nature. He did not imagine that in assuming the office of a preacher of the Gospel he was bound to quench all the natural instincts of humanity. He loved children. Of a candid and truthful moral disposition, generous in his sympathies, just in his desires, an ardent and eloquent preacher, he was a man who seemed to be, above all his contemporaries, born to be the apostle of the new religion. Had the King and he lived, the Reformation would probably have been completed, and the Church of England would not have been the daughter only of Tudor pride and lust, and the mother chiefly of those whom she denounces as heretical schismatics.

For Hooper to be offered a bishopric under the first Act of Uniformity, was for him to refuse it. He declined to take the oath of supremacy, and he "scrupled the vestments." The oath was altered by the King, and large personal liberty in wearing the "garments of Popery" was, it must be said, generously offered him; but he loved his conscience more than any honours, and esteemed the cause of the Reformation of more value than many bishoprics. The King, Cranmer, and Ridley remonstrated with him. He took advice of the German and Swiss Reformers, and they, while holding his opinions of the habits, advised him, for the sake of religion, to take the office, but he still declined. Then he wrote against them, and was committed to the Fleet, from whence he came forth giving up a little but holding much, and was consecrated Bishop of Gloucester. Here, for four years, he visited and preached as bishop had never done in England before, and seldom, if ever since, and so won the crown of a martyr. Such was the man who sounded the first note of that controversy which was afterwards to test the English Church, and who laid the foundation of English Puritanism.

All times of persecution, and all ages which have been distinguished by an intemperate zeal for external uniformity, have been characterized by the prevalence of notorious immorality. The age of Edward the Sixth, as were the succeeding ages of Elizabeth and Charles, was no exception to this rule. While the King's council was framing theological propositions and compelling, for the first time in the history of England, "subscription" to them, enforcing laws for wearing red habits by some on some days, and white and black habits by others on other days, changing the laws themselves within two years, and burning, hanging, or imprisoning all those who could not change their consciences as fast as their rulers could theirs, immorality flourished like a green bay-tree. "Lying, cheating, theft, perjury, and whoredom," says Bucer, in his letter to Hooper,* "are the complaints of the times." Bishop Latimer said that the English nation were "infamous for whoredom" beyond any other part of the world.† "Profaneness and immorality," says a Church historian who is not given to exaggeration in the use of language, "had now an unlimited range."‡ "The courtiers and great men," writes another historian, "indulged themselves in a dissolute and licentious life, and the clergy were not without blemish."§ But trine immersion was a more important question than the state of morality, and it did not matter if people lived in adultery so long as the clergy wore albs and rochets.

* Collier, vol. ii., p. 294. † Ib., p. 295.
‡ Ib. § Neal, vol. i., p. 78.

The reformation of the English Church never passed beyond the line drawn by the death of Edward the Sixth. It has, on the contrary, rather receded from it. There can be no doubt concerning the intentions of the reformers of that reign.* They wished for a further reformation. Had they lived the royal supremacy would probably have been relinquished; the idea of enforcing uniformity by legal pains and penalties would have been surrendered; the theory of episcopacy, as it is now held and stated, would have been consigned to the pages of history only, and the Reformation would have been as complete in England as it was in the German States.

It might have been expected that the persecutions endured in the reign of Mary would have been succeeded by a rebound, and that there would have been a sudden leap from Romanism to a more extreme Protestantism, and under a monarch of any character but Elizabeth's this might have been the course of history; but the Queen had inherited too much of the disposition of her father, for her to surrender the smallest of her royal prerogatives. Her unwillingness to assume the title of "Supreme Head" of the Church, while she retained the whole prerogative of headship, and her willingness to take the title of "Supreme Governor" only, have been much commented upon, but it requires an intellect of peculiar character to detect any real difference between the two titles. The English legislature certainly has never recognized that difference,† and Elizabeth acted

---

* The testimony on this point is indisputable. See Neal, vol. i., p. 79.

† In the Act relating to First Fruits and Tenths (2 and 3 Anne, cap. 11), the two Houses addressed Queen Anne in the following terms:—"Inasmuch as your Majesty, taking into your friendly and serious consideration the mean and inefficient maintenance belonging to the Clergy in divers parts of

with all the supremacy of headship and all the authority of governing rule. From the reign of the second Tudor to the reign of the last Stuart, the sole object of the crown was to retain its supremacy over all the actions of the subject. In the reign of the last of the Tudors, and the first of the Stuarts, the opposition to the regal claim assumed an ecclesiastical, afterwards a civil form. It succeeded in the latter rather than in the former, partly because the majority of mankind care more for their political than they do for their religious rights.

During the forty-four years of the reign of Elizabeth the whole power of the crown was exercised, in regard to ecclesiastical matters, with two distinct purposes. The first was to subject the Church to its "governor," the second to suppress all opinions differing from those which had received a special patent of protection. The first wholly succeeded; the second wholly failed. The Prayer Book and Articles of Elizabeth do not materially differ from those of Edward. The only difference of any importance relates to the vestments, which were ordered to be the same as those in use in the second year of Edward. This change was against a further reformation, and it was confirmed by a third Act of

---

this your kingdom, has been most graciously pleased out of your most religious and tender concern of the Church of England (whereof your Majesty is the 'Supreme Head' on earth)." On May 3rd, 1717, the Lower House of Convocation made a representation to the Upper House relating to Bishop Hoadly's Sermon on "The Nature of the Kingdom and Church of Christ," —a sermon, the doctrine of which was that Christ alone was Head of His Church. The Lower House, on this occasion, condemned Bishop Hoadly's sermon, because its tendency was to "impugn and impeach the regal supremacy in causes ecclesiastical," in maintenance of which, said the House, "we offer the following particulars:—That whereas His Majesty is, and by the statutes of this realm, is declared to be 'Supreme Head' of the Church." Palin's "History of the Church of England," cap. 17.

Uniformity. The Queen soon let it be known that this Act was not to be a dead letter. She heard of some who did not wear the habits, and who even preached against them, and Parker was at once ordered to enforce the law. Then the exiles who had returned from the Continent, flushed with hope, and ardent in the cause of the gospel, found the paw of the lion's cub as heavy as that of the royal beast himself. The Primates of the English Church have always been selected for their willingness to be the passive instruments of the government. The dignity of their office has, in their judgment, culminated in obedience to the policy and the passions of the Sovereign. Cranmer's chief work had been to celebrate and then to undo royal marriages, to carry out the law of the Six Articles, to publish the Bible, when it pleased the king that his subjects should read it, and to recall that Book when the king found that its circulation was becoming dangerous to his pretensions; Parker's office was to carry into execution the law which made it criminal not to conform to the Prayer Book, and high treason itself to refuse to take the oath of spiritual supremacy. A hot-headed, intolerant, arbitrary, and vindictive man, he was the model of an Elizabethan archbishop. So zealously did he set about his work, that he shocked the statesmen of his age,[*] and at last shocked even Elizabeth herself. Not being an ecclesiastic, there was a limit to the Queen's capacity of creating and afterwards enjoying the sight of human suffering. There was no such limit in Parker. The jackal's appetite was, for once, stronger even than that of the lioness.

[*] Burleigh's Letter to Grindal in Strype's "Grindal," p. 281.

The attempt to enforce the Act of Uniformity excited instant resistance, and the Church was "turned into a great shambles."* Those who, soon afterwards, came to be denominated "Puritans" were the first to suffer; but at Oxford one rose whose character, genius, controversial ability and persistency of purpose made the Puritan controversy famous throughout Europe. Thomas Cartwright, the leader of the Puritans in the reign of Elizabeth, had preached the doctrines of Puritanism with boldness and vigour for some time before he was silenced. Thousands in the University town and its neighbourhood crowded to hear him, for he united in an equal degree the finest qualities of the scholar and the preacher. "The sun," said Beza, "doth not see a more learned man."† The Church historian Fuller does not hesitate to bear similar testimony to his high character and his great abilities.‡ Whitgift, an almost equally able disputant, attempted to answer him, and failing to convince either the preacher or his hearers, used his power as Vice-Chancellor to dismiss him from the University. Cartwright, indeed, held doctrines more dangerous to the established order than many of the Puritans. He seems to have attached no importance to the controversy respecting the habits, and had avoided speaking on that subject; but he objected to the whole order of Church government and patronage. He denounced the hierarchical system, and demanded that the people should have liberty to choose their own ministers. On other subjects he anticipated most of the

---

* Sherlock on "Judgment," p. 119. † "Clark's Lives, p. 19.
‡ "Church History," b. x., p. 3.

views and practices which were afterwards enforced by the Presbyterian party in the time of the Commonwealth. The controversy between Cartwright and Whitgift was carried on with equal vigour on both sides; but Whitgift had one advantage,—he was in power.

It does not come within the scope of this work to review at any length the progress of the Puritan struggle. It was characteristically a struggle against all that was Romish in origin in the Protestant church. Every doctrine and ceremony which could not be authenticated by reference to the Scriptures was assailed. Diocesan episcopacy was the question of first magnitude; then came the baptismal ceremonies, the churching of women, church discipline, episcopal ordination, the use of the cross in baptism, of caps and surplices in preaching, of the ring in marriage, and of organs in church music. It may be a matter of wonder at the present time how some of these questions could have been debated with such excitement; but there lay at the bottom of all of them the greater question of the ultimate supremacy of the Divine or of human law. And, besides, the Puritans knew, or thought they knew, that each and every one of the doctrines and practices which they condemned was a side portal back to the Church of Rome. Hence they felt that they were fighting both for their God and for their country; for what greater curse could fall upon England than a revival of Papal rule, and what greater sin could a Christian commit than to add to the inspired Word of God?

The greatest struggles took place on two questions— that of episcopacy and that of the habits, and on both these questions the persecuted had the private sympathies of the men who persecuted them. The doctrine of Episcopacy had not then become hardened into an absolute theory. The present theory of the Church of England on this subject was held, at that time, only by members of the Roman Catholic Church. Cranmer held Wycliffe's doctrine that bishops were not a distinct order. In the " Necessary Erudition "—a book drawn up by a Committee of Bishops and Clergy, and published by Royal command, as an authoritative exposition of the doctrines of the Church, it is stated that there are only two orders of the Christian ministry,—presbyters and deacons, and that the episcopal character is included in the former. Archbishops and bishops were declared to be of human appointment only.* Whitgift treated the whole question of the form of Church government as a matter of indifference, maintaining, in reply to Cartwright, who advocated the exclusive authority of the presbyterian system, that Christ had left the external polity of His Church an open question.† It was not until near the close of Elizabeth's reign that the theory of Episcopacy which now prevails in the Established Church was even mooted. It was in A.D. 1588, when all the fathers of the Reformation were dead, that Bancroft, then chaplain to Whitgift, first maintained that bishops were an order distinct from presbyters, or as he called them priests, and were superior to them by Divine law, and that it was heresy to deny the doctrine.‡

---

* Records of the Reformation in Burnet.
† Whitgift's "Answer" (A.D. 1572); and "Defence of the Answer," (A.D. 1574.)
‡ Neal, vol. i., p. 494.

Whitgift acutely said that he wished this were true, but could not believe it. A theory so flattering to human vanity was not, however, likely to remain unrecognized by those whose position it would most favourably affect; and accordingly, in another generation, Diocesan Episcopacy was claimed to be of divine institution, and the only Scriptural form of Church government.

The Puritans denied not merely the expediency but the lawfulness of this form. They preached and wrote against it with the same vigour that they preached and wrote against the "Popish garments." The difference between the two parties was not so wide then as it afterwards became, but Episcopacy was part of the system established by law, and no mercy was shown to any man who dared to oppose the smallest part of that system.

It was the same with respect to the habits. Neither the bishops nor the clergy were very zealous for them; they would have given them up as willingly as they would have retained them, but they wore and therefore defended them. Latimer, Ridley, and Cranmer derided them; Jewel could compare them only to actors' dresses; Grindal tried to get them abolished; Parker gloried in not having worn them at his consecration; Sandys, Bishop of Worcester, said that they "came from hell;" the laity hated them, and, says Whitgift, would "spit in the faces" of the men who wore them, but they, too, were part of the system established under the Act of Uniformity, and, although Parker himself disapproved of them, he hunted to banishment, to prison, or to death, all who openly did the same. The question of the habits has, since that time, undergone a change somewhat similar to that which has come over the question of Episcopacy. An "ultra-ritualist" could not have been met with either in court or church in Queen Elizabeth's days, but in the days of Queen Victoria, Ritualism is a gospel in itself.

Public opinion was thus clearly on the side of the Puritans, and yet they failed to do more than to create a party. They did not shake, for one moment, the foundations of the Church, or the smallest of its ornaments. Not a single concession was made to them. Looking at their controversy, from this distance of time—for distance does not lend enchantment to controversy—it would be harsh and ungenerous to say that they did not deserve success. They were men of the noblest intellectual attainments, the greatest scholars of their age, and of the loftiest piety. Like their successors, also, a hundred years later, they must have been aware that for them to be suspended from preaching, was for the best preachers to be silenced, and that at a time when preaching was never so much needed. For, thousands of the pulpits were empty, and in many parts of the country a sermon could not be heard within a distance of twenty miles, or from one six months in the year to another. They must have reckoned on this amongst other deprivations, or did they, knowing the extent of public sympathy with their views—having repeated evidence that the House of Commons agreed with them, and aware that all the foreign reformers were pleading their cause—expect a relaxation of the laws? There is no evidence to this effect. There is not a sentence in all their writings expressing the assurance of ultimate victory. They do not seem, at any time, to have had a gleam of certain hope. They acted as they did, with a forlorn courage, knowing that there was no issue for them but punishment or death, yet meeting both when they came with an abounding happiness which was certainly denied to all their persecutors. Probably not one of these, Henry, Elizabeth, Parker, or Whitgift, but would gladly have exchanged his death-bed for that of the commonest Puritan that was dying in the Gate prison or the Compter.

There must be a reason, apart from the character of the governing power, why Puritans within the Church have never succeeded. The reason is probably to be found in the fact that they never essentially differed from the dominant party. Both were almost equally intolerant. Parker and Whitgift persecuted the Puritans; but if Cartwright had been in Whitgift's place he would have dealt out equal persecution to Baptists and Independents. They, who had suffered imprisonment on account of their opinions, actually remonstrated with statesmen for releasing Roman Catholics from confinement. They held a purer doctrine that their opponents held, but none the less did they require it to be enforced by the "authority of the magistrate." It seems strange that men who devoted so much time to the study of the Scriptures, and whose knowledge of them was as extensive as it was profound, should have missed the one study which, to a Christian, would seem to be the most obvious, the life and character of the Founder of their religion and the nature of His mission. But, habits of thought are more tyrannical than habits of action; and the habit of theological thought was then, as for generations afterwards, essentially dogmatical. The best of the Puritans looked to the Scriptures for rules rather than for principles, for propositions rather than for examples. Christianity was, with them, merely an historical development of Judaism; and therefore, while they believed in the sacrifice of Christ they equally believed in the laws of Moses. The Sacred Writings were rough materials out of which they might hew their own systems. The stones were taken in equal parts out of the books of the Old Testament and the New, the latter being dug for doctrine and the former for precept. Amongst all the works of the early Puritans, there is not one on the character or life of Christ, nor one which gives any indication that they had even an imagination of the wholly spiritual nature of His kingdom. Whatever that kingdom might be in the place Heaven, on the place Earth it was to be fenced and extended by pains and penalties, threatenings, and slaughter. They denied the supremacy of the civil magistrate in religion, but it was only in order to assert their own supremacy. They pleaded with tears for liberty of conscience, and would have denied it to the first "Anabaptist" whom they met. It was no wonder that they did not gain their end, and no wonder that they scarcely hoped to gain it. It would seem that the English race required to be transplanted before it could bear a more perfect flower and fruit than any of which Puritanism only was capable. That service was effected by Elizabeth.

For, there were men who were esteemed guilty of a greater crime than Puritanism. A Presbyterian church had been formed at Wandsworth in 1572, and it had the honour of being the first silenced "conventicle." Wandsworth was then a quieter and a pleasanter place than it is now, and those who went there may have gone for rural retirement as well as for personal safety; but Parker's hounds of law had tracked them and they were dispersed. No greater punishment, at that time, awaited them, for they were not "Anabaptists," or "Brownists." Dutch Anabaptists* had been caught and burned in Henry the Eighth's time, and had perished in the same way under Elizabeth, but the English Baptists and Independents had not hitherto attracted much public notice. It has been asserted that a Baptist Church existed in England in A.D. 1417.† There were certainly Baptist "Churches" in England as early as the year 1589,‡ and there could scarcely have been several organized communities without the corresponding opinions having been held by individuals, and some Churches established for years previous to this date. With respect to the Independents, certain "Congregations" are spoken of by Foxe,§ as established in London in A.D. 1555, and it is possible that they were Independent, but more probable that they were Puritan. It is now clearly established that an Independent Church, of which Richard Fitz was pastor, existed in A.D. 1568.‖ In A.D. 1580, Sir Walter Raleigh spoke of the Brownists as existing by "thousands." In A.D. 1583, Brownists and Anabaptists are freely classed together.¶ Which

---

* The Dutch Anabaptists of this period had little in common with English Baptists, excepting an objection to infant baptism. These and the Münster Baptists are no more to be confounded with English Baptists, than are Greek with English or Armenian Episcopalians. It served an obvious purpose, however, in Elizabeth's reign, to do so.

† Robinson's "Claude," vol. ii., p. 54.

‡ Dr. Somers' Reply to Barrowe, quoted in Ivimey's History, vol. i., p. 109.

§ Vol. iii., p. 114.

‖ "Congregational Martyrs." Art., Richard Fitz, *pass*.

¶ Strype's "Annals," iii., p. 264.

really appeared first in point of time can be only a matter of conjecture.

But although Richard Fitz was the first pastor of the first Independent Church in England, to Robert Browne belongs the honour of founding the denomination. This man's character has been assailed with almost equal virulence by Church and Nonconformist writers; but, although he is proved to have been naturally of a passionate, dogmatic, and weak nature, no charge against his piety has been successfully established.* His moral courage and his willingness to bear suffering in testimony of his sincerity, were amply shown by his life. If, like Cartwright, he eventually returned to the Church, he did what ought not to excite surprise. The wonder is, not that human nature was so weak in him, but that it was so strong in others.

With one exception Browne held all the views which distinguish modern Independents. It was many years before this body adopted the principles of religious freedom in their widest application. Browne himself, who was extravagant in many of his views, believed that the power of the civil magistrates ought to be exercised in favour of a Scriptural religion. Barrowe and Greenwood, next to Penry, the noblest martyrs of Independency, fully acknowledged, together, the supremacy of the crown in Ecclesiastical matters. Barrowe's opinion separately expressed, was that the magistrates' sword only wanted "an eye to guide it."† Greenwood maintained that "both the magistrates ought to compel

---

* The best estimate of the character of Browne, is to be found in Fletcher's "History of Independency." Vol. ii., cap. 3.

† "Plain Refutation," p. 141.

the infidels to hear the doctrine of the Church, and also, with the approbation of the Church, to send forth men with gifts and graces to instruct the infidels, being as yet no ministers or officers unto them." It is the singular and distinguished honour of the Baptists to have repudiated, from their earliest history, all coercive power over the consciences and the actions of men with reference to religion. No sentence is to be found in all their writings inconsistent with those principles of Christian liberty and willinghood which are now equally dear to all the free Congregational Churches of England. They were the proto-evangelists of the voluntary principle.*

On Independents and Baptists the hand of the Jeffreys of the Episcopal bench, Archbishop Whitgift, fell with double vengeance. He choked the prisons with them, and from prison hailed their most eminent leaders to the scaffold. None of these can be said to have committed a very grave offence. The greatest crime of which they were guilty was that of denying the supremacy of the Crown as it was then exercised. In the eyes of Churchmen, however, the Independents and Baptists were heretics beyond any of their age. The one party denied the Scriptural warrant, and even the priestly efficacy of Infant Baptism. The doctrine of these men cut at the roots of Priestism, and was fatal to the very idea of a National Church. For, how could there be a National Church, if only "believers" were to be baptized; and if priests did not, by the

---

* The Author is not connected with the Baptist denomination; and has therefore, perhaps, greater pleasure in bearing this testimony to undoubted historical fact.

magic of baptism, make all infants Christians, was not their principal function gone? The frantic opposition of the clergy to these revolutionists can be easily understood. Even the best of the Puritans could not endure them, and employed their pens to revile both their characters and their opinions. With scarcely less violence were the "Brownists" attacked. The characteristic creed of the Baptists was adult believers' baptism. They were as thorough Independents as were the Brownists, but Independency was not the most prominent feature of their belief. Browne, however, had given such conspicuousness to this distinctive doctrine that those who accepted it were publicly marked off, both from Puritans and from Episcopalians. It was, as even then taught, a doctrine which was fatal to an order as distinct from an office in the Christian ministry. The Puritan system was one of a mixed ecclesiastical oligarchy, in which the clergy held life-peerages, and were the superiors in rank, as well as in work, to the people. The Independents denied the scripturalness of any such distinction. A man, with them, was a minister no longer than he had the care of a separate congregation. The sole authority for his office was his spiritual fitness and the consent of the people to whom he ministered. Other ministers and churches had nothing to do either with him or with them, but they gladly, and from the first, welcomed the co-operation and approved of similar organizations in their choice and work. They differed therefore, as much or more from the Puritan clergy as the Puritan clergy differed from the Episcopalians, and the Puritans took pains to let it be known that they had as little sympathy with the "schism" of the

Brownists as they had with the "heresy" of the Anabaptists.

The doctrines of these men were set forth with great clearness in their defences before the ecclesiastical authorities as well as in their works. Their mode of stating them, if sometimes offensive,* was generally, from its extreme simplicity, exceedingly winning. Jeered at and browbeaten in Courts of High Commission and Star Chamber by archbishops and bishops, they defended themselves with a humility which became as well as adorned their belief. " And what office," inquired Fanshawe, of Penry, "had you in your Church, which met in woods and I know not where?" " I have no office," replied Penry, " in that poor congregation; and as for our meeting in woods, or anywhere else, we have the examples of our Saviour Jesus Christ, and of His Church and servants in all ages, for our warrant. It is against our will that we go into woods or secret places; as we are not ashamed of the Gospel of Christ, so our desire is to profess the same openly; we are ready before men and angels to show and justify our meetings, and our behaviour in them, desiring earnestly that we may have peace and quietness to serve our God, even before all men, that they may be witness of our upright walking towards God and all the world, especially towards our prince and country. We know that meeting in woods, in caves and mountains, is a part of the Cross and baseness of the Gospel, whereat it is easy for the natural man to stumble, but we are partly partakers of this

---

* Barrowe, when before the Commission, called Whitgift a "beast" and a "monster," to his face. It was true; but the words, probably, cost him his life.

mean estate for the Lord's sacred verity; and the question should not be so much where we meet, as what we do in our meeting?"*

These were the men whom the civil and ecclesiastical authorities of the latter part of Queen Elizabeth's reign judged to be not fit to live. The laity, generally, cared little for them, and the Queen suffered herself to listen to the promptings of her clerical advisers.† They were therefore imprisoned for months and years in the foulest gaols—fouler even than those which John Howard, two centuries later, exposed to the shame and indignation of the world—beaten with cudgels, some left to die of fever and sores, while others were committed to the gallows. Barrowe, Greenwood, and Penry, the three great witnesses for Independency, met the latter fate. They were all just and holy men, but the character of Penry was of an order which only times of the fiercest persecution apparently can produce; for, only at such times are certain characters tested to their utmost. Penry seems to have stood that test until his soul was purified from all the dross of human nature. He was a man of a Johannine disposition, yet of a most indomitable energy; a scholar, but also an evangelist; of as intense reflective faculty as a mystic, yet as active as a pioneer; overflowing with domestic affections, but absorbed with

* "Examination of Barrowe, Greenwood, and Penry," p. C. 4.
† "The Queen hearkened to the suggestions of the clergy, who represented the Puritans as seditious persons who rebelled against the laws, and by their disobedience shook the foundation of the Government. There is scarcely a Christian state where the prevailing sect will suffer the least division or the least swerving from the established opinion; no, not even in private. Shall I venture to say, it is *the clergy chiefly* who support this strange principle of non-toleration, so little agreeable to Christian charity?"
—"Rapin," vol. ii., p. 141.

the love of the souls of his countrymen, and serving his Divine Master, as though that Master had no other servant to do His work. He was the Christian apostle of Wales, a country then, although four bishops had charge of it, and "livings" abounded, in a state of worse than heathen barbarism, for the clergy set an example of the grossest vices and of the foulest living.* Better that Penry should be hanged and the people left to perish in their ignorance, than that their self-indulgent lives should be exposed and disturbed,—a feeling, unhappily, not confined to that age or country. Penry was hanged, and Whitgift was the first to put his signature to the warrant for his execution.

The Independents and the Baptists took up the weapons against the Established Church as the Puritans were dropping them. The vestment controversy had worn itself out. The old leaders of it were dead or had conformed. What law failed to do with many others, the power of a master intellect had accomplished. Jewel had, in the early part of this reign, in an "Apology" for the Church of England, built a barrier of reason and Scripture against the pretensions of the Church of Rome; Hooker now undertook a similar work in behalf of the principles of an Established Protestant Episcopalian religion. Most churches have been fortunate enough to possess one man of commanding intellectual ability to do its needed intellectual work, but no Church has been more fortunate in this respect than the Church of England. Jewel, Hooker, Burnet, and Pearson have probably done more to hold that Church together than

---

* Rees' "History of Nonconformity in Wales." Int. chap.

all its Acts of Uniformity. Hooker was, to the communion to which he belonged, what Bellarmine was to the Papacy, and what Owen, in a subsequent age, became to the Independents. Like Bellarmine, however, he required his first principles to be granted. That done, and his work is a masterpiece of reason; as it is, it must be acknowledged to be, in compass of thought and dignity of style, one of the greatest of all the works in Christian literature. In an age when nearly all learning and culture were on the side of the Puritans, Independents, and Baptists; when most of the ministers of the Established Church "were the basest of the people," and had been taken from the lowest occupations,[*] Hooker must have seemed an ecclesiastical Ajax, and it is no slight testimony to his greatness to say, that time has not diminished his proportions.

It is unfortunate for Hooker's reputation, that in the controversy which occasioned the writing of the "Polity," he should have so closely imitated his archdiocesan Whitgift, in his controversy with Cartwright. Not being able to silence Cartwright by argument, Whitgift had silenced him by authority. Travers was as learned a man as Hooker, and as great a scholar. He was predecessor to Hooker in point of time, as a Temple lecturer, although inferior to him in position. It might be an unseemly thing, and it was illegal, for the same pulpit to be used in the morning by Hooker to preach Conformity, and in the evening by Travers to preach Puritanism, and it was unseemly that they

---

[*] "Supplication of the Puritans to Parliament." Neal, vol. i., p. 483; and "Survey of the State of Religion." Ib., pp. 477-78.

should attack each other. But wars of oral disputation were at that time as common as pamphlet wars have since become. They were arranged beforehand with all the formality of a tournament. Luther had engaged in one such war; Bucer in another. They were still more common a century later, when Pœdobaptism and anti-Pœdobaptism divided the Nonconformist body, and public disputes were invited on both sides. But Hooker became annoyed. Travers was a man of quicker if not profounder intellect than he, readier at attack and more adroit in fence. Hooker moved slowly. His thought might be, as it was, majestic in its march and grand in its sweep, but it was deficient in celerity of action. He complained to the authorities, and Travers was silenced and ejected, but afterwards Hooker seems to have become ashamed of the course which he then took. His "Polity" occupied the whole of his subsequent life, and those who, since then, have maintained the power and authority of the Church to command human obedience, and to enforce penalties for the non-observance of her laws, have always drawn the best of their arguments from the great armoury of the "Ecclesiastical Polity."

The foundations, rites, and ceremonies of the Church being settled against Roman Catholics on the one hand, and Puritans, Independents, and Baptists on the other, and the press and pulpit closed against any replies, an attempt was next made definitely to settle her particular system of theological doctrine. Whether, as has been supposed, the language of the Articles was so chosen as purposely to leave them open to different interpretations, is, and always will be, a matter of dispute. Like the Catechism, they are of Lutheran origin,* and are therefore not essentially Calvinistic. As far as they go they will bear a Calvinistic interpretation better than they will bear any other; but where Calvin's system, as on the doctrines of Predestination, the Atonement, and Inspiration, is particularly explicit, the Articles are particularly vague. The presumption is that, like every thing else connected with the new Establishment, they were intended to be a compromise. But theological compromises, however they might have suited Cranmer, did not suit Whitgift. A preacher of the University of Cambridge, sympathizing with the doctrines of the lately-risen Arminius, had ridiculed Calvin's theory of Predestination and Perseverance. Whitgift, to settle the controversy, issued the nine propositions known as the "Lambeth Articles," in which the doctrine of Predestination is stated with a naked repulsiveness of language only since surpassed by Toplady. "God," said Whitgift, "has, of his own good will and pleasure, from all eternity, reprobated some men to death; men cannot be saved if they will, and a person predestinated to life, whatever his sins and relapses, shall inherit that life." Whitgift, however, was not supreme head of the English Church, and he had no sooner published his dogmatic decisions as to the counsels of the Almighty from eternity, and which he declared to be "already established by the laws of the land," than Elizabeth commanded them to be recalled. The Queen might, or might not, have been a "hyper-Calvinist." She was, on the whole, likely to be one. Her government was based upon the Calvinistic prin-

* This is conclusively shown in Archbishop Lawrence's "Bampton Lectures."

ciple of politics. She predestinated sound Churchmen, whatever might be their personal profligacy, to a heaven of place and profit, and Puritans and Anabaptists, whatever might be their personal piety, to human hells. She might naturally, therefore, be supposed to approve of Whitgift's Articles; but they raised painful and troublesome questions. Perhaps they made her ask herself whether she was a "justified person," having, as such, "full assurance and certainty" of the remission of her sins, and, doubting it, may have decided that a system which doomed herself to a worse punishment than she had been able to inflict on all the heretics in her kingdom—from Wiel-macker and Ter Voort, the unhappy Anabaptists whom she had burned at the stake, to Penry, the last Brownist whom she had hanged—however true it might be, should not be declared to be the doctrine of the Church of which she herself was the supreme head.

The controversy between Calvinists and Arminians, although never entirely ceasing, and never likely now to cease, did not again attract prominent notice until the Arminian Laud succeeded the Calvinistic Whitgift, when an Irish Episcopalian Synod framed articles in exact accordance with Whitgift's, a House of Commons decided in favour of Calvinism, and the question was so debated at solemn public conferences that no one, we are informed, left them as Arminians, who had not gone thither in the same opinion,* which is not at all unlikely. But from Whitgift's time the Puritans were distinguished by their rigid creed as well as their rigid

* Neal, vol. ii., p. 170.

life, and the Archbishop, who had spent his most vigorous years in rooting out that party, must have found, just before he died, that in his last attempt at enforcing uniformity, he had given greater unity to his own adversaries. Calvinistic Puritans afterwards brought to the block an archbishop whose Arminianism was, in their eyes, one of his greatest sins, and Whitgift was one of their authorities.

It was just previous to this controversy that Elizabeth took the step to which reference has already been made. She cleared the gaols, and, by substituting banishment in place of imprisonment for non-attendance at Church, drove both Brownists and Anabaptists from her kingdom. No event has had a greater influence on the human government of the world and the success of the Christian religion than the transplantation of the English race which then commenced. What Elizabeth intended to do, and no doubt thought she had done, was to secure her dominions, for all time to come, from being troubled by Separatists. But absolutism in a State is as short-sighted as intolerance in a Church, and in the Tudor Queen absolutism and intolerance were combined. What, therefore, she did do was to plant nurseries of freedom, destined, in a future period, to be fatal to the very principles of political and ecclesiastical government whose permanency she had thought to secure.

Amongst those who went forth to find new homes in the free cities of the Continent were Francis Johnson and Henry Ainsworth, who, in A.D. 1596, published " A Confession of Faith of certain English people living in the Low Countries, exiled." The Church at Amsterdam, of which these men were joint pastors, was apparently the first English Independent Church founded on the Continent; and was the first which issued a public confession of its faith. This document, which consists of forty-five articles, contains an elaborate explanation of the views of the English Independents at that period. It commences with a protest against the constitution and worship of the Established Church, and the means by which that Church was upheld. It then goes on to expound the nature and constitution of a Christian Church, the exposition being supported by numerous Scripture proofs. The articles on this subject differ materially, on only two points, from the principles and practices of most modern Congregationalists. All infants, it is stated, should be baptized or received into the Church, " that are of the seed of the faithful by one of the parents, or under their education and government."* On this subject great difference of opinion afterwards arose, but the first Independents held the creed of the Presbyterians, both of that and of the present age. They also adhered to the doctrine that it was the official duty of princes and magistrates to "suppress and root out, by their authority, all false ministries, voluntary religions, and counterfeit worship of God. Yea, to enforce all their subjects, whether ecclesiastical or civil, to do their duties to God and men."† Worshipping in a back lane in Amsterdam, and having had experience beyond most men of what was meant by the " suppressing " and " rooting out " of religious opinions,

---

* Articles xxxv. and xxxvii. Hanbury's " Hist. Memo." Vol. i., pp. 96, 97.

† Art. xxxiv., Ib.

this Church was yet as intolerant as that which it so fiercely assailed. If Ainsworth and Johnson had been entrusted with power they would, in all probability, have been the Whitgifts and Bancrofts of Independency. Happily, they were not the persecutors but the persecuted, and their reputations are stained by their doctrines, but not by blood.

What influence it was which, for a time, stayed the more active persecution of the Nonconformists towards the end of the reign of Elizabeth can only be conjectured; but there is evidence that as the Queen grew older her disposition became more tender. She had endured much pain and remorse, and had not the old hard courage to inflict pain on others. With Parker and Whitgift to carry out her behests and find new victims to the law, she had left Fox and Coverdale to linger out their lives in misery and die in poverty. She had silenced the best preachers of Christian truth; and she had filled all the prisons in England with the men of most eminent piety and learning. Then, until her death, there was a limited toleration. There was reason to expect that, when James came to the throne, this toleration would be continued, or perhaps extended, but none as yet knew the character of Elizabeth's successor. James the First has to be considered, in these pages, only as the head of the Established Church. That Church had already enjoyed the honour of having the grossest of voluptuaries for its supreme head; it was now to enjoy the honour of having the greatest liar and one of the greatest drunkards of his age in the same position. The prelates accepted him with devout gratitude. The more his character became revealed to them the greater was their satisfaction. When he almost swore at the Puritans, Whitgift declared that his Majesty spake by the especial assistance of God's spirit, and Bancroft, that he was melted with joy, for that since Christ's time such a King had not been. When he drivelled they held up their hands in amaze at his wisdom. The two parties fully understood each other. James had quite sufficient cunning to detect the ambitious designs of the prelates, and the prelates had sufficient learning, and sufficient knowledge of the theory of morals, to know that they were dealing with a dissembler and a fool. But it served their purposes to play into each other's hands. The king could put down Puritanism in the Church and "harry" all Brownists and Anabaptists out of the land, and the bishops, in their turn, could exalt the supremacy of the monarch.

The Puritans of James's reign were a different order of men from those of Elizabeth's. They were more numerous, but they were more moderate, and very few of them went as far as Cartwright had gone. The grievances complained of in the "Millenary" petition from the Hampton Court Conference, included, certainly, the cap and surplice, and the ring in marriage, but they did not touch on the regal supremacy or on episcopacy. They objected to portions of the baptismal service and to confirmation; they wished the Lord's-day to be kept more holy; they asked for a more godly ministry and for a restoration of Church discipline; for pluralities to be abolished, and lastly, that the Calvinistic Articles of Whitgift might be declared to be the creed of the Church of England, and that uniformity of doctrine might be prescribed. The King answered them at the Conference with denial and abuse. Church writers, in dealing with this subject, have felt compelled to employ language of shame and indignation at the conduct of the King and the bishops at this period which a Nonconformist would almost hesitate to use.* It is obvious from the whole proceedings, that the Conference was summoned for a purpose opposed to its ostensible aim. It was not intended to bring the two parties in the Church in harmony, but to give occasion for casting out one of them. It led, however, to results which none probably had anticipated. Reynolds, the Puritan, had suggested a new translation of the Bible, by His Majesty's special sanction and authority. The vanity of the King was touched, and the great work was executed. If the knowledge of the Gospel was extended, and practical religion was strengthened by this act, the next step had a contrary tendency and effect. In the year after the Hampton Court Conference, Convocation met to frame a new set of Canons. These laws—laws so far as the clergy are concerned—still deface the constitution and character of the English Episcopalian Church. Most of them are obsolete, for they have been virtually repealed by the Legislature, and only those which can be brought to bear against Dissenters are observed by the clergy, who have sworn to obey them all. They are now little else than monuments of a past age of intolerance, and of the combined immobility and timidity of the ecclesiastical establishments of the present day. Old bloodhounds of the Church, with their teeth drawn

---

* Marsden's "Early Puritans," chap. x. Hallam's "Const. Hist." i., 404.

and the force exhausted, they are gazed at with as much contempt as they once excited fear.

The exiles also addressed a humble supplication to the King, in which, in admirably chosen words, they stated their faith and asked for toleration. One article of this statement relates to the maintenance of the Christian ministry, and is decisive as to the opinions of the earliest Independents in favour of the voluntary support of religious worship. They declare their doctrine to be, "That the due maintenance of Christian ministry should be of the free and voluntary contributions of the Church; that, according to Christ's ordinance, they which preach the Gospel may live of the Gospel, and not by Popish lordships and livings or Jewish tithes and offerings." * This doctrine, as will be seen, was subsequently re-affirmed, while unlimited religious freedom was still unrecognized. In the course of their history during the next hundred years this position of the Independents was reversed. They allowed the lawfulness of tithes, and of a compulsory support of the Christian religion, but claimed a more perfect liberty of worship.

The King did not consider this petition worth his notice. Once more, therefore, uniformity was rigidly exacted, and once more, but for the last time, the fires of Smithfield were lighted. Bartholomew Legget, who had been convicted of Arianism, was the last to suffer in this place, and a month later, in May 1612, Edward Wightman met the same death at Lichfield. He had been convicted of a multitude of mysterious heresies, the

---

* Fletcher, vol. ii., p. 235.

principal of which were Anabaptism and Arianism. After this, imprisonment was substituted for death, and books instead of bodies were burned. The change marks one step towards increased religious liberty; Puritans were now tolerated, but to Brownists and Anabaptists a severer measure was dealt out. Archbishop Bancroft was to James what Parker had been to Elizabeth, and those Separatists who could not be imprisoned were compelled to banishment. "Things in a manner recovered to the first settlement under Elizabeth."*

It was under this new reign of terror that a second exodus took place to Holland from inhabitants principally of London and Lincolnshire. Amongst them and their followers were some whose names are written in many histories,—John Robinson, the scholar and pastor,* whose figure so often adorns the annals of Independency, and stands so prominent in the history of the Pilgrim Fathers, William Brewster, the future governor of the new colony, and John Smyth and Thomas Helwys, the most prominent of the Baptists of this period. A historian of the Free Churches of England, in referring to some of these names, approaches questions which have afforded matter of controversial debate between the writers of the Independent and the writers of the Baptist denominations. When Smyth joined the Church at Amsterdam, it was already torn with dissension, and the course which he took added to its divided state. He declared himself to be a Baptist, and because the Church allowed

* Collier, vol ii., p. 687.

infant baptism denounced it as participating in spiritual adultery. The Independents, in their turn, denounced Smyth and his party as "heretics," and excommunicated them.* This act has been reprobated in strong language, but it is impossible to say how it could have been avoided. If the whole controversy on both sides is read, most persons will come to the conclusion that the blame of this first and fatal division of the Independent body into Pædobaptists, and Antipædobaptists, ought to be equally divided amongst both parties. If one more than another should be condemned, it is Smyth, whose violent language alone would have justified the violent measure by which he was expelled. Then followed the usual pamphlet war, and the two parties of exiles employed their pens to attack each other, with more or less of sound argument, but with unlimited abuse.

Smyth and Helwys at once formed a Baptist Church, Smyth baptizing himself in order to commence it.† The members of this Church, forty-two in number, drew up a confession of their faith, which is remarkable for two points—its Anti-Calvinism, and its Anti-State Churchism. The former is exhibited in treating of Original Sin, Predestination, and Free Will, on which subjects the Arminian view was taken; the latter in the declaration that the office of the magistracy is not ordained in the

---

* Francis Johnson writes:—"About thirteen years since, this Church, through persecution in England, was driven to come into these countries. Awhile after they were come hither, divers of them fell into the heresies of the Anabaptists, which are too common in these countries; and so persisting, were excommunicated by the rest." Hanbury, vol. i., p. 110.

† Whether Smyth did or did not baptize himself has been the subject of much controversy. The most satisfactory statement of the case is to be found in Dr. Evans's "Early English Baptists," vol. i., pp. 203—218.

Church. Smyth and his followers held, also, some doctrines nearly approaching to those afterwards affirmed by the Society of Friends. "Christ," they said, "hath called his servants to their own 'unarmed and unweaponed life.'" In one respect they went beyond this; they denied the right of a Christian to assume the office of the magistracy in any rank. On the subject of the relation of the magistrate to the Church, as on other subjects, Smyth himself afterwards published a fuller confession, in which he writes, "That the magistrate, by virtue of his office, is not to meddle with religion or matters of conscience, nor to compel men to this or that form of religion or doctrine, but to leave the Christian religion to the free conscience of every one, and to meddle only with political matters, namely, injustice and wrong of one against another, such as murder, adultery, theft, and the like; because Christ alone is the King and lawgiver of the Church and of the conscience."* The contrast between this doctrine, where the line, beyond which the magistrate, as such, may not step, is drawn as clearly as it is by all the Free Congregational Churches of the present day, and the doctrine of Johnson and Ainsworth is decisive as to the more advanced opinions on this subject of the Early Baptists.† Helwys returned

---

* Evans, vol. i., p. 270. Art. xxxvi.

† In writing this, I have not overlooked the Humble Supplication for Toleration, attributed to Jacob, published on behalf of the Independents in 1609; nor the Pamphlet entitled "Religion's Peace; or a Plea for Liberty of Conscience," by Leonard Busher, a Baptist, and published in 1614. Mr. Hanbury ridicules Dr. Price for having, in his History of Nonconformity (vol. i., pp. 522-23), taken credit to the Baptists for being the first, as shown in Busher's Pamphlet, to bring forth to public view, the principles of religious liberty, and refers to the "Humble Supplication," published five years before, as proof that the Independents were the first

to England about 1612, and formed in London the first General or Anti-Calvinistic Baptist Church. All Baptists at that period apparently held the sentiments of Smyth and Helwys on the subjects which divide the Calvinistic and Arminian sections of the Christian world.

John Robinson had joined the Church at Amsterdam, but soon afterwards left it to found in Leyden a new Independent Church, the mother Church of the Pilgrim Fathers of New England. No name in the history of Independency shines with greater lustre that his. To him the Churches of that communion were indebted, until the time of Owen, for the ablest vindication of their principles, both as against the Church of England on the one hand, and Baptists on the other. He was a man of profound scholarship, high culture, and of a largeness of heart which was, at that time, less common amongst the Separatists than many other qualities. As a theological disputant he was quick and vigorous. None of the Separatists lacked moral courage, but Robinson had a higher courage than most, if not any, of his brethren. The most conspicuous fault of the Separatists was excessive dogmatism. It was impossible for any of them to err; impossible for any who differed from them to hold the truth. They

---

to do this; but Mr. Hanbury does not distinguish between even toleration and liberty, much less between toleration and equality. The "Humble Supplication" acknowledges the power of the Sovereign in "overseeing, ruling, and censuring particular Churches," and requests that subordinate civil officers may be appointed to demand and receive of each Church, accounts of their proceedings. This is not asking for, or dreaming of religious liberty, and only for toleration in a most limited and degraded sense. The doctrine of "Religion's Peace," on the other hand, is as unequivocal as is that of Smyth.

were all infallible in their judgments, and none knew the whole counsel of God but they. When this failing did not become a vice, as it sometimes did, it was not without its service. It was the almost inevitable result of the circumstances in which the Separatists were placed. They were in constant conflict with a supreme authority, which was not exercised in favour of what they judged to be the truth. They were pressed down, limited and restrained by it on all sides. Against it they could oppose only their faith and confidence in their own convictions. If they had not been doubly sure that they, and they alone, held the truth, they could never have withstood the power which was arrayed against them. If that faith and confidence often, or, indeed, generally, degenerated to dogmatism, was it not natural that it should do so ? To doubt was, with them, to be lost; to entertain a single suspicion that, after all they might be wrong, would have paralysed them in conflict with such foes as the ecclesiastical law-makers and laws of the Tudors and the Stuarts. Just when it might be necessary for them to strike a blow on behalf of their principles or their rights they would have been dropping their weapons, or striking with a faltering purpose and a weakened arm. Dogmatism was their early shield of faith hammered into what it had become by the blows of opponents. There was little of art in their controversies. They did not fight with the measured pace and nice rules of courtier duellists, but Agag "was hewed in pieces," and the Christian Hector was dragged round the applauding field by the Christian Achilles who had slain him.

Robinson was a man of finer mould and higher temper.

He could strike with equal swiftness, and generally with surer accuracy than most of his rivals; but his courage resembled less that of a common soldier than did most men's. He is unworthy of himself in his controversy with the Baptists,* but who has been worthy of himself in that controversy? In most of his controversial, and in all his ethical writings, there is an equal breadth and purpose. He could assail the Church of England without reviling her in language coarse enough—save the gentle Abbott—for even a prelate of the Stuart dynasty. He could treat of morality and philosophy with a learning, a wisdom, and a calmness second only to Bacon's. His faith was perhaps more assured than that of some who used more assertion, but it was further removed from dogmatism. He could write—a great thing in those days to do— "If in anything we err, advise us brotherly. Err we may, alas! too easily, but heretics, by the grace of God, we will not be." And when he bade the Pilgrim Fathers God speed, his memorable last words were— "I charge you, before God and His blessed Angels, that you follow me no further than you have seen me follow the Lord Jesus Christ. If God reveal anything to you by any other instrument of His, be as ready to receive it as you were to receive any truth by my ministry, for I am verily persuaded the Lord hath more truth yet to break forth out of His holy word. For my part, I cannot sufficiently bewail the condition of those reformed Churches which are come to a period in religion and will go, at present, no further than the instruments of their reformation. The Lutherans cannot be drawn to go

---

* He denounced all Anabaptists as "Vile heretics and schismatics"

beyond what Luther saw. Whatever part of His will our God has revealed to Calvin, they will rather die than embrace it; and the Calvinists, you see, stick fast where they were left by that great man of God, who yet saw not all things. This is a misery much to be lamented." No man, probably, but Robinson could have given expression to thoughts such as these, for no other man possessed his spirit. He was honoured to be the Pastor of the Pilgrim Fathers, and from his Church went forth those also who founded anew in England the Independent denomination. From John Robinson's congregation at Leyden came Henry Jacob, to form in London in A.D. 1616 what, at one time, was termed the first Independent Church. Probably it was the only Church at that period, those that went before having been rooted out by James and his prelates.

We now see two, but only two, Free Churches certainly established and existing in England in the latter part of the reign of James the First. And at this period we see two questions rising into prominence, the discussion of which served, in no small degree, to aid in the development of a freer thought, and a more devout religious life. The first of these questions was the history and origin of tithes. Selden had written his book, proving the purely human authority for this imposition, which so exasperated the prelates, that the author was compelled to apologize for its publication. Yet his work is now the highest authority on its subject, and its principal doctrine has been accepted by the greatest jurists and statesmen of England. In the same year another question was forced before the people. One of the petitions of the Puritans had been for a better observance of the Sabbath. This question had begun to excite attention in Elizabeth's reign by the publication of Dr. Bound's work on the obligations of the Sabbath-day. Bound was inclined to Jewish Sabbatarianism, but so were the Puritans, and his work had, for that age, an extraordinary circulation. There was certainly a necessity for the moral obligations of the Christian day of rest being explained and enforced. Sunday, in England under Elizabeth, was what Sunday is in France under Napoleon the Third. It was the gala day of the week, a day for sport and pleasure, dancing and theatrical entertainments, riot and debauchery. Bound's work was exercising great influence, but it was an influence which tended in favour of Puritan doctrine and life. This was enough for Whitgift, and it was at once prohibited. The Archbishop declared that the doctrine of the Sabbath did not agree with that of the Church; every copy of the book was called in, and the author was ordered not to reprint it. Bound's work holds the same position in this controversy that Hooker's holds in the controversy relating to Church Establishments. It gave an impetus to what have been denominated Sabbatarian views, which has never ceased, and it was the text book of the Puritans in the next and succeeding reigns. The author's views, as was likely to be the case—for one extreme causes another—would, by most persons, now be considered somewhat too Judaical, and the contrast between them and those set forth in the most recent work on this subject* is a fair measure of the gap which lies between the style of Puritan thought in the sixteenth

---

* Dr. Hessey's "Bampton Lectures."

and seventeenth centuries and the style of religious thought in the nineteenth century. Bound's book was reprinted in A.D. 1606, and it largely influenced the Puritanical observance of the Sunday. It appears to have been some time before James saw this, but when he saw it he determined to counteract it. The "Book of Sports" was issued, and the people were informed by royal authority that Sunday was not to be a day mainly of religious rest and worship, but of games and revels. What there was, however, of religious sentiment and feeling in the nation, revolted at the order to publish, from the pulpits of England, this indulgence, and even Whitgift's successor, Archbishop Abbott, himself forbade it. The Puritans now, for the first time, defeated the King, and, for the first time, royal authority was set at nought. Elizabeth would have known how to deal with such subjects. She would have "unfrocked" Abbott, dispossessed the clergy of their benefices, and tried the whole of them before the Star Chamber, but James was cowed. In conquering him the Puritans first became conscious of their real strength and power, and learned that resistance to a monarch might, after all, be successful.

The events of no period of English history have been more fully described than those of the reign of Charles the First and the Commonwealth. Charles prepared the way for his own defeat and execution by his lofty pretensions and his habitual perjury. It has been said that lying is the peculiar vice of the lower classes; but history indicates that it has been the more peculiar vice of monarchs. The fountains of what is termed "honour" have been usually the fountains, at the same time, of all vice and uncleanness. In three centuries, until the reign of Queen Victoria, only three supreme rulers appeared in England of a character calculated to command even common respect. Elizabeth was one of these, and the respect accorded to her has its foundation solely in the strength of her will and her courageous patriotism. In the virgin purity of her character no one now believes, and her ordinary language was such as would, at the present time, disgrace a betting room. Of Cromwell and William the Third we shall have soon to speak: no others can be named. Charles the First lied on system; other Stuarts liked lying, but he approved of it, and the vice cost him his crown and his life.

At the same time the way was prepared for the sacrifice of the Established Church. The "Book of Sports" was again issued, "out," said the King, "of a pious care for the service of God." Scotland was excited to rebellion by the imposition of Episcopacy, and Convocation was invested with unlimited power to make ecclesiastical laws. All "sectaries" were again brought under the extreme penalty of law, and the doctrine of the divine right of Kings and of passive obedience assented to without reservation. There was some occasion, apparently, for new laws against the sectaries, if toleration was not to be allowed. The Independent Church formed by Jacob, but now presided over by another pastor, was still in existence. From it, in 1633,* a separation of Baptists took place, who formed the first Particular or Calvinistic Baptist Church in England, and who were the first to practise baptism by immersion, for,

---

* Wilson's "Dissenting Churches," vol. i., p. 41.

hitherto, the controversy between Baptists and Independents had had relation to the subjects only of baptism, and not to the mode. There were, at this period, four other Baptist Churches in England, one at Lincoln, one at Salisbury, one at Coventry, and one at Tiverton,* and probably also one at Olchen in Wales.† A little later Laud notices vindictively the existence of "several Anabaptists and other sectaries" at Ashford, in Kent,‡ while Bishop Hall, in 1641, called attention, in the House of Lords, to the existence in London and the suburbs of "no fewer than four score congregations of several sectaries, as" he says, "I have been too credibly informed, instructed by cobblers, tailors, felt makers, and such like trash."§ Hall was alarmed at such a state of things, and prophesied the rise of Jack Cades, Jack Straws, and Wat Tylers, if such people were not put down.‖

But it was not the "sectaries" who rose against Charles. The House of Commons, which declared war against him, was a house of Churchmen only,¶ gentlemen of rank, wealth, and territorial position. The bishops, and afterwards the clergy, suffered with him, for the reason that they had identified themselves with his cause, and that their pretensions were as opposed to the preservation of liberty as were the King's. There can be no doubt that the Episcopal form of Church govern-

---

* Evans' "Early Baptists," vol. ii., p. 26.
† "Thomas's History," p. 3.
‡ Collier, vol. ii., p. 791.
§ Works, vol. x., p. 65.
‖ Ib., p. 66.
¶ The testimonies of Clarendon and Baxter, on this point are too well known to be cited.

ment is more consistent with a civil tyranny than any other form. Wherever it has existed its adherents have cast the weight of their influence into the scale of despotism. It would not be difficult to explain the reason of this. It consists in the fact that the Episcopal form of government demands a greater surrender of personal liberty in religion than any other system. It exalts authority at the expense of right. Its chief officers are a superior order of men, invested, according to their own theory, with functions belonging to no other men on earth. They, too, are "fountains of honour," and their will is supreme, and their judgment final concerning some of the highest interests of mankind. A spiritual oligarchy, though sprung from the people, or, rather, because sprung from the people, they have never associated the people's interests, either civil or religious, with their own. Hence the Episcopal system has flourished best where religion has flourished least, and has found most favour wherever Christianity has been least removed from heathenism. Nothing of this is necessary to the system. It would be possible to imagine a Bishop as an active, humble, and zealous co-worker with other Christians, identifying himself with all their interests, and, seeking to advance rather than to retard them, to be the wise guide of the people rather than their bigoted opponent. But, excepting in a few rare instances, this has not been the character or the work of the English Episcopacy; and in Charles's time, as often since, it sought the apparent interests of its order, and of its order only. If self-preservation be a law of human nature, and self-abnegation a law of Christian nature, the bishops of the English Church have been intensely human and intensely heathen. What wonder that, with their recent history in view, the people should have determined, while they held the King in check, at the same time to suppress the Episcopalian religion and all connected with it?

The progress of Free Christianity can be clearly traced through the period which followed, but it was far more apparent than real. The religion partially established by Parliament and the Westminster Assembly of Divines was simpler, more strict in form, and finer in essence than that which had been overthrown, but this is the best that can be said of it. Politically, its establishment was expedient, for the sympathy and aid of the Scots could scarcely, at that time, have been dispensed with, but religiously it was a blunder. The Presbyterian State Church, where, as in London and Lancashire, it enjoyed coercive power, proved to be quite as intolerant as, and, to the majority of the people, less pleasant than the Episcopalian had been. Assemblies of Divines have never been celebrated for practical wisdom, moderation, or charity, and of all assemblies, that of Westminster, which sat for six years, and held one thousand one hundred and sixty-three sittings, showed the least of these qualities. The imposition on the nation of the Solemn League and Covenant was a more odious infraction of religious liberty than the imposition of the whole of the Prayer Book and thirty-nine Articles, for it was enforced on laymen as well as on the clergy. The longer and shorter Catechisms are admirable summaries of the doctrines of ultra-Calvinism, and the Confession of Faith is a work of masterly theological exposition; but what is to be said of the proposed enforcement of these on a whole nation?

The Baptists took no part in this Assembly, for it was tacitly decided that their doctrine concerning Infant Baptism excluded them from sitting in it. The position taken by the few Independents, five or six in number, who were nominated to it, has only lately been thoroughly understood.* It was not favourable to a very extensive degree of religious liberty. How could it be, when, at their entrance, they had signed the Solemn League and Covenant, by which they engaged to extirpate all "heresy and schism" from the land? And they let it be distinctly understood that they were not in favour of complete toleration. A petition was presented to the Assembly by " an old Anabaptist at Amsterdam" against the Covenant, and in favour of "full liberty of consience to all sects." It contained, no doubt, some wild sentiments, but not so wild as the Covenant must have appeared to the majority of Episcopalians. Nye and Thomas Goodwin, the leaders of the Independent party, were the most vehement in their denunciations of it. The Independents also prayed to be included in the proposed new national Church, the conditions being that the power of ordination should be reserved to their own congregations, and that they might be subject, in Church censures, to Parliament, but not to any Presbytery. They offered, if this were conceded, to allow the State to limit the number of their congregations. The Presbyterians replied, saying that if such a toleration were allowed to Independents it must be allowed to all other sects, and taunted Nye and his party with the fact that they were asking for more than their brethren

---

* See Fletcher's "History of Independency," vol. iv., cap. 1.

in New England were willing to permit.* The noblest words uttered by the Independents in this assembly were by Jeremiah Burroughes, in reply to the refusal of the Presbyterians to grant even this concession. " If," he said, " their congregations might not be exempted from that coercive power of the classes, if they might not have liberty to govern themselves in their own way, as long as they behaved peaceably towards the civil magistrates, they were resolved to suffer, and to go to some other place in the world where they might enjoy their liberty. But while men think that there is no way of peace but by forcing all to be of the same mind ; while they think the civil sword is an ordinance of God to determine all controversies of divinity, and that it must needs be attended with fines and imprisonment to the disobedient; while they apprehend that there is no medium between a strict uniformity and a general confusion of all things; while these sentiments prevail there must be a base subjection of men's consciences to slavery, a suppression of moral truth, and great disturbances in the Christian world."† With these words the endeavour to comprehend Independents in the proposed new national church came to an end. Few though they were in number, the Independents probably prevented this establishment. They were incessant in

---

* There are many misunderstandings concerning the persecution of the sects by the New England Independents arising from the confusion between the Pilgrim Fathers and the Puritans. The former never persecuted. The latter, as in England, were avowed State Churchmen. The distinction is pointed out in Palfrey's " History of New England ;" and in a Tract entitled, "The Pilgrim Fathers not Persecutors." By B. Scott, F.S.A. London, 1866.

† Neal, vol. iii., p. 309.

exposing the evils of a coercive Presbyterianism, and in this they succeeded. When it is said that this is all that they did, more is said than can now be realized. Before the nation they were the sole advocates of greater liberty of conscience. They stood in the breach against the advance of a new State Church, which, if better in many respects than the old, would have been worse in other respects. For the Puritans contended for a stricter uniformity of life, if not of belief, than the Episcopalians had ever demanded. The effect of the old system was to make martyrs; the effect of the new would have been to make hypocrites. The final result was, that while uniformity of external worship by the imposition of the "Directory," was enforced, no system of Church government was established. Episcopalianism was made impossible; but neither the bishops nor the ministers of the old persuasion were rooted out, as the sectaries had been under all previous governments.

The attempt at comprehension had thus signally failed. Almost as soon as this was evident, both the Parliament and the Assembly were dispensed with. The latter had long lost all moral influence. The wit of Selden had made it ridiculous, and the denunciations of Milton had exposed its tyrannical tendency. And there was growing a public distrust of Puritanism. The instruction to the Assembly to frame, if possible, a scheme of comprehension which should allow full liberty of conscience, had been moved in the House of Commons by Oliver Cromwell, and its failure was certainly one of the leading causes of his assuming the reins of government. With the liberty then allowed to them by law the Nonconformists had recently increased both in numbers and in influence. They had what they had never before enjoyed—a clear stage. The greatest statesmen were Independents; the army was filled by members of the same body, Fairfax's regiment especially, being almost entirely composed of them. Led by Cromwell, St. John and Vane in Parliament, with Milton as their literary champion, they had nothing more to fear. If the Baptists were not so well represented in the legislature, they had large influence in the army. The Lord Deputy Fleetwood, Oliver Cromwell's son-in-law, Major-General Harrison, Major-General Ludlow, and Colonel Hutchinson were Baptists. It is scarcely to be wondered at that an army so composed should resent the proceedings of the Parliament and the Assembly. At the time, therefore, that the power of both these bodies seemed to be at their height, the army made complaint and demanded a general indulgence for tender consciences. They asked that the taking of the Covenant be not imposed, and that all orders and ordinances tending in that direction should be repealed. They protested against any "compulsory" religion, stating that "the ways of God's worship are not all entrusted to us by any human power." The Presbyterians on the other hand insisted on the establishment of their own religion only, upon "a covenanted uniformity," and upon the extirpation of the sects. A third party was represented by the King, who, after two years' treaty, consented to most of the views of the Presbyterians. It was at this period that the army, seeing that everything for which they had fought, including liberty of conscience, was about to be wrested from them, sent in a remonstrance to the legislature. It was not attended to; Fairfax at once marched on London, and on December 6th, 1648, Pride "purged" the House of Commons. From this time Cromwell and the Independents held the reins of government.*

If the Presbyterians protested against one thing more vehemently than another in the prospect which was now before the nation, it was against toleration. The army had asked for a conference on the subject of the coercive power of the magistrate in matters of religion. The Presbyterians, instead of granting the request, drew up two formal documents, warning them of the consequences of men being guided by the "impulses of the Spirit." "We will not," said the army, "have any restraint laid on the consciences of men for religious differences." The Presbyterians replied that this would but make way for the "toleration of all heresies and blasphemies." It is significant to notice amongst the names of those who gave their assent to these views some of the most eminent of the men, who, with the two thousand ejected ministers were, fourteen years later, thrust from the Established Church because the toleration which they had denied to others was now denied to them. William Gouge and Thomas Manton, Edmund Calamy, William Spurston, Edmund Stanton, and Andrew Janeway believed, at that time, that toleration was a doctrine born of hell.

---

* It is remarkable that so few modern writers should have drawn attention to the intimate connection of the question of religious liberty with the events which led to Pride's "purge," the execution of Charles, and the establishment of the Commonwealth. Rushworth, and Neal following him, have clearly pointed it out.

The establishment of the Commonwealth was an era in religious liberty, and England, under Cromwell's government, experienced a degree of freedom which had hitherto been unknown. All who petitioned for liberty of conscience received it. Considering the political position which they occupied, the Episcopalians were, on the whole, tenderly treated—much more tenderly, indeed, than they had ever treated those who differed from them. In many parts of the kingdom the reading of the Book of Common Prayer, although contrary to law, was suffered. The few who left the Church were mercifully dealt with. They were not deprived of all means of living, and Usher and Pearson were still allowed to preach. Political Presbyterianism had received its death blow at the battle of Dunbar, but although its adherents were the worst enemies of the Commonwealth and the Protectorate, they were allowed freely to disseminate their views, and to defend the "Solemn League and Covenant." They were associated with Independents and Baptists, as "Triers" of the qualities of ministers, and by their "trials" they purged the pulpit of the vicious, the profane, and the ignorant,—in other words, of men who were ordinarily found to be the possessors of the old livings. Presbyterians and Independents, and a few Baptists, took the places of these men, and Christianity was preached throughout the land with a zeal and an energy which had never before been known. The doctrine of the State on the subject of religious toleration was indicated in the declaration of the Council of State in 1653, the thirty-sixth and thirty-seventh articles of which provided "that none be compelled to conform to the public religion by penalties or otherwise; but that endeavours be used to win them by sound doctrine, and the example of a good conversation," and that "such as profess faith in God by Jesus Christ, though differing in judgment from the doctrine, worship, or discipline publicly held forth, shall not be restrained from, but shall be protected in, the profession of their faith and exercise of their religion, so as they abuse not this liberty to the civil injury of others, and to the actual disturbance of the public peace on their part, provided this liberty be not extended to Popery or Prelacy, or to such as, under a profession of Christianity, hold forth and practise licentiousness." Tithes also were proposed to be abolished, in order that "a provision less subject to scruple and contention" might be made.* The views of the State on this subject were unquestionably in advance of those of the nation, and it is probable that they were in advance even of the opinions of most of the Independents of that period. For Burroughes thought that if the magistrate should choose to interfere, it was lawful to assist and second the sentence of subverters of the faith. Owen, in his sermon on "Toleration," went no farther than the title of his discourse, affirming in it his adherence to the principle of a State Church, while the

---

* I cannot refrain from quoting the words of a Church historian, the Rev. J. B. Marsden, on these declarations:—"Wise men," he says, "musing in their closets, had for some time questioned the wisdom, if not the justice, of compelling the dissatisfied to embrace the religion of the greater number, and making their dissent a crime. But Cromwell was the first who dared, not merely to give expression to the doubt, but to enrol the principle itself with the fundamental laws of England. Received with hesitation at the time, denounced by Presbyterians as little short of blasphemy, spurned by the Parliament of Charles II. with the same indiscriminate contempt with which all Cromwell's legislation was trampled under their feet, it still survived. The plant grew, for it was watered by the rains of heaven, and tens of thousands have reposed beneath its quiet shade."

Savoy Conference of 1658, which was attended by more than two hundred ministerial and other delegates from a hundred Independent Churches established throughout England and Wales, and of which Owen, Goodwin, Nye, and Caryl were members, said, only, that "professing Christians, with their errors, which are purely spiritual and internal, and overthrow not civil society, are to be borne with, and permitted to enjoy all ordinances and privileges, according to their light, as fully as any of their brethren who pretend to the purest orthodoxy." They further declared that "if they had the power which any of their brethren of different opinions had desired to have over them, or others, they would freely grant this liberty to them all." * This seems to be unexceptionable, and, as far as toleration only is concerned, it is so; but when Dr. Thomas Goodwin delivered this declaration to Richard Cromwell, he said, on behalf of the Savoy Assembly, "We look at the magistrates as custos utriusque tabulæ, and so commit it [the Gospel] to your trust, as our chief magistrate, to countenance and propagate." † It was such sentiments which drew down upon the Independents the scornful rebukes of Milton. The laymen, in fact, as has generally been the case, were in advance of the clergy on this subject. Vane, one of the greatest of the Independent statesmen, had said, "The province of the magistrate is this world and man's body; not his conscience or the concerns of eternity."‡ Cromwell probably only waited for time in order to apply this principle to the practical government of the nation.

* Orme's "Owen," p. 180. † Ib., pp. 182-183.
‡ "Meditations," A.D. 1655.

No just estimate of this period of ecclesiastical history can be formed without taking into consideration, first, the characters of the principal actors in it and their intentions, and, secondly, the results of their work. The figure of Cromwell stands in the foreground. No man's character was better indicated than his by his features and his attitude. He was notably a rugged, firm, enthusiastic, sincere, and affectionate man. That he was not a hypocrite, as some have judged, is proved by the fact that his feelings retained their natural force and freshness to the last moment of his life, and this can be the case with no hypocrite. Of all his qualities his will was the strongest, and, next, his family affections. Occasionally, his enthusiasm seemed to overbalance his judgment, but this was not really the case; for although it appeared to excess in his words, it never influenced him to a rash act. What is remarkable in such a character, considering his ecclesiastical relationships, is, that while he imposed, from temporary necessity, his own form of civil polity on the nation, he never cared to impose upon it his own form of ecclesiastical polity. The explanation is that he was not, in any sense, a theorist. The breadth of his intellect was equal to its strength, and though not a cultured man, he had all the essential qualities of cultured men. He could bear with differences of opinion, and although he had power to suppress, he chose to tolerate and encourage them. Politically, he was a monarchist both by tradition and feeling, and would have restored Charles if he could have done so with safety to the nation. He became a dictator from necessity. There is no evidence, however, that he cared for power as such, and he never used it but for what he judged—with a larger judgment than any man who had gone before him was capable of exercising—to be for the good of the nation. Ecclesiastically he was an Independent, but he never forced Independency on the nation. He was willing to tolerate even Jews—a thing at that time almost unheard of in Christendom; and he allowed Usher to preach almost within a stone's throw of Whitehall. With a sagacity which would have been justified by events had he lived longer, or had his son been competent for government, he used his influence mainly for the better political education of the nation. He cast off even his oldest friends for this, and made enemies equally amongst pure republicans, democratic levellers, and army leaders. It was the same with respect to religion. He would not impose Presbyterianism, and the Presbyterians therefore hated him. Many of the Baptists were "red republicans," and they, in their turn, were estranged. He, himself, kept in the way which he judged would be for the permanent advantage of his country, actuated in his work by a strong patriotism and a fervent religious feeling. Such a man, dying before half his task was accomplished, was not likely to be well reported of by many, either of his contemporaries or his successors. What he hoped to have done was to change the character of the nation, and he lived only long enough to disturb it. As soon as he was dead "the sow went back to her wallowing in the mire."

As Cromwell was at the head of the government of his age, so Milton was at the head of its literature. One remark applies to both,—they stood, from the greatness of their genius, comparatively alone. Milton appears to have been an Independent in Church government, a Baptist so far as the distinctive creed of the Baptists was concerned, with theological beliefs inclined to Arianism. He cannot be identified with any of the denominations, and in the latter years of his life he attended no place of public worship. He was above the sects, and appears to have loathed their mutual jarrings. Of his controversial works the utmost that can be said is that he defended the Commonwealth with his pen as successfully as Cromwell defended it with his sword. He gave to the Government the services of the loftiest genius and the most varied scholarship, adorned by all the manners of a courtier. What is most pertinent to remark in connection with his support of Cromwell and Cromwell's government is, that they could not have been of the character which it was once the fashion to ascribe to them, or Milton would not have identified himself with their cause.

The names and labours of the religious leaders of this age belong to the Christianity of the English nation. Foremost amongst them were the disputatious but zealous Baxter, the scholarly Owen, the gentle Howe, the liberal Goodwin, the solid Manton, and the active Powell. The Church of Christ never possessed abler or purer ministers than those of the Commonwealth, or men who gave themselves up with greater ardour to the work to which they had consecrated themselves. They gave a new character to the religious life of their country.

Much has been written of the vulgar and hypocritical character of the religion of this period. No doubt religious affectation prevailed to a great extent; but the representations which have come down to us from Tory writers are charged with the grossest exaggerations. The religious leaders of the Commonwealth have been stigmatized as a company of ignorant and canting fanatics. Ignorant they were not, canting some of them probably were, and they were not more fanatical than the High Churchmen of their age. Their learning alone has made their time as illustrious as any in the history of their country. No man was a greater patron of letters than the Protector. Oxford and Cambridge became, under his auspices, seats of study more profound and exalted than had been known since their foundation. "The love of deep learning was now, for the first time, widely diffused."* Under Owen's Vice-Chancellorship at Oxford, Wilkins and Boyle were pursuing their philosophical studies, and Locke and South were being educated. Goddard the physician, Gale the philologist, Seth Ward the mathematician, Pococke, the greatest Oriental scholar in Europe, with John Howe and Stephen Charnock, were in the same University. Some of these men were Independents, some were Presbyterians, and some were Episcopalians, for Cromwell never sacrificed the interests of learning to the prejudices of the sects. At Cambridge, Cudworth was teaching, and Poole, Stillingfleet, and Tillotson obtaining that learning with which they were subsequently to adorn their Church. If a comparison of times be made, it will be found that no time was more fruitful in the most exalted genius and the most profound scholarship than the time of the English Commonwealth.

Nor were the manners of the age as destitute of dignity and grace as is generally supposed. The Non-

* Marsden's "Later Puritans," p. 386.

conformists were not the melancholy and sour-visaged race that historians have delighted to portray. Addison has handed down to us* a picture of Puritan manners in the person of a " very famous Independent minister " who lived in funereal state, and exhibited nothing but "religious horror" in his countenance. The genial humourist describes a saint of that age as abstaining from all appearance of "mirth and pleasantry," and as "eaten up with spleen and melancholy;" but no such impression as this is to be obtained either from their portraits, their writings, or the memoirs of their lives. Gravity was certainly a characteristic of their manners; but it was not unmixed with pleasantry and humour. Some, like the leaders and followers of the highest fashion in the present day, chose to wear their hair cropped, but the majority of those whose portraits have come down to us were remarkable for their flowing ringlets. Milton, Colonel Hutchinson, Selden, and Owen are fair representative men, and they were all distinguished by their graceful dress, their curling hair, and their polished manners.† In their own times, indeed, they were abused for their gaiety. "Yea," said Bastwick of the Independents, "you shall find them with

---

* "Spectator," 494. The divine is supposed to be Dr. Thomas Goodwin.

† The following is Mrs. Hutchinson's portrait of her husband :—" He could dance admirably well, but neither in youth nor riper years made any practice of it; he had a skill in fencing, such as became a gentleman; he had great love to music, and often diverted himself with a viol, on which he played masterly; had an exact ear and judgment in other music; he shot excellently in bows and guns, and much used them for exercise; he had great judgment in paintings, graving, sculpture, and all liberal arts, and had many curiosities of value in all kinds. . . He took much pleasure in improvement of ponds, in planting groves, and walks, and fruit trees, in opening springs and making fish ponds." "Memoirs," p. 23. Col. Hutchinson was an " Anabaptist."

cuffs, and those great ones, at their very heels, and with more silver and gold upon their clothes and at their heels (for these upstarts must now have silver spurs) than many great and honourable personages have in their purses."* Anthony Wood brings a charge against Owen that, instead of being a good example to the University, he scorned all formality, and describes him as "like a young scholar, with powdered hair, snake-bone band-strings, or band-strings with very large tassels; a large set of ribands pointed at his knees, and Spanish leather boots, with large lawn tops, and his hat mostly cocked."† Cromwell himself, when Whitelocke told him, on his return from Sweden, how he had amused the members of his Embassy with music and dancing in the long winter nights, expressed his emphatic approval of "such very good diversions."‡ The sermons of some of the most popular preachers of the Commonwealth abound like Latimer's, in broad English humour. Milton, who appears to have thought that his works would be read only by the Puritan section of his countrymen, wrote for them not only the "Paradise Lost," but "L'Allegro" and "Comus."§ The controversial writings of the age are distinguished by

* "The Utter Routing of the Independents." Preface.
† "Athen." Oxon. ii. 556.
‡ "Whitelocke's Embassy," ii. 438.
§ "Eaten up with spleen and melancholy," and "abstaining from all appearance of mirth and pleasantry:" this is the popular picture of the Puritan. For such men Milton wrote:
"Hence loathed Melancholy—
. . .
But come, thou goddess fair and free,
In heaven yclep'd Euphrosyne,
And by men heart easing Mirth—
. . .

their quickness of wit and their felicity of classical illustration. It is true that some sanctioned laws for the suppression of certain pastimes, revels, and theatrical entertainments; but those amusements had been conducted in a manner which no decent man would now tolerate. The difference in morals and manners between the Nonconformists and the Cavaliers was, that while the former anticipated the pure and refined life of the English gentleman of the nineteenth century, the latter were as dissolute and licentious as the ancient heathens.

The Baptists of this period were inferior as a sect to others in learning, but their activity in preaching the Gospel, and their zeal in defence of religious freedom, were probably superior. The mantle of Penry had fallen on Vavasour Powell, who was evangelizing Wales and forming Churches, most of which appear to have been of an unsectarian character, in various parts.* William Kiffin, a wealthy London merchant, was their chief pastor in the metropolis, and had great influence with Cromwell, as well as, afterwards, with the two Stuarts. John Canne and Hanserd Knollys were using their pens with vigour and success in favour of a free Nonconformity, and

> "Haste thee, nymph, and bring with thee
> Jest and youthful Jollity—
> .   .
> Sports that wrinkled Care derides,
>   And Laughter holding both her sides;
> And, if I give thee honor due,
>   Mirth admit me of thy crew."

* This was the case with many of the early Nonconformist Churches. The Pilgrim Fathers' Church, at Southwark, was originally an unsectarian Church, and had Baptist ministers. Wilson's "Dissenting Churches," vol. iv. p. 122, and "Crosby," vol. iii. p. 40.

Tombes, a man of learning and great controversial ability, was defending Baptist views against Baxter, and preaching with vigour in the Midland Counties. All through England the activity of religious effort was unsurpassed, and it was adorned, for the most part, by such human graces as commonly attend profound scholarship and unaffected piety. Nor ought it to be forgotten, in justice to the Independents of the Commonwealth, that it was they who first conceived the duty of foreign missionary effort. It was on July 27th, 1648, that an ordinance was passed in Parliament,* constituting a corporation under the title of "The President and Society for the Propagation of the Gospel in New England." The preamble of this ordinance recites "that the Commons of England assembled in Parliament, having received intelligence that the heathens of New England were beginning to call on the name of the Lord, felt bound to assist in such a work." They therefore gave power for the formation of a special corporation for the propagation of the Gospel, and ordered that the Act might be read in churches and collections thereafter made. This Society was the first Missionary Society formed in England, and was the parent of the present Society for the Propagation of the Gospel in Foreign Parts.

A new faith, however, now appeared. It had the reception usually accorded to new faiths, and its leaders appeared even to court persecution. The Society of Friends dates its origin from this period. No religious community ever had more vigorous or consistent founders. George Fox, to whom it owes its origin, was

* Scobell's "Acts," cap. 45.

no doubt an indiscreet man; but such indiscretion as his may well be overlooked, in comparison with the purity the enthusiasm, and the piety of his life. No man was more maligned than he; and the creed of no sect was so grossly caricatured and misrepresented as the creed of the " Quakers." The doctrines of the Baptists had only lately been tolerated ; but here were doctrines that went far beyond those, which, to many, had once appeared to be utterly inconsistent with Christianity. The demand made upon the charity of Christians of all sects was greater than they could bear, and there was, for once, unanimity in denunciation. Baxter, not for the first time in his life, became the bell-wether of theological detraction. He was always ready for controversy; but in controversy with the Quakers he was not merely ready, but eager. He had some hope of the ultimate salvation of Baptists, but he doomed all Quakers, without reserve, to utter damnation. " I had rather," he wrote, " that men continued Separatists and Anabaptists than turned Quakers or plain apostates, and therefore would do all that I can to hinder such an emptying of their Churches as tendeth to the more certain filling of hell. It is better to stop them in a condition where we may have some hope of their salvation than to let them run into certain perdition."* Owen, also, used his authority as Vice-Chancellor at Oxford to sanction the whipping of two Quaker women for speaking in church, denouncing them, at the same time, as blasphemers and abusers of the Holy Spirit.† Much of this language was simply

---

* Preface to the "Quaker's Catechism."
† Sewell's " History," p. 90—91.

retaliative, for George Fox and those who became his disciples denounced all the forms of worship then in practice, and "bore testimony" against them in a manner which was calculated to excite both anger and revenge. "Steeple houses," as they termed the Churches, were an abomination; a paid ministry was unscriptural; tithes were without warrant either from religion or from justice;* the Sacraments were done away with, and, above all, they declared that men had not merely the light of Scripture, but an "inward light" communicated by God's spirit, whereby they might discern the truth. Allied to these opinions were some that were not less unpalatable to those who heard them. Such was the doctrine that all oaths are sinful; that priests should have nothing to do with marriage; that no extravagant respect should be paid to rank; and that it was unlawful for a Christian to take up arms, or even to make use of physical force, for his own or his country's protection. The characteristic doctrines, however, of Quakerism resolved themselves into two,—those of the "inward light" and of the essential spirituality of religion. Religion, they maintained, had its origin in the communion of the Spirit of man with the Spirit of God, and therefore neither needed, nor could properly be expressed by, forms and ceremonies. They abjured all that was traditional, and all that was merely external in worship. Had they abstained from attacking other sects they would probably, in the time of the Commonwealth, not

---

* The Quakers were the first people who assailed with anything like power or persistency the injustice of tithes and Church-rates. They did this from their first origin. In their early tracts all the modern arguments on these subjects are anticipated.

have been attacked; but when they attended places of worship, and publicly assailed both the preachers and their doctrines, they excited an animosity which fell little short of fury. They were whipped and imprisoned, put in stocks, pilloried, and made subject to every personal indignity, but they still increased in numbers with an unexampled rapidity. During the Protectorate three thousand one hundred and seventy three persons of this denomination were imprisoned, thirty-two of whom died in confinement. Their persecutors were, for the most part, Presbyterians and Independents. Whenever their sufferings were brought officially before Cromwell he appears to have given orders for their relief. It was at the time of one of Fox's numerous imprisonments that he first met the Protector. The two men, each equally remarkable, and each capable of appreciating the peculiar greatness of the other, talked largely of God's ways, and Fox was dismissed and set at liberty with an expression of Cromwell's personal good-will. All Quakers were then ordered to be set free, and men were forbidden to harm them. Liberty of public meeting was, however, denied them, but Quakers were the least likely of all men to obey such a law. They defied the law, met and preached, and from the Baptists especially, gathered large numbers of converts. So they laid the foundation of one of the most respected and useful of all the Christian communities. Those who will be at the trouble of reading their own expositions of their own faith will hardly fail to acknowledge that the Quakers obtained a firmer grasp than others of one or two central Christian truths, and that their "testimony" was necessary to the complete exhibition of the Christian religion. Much of their distinctive theology has unconsciously been absorbed into the theology of the present day. Their appearance was a test of the degree of religious liberty enjoyed under the Commonwealth and the Protectorate. Fox, Burroughes, and their co-adjutors, whatever might have been their peculiarities, were men in whose character and work any society of Christians might rejoice. One duty they had certainly learned long before others had dreamed of it, namely, to tolerate the intolerant.

No one can doubt that the Restoration under Charles the Second was popular with the nation, and especially popular with the Presbyterians, to whom, indeed, he owed his return. Cromwell had offended this body, beyond forgiveness, by frustrating their schemes for ecclesiastical domination. They had hated the tolerant character of his government, and they now, with all his debauched habits, welcomed the Stuart. They again looked forward to a modified National Church, in which they might retain their livings and probably regain their coveted ascendancy. They were assured not merely of toleration, but of indulgence for tender consciences. Had not the King given his word? Had he not said it in the Declaration from Breda, which was signed with his own hand? Their joy was great when ten of their number were appointed Court chaplains, and greater when they knew that five bishoprics were kept open for them. Although the old Liturgy and all the old clergy had been restored, they were sanguine enough to wait upon the King, and ask his interposition for removing the differences in the Church—that is to say, the differences between the Episcopalians and themselves. They obtained, in reply, a second Declaration, in which a modified and temporary liberty of Nonconformity was granted, which the House of Commons refused to sanction.

There can be little doubt that Charles would have consented to a large degree of religious freedom. Like most men of his class, he had a generous and easy nature, and preferred not to be troubled with ecclesiastical matters. This, however, was not Clarendon's disposition, nor was it Sheldon's. While the King sported with his mistresses, the statesmen and the ecclesiastics ruled the people, and there was no intention on their part to allow the smallest indulgence to the most tender conscience.

It was probably only to save the public honour of the King that the Savoy Conference was held. This Conference was a repetition of that at Hampton Court, and its object was the same, namely, to keep all Puritans and Presbyterians out of the Church. The presence of Baxter, with his argumentative disposition, would have prevented the success of any such assembly; but had Baxter not been a member, and the most conspicuous member, of the Conference, its issue, while it might have been delayed, could scarcely have been of a different character. His demands were not dissimilar from those of the earlier Puritans,* and their reception was the same. The Book of Common Prayer was made less, rather than more, palatable. The ecclesiastical authorities decided, with expressions of hatred and contempt for those who were suing to them, that there should be no alteration in the formularies of the Church, which would

---

* See "Documents relating to the Settlement of the Church of England under the Act of Uniformity," edited by the Rev. George Gould, 1862.

be likely to keep within its borders any who differed from the old ecclesiastical constitution.

Neither the Independents nor the Baptists took any part in the Savoy Conference. They did not ask for, nor apparently, did they desire, any comprehension within the Church. They pleaded only for toleration. The Presbyterian Commissioners took no note of their existence. They do not appear even to have considered what effect their proposed revision of the Prayer Book would have on other Christian communities. No one who has read Baxter's controversial works—the most abusive even of that age—will believe that he would willingly have consented to the toleration of Baptists or Quakers. Had the Church of England been reconstituted in accordance with the desires of the Presbyterian party in this Conference, the result, in all likelihood, would have been such a State Establishment as was contemplated by the Westminster Assembly, which refused to allow of more than a limited toleration, even to Independents. As it is not in the nature of ecclesiastics to become more liberal in proportion as they are invested with power, it is very possible that the Act of Uniformity, which must have been passed to give authority to the revised Prayer Book, would have been followed by other Acts, not very dissimilar in character from those which followed the establishment of the unreformed Book. The Puritans were saved from this disgrace by their own ejectment.

The history of this ejectment has been often and eloquently told. Considered as an act of the State Church, it was a fatal blunder; considered as part of the history of the Free Churches of England, it was the most happy event which could have taken place. For, where

Nonconformists could formerly be counted only by the score, they could now be told by the thousand. Until the year 1662, the opponents of the State Church were few, and those few were localized. They were now spread throughout every part of the kingdom, and wherever there was an ejected pastor there was public sympathy with him. But the lives and the preaching of Howe, and Owen, and Baxter, and Caryl, and Bates, and Manton, with their two thousand brethren, would have counteracted all the external influences which the authority of the State had given to those who had conformed. Sheldon, in spiritual power, could never have successfully competed with any of the men whom he had aided to cast out of the Church. He, and the majority of his episcopal brethren, were ecclesiastics only —unscrupulous politicians with clerical titles, who, to aid their own ambitious purposes, banded themselves together to uphold the worst of all the Governments of England. It was seen by these men that the Act of Uniformity had not decreased the influence of the ejected ministers. It had, on the contrary, increased it. In many cases, perhaps the majority, the ejected remained where they were, and preached to the same people. The chief difference between their former and their present position was a difference of external circumstance. They did not preach in a certain building, nor had they a fixed maintenance ; all besides remained as it had been, excepting that the sacrifice which they had made for conscience' sake had increased towards them the respect and affection of the people.

It was resolved to break this spiritual power. During the remainder of Charles the Second's reign the aim of the ecclesiastical authorities was to effect the extinction of Nonconformity. First, in A.D. 1661, had been passed the Corporation Act, after which no Nonconformist could hold office in any municipal body; in A.D. 1662, the Act of Uniformity silenced their ministers; in A.D. 1663, the Conventicle Act was passed, and no Nonconformist could hold a meeting at which more than five persons in addition to the family were present; in A.D. 1665, all Nonconformist ministers were prohibited, by the Five Mile Act, from coming within five miles of any corporate borough; in A.D. 1670, the Conventicle Act was extended, the penalties under it increased, and informers encouraged; in A.D. 1673, the Test Act was passed, after which all employment, civil, naval, or military, under the Government, was denied to Nonconformists. The revival of the Act for the burning of heretics would have been an appropriate addition to these laws, but Sheldon did not suggest it. Long and weary imprisonments, banishment and starvation satisfied the Episcopal bench, and to this moderation England owes the continued existence of her liberties and her religion.

Some hundreds of Free Churches date their existence from this period. It was the period, also, when the distinguishing principles of the various sects may be said to have been finally established in literature. Stillingfleet, the greatest ecclesiastical lawyer and antiquarian of his age, was beginning to denounce the sin of schism; Baxter, as though he were a whole college of divines, poured forth defences and expositions, answers and rejoinders, at the rate of sometimes eight and sometimes ten in one year, on Conformity and Nonconformity, Peace and Schism, Baptism and Popery, Calvinism and Arminianism; David Clarkson, with a mind stored with patristic lore, assailed the theory of diocesan Episcopacy; and John Owen, with massive and sinewy brain and exhaustless learning, so built up the principles of Congregationalism, that if all the works on that subject which have since been written were destroyed, the Congregational Churches of England could stand behind his treatises as behind an impregnable rampart. Amongst the Baptists, Benjamin Keach did eminent service by the publication, amongst other works, of a Christian Catechism, for which he was sent to the pillory, and from thence to gaol; Delaune perished in prison for his "Nonconformist's Plea," and John Bunyan arose to expound and defend the principles, if not of a liberal theology, at least of a liberal ecclesiastical rule.* The Quakers were represented with equal ability. To this period are owing the Catechism and the "Apology" of Robert Barclay, a man of eminent piety and equally eminent learning, and the first treatises of William Penn. Exegetical and devotional theology were cultivated with similar zeal. The "Pilgrim's Progress," the "Saint's Everlasting Rest," the "Redeemer's Tears," the "Living Temple," and " No Cross No Crown," belong to the time of Stuart persecution.

The sufferings of ministers and people during this period were unspeakable. Their congregations were scattered; they were fined, pilloried, imprisoned, and banished. Many Presbyterians took refuge in the Church; others identified themselves more closely with the Independents, and the denomination, as such, began to decline. The Independents and Baptists gave up their

---

* Bunyan advocated "mixed communion" principles, and his Church was an unsectarian one.

meetings or met by stealth, while watchers, stationed on roofs, or as outposts in the streets, were ready to give warning of the approach of informers. The members of one denomination alone continued, by meeting openly and without concealment, to defy and not to evade the law. These were the Quakers. The brutality with which the members of this sect were treated exceeded anything which had been known in the recent history of persecution in England. Their meetings were broken up by the military, and their attendants stunned by bludgeons and hacked by swords. The female members were stripped and flogged with shameless indecency. This was almost mild treatment compared with the usage they received at the hands of the Puritans of New England, where, tied to a cart-tail, women were flogged naked for eighty miles; where Quakers' tongues were bored with a red-hot iron, their ears cut off, and themselves finally hanged; but it was more savage treatment than had been experienced in England since Laud was led to the block. In A.D. 1662, more than four thousand of this sect were in prison in England, five hundred of whom were crowded into the prisons of London.* Hundreds died, and many more were banished to the West Indian settlements. In spite of all this, they continued openly to meet and preach, not once reviling their persecutors. And when, in A.D. 1672, an " Indulgence " was granted to Dissenters, and a return ordered of all such prisoners as should be released, George Whitehead, a Quaker, waited on the King, and obtained his promise of pardon to such as were imprisoned. None had been

---

* Sewell's " History," vol. ii. p. 2.

more vehement against the Quakers than Bunyan, yet he obtained his release from gaol through Whitehead's exertions. "Our being of different judgments," said Whitehead, "did not abate my compassion or charity, even towards those who had been my opposers in some cases. Blessed be the Lord God, who is the Father and fountain of mercies; whose love and mercies in Christ Jesus to us should oblige us to be merciful and kind one to another."* Bunyan was the first Nonconformist minister licensed to preach in England. It was fit that a man whose genius and pulpit eloquence were of matchless order should occupy such a historical position, and it is a proof that no degree of persecution, short of extermination, will root out religious opinions, that in ten months after the "Indulgence" was issued, three thousand five hundred licenses to preach and to hold meetings were granted.†

It was previous to this that another and probably sincere endeavour towards comprehension was made. The initiative was taken by the Government, and immediately responded to by the leaders of the Presbyterian party. Baxter and Manton did not, on this occasion, forget the Independents. Baxter informed the Lord Keeper that it was now possible to include this body and all sound Christians in the Establishment, but the suggestion was received with no favour. Terms of comprehension were however agreed upon, one of which was that ceremonies should be left indifferent. All who were not comprehended were to be indulged, the names of the

---

* Offor's "Bunyan," Hanserd Knollys' ed. pp. 62—65.
† Ib. p. 62.

ministers and of every member of their congregations being registered.

It is impossible to say whether Howe and Owen gave authority to Baxter to make such concessions, but Baxter in A.D. 1667, was in correspondence with Owen concerning a union between Presbyterians and Independents. Baxter took the first step towards this object. Christian union may be said to have been his hobby, but no man was less fit to promote it than himself. He was for ever framing concordats, but never yielding either to Episcopalians or to Independents the smallest of his proposals. He was induced to open a correspondence with Owen in consequence of the publication, by the latter, of a Catechism of Church Worship and Discipline, in which Owen laid down the doctrine that Christian Churches have not the "power of the keys," or, in other words, that ministers of the Gospel do not derive their office to preach and rule from the Churches, but from Christ himself.* Twice before had Baxter made similar proposals, and now he was engaged in another scheme of general comprehension. Nothing came of either, and the purity of the Independent Churches, if it was ever endangered, was saved from compromise.

In the years A.D. 1673 and 1674 Baxter made new proposals for union with the Church, which he again thought might "take in the Independents," but he must have known, after all, little of their doctrines, if he supposed, as he appears to have done, that they would have accepted, in its substance, the Book of Common Prayer, and subjected themselves to the authority of a political

* Orme's "Owen," pp. 235—237.

hierarchy. It is noticeable that the whole of these proposals were made, on behalf of the Church, with the view of "strengthening the Protestant interest," and counteracting the growth of Popery. The statesmen and bishops of those days felt, what has been manifest ever since, that the Established Church alone is no preservative against the errors of Roman Catholicism. Baxter's amendments to the Prayer Book would have taken out of that volume all, or nearly all, that is distinctively Roman Catholic in origin and influence. That they were accepted, at the time, by such men as Tillotson, Morley, Stillingfleet, Sir Matthew Hale, the Earl of Orrery, and the Lord Treasurer, is a sufficient indication that the Prayer Book was considered, not by Presbyterians and Independents alone, to encourage the growth of Popery.

During the next fifteen years Protestant Dissenters were alternately persecuted and coaxed. James the Second, whatever may have been his vices, was on the whole in favour of religious liberty. It is customary to state that his sole design in the permission of toleration was to gain an ascendancy for his own sect, but there is trustworthy evidence of the general liberality of his opinions. Almost as soon as he ascended the throne he released all who were in prison for conscience' sake; by this act no fewer than fifteen hundred Quakers alone were set at liberty. When, in A.D. 1687, this body sent a deputation to thank him for his tolerant spirit, the King replied, "Some of you know, I am sure you do, Mr. Penn, that it was always my principle that conscience ought not to be forced, and that all men ought to have liberty of their consciences, and what I have promised in my declaration I will continue to perform as long as

I live; and I hope, before I die, to settle it so that after ages shall have no reason to alter it." * Unfortunately the King, while right as to the end he had in view, was wrong as to the means which should be adopted to attain it. He believed in governing without a Parliament, and the English people had decided, in the time of the Commonwealth, that the prerogative of the houses of legislation was superior to that of the monarch. The King could pardon offences against the law, but he could not suspend the law.

The attitude assumed by some Dissenters towards the Crown at this period has been the subject of severe denunciation, and the conduct of William Penn and the Quakers especially has been held up to the most unmerited opprobrium. The great historian of this and the succeeding reign was not the first who accused Penn of partiality to the Stuarts. The accusation was made in Penn's lifetime, and replied to by him. He acknowledged his daily visits to the palace, and states how it was he became so intimate with the monarch. His father had been admiral when the King was lord-high admiral, and had left Penn to James's guardianship, receiving from him a promise to protect the young Quaker as far as possible from the inconveniences to which he would be subjected in consequence of his religious profession. Penn made use of his friendship to promote the progress of religious freedom. Writing of the accusations made against him, he says, " I am not without apprehension of the cause of this behaviour towards me ; I mean my constant zeal for an impartial liberty of con-

* Sewell, vol. ii. p. 333.

science."* No man had done more than Penn to prove his faithfulness to this principle. Like the Barclays— David and Robert— he was born a gentleman, and had received the most cultured education which Oxford University could bestow. He was a fellow student with Locke and Villiers at Christ Church, when John Owen was Dean. He had all the polished manners of a courtier. His father was a favourite with Charles and James, and no man had better prospects of receiving substantial proofs of royal friendship. From a sense of religious conviction, he gave up the whole of this, and attached himself to the most unpopular sect in Christendom. What influence he had he afterwards used to shield the members of his own denomination from the vengeance of the law. As the founder of the Commonwealth of Pennsylvania, he has made himself a reputation immortal in the history of the world. His wisdom and justice as a legislator gave a new revelation of humanity and religion to the savages by whom he was surrounded. His consistency as a friend of religious equality was made evident by the constitution of his Commonwealth, the first words of which were as follows:—" In reverence to God, the Father of light and spirits, the author as well as the object of all divine knowledge, faith, and worship, I do, for me and mine, declare and establish, for the first fundamental of the government of this country, that every person that doth or shall reside therein shall have and enjoy the free profession of his or her faith and exercise of worship towards God in such way and manner as every such person

* Sewell, vol. ii. . 44.

shall in conscience believe is most acceptable to God." The man who could first originate and then impose such a statute was not likely to be a favourite with many of the ecclesiastical parties of James the Second's time.

But Penn and the Quakers were not the first to thank the King for his lenity. The Presbyterians, Independents, and Baptists were before them. When the Declaration of A.D. 1687 in favour of liberty of conscience was issued, and the prison doors thrown open, it was natural that there should be a spontaneous burst of gratitude to its author. At first the Dissenters did not see what would be the consequences of recognizing the legality of the Declaration; when they did, notwithstanding the renewed sufferings to which they might be exposed, they took part against it. It was owing solely to the persecuting spirit of the Church that a general toleration had not long before been granted. Yet when the seven bishops refused to read the Declaration, and were sent to the Tower, Independents, Baptists, and Quakers vied with each other in showing them their sympathy. There can be little question but that they acted, at that time, from mixed motives. None of them—not even Penn—was in favour of the toleration of Roman Catholicism. No man who valued the civil liberties of England dreamed of giving a foothold to the professors of that intolerant creed. Three generations had not sufficed to wipe out the memory of its curse on England. Thousands still living could recollect the Vaudois massacres; and the streets of London were at that moment crowded with sufferers from the revocation of the Edict of Nantes. Is it a wonder that the most tolerant refused to tolerate the creed of men who, whenever they were in power, persecuted to the utmost limits of persecution?

It is stranger that the Nonconformists should have declined to recognize the legality of the Indulgence because its exercise was opposed to the constitution of England. What was the constitution to them, that they should have been willing to make even the smallest sacrifice for it? Its history was written with their own blood. They were excluded from its pale. They existed but to be fined, imprisoned, and banished. The law was, to them, a savage tyrant. In place of protecting their rights, it was never exercised excepting to violate them. Yet they freely and almost unanimously resisted any encroachment upon it, even when that encroachment was made in their own favour. There were, however, reasons for this attitude. The first was a fear that, if the King's claims were not resisted, his prerogative might ultimately be exercised in favour of the restoration of Popery as the established religion. They would not have suffered much more, in such an event, than they had recently suffered from the establishment of Protestant Episcopalianism, but they believed that religion would suffer. The second reason was of a political character. The Dissenters were the brain and muscle of the constitutional party. The right of resistance—passive or active—to despotism had come down to them as their most precious inheritance. All their ecclesiastical organizations were founded on a recognition of the rights of the people, and it was not probable that they should surrender those rights to a Stuart. By their co-operation with the bishops, when their weight might have turned the scale of public opinion in favour of the King, they assisted to save the liberties of their country. From the time of the arrest of the seven, James's authority as a monarch was gone, and the temporary union, in a period of common danger, of Conformists and Nonconformists, for the safety of the State, gave promise that when a new Government should be instituted, the legal security of toleration would be one of its first works.

With the end of the reign of James the Second, the experiment of forcing one form of religion upon the English people ceased. Every means which the despotism of the State and the intolerance of the favoured sect could devise to secure an entire conformity, had been adopted. The Crown and the dignitaries of the Established Church had united to put down all freedom of opinion. The fire of the stake had been lighted, the gallows had been erected, and the prisons choked, in order to strike terror into the minds of all who dissented from the privileged sect. During the whole of this period not one bishop or clergyman had lifted up his voice against such inhumanity. The hierarchy of what was declared to be the only Christian Church in England employed all their influence to make the fires hotter, to give increased employment to the hangman, and to swell the numbers in the gaols. Yet the Nonconformists grew and increased. Their doctrines became, every year, more readily accepted, until it was seen that a despotic Church was as opposed to the interests of religion and humanity, and as inconsistent with the rights of mankind, as a despotic State. And, in looking back upon the history of their country, it must have struck the most superficial observers that the worst instruments of bad government had always been the instruments which had been employed for ecclesiastical purposes. Elizabeth and Whitgift, James the First and Bancroft, Charles the First and Laud, Charles the Second and Sheldon, were names that could not but be associated together. The sympathy of the Established Church with the despotic rule of the Tudors and the Stuarts was now a matter of history. It remained to be seen whether it would oppose or support a practically new dynasty, which entered on its reign with the promise of a constitutional government and the toleration of ecclesiastical differences.

CHAPTER II.

THE REVOLUTION TO THE COMPREHENSION BILL,
A.D. 1688—89.

It is seldom that those who fight the battles either of political or of religious liberty live to see the reward of their labours, and this was especially the case with many of the most eminent of the earlier advocates of religious toleration. When James the Second was expelled from England, those who had laboured with the most ardent zeal and untiring devotion for this consummation of their work had entered into their rest. John Milton had died, "in mean circumstances," eleven years before King Charles the Second's death, and immediately after that monarch had formally recalled the Indulgence of A.D. 1672, and given orders for the effectual suppression of all conventicles. If not gifted, as he may have been, with prophetic foresight of the necessary termination of a prolonged Stuart government, the death-bed of the great defender of the liberties of his country must have been visited with mournful reflections concerning the apparent vanity of virtuous human labour. Three years afterwards, in A.D. 1677, Dr. Manton, who had been one of Cromwell's chaplains, and who had suffered imprisonment for his Nonconformity, also died. Two years later died Matthew Poole, a professor at Oxford University with Owen, and whose labours in Biblical criticism remain, at the end of two centuries, undimmed in splendour, and, at the same time, Dr. Thomas Goodwin, president of Magdalen College during the Protectorate, and who had attended Cromwell's death-bed. The next year died Stephen Charnock, chaplain to Henry Cromwell, and one of the greatest preachers of his age. In A.D. 1681, Thomas Gouge, who had devoted his life and fortune to the evangelization of the Welsh, who gave to that people a Welsh Bible, and whose character Archbishop Tillotson compared, for his eagerness in doing good, to "the glorious character of the Son of God," also died. Nearly six years before the Revolution died Dr. John Owen, the greatest champion of their principles who has ever adorned the Independent denomination. David Clarkson, Owen's successor in the ministry, and almost his equal in learning and in public service, died in the year before the Revolution. Delaune the Baptist had perished in prison, and Canne, of the same denomination, had not lived to see one of his principles obtain, after the Protectorate, public toleration. Only a few months before William the Third landed in England John Bunyan, who had suffered more than any, also died. The greatest popular preacher in England since Latimer and until Whitfield; who had endured Jeffrey's abuse, and who had spent a fifth portion of his life in gaol, lived neither to see his preaching legalized, his persecutor meet his reward, nor one of the laws under which he had suffered repealed. These, and the thousands who had died in prison without leaving a name behind them, were the men who had made the continuance of an intolerant ecclesiastical policy impossible, and who had prepared the people for a more liberal and patriotic government.

But if the principal "witnesses" for religious freedom did not live to enjoy that rest from controversy which is so refreshing to the Christian man who is a controversialist only from necessity, and that peace which none enjoy so well as those who have had experience of war, neither did their opponents live to see the triumph of their adversaries. The race of intolerant prelates and arbitrary statesmen had also died out. Sheldon, the last conspicuous representative of the principle of intolerance, had long lain beneath his monument in the parish church of Croydon. Their successors had, for the most part, been chosen on account of the moderation of their ecclesiastical sentiments. Clarendon had died in exile and disgrace fourteen years ago, and no statesman of equal power, ability, and independence, holding his principles, had succeeded to him. The high character, the zealous labours, the controversial ability, the steadfast adherence to their views, and the unselfish patriotism of the Nonconformists, had changed the temper of all parties. In a time of common danger, even the bishops had welcomed them as their friends, and had loudly declared their desire for more liberal ecclesiastical laws.

They went, indeed, almost beyond this. In their petition to James against publishing the Declaration for liberty of conscience, they had declared that their "averseness" proceeded not from any want of due tenderness to Dissenters, in relation to whom, they said, they "were willing to come to such a temper as shall be thought fit, when that matter shall be considered and settled in Parliament and Convocation."* After their acquittal, Sancroft, Archbishop of Canterbury, publicly counselled the bishops and clergy of his province to have a very tender regard to "their brethren" the Protestant Dissenters, to visit them at their houses, and to receive them kindly at their own; to discourse to them civilly; to persuade them, if it was possible, to join the Church, but, under any circumstances, to unite heartily and affectionately with them in prayer for the blessed union of all the Reformed Churches.† Privately, the bishops told every one that they were about to adopt a new policy towards Dissenters.‡ "I do assure you," said one writer of the time, "and I am certain I have the best grounds in the whole world for my assurance, that the bishops will never stir one jot from their petition; but that they will, whenever that happy opportunity shall offer itself, let the Protestant Dissenters find that they will be better than their word."§ Another writer, who was afterwards elevated to the Episcopal bench, candidly acknowledged the errors of the Church in her former persecutions, and confessed that "the wise and generous behaviour of the main body of Dissenters had given them so just a title to our friendship, that we must resolve to set all the world against us if we can ever forget it, and if we do not make them all the return of ease and favour, when it is in our power to do it."‖ Such promises, made in

* Burnet's " Own Times," p. 470, *note*.
† "Papers relating to the Affairs of England," vol. i., 1688. Birch's "Tillotson," pp. 155, 156.
‡ " Wharton's Diary."
§ "Calamy's Abridgement," pp. 629, 630.
‖ Burnet's "Apology for the Church of England with relation to the Spirit of Persecution," p. 6, 1688.

foul weather, were destined to receive only the ordinary fulfilment.

The condition of Protestant Dissent at the commencement of this reign was remarkable for its strength and purity. Some estimate of the number of its adherents may be formed from the circumstance that two hundred and seventy-three Congregational and one hundred and twenty-two Baptist Churches now existing date their origin from before this period.* The Presbyterians existed probably in still greater numbers,† and in London, Lancashire, Yorkshire, and Cheshire, and the Northern counties generally, predominated over all the other denominations. The Quakers appear to have been almost as numerous as either the Baptists or the Independents. Their places of worship, especially in the metropolis, were large and well attended,‡ and their missionary spirit was inferior to that of no other sect. With the exception of the Quakers', the "meeting-houses," as they were termed, of the denominations were secured by trusts of a general character, which neither specified the sect to which they belonged, nor the doctrines which were to be preached.§ They were secured by deeds to the congregations of " Protestant Dissenters " worshipping in that place, who were allowed to choose such person as minister as a majority might elect. No creeds, confessions, or articles of belief were subscribed to by either ministers or Churches,‖ but declarations of

* Reckoned from the Congregational Year Book and the Baptist Hand Book for 1866.
† Burnet says that the Presbyterians and Independents were three-fourths of all Dissenters. "Own Times," p. 438.
‡ "Gouge's Sufferings." § Hunter's "Historical Defence," p. 10.
‖ Wilson's "Historical Inquiry," p. 3.

their faith, made at general assemblies or conferences, were common to all the sects. The creed of the Presbyterians and Independents was in accordance with the Westminster Assembly's Catechism; while the Baptists were perhaps equally divided between Calvinism and Arminianism. Arianism, or Socinianism had, as yet, only individual professors. It had existed in England from the time of the Dutch Anabaptists, but no attempt had been made to found an organization on its basis.

The form of public service of all the denominations, excepting the Baptists, was the same as that which prevails at the present day. The Baptists, like the Quakers, had conscientious scruples against public singing, which were scarcely overcome at the end of half a century from this time.* Books were written to prove that the only Scriptural singing was from the heart, and that women especially ought no more to sing than to speak in Church.† In one or two places where singing was at all allowed, it was agreed to sing only once, and that after the last prayer was ended, so that those who disapproved of the practice might have an opportunity of leaving the meeting; but even this compromise created dissatisfaction.‡ Anointing with oil seems to have been common amongst the Baptists of this period, and it is related of Kiffin how, on one occasion, he so anointed a sick person.§ The denomination was also already divided on the subject of open and strict communion.

Of the general character of Nonconformist preaching, if judgment may be given from such printed sermons as

---

* "Ivimey's History," ii. 373.   † Marlow's "Discourse against Singing."
‡ Keach's "Breach Repaired," 1689. The practice described existed in Keach's own Church at Horsleydown, but it divided the Church.
§ "Kiffin's Life," p. 33.

have come down to the present time, it may be said that the Presbyterians excelled in doctrinal, the Independents in exegetical, and the Baptists and Quakers in experimental discourse.* Neither of the former was remarkable for brevity, while the minuteness with which they divided and subdivided their sermons has made it difficult for modern readers to take any pleasure in them.† "My next," wrote Bolingbroke to Swift, "shall be as long as one of Dr. Manton's discourses, who taught my youth to yawn, and prepared me to be a high Churchman, that I might never hear him read, nor read him more."‡ Yet Manton was not one of the most tedious of preachers. The length of their religious services was not, probably, so great as it was in the time of the Commonwealth, but, according to modern tastes, it was exorbitant. Philip Henry, one of the purest men and most instructive preachers of that age, began family worship, on Sunday, at eight o'clock, "when he read and expounded pretty largely, sung a psalm, and prayed," and this service was eagerly attended by others than the members of his own family. At nine o'clock, public service began, which did not conclude before noon, after which there was a rest of an hour and a half. He then read and commented on a chapter of Scripture, catechised the children, expounded the catechism, and preached another sermon.§ This is a

* A curious work was published in 1657, by Abraham Wright, Fellow of St. John's College, Cambridge, and Vicar of Okeham, entitled "Five Sermons in Five several Styles or Ways of Preaching," in which the Episcopalian, the Presbyterian, the Independent, &c., styles were cleverly imitated. The fairest specimens of the pedantic Episcopalian style with which I am acquainted are Archbishop Sancroft's "Occasional Sermons."

† This methodical style is well described by Burnet, "Own Times," p. 102. ‡ Burnet, *note*, p. 106.

§ Matthew Henry's "Life of Philip Henry," p. 105.

fair example of public religious service amongst Nonconformists at this period.

But whatever might have been the minor characteristics of their preaching, the eminence of the intellectual and spiritual power of the older Nonconformist preachers can even now be seen, and it was fully recognized not only by that "middle class" which is ordinarily said to be the support of the Nonconformist interest, but by the most refined and cultivated sections of society. The barrier which, through the lust of social as well as ecclesiastical predominance, and the consciousness of a prolonged course of injustice, the Established Church has, since, successfully raised between the Nonconformists and the upper classes of society, was, at that time, neither so high nor so impregnable as it is now. Owen's Church, while it included some of the still living leaders of the Commonwealth, such as Lord Charles Fleetwood, Colonel Desborough, and Colonel Berry, included also many of the aristocracy, amongst whom were the Countess of Anglesea, Sir Thomas Overbury, and Lady Haversham, whilst amongst Owen's most intimate friends were Lord Orrery, Lord Willoughby, Lord Wharton, the Earl of Berkeley, and Sir John Trevor.* When Manton preached in Covent Garden Church, the Duke of Bedford was his constant hearer, and remained his friend until his death.† Dr. Bates was in intimate intercourse with King William, Archbishop Tillotson, the Earl of Nottingham, and his father, the Lord Chancellor Finch.‡ Baxter was acquainted with all the leading men of his age,

---

* Orme's "Owen," pp. 277—89.   † Calamy, p. 210.
‡ Calamy, p. 216.

and would be found discussing philosophy at Acton with Sir Matthew Hale; terms of concordance, at Dublin, with Archbishop Usher; politics, in London, with Lord Lauderdale, and divinity with the Earl of Balcarres; while Oxendon Street meeting-house was built, in large part, through the contributions of the aristocracy.* Howe held an equal social position to that of either Baxter or Owen. He was on visiting terms with many of the aristocracy, was a close correspondent of Lady Rachel Russell, and a personal friend of Archbishop Tillotson.† All the leading Nonconformists had free personal access to the monarch.

This intimacy, although it did not result, on either side, in any compromise of opinion or of position, had the effect of moderating the spirit of controversy. Illustrations of this are to be found in the controversial works of Stillingfleet and Tillotson, and Baxter, Howe, and Owen. Stillingfleet, by his repeated charges of schism on the Nonconformist, provoked replies from the leading Presbyterian and Independent divines, but even Baxter met him with moderation, and Owen was chivalrous. Tillotson, in a sermon preached before the King, had indiscreetly committed himself to the statement of opinions which, in their logical issue, involved the persecution of all Nonconformists. While it was necessary, on account of the royal command, to print this discourse as it was delivered, the author candidly stated to Howe his regret at having so expressed himself, and in a subsequent edition of the sermon, carefully modified its

* Calamy, p. 688.
† Birch's "Tillotson," and Rogers's "Life of Howe."

language. It was the suggestive and acute remark of a writer of that age, that the high personal honour and piety and the generous dispositions of such men as Stillingfleet and Tillotson worked greater harm to the Nonconformist interest, as such, than anything which mere policy could have devised.*

The education of Dissenting ministers was conducted in private academies. One of the first resources of those who had been ejected by the Act of Uniformity was to establish themselves in teaching; and although contrary to law, they formed schools in all parts of the country. The Universities, for the first time in English history, were closed against a section of the people, but no laws could recal the learning which the ejected ministers had received from them. Their academies appear to have been numerously attended, and their students, drawn from all sections in society, to have received an exact and a "liberal" education. It was scarcely to be expected that such proceedings should not be looked upon with jealousy, and accordingly we find even Tillotson approving of the suppression of such academies as were conducted by members of either of the Universities.† It was thought that no person who held a University degree could legally, without breaking the oath which he had taken not to lecture at any place in England excepting in Oxford or Cambridge, assume the office of a teacher. The Nonconformists objected to this interpretation of the oath, and, although sometimes obliged to remove their residences, maintained their academies in large numbers and great efficiency.

* Birch's "Tillotson," p. 32, *note*, and Du Moulin's "Appeal."
† Birch's "Tillotson," p. 246. Toulmin's History, chap. iii.

Amongst the most memorable of such teachers were William Jarieway and Philip Henry. Upwards of twenty academies are known to have been in existence at the time of the Revolution.*

Of the character of the religion both of Nonconformists and Churchmen, the impartial testimony of one of the most moderate and charitable of Churchmen may be accepted without question or reserve. The gentle and sainted Archbishop Leighton had remarked of the Church of England, in Charles the Second's reign, that its administration, both with relation to the ecclesiastical courts and pastoral care, was the most corrupt which he had ever seen; that it was a fair carcase without soul, and that the clergy were equally destitute of strictness in life and zeal and laboriousness in work.† Bishop Burnet observes of the clergy of his own time, that, of all whom he ever knew, the English clergy were the most remiss of any in their labours amongst the people.‡ "I must own," he adds, "that the main body of our clergy have always appeared dead and lifeless to me, and, instead of animating, they seem rather to lay one another to sleep."§ The Nonconformists, on the one hand, he commends for their "great zeal,"‖ and observes of the Baptists especially that they were generally "men of virtue, and of an universal charity."¶ The predominants and the predominated differed as it was natural that they should differ. In the one party, persecution had ensured piety, and in the

---

* Dr. Toulmin has given the most complete account of the early academies of Dissenters. See chap. iii. of his History.
† Burnet's "Own Times," p. 381.
‡ Ib. 438.   § Ib. 907.   ‖ Ib.
¶ Ib. 446.

other, privilege had begotten indifference, luxuriousness, and pride.

While the intentions of the Prince of Orange and his party were as yet unknown to or discredited by the Court of St. James', Fagel, the pensioner of Holland, had written a letter explaining the Prince's and Princess's sentiments on the subject of religious toleration. In this letter, which was soon circulated throughout the kingdom, it was stated that the Prince and Princess consented to grant " a full liberty to Dissenters, but that they would not consent to the repeal of the laws which tended only to the securing the Protestant religion, such as those concerning the tests, which inflicted no punishment but only an incapacity of being in public engagements, which could not be complained of as great severities."* In writing this, Fagel wrote what he knew would be acceptable to Dissenters. In the first place, it was at that time fully intended to bring about a comprehension of the Presbyterians and the Independents in the Established Church, and it was known that these two principal sections of the Nonconformist body, providing that the Church services were modified, were willing, for the sake of Christian unity, and what was considered to be the strength of the Protestant interest, wholly to unite with the Church. In such an event, the tests which it was proposed to retain would bear only upon the Baptists, the Quakers, and the Roman Catholics. The two former parties had little political influence; the latter, it was unanimously agreed, could not, without putting the State itself in peril, be trusted with any civil

---

* Declarations issued by the Prince of Orange, 1688.

or political power. This letter satisfied equally the Dissenters and the Church party. The former saw, at last, an end to the persecutions which they had suffered; the latter felt that, with the tests still in force, their position of supremacy could not be endangered by any ecclesiastical party which might choose to remain out of their own pale. The people saw in it the assured safety of the Protestant religion, and a promise of peace to the kingdom. These pledges were renewed and extended on the landing of the Prince in England. The first public act of William, on setting foot on English ground, was to issue a declaration, in which he stated that it was his intention to preserve the Established religion; to unite to the Church, by the best means which could be devised, all such as were divided from it, and to suffer all others, who would live peaceably, to enjoy a due freedom of conscience. No one doubted that the Prince would keep his word, and those who enjoyed his most intimate confidence well knew that he was prepared to go beyond it.

William had not been many days in England before he received decisive proof that some of the clergy were not disposed to welcome him. The Bishop and the Dean of Exeter left that city as soon as he entered it, while the whole of the clergy stood aloof from him.[*] When the Declaration was read in the cathedral, all the officers hurried from it. On the first Sunday, Burnet, his chaplain, was obliged to preach. No man more merited this honour, for none was more devoted to William's interests or had been more useful in promoting them

---

[*] Burnet's "Own Times," p. 500.

than this able, skilful, and large-minded man. James, at this very time, was expressing his own confidence in, and obligations to the bench of bishops, telling them how sensible he was that they had shown themselves, "zealously concerned" for him.* When, however, James had left England, and the loss of his cause was patent to almost every man, the bishops did not hesitate to throw themselves, for the time, into the arms of William. Sancroft, Archbishop of Canterbury, Lamplugh, Archbishop of York, and five bishops, were amongst the peers who met at the Guildhall, in the city of London, on the 11th of December, 1688, to take upon themselves the government of the country until William should arrive. They issued, at once, a declaration that they had determined to join with the Prince of Orange, both for the protection of the Church, and for securing a due liberty of conscience to Dissenters.† Lamplugh was the bishop who hastened to James when William entered Exeter, for which service he was promoted, on the 15th November, to the archbishopric of the northern province. Twenty-six days afterwards he thus publicly joined the standard of the Prince. Nothing, however, was more remote from the intentions of the bishops and the clergy than to accept the Prince of Orange as King. The highest post which they were inclined to assign to him was that of Regent; while many would have been satisfied if, after doing duty as an armed mediator between the Church and James, they could have sent him back to Holland. The opinion of this party was that it was the Prince's prime duty not to look to the

* "Kettlewell's Life," p. 81.
† "London Gazette." December 13, 1688.

general interests of the nation, but to the special interests of the Established Church.

It was quite consistent with such views that the bishops and the clergy should personally welcome the Prince. The day after William's arrival in London, all the bishops who were in town, with the exception of Sancroft, who declined to go, waited upon him. The clergy of London, with Bishop Compton at their head, and several Dissenting ministers, followed. The Dissenters had not had time to organize a separate deputation. The bishop, therefore, spoke of their presence, stating that they united with the clergy in welcoming the Prince to England. Compton had always treated the Dissenters with respect, and, excepting Trelawney, Bishop of Bristol, was probably the only prelate present who was disposed to enter heartily into the Prince's views. Scarcely a month after this Evelyn visited Sancroft at Lambeth Palace, where he found the Bishops of St. Asaph, Ely, Bath and Wells, Peterborough and Chichester, debating the state of the nation. " They were all," he says, " for a regency."* The Dissenting ministers waited some days before they presented a separate address; but on January 2nd they waited on the Prince. The Duke of Devonshire and Lords Wharton and Wiltshire introduced them; Howe acted as their spokesman. The illness of Baxter and Bates prevented their being present, and they could take no part in a ceremony which could not but have yielded to both a peculiar and intense gratification. In their address, the Nonconformist ministers expressed their

---

Evelyn, iii. 263.

"grateful sense of the Prince's hazardous and heroical expedition," and of the "favour of Heaven" upon it; they esteemed it "a felicity that the patriots of the nobility and gentry had concurred in the design," and that the administration of public affairs "was devolved into hands which the nation and the world knew to be apt for the greatest undertakings;" they promised to promote the views of the Prince to "their utmost endeavours;" they prayed to the Almighty to preserve his person, and to grant success to his efforts for "the defence and propagation of the Protestant interest throughout the world;" they apologized for not having paid their duty earlier, and stated that they did not now appear "on a distinct account, but on that only which was common to them and to all Protestants;" and lastly —referring to the absence of Baxter and Bates,—said, that while some of "eminent note" were prevented by age or infirmity from being with them, they concurred in the same grateful sense of a common deliverance. The Prince at once caught the tone of this address, and answered that he came on purpose to defend the Protestant religion, and that he should endeavour to promote "a firm union amongst Protestants."* Nothing could have been in better taste than the language of the ministers. While the bishops and clergy could never keep out of sight the defence of the religion as established by law, the Dissenters made no reference whatever to their own painful position. They disclaimed appearing on a distinct account of their own. They spoke as Protestant Englishmen only, anxious, before

* Gazette, Jan. 5, 1688-9.

their own grievances were considered, that the government of the nation should be placed on a safe and satisfactory basis. Their reference to "the propagation of the Protestant interest throughout the world," whatever meaning such words might cover, was only natural in addressing a Prince who had been, during the whole of his life, and was now especially, looked up to as the great champion of that interest, the embodiment of the Protestant thought, and the leader of the Protestant armies of Europe. It was more than a skilfully designed reference to the Prince's secret object of ambition; it was an acknowledgment of his great public services as a European statesman, and an expression of trust in his capacity and his policy. William frankly accepted it as such, and at the same time gave expression to what he knew was in their thoughts, although, from delicacy of feeling, it was not expressed. When he said that he should promote a firm union amongst Protestants, he gave a renewal of the promises contained in his declaration, that he would do all that was possible to unite to the Establishment such as were divided from it.

When, on January 22nd, the Convention Parliament met, the state of feeling existing amongst the bishops and clergy was more fully disclosed. Sancroft refused to appear in it. Nothing could move him from that determination. It was in vain that Halifax, who had been elected to preside over the proceedings of the peers, conjured him, as the primate of the Established Church, to attend.* It was in vain that the House of

---

* Tanner, MSS. 28, 352.

Lords sent him an order to appear in his place. It was in vain that his friends remonstrated with him, and plainly hinted that he was guilty of a cowardly desertion of them all.* Sancroft saw the tendency of events, and was determined to be no party to any course of action which would lead to the deposition of James. His stubborn and persistent refusal proceeded from the mixed obstinacy of a weak man, and the weakness of an obstinate man, whose weakness was strengthened, and whose obstinacy was confirmed by that favourite doctrine which Churchmen had so often proclaimed since the Restoration—the Divine right of all Kings. It is only doing justice to the memory of a celebrated man to add that Sancroft's course of action did not proceed from any jealousy concerning the extension of religious liberty. When he was reminded that he was pledged to the relief of the Protestant Dissenters, he answered, at once, that the bishops had no intention of evading their obligations in that respect, but that this was a matter to be settled in Convocation.† The High Churchmen were thus, before William was on the throne, giving clear indication of their intention to set up the claims and privileges of their own order as against the paramount rights of the State. The laws of England respecting the religious liberties of the subject were, in their judgment, to be settled by the spiritual peers only, and the few score country clergy who formed the Lower House of Convocation. Sancroft's declaration was a fresh statement of the old doctrine, that the interests of the nation and the rights of subjects were to be

---

* "Clarendon Correspondence," ii. 248. Tanner, MSS. 27, 16.
† Ib., ii. 240.

subservient to what an already privileged order might consider to be the interests of their own section of society. No class of men in history have so often forgotten that they are Englishmen as the clergy of the Established Church.

But although Sancroft did not attend in his place, many of the other prelates had no such hesitation. The primate could move in neither direction; but he could and did influence the conduct and the votes of others. This influence, however, was not felt in the House of Commons, which, in one sitting, resolved, without going to a division, that James had abdicated the government, and that the throne had thereby become vacant. This resolution was at once communicated to the other house, and its concurrence in it desired; but it was only after prolonged debates and conferences between both houses that this concurrence was secured. When the first vote was taken on the question that the Prince and Princess of Orange be desired to accept of the Crown and be declared King and Queen, fourteen bishops were present, of whom twelve voted against it, and only two, Compton and Trelawney, in its favour.* These two gave to the vote the small majority which it received, the numbers being forty-nine against and fifty-one for it.

By this time it had become evident that the clergy, as a body, were opposed to the new settlement. They had supported the bishops in their arguments in favour of a regency,† and were now in an "ill-humour" with everything.‡ So manifest was their disaffection that

---

* "Clarendon Correspondence," ii. 256.
† Burnet, p. 513.   ‡ Ib., p. 517.

members of the House of Commons felt compelled to notice it. Sharp, Rector of St. Giles and Dean of Norwich, had preached a sermon on Popery before the House, on January 30th, and had had the bad grace, notwithstanding that the legislature had declared the throne vacant, to pray for " his most excellent Majesty." Maynard, the Nestor of the House, who had sat in all the Parliaments from the first of King Charles the First, charged the Dean with a breach of the vote, and expressed his opinion that he should not receive the thanks of the House for his sermon. " Almost all the clergy," cried Sir John Thompson, " do the same thing." The Speaker ruled that the preacher had contradicted the vote of the House.* The temper of the clergy was again alluded to in the debates on the King's speech. " I think," said Maynard, " that the clergy are out of their wits, and I believe if the clergy should have their wills, none of us would be here again."† It is not difficult to assign a cause for this feeling. Neither William nor Mary was a hot Episcopalian. William had, on the first Sunday after arriving in London, attended the worship of the Established Church, and partaken of the Communion. He pledged the word of a man, whose honour both as a gentleman and a statesman had never been impeached, that he would maintain the religion established by law, but it was well known that he was not a Churchman by conviction. In his own country he had been a Presbyterian; but he attached little, if any, importance to forms of worship or Church constitutions. He would listen to preachers of any sect, and

---

* Grey's Debates, Jan. 30. † Ib., Feb. 20.

although holding most of the Evangelical tenets was inclined to Latitudinarianism. But, while he did not drink or swear like James the First, was not untruthful like Charles the First, was not dissolute like Charles the Second, nor a tool of France and the Jesuits like the second James, he was liked by the clergy less than either of these men. It was natural that he should be accused of favouring the Presbyterians,* although it would be difficult to tell in what manner he favoured them. His fault was, that he intended to keep faith with Dissenters as well as with the Church; and the clergy, as soon as they saw him, knew that he would keep it. They had probably imagined that his declarations were of no more value than that from Breda, and that, as soon as he came amongst them, they would be able to make him, as they had made Charles, swerve from his purpose, and give himself wholly up to their own exclusive and sectarian interests. They never accomplished this, but they effectually succeeded in thwarting his highest desires. Ecclesiastical intolerance in the clerical order is generally, although not always, co-existent with negligence in the performance of religious duties. The clergy of this period are described, by one who knew them well, as pluralists, as non-resident, as busy-bodies, news-mongers, frequenters of ale-houses, intemperate, and as of weak and small understanding.† The moral power of such men could have been very little, but the nature of their office appears, notwithstanding, to have cast, as it has so often and so strangely done in history, a glamour over the minds both of

---

* Ralph, vol. ii. p. 7.   † "Kettlewell's Life," p. 91.

statesmen and people. One man, however, was insensible to this charm; this man was the Prince of Orange.

The feeling with respect to the Established Church as a part of the Constitution of England, was first manifested in the debates on the Coronation Oath. In what words should the King and Queen declare their intention to support the Church as established by law, and how could the legislature most firmly bind the Sovereigns of England, under the new settlement, to such a support? It was moved, as an addition to the old oath, that the King should swear that to the utmost of his power he would maintain the Protestant religion established by law, to which it was replied that he should also maintain the Protestant religion not established by law. But what was meant by "law"? Did it mean the laws in being when the oath was taken, in such a strict sense that the Sovereign was never to consent to an alteration in them,* or did it mean such laws as the legislature might, from time to time, see fit to make? In order to settle this point it was further moved that the King should swear to maintain the Protestant religion, as it is, or shall be, established by law. But what was meant by "established," and might not these words be as effective with regard to all as to one particular Church? Were not Quakers and Baptists of the Protestant religion, and were not they also, in a certain sense, established, or about to be established, by law? "What," said one speaker, "is established by law, may be overthrown by law;" and he suggested the use of the words "according to the laws for the

---

* This, as is well known, was the view taken by George III. and George IV. in the case of the Irish Church and the laws affecting Dissenters.

time being." A curious alternative, and one which, if it had been adopted, would have led to singular results, was then suggested. Major Wildman moved that the King should swear only to maintain "the doctrine established by God and Jesus Christ," but no one appeared to think that these words were at all synonymous with the doctrine established by law. Ultimately, and notwithstanding a warning that they would imply a forgetfulness of the promises made to Nonconformists, the Commons agreed to the words "as it is now established by law." An amendment adopted in Committee, substituting the words "Protestant religion professed by the Church of England," was subsequently rejected. On the third reading, Mr. Pelham moved a further proviso, to the effect that no clause in the Act should be understood so as to prevent the Sovereign from giving his assent to any measures for alterations in the discipline or the forms of the Church, but it was unanimously considered that the words already adopted did not restrict his liberty in this respect. Mr. Pelham's amendment, therefore, was not persisted in.* The tone of the debates on this question indicated, throughout, a recognition of the just claims of Dissenters; and it is evident that the words of the oath were not intended to prevent any subsequent alteration in the constitution of the Established Church.

The Oaths of Allegiance and Supremacy were next debated. It was proposed, on the introduction of this question, that the Corporation Act should, at the same time, be abolished; "an Act," said one speaker, of "as

* Grey's Debates, March 25—28, 1689.

much intrinsic iniquity as any Act whatever;"* but it was thought desirable to deal with this question separately. No debates excited greater interest than the debates on this important measure. It was well known that many of the bishops and clergy entertained conscientious scruples against taking the oath to William and Mary. Amongst them were some of the highest influence and the most spotless integrity, — men who considered that no earthly power could absolve them from the oath which they had already taken to King James. Were they and their whole order to be exempted, and so to be allowed, if they should think proper, to conspire together for the return of the Stuart? There was no difference of opinion in the legislature on this point. In the House of Commons there existed a strong feeling against the clergy as a body, and it was resolved to make no exceptions in their favour. But there is more than one way of imposing an oath. The Lords were in favour of the oath being privately tendered to the clergy by an Order in Council, a course which might have led to some persons being omitted. The subject was gravely debated in formal conferences between both houses, but the firmness of the Commons triumphed. The Act provided that those who did not take the oaths before the 1st August, 1689, should be dispossessed of their benefices, the only modification being that the King was at liberty to allow such of the clergy, not exceeding twelve in number, as might refuse to take the oaths, an allowance of a third part of their present income.†

* Speech of Sir Robert Howard, Grey's Debates, Feb. 25, 1688-9.
† The proceedings of the conferences are fully reported in Grey's Debates, April 19-25, 1689.

The wisdom and magnanimity of William were never more conspicuously shown than on this occasion. On March 16th, he went down to the Houses of Legislature, and earnestly recommended that the Test and Corporation Act should be abolished, and that all Protestants might be admitted to public service. If this were done he was willing to dispense with the Oath of Allegiance from the bishops and clergy who were already in possession of office. No one has charged the King with mixed, much less with unworthy motives, in making this proposal. It was the natural suggestion of a generous and trustful mind. It may, indeed, have occurred to him that, with the aid of Dissenters in office,* he need not fear the enmity of a portion only of the clergy, and, on the other hand, he might have been confident that even the most bitter of his enemies in this order could not but be favourably affected towards him by this expression of his trust in their loyalty, and his consideration for the tenderness of their consciences. But William did not yet know the English people. By asking greater liberty for Dissenters he enraged all Tory Churchmen, while, by suggesting a generous treatment of the bishops and clergy, he offended his own friends, who knew better than he, the danger of trusting implicitly to the forbearance of the clerical order. His speech, therefore, did harm to both the parties whom he would have befriended. The Act took no notice of Dissenters, and bore with all the justice of the severest law on the position of the clergy.

* "It was their (the clergy's) disaffection that made the King more inclinable to favour the Dissenters, whom he generally looked upon as better affected to his person and title."—Kennett's "History," iii. 518.

Eight bishops and more than four hundred of the clergy refused to take the oaths. It should be possible, at this distance of time, to pass an unprejudiced judgment on the characters and the acts of the non-jurors. At their head, was Sancroft, Archbishop of Canterbury, a man of unblemished moral and religious character; but weak in purpose, and narrow in his judgment and his sympathies. Next to him in influence, and superior to him in spiritual character, was Thomas Ken, Bishop of Bath and Wells, the author of the "Morning, Evening, and Midnight Hymns." A man of gentler disposition, or more saintly life than Ken, never adorned the Christian Church; and none can suspect the motives which induced him to throw in his lot with the non-jurors. In the midst of the tempest of passion which characterized these agitated times, he quietly justified himself by writing, "Though I do daily in many things betray great infirmity, I thank God I cannot accuse myself of any insincerity; so that deprivation will not reach my conscience, and I am in no pain at all for myself."* The remaining bishops were Thomas, of Worcester; Lake, of Chichester; Turner, of Ely; Lloyd, of Norwich; Frampton, of Gloucester; and White, of Peterborough. Thomas and Lake died immediately afterwards; and Sancroft, who somewhat ostentatiously retired to a cottage at Fressingfield, soon followed them. Turner implicated himself in a conspiracy to restore James, and the sympathies and prayers of all of the new sect were unhesitatingly given to the dethroned monarch. Ken refused to dissever himself from the

---

* "Ken's Life." By a Layman. Page 364.

Church, but Sancroft had no hesitation in denouncing the whole of the hierarchy and clergy who took the oath as schismatics. He joined with the other nonjurors in obtaining James's license to proceed with the consecration of new bishops,* thus defying the government, and inviting persecution from it. There was no occasion, however, for the State to stretch out its arm in order to punish the members of the new sect. Some reverence was felt for the personal character of many of them, but public opinion was not in their favour. If the rank of a few was high, their number was small. During the time of their probation, the press groaned with pamphlets concerning the injury which might result to the State and the Church if they refused to take the oaths. Burnet used his persuasive powers to the utmost. Stillingfleet forgot the sin of schism in Dissenters, and turned the whole of his controversial battery against the stubborn members of his own Church. When the day of probation passed, it was found that the government was not endangered, nor the Church rent in twain by the defection of even eight bishops. The State was, in fact, the stronger for the slight danger to which it had apparently been exposed. It had asserted the superiority of the civil to the ecclesiastical power in the Church of its own creation; it had ventured to depose from office men who claimed the authority of their office from God himself, and to deny to them the right of exercising any of their functions.

The non-jurors were pre-eminently the sacerdotalists of their age. Their favourite doctrine was, that the

---

* " Lathbury's " History of the Non-jurors," p. 97.

clergy were independent of the "lay power,"* a doctrine true of the Church, but not of the clergy of any State-established Church. In the course of years this doctrine blossomed into semi-Romanism, and the non-jurors claimed to be members of the "Catholic," as distinguished from the Protestant Church; advocated Transubstantiation; the mixing of water with wine in the Communion; and the supreme authority of the Church over all persons, "though never so great."† Finding themselves to be cut off from intercourse with Episcopalians at home, they fruitlessly endeavoured to promote a union with the Greek Church. Reduced in number, and brought into general contempt, they eventually quarrelled amongst themselves; and what little respect had been accorded to them was lost by their participation in the rebellion in favour of the Pretender in A.D. 1745, after which they gradually sank into oblivion. A non-juring bishop, however, who refused to recognize the Hanoverian succession, was living as late as the year 1805.‡ The history of this sect bears some resemblance to that of the "Cameronians" of Scotland, who, even now, in American republics and English colonies, bear witness to the Solemn League and Covenant. This resemblance extended to morals as well as to historical relationships. Like all zealots, the non-jurors were as severe in life as they were in doctrine. Whatever may be said of their disaffection to the State, none can attaint them of spiritual heresy. Although intolerant amongst

---

* Dodwell's "Independency of the Clergy of the Lay Power," 1697.

† Lathbury's "History of the Non-jurors," pp. 313—15.

‡ The name of the last was Boothe, who died in that year. Lathbury, p. 412.

the intolerant, they were pure in life, correct in morals, and numbered amongst them men of the most studious learning.*

It became evident, in the debates on this Bill, that there was no disposition in either House of Parliament to do justice to those who had so admittedly contributed to save the nation. When the Bill had been read a second time in the House of Lords, it was resolved that a Select Committee be appointed to draw up a clause which should abolish the Sacramental Test as a qualification for enjoying any office, employment, or place of trust under the Crown. The Committee drew up this clause, but it was at once rejected by a large majority. Seven peers—but seven peers only—Delamere, Stamford, North and Grey, Chesterfield, Wharton, Lovelace, and Vaughan, entered their protest against this vote, in which they expressed their opinion that a hearty union amongst Protestants was a greater security to the Church and State than any test that could be invented; that this union was now indispensably necessary, and that greater caution ought not to be required from such as held office under the Crown, than from the Members of the two Houses of Parliament, none of whom were required to receive the Sacrament in order to enable them to sit in either House.† A more moderate motion met with a similar fate. It was moved that any person should be sufficiently qualified who, within a year of his admission to

---

* Two of the ablest and most accurate of our national historians were non-jurors—Jeremy Collier, the author of the "Ecclesiastical History of England," and Carte, the author of a history of England. Law, the author of the "Serious Call," was also a non-juror.

† "Collection of Protests," pp. 62, 63. Birch's "Tillotson," 2nd ed., p. 158.

office, should receive the Sacrament of the Lord's Supper, either according to the usage of the Established, or any other Protestant Church. The terms of this motion were fixed so as to prevent the qualification of Roman Catholics. It was obviously open to serious objection on religious grounds. Had it been adopted it would have operated as a premium on the profession of personal religion amongst Dissenters, as well as in the Church, and although Lord Wharton, himself a Presbyterian of sincere religious character, voted for it, it must be doubtful whether it could have received the sanction of the leaders of the Dissenting interest. It was, however, like its predecessor, rejected by an overwhelming majority, six peers protesting against the rejection. These were Lords Oxford, Lovelace, Wharton, Mordaunt, Montague, and Paget, who argued that it was a " hard usage" of Dissenters; that it deprived the kingdom of the services of many fit and able men of unquestionable loyalty; that it raised a suspicion of the insincerity of the many promises which had been made to them; that it was an unjust humiliation of them, a profanation of the Sacrament, a violation of the spirit of Christianity, and an infliction of punishment where no crime had been committed.* The protest had, however, no effect beyond the vindication of the personal sincerity of the protesters, and the reward of Parliament to Dissenters was to affix upon them anew the ban of dishonesty and disloyalty.

A similar fate awaited them in the Commons. A Bill was introduced into this house for the repeal of the

* "Collection of Protests," pp. 64, 65.

Corporation Act which obliged all persons to receive the Sacrament as a condition of holding office, or discharging the functions of the magistracy in any municipal corporation. It was allowed to pass a second reading, but, as it was going into Committee, a motion was made that it should be an instruction that no alteration be effected in the laws respecting the Sacrament. As this motion, if carried, would have defeated the sole object of a Bill which the House had already sanctioned, it could scarcely have seemed probable that it would meet with any success. But, while there was a vindictive opposition to the measure in the Tory party, there were trimmers and half-hearted men—waiters on the opinions of the ministers—amongst the Whigs. It was agreed amongst these that no vote should be taken on the merits of this motion. In place of it, the adjournment of the debate was moved and carried by a hundred and sixteen to a hundred and fourteen votes. The same influence which brought about this division kept the Bill from making any further progress. It therefore became a "dropped order." Once and only once in the lifetime of the generation who then sat in the House of Commons was this subject revived. This was after the Toleration Act had been passed, when the Corporation of London appeared by its Sheriffs before the bar of the House with a petition that Dissenters might bear offices as well as others.* This city, which had sheltered the "Five Members;" which had set the example of public addresses to the head of the State by expressing its confidence in the Protector's government; had found

* Grey's Debates, June 24th, 1689.

money to carry on the war of the Parliament; had taken the first step to secure the government on the flight of James, and which had been the bulwark of civil and religious freedom for generations, made the only public protest which was given at that period against the injustice of the laws to which Dissenters were subjected.

The explanation of the course taken on these questions is to be found in the position of parties in the State and the Church. Whatever amount of indebtedness might have been felt towards the King, it is certain that he was not personally popular. His grave, cold and reserved manners repulsed the courtiers who remembered and had participated in the revels of the court of Charles the Second. He cared nothing for the gaieties of the palace. His ill-health obliged him, almost as soon as he came to England, to seek a residence out of the metropolis. He cultivated no personal intimacies among Englishmen, confided to them as few of his purposes as possible, and seldom took their advice. This course could not, as is generally represented, have proceeded wholly from temperament, for he could confide without reserve in those in whom he had confidence. But unfortunately, excepting Burnet and Tillotson, these persons were not Englishmen. Like many men who have consecrated themselves to a great public work, he had very few personal sympathies. What he most cared for was sympathy with his ideas, and his ideas were not those of the people by whom he was surrounded in England. They followed him in his foreign policy because they knew that he was the only man in Europe who could cope with the French King, and that the safety of

England as a State, and the permanency of the new government, depended on the manner in which that policy was carried out. William the Third brought to the consideration of domestic matters the same breadth and strength of intellect which enabled him to be the master of the political future of Europe, but not quite the same sagacity. Foreigner though he was, he had larger and more patriotic purposes respecting the country, the government of which he had undertaken, than almost any of the statesmen who sat in his council. His was the only vision that was not disturbed by party and personal prejudices. He indicated his want of sagacity by not taking such prejudices into sufficient consideration. Although a greater statesman than any Englishman of his day, he was by no means so great a politician as many men of smaller intellect. Yet it is probable that if he had not been a foreigner he would have had his own way in every matter of importance. Englishmen had, before this time, submitted to both the caprice and the arbitrary dictation of their Sovereigns; but those Sovereigns had, as a rule, no sympathies which were opposed to the national prejudices. William did not care to conceal the fact that he had such sympathies; and still less did the statesmen by whom he was surrounded care to conceal their intention of thwarting him. They made him miserable by their opposition to his plans and preferences. They took advantage of every occasion to prove to him that his wishes, however harmless they might be, were not to be considered law. They seemed to delight in humiliating him. No Sovereign of England, before or since his time, ever endured so much personal mortification as this great "deliverer" of the nation from the despotism of the Stuarts and the anarchy of another civil war. What real gratitude was felt towards him was shown by the manner of his burial. He had the meanest funeral of any King who ever sat on the English throne.

Considerations of public policy, occasioned, no doubt, much of the treatment to which William was exposed. It was desirable to show, and show frequently, that the relations of ruler and people were changed from what they had been; that, in fact, the King was now only nominally a ruler; that the three branches of the legislature held the sovereign power; and that the chief magistrate's functions were limited by their will and pleasure. The despotic powers of the Tudors and the arbitrary pretensions of the Stuarts were gone, and gone for ever. The statesmen of the Revolution had the difficult and delicate task committed to them of adjusting the new relations. To their firmness are owing the solidity of the throne and the liberty of the nation, but little can be said in praise of their delicacy. If the people had cared to think much about the subject, they would have found that nearly the whole power formerly claimed by the monarch of the country was now becoming lodged in the great territorial families, and that their chief safety consisted in the ambition and the mutual jealousies of those families. The Revolution practically substituted a mild oligarchy for an intolerable despotism, and from that time to the present this feature of the government of England has undergone but little modification. During the reign of William the great Whig families, with a few exceptions, were naturally the rulers of the nation, and their sympathies were, as they had always been, with the Nonconformists. But even amongst these men, the influence of the clergy, Jacobite although it was, was powerful. It was better for the sake of the public peace that this body should approve than that it should disapprove of their measures, and that, as far as might be consistent with the general welfare, or even a little beyond such pure patriotism, their good will to the new government should be conciliated. Such families as the Devonshires and the Bedfords would nearly always be found voting right; but the Halifaxes, who had joined the new government simply because it was successful, would, as it suited their own purposes, support an increased religious liberty one day and deny it the next, while the Earl of Nottingham, Secretary of State, who had the largest influence amongst the peers, was a Tory. The clause for abolishing the Sacramental Test was thrown out in the Lords by the votes of Whigs, and the votes of Whigs decided the fate of the Corporation Bill in the Commons. Both these decisions were probably given, not on the merits of the question at issue, but from a desire to conciliate the growing disaffection of the Church and the clergy.

There were churchmen and clergymen, however, of large mind and generous temper, who did not share in the general feeling respecting either the government or the Dissenters. The best representative of the political feeling of the general body of the clergy at this period was South, Prebendary of Westminster, whose rich and lofty, if sometimes coarse and turgid, eloquence has earned for him the deserved distinction of one of the greatest orators of the English Church. No preacher of his day, and few preachers since, could decorate Christian truth so gracefully and gorgeously—could make the love of God seem so winning, or the powers of the world to come so terrible as this man. But he loathed Dissent and Dissenters. The coarsest words in the English language were scarcely coarse enough for him to express his scorn and hatred of those "schismatics" and their schism. He had more charity for the greatest sinner before him, than he had even for a Howe or a Bates. When he spoke on this subject he became inflamed with passion, and his mouth poured forth a torrent of invective. What South said, five-sixths of the clergy felt, but there was a minority which included in its ranks men of equal, though of a different order of ability from South, who were possessed of very different feelings. Most prominent in this section was Burnet, who, in acknowledgment of his sincere Christian character, his devotion to the duties of his ministerial office, as well as in reward for his great services in forwarding the Revolution, had now been created Bishop of Salisbury. An ardent Whig and a severe rebuker of the vices of the greater portion of the clergy of his time, no man was both more respected and more hated than this active, learned, and liberal-minded prelate. His weaknesses undoubtedly drew upon him some contempt. He was garrulous, and like all garrulous men, sometimes too plain-spoken. He was also credulous, and too easily prejudiced against persons; but these faults diminish to nothing in comparison with the excellences of his character, and his great public services. He was the personal confidant of both William and Mary, and his suggestions and advice contributed in no small degree to the success of their enterprize. A Whig of the Whigs, when Whiggism meant devotion to one's country at the risk of life and fortune, he was an unswerving advocate of popular rights as opposed to arbitrary authority. His Protestantism was more than a creed: it was a principle of his religion. His liberality of sentiment would be esteemed even in this age: in his own it was exceptionally conspicuous. While he deplored any separation from the National Church, he advocated, with a zeal and energy which was the secret of half the hate of which he was the object, an unlimited toleration. "I think," he says, "it is a right due to all men; their thoughts are not in their own power, they must think of things as they appear to them; their consciences are God's, He only knows them, and He only can change them. And as the authority of parents over their children is antecedent to society, and no law that takes it away can be binding, so men are bound antecedently to all society to follow what to them appears to be the will of God; and, if men would act honestly, the rule of doing to all others what we would have others do to us would soon determine the matter; since every honest man must own that he would think himself hardly dealt with, if he were ill-used for his opinions, and for performing such parts of worship as he thought himself indispensably obliged to. . . . . I add not here any political considerations from the apparent interest of nations, which must dispose them to encourage the increase of their people, to advance industry, and to become a sanctuary to all who are oppressed. But though this is visible, and is confessed by all, yet I am now considering this matter only as it is righteous, just and merciful in the principle."* In the pulpit, in his place in the House of Lords, and in the press, through good report and through evil report, from the first Liberal administration of King William to the last Tory administration of Queen Anne, he never failed to advocate the application of this principle to the legislation of his country. His works on the "Thirty-nine Articles," the "History of the Reformation," and the "History of His Own Times," are part of the national literature, and his example as a bishop was a legacy to his Church. A more laborious, charitable and useful prelate, or a more active preacher never adorned the English Episcopacy. If, considering his admitted weaknesses and prejudices, this eulogy may seem extravagant, it has to be remembered that Bishop Burnet lived in an age when his opinions were as unfashionable as his virtues were uncommon.

Next, in personal, and superior in some respects in public influence to Burnet, were Tillotson, Tenison, and Stillingfleet. Tillotson and Tenison, successively Archbishops of Canterbury, had much in common. Both were liberal men; but Tillotson was by far the greater man of the two. He was one of the most chaste and pious, and at the same time, one of the most popular of preachers; he was active in promotion all measures tending towards an increased toleration; he cultivated largely the personal friendship of Dissenters, and was the leader of the Liberal Church-party who sought, by a revision of the formularies and the constitution of the Church, to bring back those who had left it to her fold. Tenison possessed

* History of His Own Times, p. 906.

less mental power, but was of equal liberality of sentiment. Stillingfleet, Bishop of Worcester, was superior to both of the archbishops in learning, and, in love of disputation, somewhat resembled Baxter. But although he had raised a controversy with Dissenters on the subject of "Schism," no man was more respected by them. All these, as were all William's bishops, were somewhat latitudinarian in theology; but the latitudinarianism of William's day meant nothing more than Calvinism which was not of immoderate exclusiveness. They were men who were accustomed to dwell more on the love of God than on the terrors of hell, and who lived that mild and tolerant life which is most in accordance with such a disposition.

The most cultured intellect and the most unblemished patriotism in the House of Commons were also ranked in favour of the largest degree of religious liberty. Serjeant Maynard, the veteran general of the Liberal party, now past ninety years of age, had seen too much of the fatal folly of persecution to resist any measure which had for its object the relief of conscience and the restoration of natural religious rights. The grandson of John Hampden was found on the same side. Somers, who spoke for the first time in this Parliament, and who was destined soon to attain to the highest eminence of statesmanship, never faltered in his loyalty to the principles of English liberty. In the same rank was to be found the great name of Sir Isaac Newton, who, although apparently a silent member, gave his uniform support to such measures as most tended to the higher elevation of his country. How was it that, with such a weight in favour of a more enlarged liberality, one House of Parliament decided to retain the Test Act, and the other the Corporation Oath?

The opposition of the clergy to all such measures has already been referred to; but their opposition was not the only cause of this failure. The truth is that neither the people at large nor the majority of the Dissenters cared about them. Dissent, however in certain districts it might and did command respect, in consequence of the high character of its representatives, was not popular. This was sufficiently shown on William's death, when the lower classes all over the country threatened to pull down the meeting-houses. In fact, the people far preferred the chatty, easy-going careless " parson " to either the severe and scrupulous Presbyterian, the godly and painstaking Independent, the zealous but generally unlettered Baptist, or the ardent but strange Quaker. The preacher who allowed them to live as they might choose; who did not preach too censoriously about sin; who was ready with the absolution at the last moment of life, and who professed to give them, with the sanction of the State and all the bishops, an easy entrance after death to heaven, was the preacher for them. Besides this, the English have, of all people, the strongest feeling of loyalty. The Tudors were popular with them notwithstanding their vices, and the Stuarts notwithstanding their crimes. Of the questions at issue between James and the Constitution, they could have known little or nothing. If the great statesmen, landlords, and merchants had decided for James, they too would have decided for him, and on the whole, perhaps, because he belonged to a race of English kings, have preferred him to William. Loyalty is a sentiment which, in England, it is happily difficult to change. It cannot be created by a Parliamentary vote; it was almost in abeyance until the House of Hanover became firmly seated on the throne.

The greater number and the most influential of the Dissenters were indifferent to the proceedings of the legislature from another cause. A Bill was already under discussion having for its object the promotion of a union of the Presbyterians, and possibly the Independents, with the Church. If it should be successful, the Test and Corporation Acts would not affect them; they would only affect the smaller and more unpopular bodies of Baptists and Quakers. Some amongst the Presbyterians had not, even yet, very large views concerning toleration, and they were the most conspicuous representatives of the " Dissenting interest." While, therefore, these bills were under discussion, they stood still. If the "comprehension scheme" should, as they expected, come to a satisfactory termination, their own troubles would be over; if the contrary, they were not disposed to complain so long as mere toleration was allowed. In the absence of all external pressure on the legislature, excepting from the King, and in view of the spirit of the clergy, now just beginning to raise the cry of the " Church in Danger," it cannot be a matter of surprise that these measures should have been defeated. No one in all the debates questioned the undoubted loyalty of Dissenters; the doubt was as to the loyalty of the Church. Both proposals, therefore, became a sacrifice to the twin Molochs of political disaffection and ecclesiastical supremacy.

The last act, as peers of Parliament, of the non-juring bishops was to move for the introduction of two Bills—one for the toleration and the other for the comprehension of Dissenters. In doing this they vindicated the sincerity of their promises, and furnished proof that their conduct did not proceed from personal animosity to the King, for on no questions did William feel more strongly than on these two. The Earl of Nottingham, on behalf of the Government, took charge of both these measures. The first was entitled " An Act for exempting their Majesties' Protestant subjects, Dissenting from the Church of England, from the Penalties of Certain Laws." It passed the House of Lords without objection, and reached the House of Commons in May, A.D. 1689. That House, however, had its own Bill on this subject, entitled " An Act for Liberty and Indulgence to Protestant Dissenters," and on May 11th both Bills were read a second time. There was no substantial difference between the two measures, and on the question that the House do go into Committee, it was agreed, out of respect to the Lords, that their Bill only should be proceeded with. So important a measure was probably never so briefly discussed. The first speech made upon it was by Hampden, who remarked that every man was in favour of indulgence to Dissenters, and that little needed to be said on the subject. " The empire of religion," he continued, " belongs to God," and he showed that those nations which had refused to acknowledge this principle had been injured by such a policy. He deprecated certain theological references in the Bill, but expressed his hearty agreement with the clause which excluded Unitarians from toleration. After two or three unimportant speeches, the measure was ordered to be committed. Two days subsequently the report of the Committee was brought up by Mr. Hampden. There was some debate on the proposal to allow Quakers to make an affirmation instead of taking an oath; "but," said Colonel Birch, "these sort of people have been in the shambles these twenty years;" and, he added, that he had never supposed they would have accepted such a bill.* It was also urged that the measure should be limited to seven years; but the House made no alterations in it, and, on the same day, May 17th, it finally passed.

During the passage of the Bill through the legislature, the last appeal for an enlarged toleration was issued. John Howe, in an anonymous publication, entitled "The Case of the Protestant Dissenters represented and argued," laid down, in clear and stately language, the right of Dissent. He based this right on the natural claims of conscience, on the human origin of those forms and ceremonies which divided Dissenters from the Church, on the unnatural cruelty of the laws by which the supremacy of the Church had been enforced, and on the known patriotism of Dissenters. In this publication, Howe affirmed that the generality of Dissenters differed from the Church of England in no substantials of doctrine or worship, or even of government, provided that the government were so managed as to attain its acknowledged end. He also argued against the unreasonableness of excluding Dissenters from any participation in civil affairs. "We tremble," he said, "to think of the

* There is a curious passage in George Fox's "Journal" of this month, in which he states how he attended the House of Commons and saw the members to arrange the terms for Quakers.

sacramental test brought down as low as to the keeper of an alehouse." "Never," he added, "can there be union or peace in the Christian world till we take down our arbitrary inclosures, and content ourselves with those which our common Lord hath set. If he falls under a curse that alters man's landmark, to alter God's is not likely to infer a blessing."

This Act, which has subsequently received the popular title of the "Toleration Act," gave, as may be supposed from the temper of the times in which it passed, the smallest possible advantage to Dissenters from the established religion. The only Dissent which it recognized or allowed was dissent from forms and ceremonies; it allowed none from what were supposed, at that time, to be the established doctrines of the Church. The preamble recited that its object was to give some ease to scrupulous consciences, in order that Protestants might be more united in interest and affection. It exempted Dissenters, on condition of their taking certain oaths against the Papal rule and supremacy, from the operation of those laws of Elizabeth compelling attendance at parish churches; on the same condition, it exempted them from any past defaults against those laws, and provided that they should not in future be prosecuted for their Nonconformity. No assembly of persons meeting for religious worship was allowed to hold such meeting in any place the doors of which were, at the time, secured by locks, bars, or bolts; nothing was to exempt Dissenters from payment of tithes or other parochial dues; if any persons elected to a parochial office objected to take the oaths, they might serve by deputy; all Dissenting preachers and teachers were required to take the oaths and subscribe, before a general or quarter session, all the articles of religion excepting the thirty-fourth, thirty-fifth, and thirty-sixth, or neglecting to do so, were liable to be subjected to the penalties of the Act of Uniformity and the Conventicle and Five Mile Acts of Charles the Second; the names of such persons as had so subscribed were to be registered, and they were to be charged a fee of sixpence for such registration; those who scrupled at the baptizing of infants were exempted from the obligation to subscribe to the Article respecting Infant Baptism; all Dissenting ministers so qualified were not to be liable to serve on juries or to be appointed churchwardens or overseers; any one going to a Dissenting place of worship might be called upon at any time, by a justice of the peace, to take the oaths, and if he refused, was forthwith to be imprisoned without bail, and to be punished as a "Papal recusant;" "certain other persons" — intending Quakers — who scrupled at the taking of any oath, were allowed to substitute for it a promise and declaration in the terms of the oath, subscribing at the same time a profession of their belief in the Trinity and in the Divine inspiration of the Scriptures; all the laws until that time in force for frequenting Divine service on the Lord's-day were to be executed against all persons who did not attend some place of religious worship; Dissenting as well as Church congregations were to be protected from disturbance during public service; no Dissenting congregation was to be permitted to assemble until the place of worship had been certified before the bishop of the diocese, his archdeacon, or a justice of the peace; and lastly, all Papists and all who denied the doctrine of the

Trinity were wholly excluded from the benefit of the Act. The Dissenters as a body, we are informed, received this measure with thankfulness and content.* The only people who were dissatisfied with it were the Quakers, who continued, from this time forward, year after year, to denounce, in the most emphatic language, tithes and Church-rates, and all compulsory exactions for the support of religion.† Howe, as soon as the Act was passed, addressed to Churchmen and Dissenters an exhortation to peace and charity, counselling them no longer to "bicker" about forms, ceremonies, or Church constitutions, but to adopt such a course of conduct as might lead to a closer ecclesiastical union.‡

In addition to the Quakers there was one man who did not view this Act with complacency. It has been supposed that the terms of the Toleration Act were

---

* Calamy's "Baxter," p. 653. "Life of Howe," p. 163.

† "We desire your testimony against tithes may be kept up in the peaceable spirit of Christ, as becomes true Christians, rather suffering patiently the spoiling of your goods, than any ways to strive or struggle with the spoilers, and retain them by force." "Yearly Epistle," 1689. "It is our desire that, for the sake of our Lord Jesus Christ, and His holy testimony, that all Friends be faithful to Him in their testimony against tithes of all sorts, knowing that since they were ended by Christ they were imposed by, and originally sprung from, that anti-Christian root, a Popish usurpation in Church and State." "Yearly Epistle," 1690. Similar language is used for many years in all the subsequent Epistles of this Society. In 1693 the Friends are urged to be a good example to their children in testifying against "the grand oppression and anti-Christian yoke of tithes, that our Christian testimony, borne and greatly suffered for, be faithfully maintained against them in all respects, and against steeple-house rates or lays." "Epistle," 1693. The number of persons imprisoned for non-payment of these exactions when the "Yearly Epistle" was drawn up, generally averaged about one hundred, and the goods taken to about £4,000. "Epistles, etc., from 1681 to 1857." 2 vols. London. 1858.

‡ "Humble Requests to Conformists and Dissenters touching their Temper and Behaviour towards each Other, upon the lately passed Indulgence." 1689.

negotiated by John Locke: if so, we know that he considered them to be most inadequate to the claims of justice.* Locke, although not a Dissenter, had been trained under Dissenting influences. "Educated," says Sir James Mackintosh, " amongst English Dissenters, during the short period of their political ascendancy, he early imbibed from them that deep piety and ardent spirit of liberty which actuated that body of men."† Cast out from Oxford soon after the Restoration, he took refuge in Holland, where, in A.D 1688, he composed, in Latin, his First Letter on Toleration. He came to England with the Prince of Orange. Soon after the Act was passed, this Letter was translated, and published in English. It was the first publication in which the principles of religious equality were described and defended by a Christian philosopher as well as a Christian statesman. Locke's mental constitution peculiarly fitted him for the dispassionate treatment of such a subject. His intellect, while it was clear and penetrating, was neither cold nor unsympathetic. He was endowed with the highest order of the reasoning faculty, but his breadth of vision was equal to its accuracy and its strength. The founder of a new school of English philosophy, he led the way to a revolution in the doctrines of mental science. All the strength and freshness of his intellect he brought to bear on the discussion of the relation which should subsist between civil governments and the human conscience. His motive, however, in writing on this subject, was not merely to settle a question in political philosophy. He was a devout, religious man, as

* Lord King's "Life of Locke, i. 327.
† Sir James Mackintosh's Miscellaneous Works. Art: "Locke."

well as an exact thinker; and he felt that the religion of Jesus Christ did not, and could not sanction any form or degree of persecution. He had an inflexible sense of right, and his mind revolted at the suggestion that injustice could ever promote the interests of the Christian religion.

The argument of the First Letter begins by stating the marks of a true Church. Toleration is considered to be its chief characteristic. Pomp of outward worship, reformation of discipline and orthodoxy, are rather marks of men striving for power and empire over one another than of the true Church of Christ. A person may be possessed of all these things, and yet be destitute of charity, meekness, and goodwill to all mankind ; and if so, he is "short of being a true Christian himself." It is in vain, Locke argues, for men to usurp the name of Christian without benignity and meekness of spirit. He appeals to the consciences of all persecutors, and asks them whether they have persecuted out of friendship and kindness, and whether they have dealt with members of their own communion, who were guilty of all manner of vices, as they have dealt with godly Nonconformists ? Why have they tolerated whoredom, fraud, and malice in their own flocks, and persecuted innocency of life, embodied in conscientious dissent ; was this to the glory of God ? " Let such," he says, " talk ever so much of the Church ; they plainly demonstrate by their actions that it is another kingdom they aim at, and not the advancement of the Kingdom of God." If they desired the good of souls they would, like the Prince of Peace, send men out, not armed with the sword or other instruments of force, but with the

Gospel of Peace, and with the exemplary holiness of their lives. He then proceeds to define the boundaries of the State and the Church. The office of the civil magistrate, he says, is to protect life, liberty, health, and prosperity, and does not extend, nor ought to be extended, to the salvation of souls. The care of souls is not committed to him more than to other men; for God has not committed such authority to one man over another, as to compel any one to his religion. All the life and power of religion consists in the inward persuasion of the mind; and faith is not faith without believing. The civil magistrate's power consists only in outward force, and it is impossible for the understanding to be compelled to the belief of anything by such a force. Even if the rigour of law could change men's opinions it would not help to the salvation of their souls. With regard to the Church, he argues that it is a purely voluntary society for public worship. People cannot be born members of it, and neither bishop nor presbyter is necessary to constitute it. It could not be a Church of Christ if it excluded from its communion those who would one day be received into the kingdom of heaven. With respect to toleration, it is maintained that all persons are entitled to equal rights as citizens, whatever may be their religion, and whether they be Christians or Pagans. Locke notices it as remarkable that the most violent defenders of the truth, and exclaimers against schism, hardly ever let loose this, their zeal for God, with which they are so warmed and inflamed, unless they have the civil magistrate on their side. He takes notice also of the fact, that while people are let alone in the management of all their temporal affairs, if they do not frequent Church, noise and clamour are at once excited. In his judgment, the magistrate has no power to enforce or to forbid any rites or ceremonies in the worship of God; for, though ever so indifferent in their own nature, when they are brought into the Church and worship of God, they are removed out of the reach of his jurisdiction. The motive of all such interference he ascribes to the heads and leaders of the Church, moved by avarice and an insatiable desire of dominion, making use of the immoderate ambition of magistrates, and the credulous superstition of the people to animate them against Dissenters, contrary to all the laws of the Gospel, and to the precepts of charity.

The principles laid down in this remarkable Letter are defended with the greatest force of reason and felicity of illustration. They not only strike at the root of all statechurches, but they go far to unchristianize statechurches as such, and all such members of them as act according to the spirit of their foundation. The real schismatics, Locke argues, are not the men who separate from an established religion, but the men, who, professing that religion, violate, by their want of charity, and by their carnal desire for supremacy, the precepts and the spirit of Christianity. This Letter was followed by two others, on the same subject, in which the position taken by the writer was defended with equal acuteness and power. In other writings Locke gave what may be termed the moral history of statechurches. In the religion established by Jesus Christ, he remarked, such outward ceremonies as had been common amongst the ancients, and which were always conducted by an order of men called "priests," were almost dispensed with, and pompous rites were abolished. Since then, its ministers, who, like the ancients, also called themselves priests, had assumed to themselves the parts both of the heathen priests and the philosophers, and had combined to enlist the secular power on their side. They had been the cause of more disorders and tumults, and bloodsheds, than all other circumstances put together. He traced the divisions of Christendom, and the persecution to which men had been subjected, to the assumption by the clergy, supported by the magistrates, of sacerdotal power, although the Scriptures plainly showed that there was nothing which a priest could do which any other man could not also do.* He connected with this the rise and growth of Episcopacy, and the ambition which such an office had excited.† The origin of state-churches, according to Locke, was to be ascribed to the lowest passions of humanity; their characteristics were not the characteristics of true religion, and their history had been one of inhuman cruelty and oppression.

The treatises of Locke bore the same relation to the age in which they appeared as those of Milton had borne to a previous generation. Both writers addressed the rulers of the State with a common object, and both designed their works for the establishment of sounder principles of government. While priests and presbyters alike were laying claim to supernatural power and arbitrary authority, Milton, in wrath and indignation, exposed the pretences of both parties. When the popular will had, in relation to the control of the

---

* Locke's Common-place Book. Art: "Sacerdos."
† "Defence of Nonconformity." Life, ii. pp. 215—218.

civil government, successfully asserted its power, he would have had it to assert itself, with equal intensity, against all ecclesiastical usurpation. To make sacerdotalism appear as odious to others as it did to himself, he arrayed it in the most repulsive garb which his imagination could suggest. He brought to bear against it the resources of the richest scholarship, and tried its claims by history, by experience, by Scripture, and by conscience. His writings aided to dam its doctrines against further advance, until priests and presbyters united to break down the obstacle which opposed them both. When the civil government again became unsettled, Locke endeavoured to do what Milton had done. The style and manner of Milton would have been unsuited to the circumstances of the Revolution. The possessors of power both in Church and State now professed to be animated by a conciliatory spirit. Locke therefore addressed them in the calm voice of philosophy. His purpose was not to arouse indignation, but to persuade the judgment and the conscience. As far as his own generation was concerned he failed, but the lovers of freedom in all subsequent times have drawn from his works a strength which, but for him, they could not have attained.

Nothing could have been more opposed to the principles of government laid down in Locke's writings than the ecclesiastical law of England as settled by the Toleration Act. This Act, while it repealed former laws which had had for their direct object the extinction of all Dissent, legalized it, and gave it social standing. But care was taken that this standing should be as low as possible. The right of all persons to think for themselves in matters of religion was now finally recognized by the law of England, but those who chose to exercise this right were, at the same time, deprived of a portion of their civil privileges. The State expressed its solemn and deliberate judgment that such men could not be trusted. It did not believe this; it knew that the very heart of loyalty was with the Dissenters; but it was thought expedient, notwithstanding, to punish them. It has not been the practice of statesmen to base their legislation on principles of abstract justice, but to accommodate their measures to the temper and the strength of the various parties in the kingdom. The statesmen of the Revolution sacrificed Dissenters to appease the jealousies and the fears of the lower order of the clergy. In A.D. 1687 the Dissenters had voluntarily surrendered their liberties, in order to save the State; in A.D. 1689 the State, ostensibly for its own safety, limited those liberties within the narrowest bounds which, with any pretension to honour, it could define. But if, relatively to Dissenters, the Toleration Act was an unjust and an ungenerous measure, relatively to the State it was an almost infinite concession. In passing it the civil government declared that it had been vanquished: that conscience had conquered law; that a system of absolute repression had failed, and could no longer be continued. Henceforward the Church was not to be armed with the sword to kill, but with the stave alone to punish and distress. The contest between it and Dissent was not to be one for existence on the one side and extermination on the other, but for equality in the one and supremacy in the other. In order that she might prosecute this new warfare with success the Church was armed and equipped at the expense of the State.

She had the exclusive privileges of office and power, and her endowments were anew secured to her. The Dissenters, like the Christians who were sent into the Roman amphitheatre, were defenceless. Looking at the prospect of the two parties from a human point of view, which was most likely to succeed? Looking at them from another point of view, which was most likely to perform the effective religious work of Christian Churches?

At the same time that the Toleration Bill was introduced into the House of Lords, the bill for the " Comprehension " of Dissenters in the Established Church was also introduced. Six times during the previous hundred years had steps been taken to bring about this result. Some of these proposals had failed from the insincerity of the government and the Church, and others from the want of general interest in the subject. It seemed that, on this occasion, there could be no such failure. The Crown was known to be warmly interested in the scheme, and some of the most eminent of the Church dignitaries were not merely favourable to it, but anxious for its success. The only quarters, apparently, from which opposition could be expected were the House of Commons and the clergy—whose influence could so effectively be brought to bear on the composition of that House. The bill introduced by the Earl of Nottingham to the House of Lords was entitled " An Act for uniting their Majesties' Protestant subjects."* The preamble recited that the peace of the State was " highly con-

---

* When Lord Macaulay wrote his History this Bill had not been seen by more than "two or three living persons" (chap. xi.) It has since been reprinted in the " Report of the Subscription Commission for 1865." Parl. Paper, 3441. Sess. 1865.

cerned" in the peace of the Church, and that it was most necessary, in the present conjuncture, for that peace to be preserved. In order, therefore, to remove occasions of difference and dissatisfaction amongst Protestants, it was provided that no subscription or declaration should be required from any person but the declaration against the Papacy, and that the declarant approved "of the Doctrine and Worship and Government of the Church of England by law established as containing all things necessary to salvation," but this was subsequently altered to an engagement to "submit to the present constitution of the Church of England" with an acknowledgment that "the doctrine of it contains in it all things necessary to salvation," and a promise "to conform to the worship and the government thereof as established by law." The declarant was also required to promise that, in the exercise of his ministry, he would preach and practice according to such doctrine. No oaths were to be required on admission to a benefice but the oaths of fidelity to the present settlement of the Crown, and the oaths concerning residence and simony. Schoolmasters, also, were required to take the two former oaths. Persons taking any degree, fellowship, headship, or professorship in the Universities were to take the same oaths, and also to engage, in the words required of clergymen, excepting, in the case of laymen, the latter portion of them, to conform to the Established religion. There was also a clause to the effect that, with the imposition of the bishop's hands, Presbyterian ordinations should be considered valid, but this clause was struck out. It was next provided that, excepting in the Royal Chapels and the cathedral and collegiate churches, no person should be compelled to wear a surplice during the performance of any of his ministerial duties, but only a black gown. Compulsion to use the sign of the Cross in Baptism was abolished, and parents were allowed to take the office of godfathers and godmothers. Kneeling at the Sacrament of the Lord's Supper was left to the option of the communicant. Lastly, as the liturgies and canons of the Church were capable of being altered so as to "conduce to the glory of God and the better edification of the people;" as the ecclesiastical courts were defective in their jurisdiction, particularly in respect to the removal of scandalous ministers; as Confirmation should be solemnly administered, and a strict care exercised in the examination of candidates for the ministry, their Majesties were petitioned to issue a Royal Commission to the bishops and clergy, not exceeding thirty in number, for the purpose of making alterations in the liturgy, the canons, and the ecclesiastical courts, and to present such alterations to Convocation and Parliament "that the same may be approved and established in due course of law." This Bill did not pass the Lords without some difficulty. The clauses relating to kneeling at the Sacrament occasioned, says Burnet, "a vehement debate,"* and a strenuous opposition was made to the proposal to include only members of the clerical order in the Commission. When the vote was taken on this proposal, the numbers were found to be equal, and therefore, according to the rule of the house, the amendment was negatived. The Marquis of Winchester, Lord Mordaunt, and Lord Lovelace entered,

---

* "Own Times," p. 531.

however, their protest against this vote, in which they expressed their opinion that it was a humiliation of the laity; that it unduly exalted the clerical order; that it was a recognition of the Romish principle of the clergy alone having a right to meddle in religion; that it would be a greater satisfaction both to Dissenters and to the legislature if lay lords and commoners were included in the Commission, that the clergy had no authority but such as was given to them by the laity in Parliament, and that it was contrary to historical precedents.

When the Comprehension Bill reached the Commons it was allowed to lie on the table without discussion. Instead of proceeding with it, the house passed a resolution requesting the King to summon a meeting of Convocation, and the Lords seconded the request. Tillotson was, at the time, in intimate intercourse with the King, and the blame of summoning this body has been uniformly charged on the advice given by him. While the measure was being discussed by the Lords, Tillotson himself suggested to the King that Convocation should be summoned to deal with it.* In all probability, therefore, the clause in the Bill relating to Convocation was inserted at his suggestion. Tillotson's sincerity in promoting Comprehension cannot be questioned, but the step which he advised proved, as it was prophesied it would be,† fatal to the success of the scheme. Tillotson's motives had reference to the character of the

---

* Birch's "Life of Tillotson," pp. 165, 166.
† Burnet was very angry at the address of the Commons and prophesied that if Convocation were summoned it would be "the utter ruin" of the Comprehension Scheme. Reresby's "Memoirs," p. 344.

Church. He thought it desirable that the stigma of its being a mere "Parliamentary religion," should be taken away from it, and that, therefore, liberty should be given to it to revise its own constitution.* The King, no doubt, saw in the suggestion a means of conciliating the clergy, and therefore yielded to it.

In accordance with the terms of the Bill the Commission was first nominated. It consisted of ten bishops and twenty divines, and included men of all parties in the Church. Amongst them were Lamplugh, Archbishop of York; Compton, Bishop of London; Burnet, Bishop of Salisbury; Stillingfleet, Tillotson, and Tenison. Tillotson and Stillingfleet appear to have taken the initiative in all the proposals which were laid before this body. Before it met Tillotson drew up a list of the concessions which, in his judgment, the Church would be willing to make. All ceremonies, Tillotson thought, should be left indifferent; the liturgy should be revised, the Apocryphal lessons left out, and the Psalms re-translated; the terms of subscription should be altered in accordance with the clauses of the Bill on that subject; the canons should be revised, the ecclesiastical courts reformed, persons ordained in foreign reformed Churches should not be re-ordained, and Presbyterian ordination should be considered valid.† The Commissioners met on October 3rd, and in six weeks held eighteen meetings, some of them of several hours' duration, besides holding various sub-committees. A diary of their proceedings was kept, and a copy of the Prayer Book used by them in their revision is still in existence.‡

---

* Birch's "Tillotson," p. 166.
† Birch's "Tillotson," pp. 168—170.
‡ These papers were inaccessible until recent years. Calamy knew of

Nothing could have exceeded the conscientious and scrupulous care, or the spirit of conciliation which characterized the labours of this Commission. They had before them all the works of Nonconformists, from Elizabeth's time to their own, in which exceptions had been taken to the services and the constitution of the Church. The whole of the Prayer Book was considered sentence by sentence, and alterations were made throughout every part. The proceedings do not appear to have been always of an amicable character. Six of the Commissioners never sat, one attended only twice, and three others left after the third meeting.* The whole of these belonged to the High Church party. The attendance, however, was still very considerable, and always included five or six bishops. Neither Burnet, Tillotson, nor Tenison was once absent. The labours of the Commission resulted in the adoption of an entirely reformed service, and in the revision of several of the most important laws and ceremonies of the Church, the whole amounting to nearly six hundred alterations. The Apocrypha was discarded; the word "priest" was altered to "minister;" the "Lord's-day" was substituted for "Sunday;" the use of the surplice was left optional; the Athanasian Creed was so explained as to diminish the effect of the damnatory clauses; there was to be no obligation to kneel at the communion, nor to use the cross in baptism; the marriage service was purged of its indecencies and the words of the contract modified; the absolution

their existence, but could not see them. Tenison desired them to be deposited in the Lambeth Library, but to be kept secret. They were published, on the motion of Mr. Heywood, M.P., in Parl. Paper, 283, Sess. 1854.

* Parl. Papers, "Alterations, &c.," p. 108.

service was so changed that it was impossible for it to sanction Romish doctrine; in the burial service the objectionable phrases relating to the " sure and certain hope " of the everlasting happiness of the departed were changed to an expression of belief in the resurrection of all the dead, and in the eternal life of all who might " die in the Lord." Ordination by presbyteries was acknowledged to be valid, and the ordination service so altered that the gift of the Holy Ghost, which the words now ascribe to the bishop, was made a matter of prayer only, the Commissioners expressing their judgment that the form then, and now, in use was imported into the Church of England service in the " darkest times of Popery." In addition to these, several alterations were made in the collects, the litany, the catechism, and other portions of the service. These changes were made not merely to satisfy Dissenters, but, as Stillingfleet remarked, they were " fit to be made were there no Dissenters " whatever.*

The Commission finished its labours on the 10th November, and on the 21st of the same month Convocation met. The Upper House was, as a whole, well disposed for peace and unity. Sancroft being under suspension, it was presided over by Compton, Bishop of London, who had been one of the most active members of the Commission, and whose antecedents were all in favour of a conciliatory policy. · The Lower House gave, at its first sitting, a proof of its opposite temper. The liberal party had hoped to secure Tillotson as prolocutor, but it appeared that the members had been

* Ib. p. 103.

already canvassed by the High Church and Jacobite party in favour of Dr. Jane, of Oxford, one of the Commissioners who had ceased to attend the meeting of that body, on the ground that he was not satisfied with its authority, and that, after having given his assent and consent to the contents of the Prayer Book, he did not see how he could make an alteration in them. Jane was elected, and with his election the hopes of all liberal Churchmen died. It was with great difficulty, after this, that the house could be prevailed upon to consent to an address to the King. It was proposed by one of its members that the non-jurors should sit with them.* The Bishop of London spoke warmly in favour of indulgence and charity, but on this question he spoke to deaf ears. All the indulgence and charity of the Lower House were accorded not to Dissenters but to those who stood in the strongest political and ecclesiastical opposition to them.† They spent their time in considering what books they should condemn, and in creating occasions of difference with the Upper House. It was useless to lay the scheme of revision before this body. To prevent unseemly spectacles, it was prorogued until the January of the next year, when, with Parliament, it was dissolved. No attempt was afterwards made to revive this subject.

The failure of this scheme perpetuated, to a great extent, Nonconformity in England. The Presbyterians never ceased to regret the issue of the labours of the Comprehension Commission. Baxter protested, in his

* Kennet, iii. 555.
† Lathbury's " History of Convocation," p. 332. Procter's " History of the Common Prayer Book," p. 159. Kennett, iii. p. 555.

latest works, that the body to which he belonged was in favour of a National State Church. He disavowed the term Presbyterian, and stated that most whom he knew did the same. They would be glad, he said, to live under godly bishops and to unite on "healing terms."* He deplored that the Church-doors had not been opened to him and his brethren, and pleaded urgently for a "healing Act of Uniformity."† Calamy explicitly states that he was disposed to enter the Establishment if Tillotson's scheme had succeeded.‡ Howe, also, lamented the failure of the scheme.§ It is uncertain to what extent the Independents shared in this feeling, but it is unquestionable that they were generally considered to be willing, on certain terms, to unite with the Church. They formed a portion of the deputation of ministers which waited on the King after his coronation, when Dr. Bates said, on behalf of the whole body, that they were now encouraged to hope for a firm union of Protestants by the rule of Christianity being made the rule of Conformity. "We shall cordially," said the ministers, "embrace the terms of union which the ruling wisdom of our Saviour has prescribed in His Word." Such an union, they added, would make the Church a type of Heaven. On the same day they addressed the Queen, and besought her to use her influence to compose the differences which then existed, and that the terms of union might be those in which all Protestant Churches were agreed.‖ It was stated, however, that the Independents

---

* Baxter's "National Churches," p. 68, A.D. 1691.
† Ib. p. 72.
‡ Calamy's "Own Life," i. 208. § Calamy's "Howe," p. 163.
‖ Calamy's "Baxter," pp. 623-24.

seemed incapable of anything but toleration, and that they could not be brought into the Church excepting by such concessions as would shake its foundations. But, in the judgment of many men, the concessions made by the Commissioners were sufficient to do this.* Calamy's assertion that the scheme, if it had been adopted, would, in all probability, have brought into the Church two-thirds of the Dissenters,† indicates the almost entire agreement of the Independents with the Presbyterians concerning the expediency of accepting it. Had Owen been alive, their sympathies might have been restrained; but no man since his death had taken, or was qualified to take, his place.

The Comprehension scheme failed not because of the disaffection of Dissenters, but because of the opposition of the Church. While it was under discussion, pamphlet after pamphlet appeared against it, in which it was denounced as tending to division rather than to union, and as undermining and "pulling down" the Church. The Universities declared against it.‡ South declaimed against "the rabble" being admitted, and compared the proposals for union to letting a thief into a house in order to avoid the noise and trouble of his tapping at the door.§ It seems, also, to be certain that the statesmen who publicly advocated it were privately opposed to it. Even those who were most eager in its promotion came afterwards to the conclusion that its failure was

---

* Dr. Comber to Dr. Patrick (one of the Commissioners), "Tanner MSS." 27, 93.

† Calamy's "Baxter," p. 655.

‡ "Vox Cleri," A.D. 1689. "Burnet's Own Times," p. 543. "Birch's Tillotson," p. 183.

§ Sermons, vol. v., p. 486.

owing to a "very happy direction of the providence of God,"* for that, in all probability, it would only have strengthened the schism of the non-jurors and have given occasion to a stronger opposition to the government. That its virtual rejection was a breach of faith to Dissenters, no one questioned. "All the promises," says Burnet, "made in King James's time were now entirely forgotten."

In a different sense from that intended by Bishop Burnet, "the happy providence of God" in this matter may be acknowledged by all Dissenters and most Englishmen. The absorption into the National Church of two-thirds, and those the most learned and influential, of the Dissenters of that period would have been a public calamity. It is true that the Church to which they would have given their adhesion would have been a reformed Church. No suspicion of Romanism could henceforth have attached to it, and it would have afforded no foothold to men whose sympathies were with the doctrines of Rome while their offices were in the Church of England. But the strength of English Protestant Dissent would have been broken, and its influence both in its political and its ecclesiastical relations,—on the religion of the people and on the character of public legislation,—have been fatally diminished in power.

* Burnet's "Own Times," p. 544.

CHAPTER III.

THE COMPREHENSION BILL TO THE SCHISM BILL.
A.D. 1689—A.D. 1714.

TOLERATED, but still under the frown of the State, all classes of Dissenters began at once to make the most active use of their newly acquired liberty. The whole body apparently constituted, at this period, about a twentieth portion of the inhabitants of England and Wales,* or a little more than a hundred and ten thousand persons. It was the opinion of some that Dissent would die out with the generation then existing;† and, looking at the age of its living leaders, and at the little prospect that there seemed of men of equal power and influence rising to take their places, this opinion may not have appeared, even to many of their own number, an unreasonable one. They did not, however, act as though there was any such probability. The most aggressive, and, in some respects, the most successful body at this period, was that of the Quakers. Fox, Barclay, and Penn, were still living. Although nearly seventy years of age, Fox's zeal was as ardent as ever it

---

* Return to an Order in Council as follows:—Province of Canterbury—Conformists 2,123,362; Nonconformists 93,151; Papists 11,878. Province of York—Conformists 353,892; Nonconformists 15,525; Papists 1,987. "Cole's MSS. in the British Museum," vol. x. p. 136. There is an evident inaccuracy in this return, for the population of England was then nearly double the aggregate of these figures. Probably the return related only to the worshipping population.

† This was Burnet's statement to Calamy as the opinion of the "great men of the Church." Calamy's "Life of Howe," p. 129.

had been. Years of imprisonment and labour were, however, telling upon his constitution. The meetings which he attended now made him feel " wearied and spent." * His work was nearly finished, and in little more than another year he, also, was to join the dead witnesses. No man then living had done more than he in preaching the Gospel, and in planting and watering new Christian communities. What was said of him by the friend of Milton was not in excess of the merits of his extraordinary character and work. He was, says Ellwood,† a "heavenly-minded man;" valiant and bold for the truth; immoveable in principle as a rock, but patient in suffering, forgiving in disposition, gentle to the erring, and "tender, compassionate, and pitiful to all in affliction." He had a wonderful acquaintance with the Scriptures, and was a bold and vigorous yet plain preacher. His zeal knew no bounds, and his love and charity were as great as his zeal. Like many great orators, Fox probably owed much of his popular power to his commanding stature, his "graceful countenance," and his admirable voice. His natural, fitted with his spiritual, qualifications to make him the founder of a sect, and he did not die until he had seen it spread throughout the world, and, in his own country, almost at the height of its vigour.

Robert Barclay, whose defence of the doctrines of the Quakers has not, during two hundred years, been superseded by any work of equal ability and scholarship, was now also approaching death; but other men were in the prime of life and the fulness of activity. Amongst them

---

* Fox's "Journal," vol. ii. p. 340. † Ib. p. 369.

were Penn, whose political influence was equal to that of any man who did not sit in Parliament, and George Whitehead, one of the most earnest of preachers. The Quakers at this period were remarkable for their extensive use of the press. Penn was equally conspicuous as a writer and as a negotiator. His history of the Society is now out of date, but his expositions of their doctrines were very numerous, and are still of value. Whitehead, however, was probably their best literary controversialist. The documents of the Society, as well as the registries of the Bishops' Courts, give proof of the rapid progress which Quaker principles made immediately after the passing of the Toleration Act. Between A.D. 1688 and A.D. 1690 licenses were taken out for no fewer than a hundred and thirty-one new temporary, and a hundred and eight new permanent places of worship for this Society. Sixty-four of these were established in Lancashire alone.* In their Yearly Epistles the Friends are repeatedly congratulated on the "prosperity of the truth in many counties," on the opening of new places of worship, and on the willingness of people to receive their doctrines.†

The old leaders of the Baptist denomination were, for the most part, men greatly advanced in years. Foremost amongst them was William Kiffin, merchant, and once alderman of London, the first pastor of the Devonshire Square Church, and the "father of the Particular Baptists."‡ Kiffin had suffered distress and imprisonments under each of the reigns of the last three Stuarts, but

* Parl. Paper, No. 156, Sess. 1853.
† Yearly Epistles, A.D. 1687, and A.D. 1690.
‡ Ivimey, ii. 296.

his great wealth and social position brought him at last into consideration at Court. Charles the Second did not think it beneath him to "borrow" ten thousand pounds from him, and James the Second endeavoured to use him as an instrument to bring over the Dissenters to his views. Kiffin, on the last occasion, gave the King a rebuke which silenced his tongue and flushed his cheek. Two of the old man's grandsons had been hung by Jeffreys in the "bloody assizes." James would have bought him over to his interests by nomination to office, but Kiffin excused himself from age, adding, with tears, "the death of my grandsons gave a wound to my heart which is still bleeding, and never will close but with the grave." The King, we are told, was struck with the rebuke. A total silence ensued, while his countenance seemed to shrink from the remembrance. He replied, however, "I shall find a balsam for that sore," and then turned away.* Kiffin was an able and faithful preacher, and a man of unbounded benevolence. At this time he was about seventy-five years of age, and he lived until the last year of King William's reign. His portrait does not bear out the once current impression concerning the Baptists of that age. With skull-cap and flowing ringlets, with moustache and "imperial," with broad lace collar and ample gown,† he resembles a gentleman cavalier rather than any popular ideal of a sour-visaged and discontented Anabaptist.

A still older man than Kiffin was Hanserd Knollys, minister of the Church at Broken Wharf, Thames Street. Knollys was originally a clergyman of the Estab-

---

* Noble's "Cromwell," ii. 463.
† See his portrait in Wilson's Dissenting Churches, i. 403.

lished Church, but had now been connected with the Baptists for fifty years. He, too, had known from experience all that persecution could tell. The High Commission Court in Charles the First's time had followed him to New England. Under Cromwell he had met with favour; but was illegally arrested for preaching in favour of baptism at Bow Church, Cheapside. After this he was stoned out of a pulpit in Suffolk by fanatical Presbyterians; but in London he gathered one of the largest of Nonconformist congregations. He was imprisoned in Newgate for eighteen weeks in the reign of Charles the Second, and again, in the same reign, imprisoned in the Compter. He was, perhaps, the most active preacher in the denomination—preaching for forty years, in prison and out of it, seldom less than three or four times a week. His scholarship adorned all his sermons and all his writings. When the Toleration Act passed he was ninety-one years of age, and he survived it for two years.*

Benjamin Keach, pastor of the Church in Goat Yard Passage, Horsleydown, was at this time in the height of his power. He, too, had suffered under the Stuarts. For publishing a Child's Instructor he was imprisoned and pilloried at Aylesbury, and for years afterwards was hunted from place to place. He was pre-eminently the controversialist of his denomination. He had defended adult Baptism against Baxter and Flavel; had engaged in controversy with the Quakers and with Baptists on the ordination question; was a writer on Popery, on ministerial support, on public singing, and on the observance of the Sabbath. His published works, some of

* Knollys' "Own Life." Wilson's "Dissenting Churches," ii. 562-71.

which are of great religious value, were more than forty in number.*

Out of London Andrew Gifford, of Bristol, occupied the most prominent position amongst Baptist ministers. Gifford, like many others of that age, had been a constant preacher in parish churches until he was silenced by the Act of Uniformity. He was the most active and intrepid evangelist in the West of England, and was remarkably popular among the colliers of the district, who, on the approach of officers to apprehend him, would disguise him as a labourer so that he should not be recognized. The narrative of his imprisonments and escapes from apprehension, and his travels to preach the Gospel, during which he would swim any river that obstructed his way, read more like romance than history. He was actively engaged in the Duke of Monmouth's rebellion, but fortunately escaped the punishment which fell on most of those who were implicated in that transaction. He appears to have had a remarkable moral power, which often awed both his gaolers and the civil authorities. Gifford took one of the most prominent parts in the organization of the Baptist body. He invariably attended the assemblies which were held in London, and when they were discontinued he established a Western Association of Churches. No man took a warmer interest in the education of the ministry, and he ardently supported all the efforts which were made at that time to improve the mental qualifications of preachers. Gifford lived until the year 1721, leaving a son and grandson in the Baptist ministry.†

* Wilson, iv. 243-250.
† Ivimey's "History," i. 432 ; ii. 541-547. Broadmead Records.

Soon after the Toleration Act was passed the Baptists held a general assembly of their churches in London. It was summoned by a circular signed by Kiffin, Knollys, Keach, and four others. The object of this meeting was to discuss the general state of the denomination. It appears from the terms of the invitation that the Baptist body was in a remarkably depressed state. Its condition was openly deplored, and it was stated that its power, life, strength, and vigour had, to a great extent, departed.* The registries of the Bishop's Courts confirm this statement. Scarcely any, if any, denomination appears to have made so little progress after the passing of the Toleration Act. While the total number of Nonconformist places of worship licensed in the two years from A.D. 1688 to A.D. 1690 was nearly one thousand,† the number avowedly belonging to the Baptists were only sixteen.‡

This assembly was attended by delegates from more than a hundred churches in thirty counties of England and Wales. Thirteen of these were in London, one in Cornwall, and no fewer than thirty-five in Devonshire, Somersetshire, and Wiltshire, where, at that period, owing mainly to Gifford's labours, the chief country strength of the denomination lay. It is noticeable that Lancashire sent only one delegate to this meeting, and that Yorkshire was altogether unrepresented, there being, at that time, no Baptist church in the whole of that county.§

* Ivimey, i. 479.
† Namely, temporary, 796; permanent, 143. Parl. Paper.
‡ The great majority (503) were registered without any specifications, and 158 were registered as "Protestant Dissenters" only. It is possible that some of these were Baptist, but I think that they were nearly all Presbyterian and Independent.
§ Hunter's "Life of Oliver Heywood," p. 413.

The proceedings of this body appear to have been marked by great humility and harmony, and they give a most favourable impression of the ardent and sincere religious character of the Baptists at this period. With regard to ecclesiastical government, it was resolved that the assembly had no authority to impose any belief or practice upon any of the Churches, and that all it could do was offer counsel and advice according to the Scriptures. It was decided to raise a common fund by way of " free-will offerings" for the support of the ministry in poor districts, for home evangelization, and for the education, in classics and Hebrew, of ministerial students. It was recommended that weak Churches existing in the same neighbourhood should unite together for the better support of the ministry, and for the better edification of each other; that ministers were entitled to an adequate maintenance; that there should be a "proper ordination of ministers; that Baptists should be at liberty to attend Churches of other denominations; but that persons who, being members of Baptist Churches communicated in the Established Church, should, after admonition, be rejected. Those who did not attend the ordinary fixed meetings of the Church were to be reported, and those who did not contribute to its expenses were to be "withdrawn from." Excesses of apparel in ornaments and dress, including "long hair and periwigs," were condemned; and the Lord's-day was considered to be sacred to worship. Two distinctively doctrinal articles were also adopted ; one in favour of the " reconciliation, adoption, or justification" of all who have a living faith, and the other in declaration of the sufficiency of the Holy Spirit alone for the continuance of a Christian ministry. A formal approbation was expressed of a book in favour of the maintenance of ministers; and, lastly, the assembly passed a declaration against the government of James and an acknowledgment of their thankfulness for that which had been established under William.* A Confession of Faith and an Epistle to the Churches were also adopted. In the latter, the general decay of religion is dwelt upon, recommendations are made in accordance with the resolutions of the meeting, and a general fast-day appointed.

The Confession of Faith, adopted by this assembly, consisted of thirty-two articles relating to theological doctrines and Christian ethics. The former would now be considered of ultra-Calvinistic tone. The doctrine of the Divine decrees is pushed to its uttermost application, even "infants" being classed in the two orders of the "elect" and the non-elect. Marriage within the degrees condemned by the law of Moses is held to be "incestuous." Liberty of conscience is declared to be a natural right, and all infringements upon it are considered to be contrary to the Word of God.†

The repeated reference in these proceedings to the necessity of a sufficient maintenance for the ministry was caused by the fact that most of the Baptist ministers of the period were supported, not by their Churches, but by some trade or profession. Some of the most eminent were schoolmasters.‡ The Churches frequently supplemented the incomes of these men by small sub-

* Ivimey, i. 478-501.
† Crosby, iii. Appendix 56, 111.
‡ The Broadmead Church at Bristol voted £20 a-year to Mr. Whinnel when his school was closed by a warrant.—" Records," 10th May, 1663.

scriptions. But although the Baptists were not mindful of their obligations in this respect, and had therefore a comparatively unlearned ministry, the incomes of all Dissenting ministers were extremely small. Oliver Heywood, one of the most celebrated of the Presbyterians of the time, received only twenty pounds a year;* Sylvester, one of the most respected of the same denomination in London, seldom received as much as ten pounds a quarter, and Calamy began his ministry with a similar stipend.† One feeling only could have sustained them under such circumstances,—the feeling that, whatever became of them, they must obey their consciences in preaching the Gospel. Some ministers, however, such as Baxter and Bates, often from having married women of fortune, enjoyed good incomes; but this was a rare exception to the general rule.

Similar association meetings were held in several following years, from the proceedings of which it appears that a project for raising a common fund for the education of the ministry and the assistance of poor Churches was attended with some success. County associations were also formed. In A.D. 1692 it was resolved, for convenience, to divide the general association into two,—one section meeting in London, and the other at Bristol. In the same year, and before the division took place, the question of public singing was brought forward. It had been agreed, between the two parties who were opposed on this subject, to submit it to the authoritative decision of seven ministers, who made their report to this assembly. The referees

---

* Life, p. 391.   † Calamy's "Own Life," i. 360.

unsparingly condemned the unchristian manner in which the controversy on this question had been conducted by both the parties to it, and told them to humble themselves before God for their mutual want of forbearance and charity. They advised that all the books that had been written should be called in, their further circulation stopped, and that nothing more should be published on the question.* No resolution concerning the merits of the points at issue was proposed. The result of this proceeding was that the public discussion of the question died out. Each church pursued the practice which it most approved, until, in the course of years, no opponents of public singing were left. The London Association meetings appear to have been discontinued in the year 1695. The Western Association, however, after rebuking their metropolitan friends for their want of zeal, continued to meet at Bristol, Taunton, Exeter, and other towns. At most of these meetings two subjects, in addition to the necessity of increased personal religion, were especially dwelt upon,—first, the fund for the sustentation of churches; and, secondly, the better education of ministers. On the latter question considerable ill feeling still existed. The promoters of it were charged with depreciating the gifts of the Holy Spirit, and the Bristol Association was compelled, in its defence, to define the precise value at which it assessed "human learning."

While the Particular Baptists were thus organizing their resources, the General Baptists were not less active. The strength of this body appears to have laid mainly

* Ivimey, i. 520—523.

in what are now called the Home Counties and in the Midland district. Of their ministers, the most eminent were Dr. William Russell and Matthew Caffin. Dr. Russell, who had been educated at the University of Cambridge, was a man of eminent scholarship and no less eminent controversial ability. Public and private disputations, indeed, seem to have been, if not his chief, at least one of his chief pleasures. He assailed Quakers with an animosity which was only equalled in the retorts which he provoked. All who held the doctrine of Infant Baptism were equally the objects of his attack. He engaged in one of the public debates with the Quakers, and was the representative of the Baptists in their last similar controversy with the Pædobaptists.* Caffin, also, was a University man, having studied at Oxford. To him, many of the churches in Kent, Surrey, and Sussex owe their existence. Caffin was at one time charged with heresy on the subject of the Trinity, and the discussion of his views appears to have given the first impulse to the subsequent movement in favour of Unitarianism amongst the General Baptists. All, however, that he did, was to define, or attempt to define, the exact relations of the divine and the human elements in the second person of the Trinity. As every attempt to do this, from the primitive ages of Christianity downwards, had provoked some metaphysical or logomachic discussion, Caffin might have felt assured that he would be assailed. He was exonerated from the charge of heterodoxy; but those who had brought the charge against him, and those who had supported it, withdrew from the

* Crosby iv. 259—261.

majority, and made a breach which was not healed for several years.*

The General Baptists had, like their brethren of the same denomination, their Assemblies, which met from time to time, chiefly in London, Buckinghamshire, and Northamptonshire. Some amongst their body appear to have keenly felt their separation from those who agreed with them on all points but such as were involved in the distinction between Calvinists and Arminians. They felt, to use their own words, that they were "looked upon as a people degenerated from almost all other baptized congregations," who, therefore, were "afraid to have affinity with them" in Christian work. In order to remove some prejudices and to open the way to reconciliation and fellowship, the churches in the county of Somerset agreed, in A.D. 1691, upon a Confession of Faith.† In this confession the doctrine of Original Sin, considered as an inherent taint, or as a sufficient cause of eternal condemnation, is denounced as both unscriptural and irrational; and the doctrine of reprobation is also abjured. The grace of God is declared to extend to the whole world, and if any man fall short of salvation it is not because God, but because the man himself, has so willed it; while the perseverance of the saints is declared to be dependent on their own conduct. This Confession, which is a clear, and in some places an eloquent, statement of the doctrines of the General Baptists, closes with a specific reference to the nature of the kingdom of Christ, and the means by which that kingdom should be sustained. "We believe," say these churches, "that

* Crosby, iv. 328—342. Ivimey, i. 548—554.
† Crosby, iii. 259; iv. Appendix i.

this kingdom ought not to be set up by the material sword, that being so exceeding contrary to the very nature of Christianity." For this reason they decline to have any communion with those "that own the setting up of this kingdom by such means; believing that His spiritual kingdom, which is His Church here on earth, ought not to be set up or forced either by the sword or any civil law whatsoever, but by the preaching of the Gospel, which is the Sword of the Spirit and the Word of God."* Clearer or more decisive language on this subject has never been held, and it cannot be a matter of surprise that no attempt was made to "comprehend" such men in an Established Church.

From the year immediately succeeding the passing of the Toleration Act to the end of the reign of William the Third the history of the Baptist Denomination, as a whole, was not a history of progression. Judging from the language held in the circular letters adopted at the Association meetings, the general state of religion was not satisfactory. The circumstance that this condition of comparative declension was so often and so urgently brought before the churches, is a proof that the leaders of the denomination and the representatives of the churches did not share in this depressed spiritual state. While, however, these representations may be considered to be correct, it is a question how far the apparent declension proceeded from actual decay of religious feeling, or how far it proceeded from the subsidence of political and ecclesiastical excitement. Under persecution the feelings of men are strongly moved. There

* Art xxvii. Crosby, iv. Appendix i. pp. 41. 42.

is a tendency to bear increased testimony to a persecuted truth, and to work with double zeal in behalf of a cause that is unjustly oppressed. The excitement of good men—however good they may be—on whom the hounds of law have been let loose, is not always of a healthy nature and may easily be mistaken for better feelings. Many a man, also, will cheerfully and heroically suffer, who will not steadily work, and it is possible that the Baptist Denomination at this period was composed largely of such men. But, if this was the fact, it is strange that the same characteristic should not have been found in the other three Nonconformist bodies. So far was this from being the case, that the Presbyterians, Independents, and Quakers made, in the earlier years of the reign of William and Mary, greater comparative progress than they have ever made since that time. The advances of Quakerism may, in a large degree, if not wholly, be attributed to the extraordinary evangelistic zeal of that body, and, where there was a Gifford or a Caffin, the Baptist body—as in the Western and the Home Counties—had met with similar success. Without a large number of such men, it was morally impossible, at that time, for a Christian sect which occupied, socially, almost the lowest position of any, to make great advances on the population; and the fact that the majority of the ministers of the Baptist body were men of other occupations prevented any general or extensive system of evangelization on their part. But it did not preclude growth in personal piety. If one cause more than another operated in this direction, it was the spirit of controversy, which seemed almost to possess the body. A Quaker writer of about this period, describes the Baptists as having great love and affection for their religion but as wanting in unanimity and agreement amongst themselves, and rash and morose towards such as differed from them.* Any testimony from this quarter, written at a time when Quakers and Baptists were engaged in hot disputes, is to be received with some reserve; but the published writings of the Baptists of the latter part of the seventeenth century substantiate the general accuracy of this description. Their zeal was, if not for the most part, to a very considerable extent, consumed in contentions amongst themselves and with other denominations. The invariable result followed. What they gained in sectarianism they lost in spirituality.

The Independents and the Presbyterians, having relinquished nearly all expectation of such a reform in the Established Church, as would enable them to enter its communion, began to open, in all parts of the kingdom, new places of worship. The trusts of many of the Presbyterian meetings were so framed that the buildings could afterwards be used by the Established Church, but the majority of their places of worship were not of a permanent character, most of the licenses taken out applying to rooms in private houses. The edifices which were erected by these, the two wealthiest sections of Dissenters, were of the plainest character and were generally situated in the meanest thoroughfares. Very few were registered as "Independent," a fact which may be accounted for by the circumstance that the two denominations were now drawing more closely together, and

---

* Gerard Croese's "Collection," p. 76. Quoted in Crouch's "Sufferings," p. 145.

making arrangements for an amalgamation on terms by which the distinctive principles of each were to be virtually sacrificed.

It is impossible to tell which party took the initiative in this project, but it is evident that both were almost equally anxious for its successful realization. The Independents were comparatively ill represented at this time. Their three most eminent ministers were Matthew Mead, of Stepney, Isaac Chauncey, of Mark Lane, who had succeeded David Clarkson as pastor of Owen's Church, and Stephen Lobb, of Fetter Lane.

Matthew Mead, whom Howe describes as "that very reverend and most laborious servant of Christ,"* occupied the highest rank amongst the Independent ministers. He had been appointed to the living of Shadwell by Cromwell, but had been ejected by the Act of Uniformity. Soon after, he went, in common with many ministers of that age, to Holland, where he became acquainted with the Prince of Orange, and earned such great respect from the Dutch community, that the States presented him with the four pillars which upheld the meeting house at Stepney. He had one of the largest of all the congregations in London, and was as indefatigable in Christian work as he was amiable in spirit. In consequence of his mild temperament, and the moderation of his opinions, he was probably more intimate with Churchmen and Presbyterians than any other minister of his denomination. He possessed, for more than forty years, the intimate confidence and friendship of Howe, and when, at the close of the century, he died,

* Funeral Sermon for Mead. Title, A.D. 1699.

the strongest personal link between the Presbyterians and the Independents was broken.

Chauncey added little strength to his denomination. Although a learned, he was not a popular man, and he alienated most of his congregation by too frequently addressing them on ecclesiastical order and discipline.* He appears to have thought that the mantle of Owen and Clarkson had fallen on his shoulders, and that it was his especial duty to continue their testimony in favour of the principles of his denomination. His zeal cannot be doubted, but he was nearly altogether destitute of the qualifications which had so distinguished his two predecessors. Lobb's character is rather difficult to estimate. Unequivocal testimony is borne by his contemporaries to his personal piety, and he had been well trained for the ministerial office. But he was a Jacobite Dissenter; he had publicly defended James in the exercise of his arbitrary powers; he had advised the King to prosecute the seven bishops, and he nearly succeeded in committing the reputation of Dissenters as a body in that controversy. He was a notorious favourite at the Court of the Stuarts, and therefore not a great favourite with his own people.† He took, also, an unhappy part in the theological controversies which arose soon after the Revolution, and in them did his best to promote division and disunion.

With the exception, therefore, of Mead, the Independents had no highly qualified leader. On the other hand, nearly all the old Presbyterian leaders were still living, and it appeared certain that if an amalgama-

---

* Wilson's "Dissenting Churches," i. 289—291.
† Ib. iii. 436—446.

tion should take place, that powerful and influential body would ultimately absorb the Independents. Baxter drawing, as he himself said, when the Toleration Act passed, "to the end of this transitory life," was now taking "half-duty" with Matthew Sylvester, and about to be confined to his house, where, however, he still preached twice a day, and from whence he was to issue, in the two years of life that remained to him, thirteen works in addition to the hundred and twenty-five which he had already published. Neither the brain nor the heart of this old Goliath of Presbyterianism had suffered with age; his immense labours had not even yet wearied him, nor, although he had grown more catholic and his charity was much more extensive than it had been,* was he tired of controversy. He had filled the largest space of any ecclesiastic of his generation, and he filled it until the year of his death. The great old man lived to see one dream of his life apparently fulfilled, in the settled concord of two at least of the Christian sects.

Next to Baxter stood Bates, the "silver-tongued," who had now taken Baxter's place in the public representation of Dissenting interests. Bates shone in the qualities in which Baxter was especially deficient. Mild, polite, affable, and courteous; full of charity; eloquent, yet chaste in his oratory, and a rare conversationalist, his social influence was surpassed by that of none. Side by side with Bates stood Howe, then in the sixtieth year of his age. This great man was one of the few who was venerated as much by his contemporaries as by his successors. Time, which commonly adds increased lustre

---

* Calamy's "Baxter," p. 677.

to the memory of the good, has not been able to magnify any of the qualities for which Howe was so conspicuous. His strong and capacious intellect; his sublime elevation of thought; his flowing eloquence; the holiness of his life; the dignity and courtesy of his manners; the humour of his conversation, won for him from the men of his own time, the title of the "great Mr. Howe." After serving Cromwell as a court chaplain, and being often engaged by him in affairs of State, Howe, at the Restoration, took his part with the ejected Puritans. Latterly he had been pastor of the Presbyterian Church in Silver Street. His Presbyterianism, however, was of the most moderate character, for his charity embraced all sects. Nor could he consent to excommunicate the Church of England, with whose most eminent scholars and divines he lived on terms of frank and friendly intimacy. He statedly communed with Churchmen, and repeatedly defended the practice.

Dr. Samuel Annesley, formerly lecturer at St. Paul's, and Rector of St. Giles', Cripplegate, one of the most humble of men, and pathetic of preachers, was now pastor of the Presbyterian Church at Little Saint Helen's. Mathew Sylvester, Baxter's biographer, with whom Baxter was co-pastor, and who was one of the most profound of theological thinkers, was minister at Carter Lane. The youngest in point of residence, amongst the Presbyterian ministers, was Dr. Daniel Williams, who had been, for about a year, pastor of the New Broad Street Church. Williams's reputation had, however, preceded him from Dublin, where he had preached for twenty years. He at once took a distinguished place amongst the city brethren, and, in matters of controversy, soon became their acknowledged leader. This eminent divine, and no less eminent scholar, was, besides Howe, the only man then living who almost invariably adorned the cause which he advocated by his combined candour and charity. His exhaustive analysis of the arguments of opponents; the clearness and order of his statements, and the learning with which they were supported, were unequalled by any contemporary writer; and his sermons were as faithful and forcible as were his written works. As the founder of the Divinity scholarships, and of the valuable library, both of which still bear his name, his memory has now been held in grateful reverence by students and scholars for nearly two hundred years.

No greater race of preachers than the Presbyterian ministers of this period ever adorned the pulpits of the metropolis. In the suburbs they were represented by men of scarcely less eminence than those who were known as the city ministers. In the south, Nathaniel Vincent, a scholarly man but chiefly remarkable for his quickness of wit and redundancy of good humour, occupied the pulpit of St. Thomas's, Southwark. Vincent Alsop, "the South of Dissent," preached at Princes Street, Westminster; while Thomas Doolittle, the principal trainer of young men for the ministry, and who built the first Dissenting place of worship in London,* was a preacher in Monkwell Street. In the provinces this denomination could boast of John Flavel, in Devonshire; of Oliver Heywood, in Lancashire; of Philip Henry, in Cheshire; and amongst laymen, of the Ashurst family in London, and Lady Hewley, in York, all of whom were

* Circ. A.D. 1666, in Monkwell-street. This place of worship has now disappeared.

steadfast adherents to, and liberal supporters of, the Presbyterian system. It would seem that so powerful a denomination must have carried all before it, and that whatever might be the history of the smaller sects, the history of Presbyterianism would be one of increasing usefulness and splendour.

The whole of the ministers in London threw themselves with great ardour into the proposals for union with the Congregationalists. Howe is said to have had a principal share in drawing up the terms of agreement, which were ultimately settled, at the beginning of the year 1691, by a committee consisting of six Presbyterian and six Congregational ministers. Amongst the former were Howe, Williams and Annesley, and amongst the latter, Mead, Chauncey, and Lobb. The terms were afterwards published, under the title of "Heads of Agreement assented to by the United Ministers in and about London, formerly called Presbyterian and Congregational; not as a measure for any national constitution, but for the preservation of order in our congregations, that cannot come up to the common rule by law established." The "heads" are nine in number. The first relates to the constitution of the Christian Church, in which the right of each particular congregation to choose its own officers is recognized; but ministers and elders are to "rule and govern," and "the brotherhood are to consent." This was an old Presbyterian formula, dating as far back as the days of Field and Wilcox, in the reign of Queen Elizabeth. The second relates to the ministry, who are to be, in all cases, elected by the churches, after the advice, "ordinarily requisite," of neighbouring churches. It is also stated to be "ordinarily requisite" that the pastors of neighbouring churches should concur in the ordination of the ministers. In this article the distinctive feature of Presbyterianism—the power of the presbytery—is entirely abandoned. "Censures" form the subject of the third article, which contains a simple statement of the nature of church discipline. In the article on the communion of churches, frequent meetings between the several Christian communities are recommended, both for worship and for counsel. The next subject dealt with is that of "Deacons and ruling Elders." Of the latter it is said that, while some are of opinion that there is such an office, and others think the contrary, "we agree that this difference make no breach amongst us." The subject of the sixth article is "Synods," and it is recommended that in order to concord, and in weighty and difficult cases, synods should be called for advice and consultation, and that particular churches should have a reverential regard for the judgment of such meetings. Obedience to civil magistrates is inculcated under the succeeding head, and it is added that "if at any time it shall be their pleasure to call together any number of us, or require any account of our efforts, and the state of our congregations, we shall most readily express all dutiful regard to them herein"—a concession to civil authority to which the descendants of these men would certainly not agree. Of confessions of faith it is remarked that it is sufficient if a Church acknowledges the divine origin of the Scriptures, and owns the doctrinal parts of the articles, or the Westminster or Savoy Confessions. Lastly, it is declared that Christians of other communities should be treated with respect; and that all who have the essential requisites to Church communion should be received without troubling them with disputes concerning lesser matters.

Both denominations, it will thus be seen, relinquished some of their distinctive opinions. The Congregationalists expressed their agreement with the Presbyterians concerning the government of each church being vested in the ministers and elders; and the Presbyterians surrendered the doctrine of the authoritative power of synods.* On the whole, however, the Congregationalists surrendered less than their brethren of the more powerful denomination. What is chiefly remarkable, however, in connexion with this attempted settlement of the differences between the two sects, is the circumstance, that the consent of the churches to the arrangements which were made, was not applied for by either party. No "lay" representative was concerned in drawing up the "heads;" and the creed and constitution of all the churches were fixed without any consultation with them. The amalgamated bodies described themselves as the united "ministers" only; and although they were pastors settled over two different classes of Christian organizations, they decided, of their own accord, to dispense with the characteristic titles which those organizations had assumed. It must, of course, be taken for granted that the churches tacitly assented to these arrangements; but the manner in which they were made contrasts as strongly with the habits of the Baptist asso-

* It is worth notice that, while the Episcopalians of the United States have accepted the revised Prayer Book of A.D. 1689, the Congregational and a large section of the Presbyterian Churches of that country are, for the most part, governed in accordance with the "Heads of Agreement" of A.D. 1691.

ciations of the same period, which were invariably attended by lay delegates, as with the modern practice both of the Presbyterian and of the Congregational communities.

The scheme of union was joyfully accepted in several parts of the country. The Cheshire, Lancashire, Nottinghamshire, Yorkshire, Hampshire, Gloucestershire, Dorsetshire, Somersetshire, and Devonshire ministers at once assented to it. In London the union was formally celebrated by a sermon preached by Matthew Mead, on "Two Sticks made One," in which the preacher declared that now the day of reproach had been rolled away from the Christian Church,* and earnestly conjured the ministers to manifest and preserve their accord. At Southampton, Mr. Chandler was appointed to preach to the county ministers. "Blessed be God," he cried, "who hath united us together."† Flavel, as soon as he saw the heads of agreement, exclaimed, "Lord, now lettest thou thy servant depart in peace;"‡ and in a subsequent sermon, alluded to them as "those blessed sheets." There can be no doubt of the sincere and great delight of most of the ministers throughout the country at this event, and although the scheme came to a quick and unhappy conclusion, the annual meetings of the two denominations, commenced at this time, were continued in some counties for more than a century.§

Two events speedily occurred to disturb this fraternal feeling, and virtually to dissolve the union. Some

---

* Mead's "Two Sticks," p. 19.
† Chandler's "Cantry's Concurrence," p. 41.
‡ Flavel's "Life and Remains."
§ Hunter's "Life of Heywood," p. 357.

Congregational ministers in London, Nathaniel Mather, pastor of Lime Street Church, and one of the committee who framed the "heads," being the most conspicuous, had never heartily accepted it. He is accused, in fact, of having been unwearied, in hindering and breaking it.* If there were any, as probably there were, anxious to seize an occasion to provoke first an ill-feeling, and then a rupture, such an occasion was soon given to them. Within a year of the formation of the union two discussions on points of doctrine and order arose. The first was excited by the preaching of the Rev. Richard Davis, of Rothwell, in Northamptonshire. Mr. Davis was a Congregational minister holding high Calvinistic or rather Antinomian opinions, believing and preaching that repentance was not necessary to salvation, that the elect were always without sin, and always without "spot before God." Notwithstanding these views, Davis was an active and untiring evangelist. He preached and made converts in all the neighbouring counties, and encouraged any unordained person to do the same. He appears to have been a man of narrow opinions, but, like many similar men, of great intensity of belief, and of undaunted zeal. Where the sustenance or the progress of religious life was at stake he made light of all ecclesiastical traditions, and all established church order. He was the first amongst the Congregationalists who broke the bounds of ordination. Wherever he made converts he justified them in maintaining Christian fellowship together, and in allowing one amongst their number to preach to them, whether they had the sanction of neigh-

* Dr. Williams's Works, iv. p. xii.

bouring churches or not. The attention of the united ministers was soon called to Mr. Davis's proceedings. The country brethren solicited their judgment upon them, and quickly obtained it. Both the doctrine and the practice of Davis were severely condemned. He was denounced and stigmatized in language which implied that he was an unruly child of the devil, who succeeded by mere "falsehood, clamour, and noise." The city ministers, acting as a metropolitan synod, sat in judgment upon him, and, as though they were a Sanhedrim, virtually cast him out from their midst as unworthy of any Christian communion, stating at the same time, as is common in such assemblies, that "they would earnestly pray for his repentance." Unfortunately, however, for the interests of the union which had but just been celebrated, their judgment was not received by all persons as of an authoritative and binding character. Davis himself repelled it. His vindication,* although characterized by what many persons would consider to be extreme theological views, was, on the whole, in better taste than the attack which had been made upon him. He successfully defended his evangelistic work, and the right of Christian men to continue what he had begun, and successfully maintained his ministerial position. The controversy threw eleven counties into disorder, and before a year had passed away, the Congregationalists had begun to be weaned from the union. The ministers could not have made a more fatal mistake than by interfering in this question. They knew, all along, that many Congregationalists were

* "Truth and Innocency Vindicated," A.D. 1691.

jealous of the union. Knowing it, they deliberately gave occasion for suspicion, that, if their authority were once acknowledged, the liberty and the independence of Christian churches, and the right even to preach the Gospel, might be fatally endangered.

In the midst of the excitement connected with this controversy, another, and a graver one, arose. Dr. Crisp, an Antinomian divine of the Commonwealth period, had written several works in defence of the views held by the school of theology to which he belonged. His son, wishing to republish his father's works, with previously unpublished manuscripts, conceived the notion of requesting some of the most eminent of the London ministers to certify to their genuine character. The ministers, Howe—strangely enough, considering his characteristic prudence—amongst them, did what was requested. Crisp's works therefore went forth to the world, with what many conceived to be a recommendation from the leaders of the moderate Calvinistic party.* Amongst those who did not sign this certificate, and who probably was not asked to sign it, was the acute and wary controversialist, Baxter. It is more easy to imagine a veteran rat deliberately entering an unbaited cage, than to imagine Baxter putting his hand to such a document. If he had hated anything more than Quakerism it was Antinomianism, which, all through his life, he had assailed with a vigour and constancy which none but himself could have exhibited. No sooner, therefore, had Crisp's works appeared than, after

* I cannot help agreeing with Mr. Henry Rogers that this was nothing but a disgraceful trick of Crisp's son; but it is incomprehensible that the London ministers should have fallen into such a trap. Rogers's "Life of Howe," pp. 271—273.

remonstrating with those who had so rashly given them such surreptitious importance, he prepared once more to enter his old and favourite field of controversy. In deference, however, to the earnest solicitations of Howe, he refrained from publishing what he had written. Howe at once cleared his own reputation, by writing a recommendation of Flavel's "Blow at the Root," a work against Antimonianism, just about to be published. This, however, did not repair the mischief which had been done, and accordingly Dr. Daniel Williams was requested to undertake a formal refutation of Crisp's doctrines. The work appeared in A.D. 1692, under the title of "Gospel Truth, Stated and Vindicated." Prefixed to the first edition was a recommendation from Bates, Howe, Alsop, and thirteen other Presbyterian ministers, to which thirty-two other signatures, including those of Doolittle, Sylvester, and Edmund Calamy, were added in the second edition.[*] No Congregationalist, however, would sign this recommendation. Both Bates and Williams requested Mead's signature, but he refused, first, on the ground that he did not judge it to be prudent to sign, and ultimately because he disapproved of its doctrines.[†] It became, therefore, very evident that the Presbyterians and the Congregationalists did not hold the same theological opinions. The variance was at once made public by virulent attacks from Chauncey, Mather, and Lobb, on Williams's doctrines relating to free grace and justification. The controversy which ensued lasted for more than seven years, during the whole of which period the London ministers were torn by the angriest dissensions.

[*] Williams's Works, iii. pp. 3, 4.   [†] Williams's Works, iii. p. 281.

In A. D. 1692, Chauncey withdrew from the united ministers. Honesty, truthfulness, and charity were now equally sacrificed. The Congregationalists denounced the Presbyterians as no better than Arminians and Socinians, and the Presbyterians retorted by fixing upon their opponents the stigma of Antinomianism. Howe tried to hush the storm by preaching on the carnality of religious contention, but this time he preached in vain. The united ministers also endeavoured to stem the torrent. In three successive years they issued three statements of doctrine to meet the various phases which the debates assumed; but each statement only gave rise to fresh disputes. They were, however, still more than sixty in number, and the whole of their moral support was given to Williams, who, it must be said, was worthy of the confidence they gave to him. Failing to silence him in argument, some persons now attacked Williams's moral character. He met the disgraceful charge by courting an examination into his whole life, from which he came out with augmented reputation. An open rupture between the two bodies now took place. In A. D. 1694, the Congregationalists excluded Williams from the Merchants' Lecture at Pinners' Hall. This lecture had been founded by some wealthy London tradesmen, for the purpose of holding week-day morning services, which should be conducted by the most eminent of the Dissenting ministers of the metropolis. It was always largely attended, and had been of eminent use, both in a religious and in an ecclesiastical sense. To prevent further contentions, the Presbyterians now withdrew, and with the aid of the majority of the subscribers, established a new lecture at Salters' Hall, the lecturers being Bates, Howe, Alsop, and Williams. The old lecture was continued by Mead, Cole, and four other Congregationalists. Mead appears to have remained with some reluctance, and he afterwards regretted that he had not gone with the Presbyterians.*

This disastrous controversy raged, at best, around doctrines the reception or rejection of which have scarcely influenced the Christian character. There can be no doubt that the Presbyterians, at this time, were more moderate Calvinists than the Congregationalists, and that the epithet of "Baxterians" was not inappropriately applied to them, but as Baxterianism included the articles of the Church of England, and the confessions of Dort and Savoy, their moderation was certainly limited. What they did not believe, was the doctrine of absolute reprobation, held in the sense that persons were condemned irrespective of their character and faith. They did not believe that sinners were pardoned without repentance. They did not believe that the Saviour so stood in the sinner's place, that God ever looked upon Him as a sinner. The last point was the point most vehemently debated in this controversy. The question was—Was there a change of persons, or only of person in the redemption; and according as this was answered, and the sense in which the answer was understood, the controversialist was classed as an Arminian, or even Unitarian, on the one side, and as an Antinomian on the other. Mather went so far as to state that believers

* The old Merchants' Lecture was subsequently transferred to New Broad Street, and is now delivered at the Poultry Chapel. The Salters' Hall Lectures are discontinued. One of the last lecturers was Dr. W. B. Collyer, of Peckham.

were as righteous as Christ himself, and the Congregational body supported Mather. By and bye the question came to be less one of doctrine than of meaning. It might be stated to be what did Dr. Williams mean? Williams replied, and was almost told that he did not mean what he said. At last a happy thought occurred to Lobb. He believed that Stillingfleet, Bishop of Worcester, the greatest controversialist in the Church, and whose views had been referred to by the Presbyterians, would not approve of Williams's views of justification, and that Dr. Jonathan Edwards, who had recently " unmasked" Socinianism, would be able to detect that doctrine in Williams. He therefore made an appeal to these divines to give their judgment on the controversy. Both men generously consented, and both pronounced without reservation, in favour of the entire orthodoxy of Williams. Lobb, not satisfied with Stillingfleet's reply, and feeling confident that the bishop must have misunderstood him, wrote again at greater length, the result of which was, that Stillingfleet, taking Williams's work out of his hands, answered Lobb himself. Stillingfleet finally advised that the Congregational ministers should formally clear themselves of the charge of Antinomianism. The advice was taken, and in A.D. 1698, a "Declaration". was published. Williams, at Lobb's request, responded in A.D. 1699, with an "End to Discord," clearing himself from the imputation both of Socinianism and Arminianism. Peace followed, and the ministers met together again, but the scheme of an organized union of the denominations was a thing of the past.*

---

* I do not pretend to have read all the pamphlets and sermons connected

The spirit of intolerance exhibited during the progress of this controversy was not confined to mutual recrimination. The Presbyterians successfully vindicated themselves from a charge of Socinianism, which could never have been honestly brought against them; but there was no doubt that Socinianism was spreading. The doctrine of the Trinity had been discussed in the Established Church. Dr. Wallis, a Professor at Oxford University, had endeavoured to prove its truth by mathematical demonstration, and had given, in doing so, ample room for a reply. The question being thus raised to the surface, the Socinians took advantage of the opportunity, and openly assailed Trinitarianism. Howe joined in an attempted explanation, but, although a master of metaphysics, lost himself in metaphysical subtleties. Sherlock, Dean of St. Paul's, defended the doctrine, but, in doing so, only laid himself open to the ironical criticism of South, that he had furnished the world with three deities. The principal Socinian at this period was Thomas Firmin, a wealthy London merchant, of high reputation for benevolence, who expended part of his fortune in the distribution of books in favour of his doctrines, and the remainder in works of charity. The literature of this small but increasing party was well written and moderate in spirit. Tillotson was never forgiven, because, while

---

with this controversy which were published during these eight years; and if, as I did, anyone should make an attempt to do so, he will, I think, do as I have done—speedily relinquish it. I have read, however, all that Williams wrote; the Declarations of the Ministers; a part of Chauncey and Lobb's publications; Stillingfleet's and Edwards's Letters to Williams; the account in Bishop Bull's "Life;" in Calamy's "Howe" and his "Own Times;" in Dr. Toulmin's "History;" and in Mr. Joshua Wilson's "Historical Inquiry." The above narrative is based on these works.

preaching against their opinions, he had once praised in high terms, their manner of conducting controversy. "They are a pattern," he said, "of the fair way of disputing; they argue without passion, with decency, dignity, clearness, and gravity." "They have," he added, "but this one defect, that they want a good cause and truth on their side, which, if they had, they have reason, and wit, and temper enough, to defend it."* The legislature, the clergy, and the Dissenting ministers, had no such charitable opinions of this sect. The first had already excluded them from the benefit of the Act of Toleration; and the House of Commons now voted an anonymous work entitled, "A clear confutation of the Doctrine of the Trinity," to be a blasphemous libel, and ordered it to be burned by the hangman. The clergy, for the most part, agreed with South, that the Socinians were "impious blasphemers, whose infamous pedigree runs back from wretch to wretch, in a direct line to the devil himself; and who were fitter to be crushed by the civil magistrate as destructive to government and society, than to be confuted as merely heretics in religion."† The Dissenting ministers appear to have held opinions of a more moderate character, but of a similar tendency. In A.D. 1697, they waited on the King, and urged him to interdict the printing of any work in favour of Socinian doctrines. In the next year the Commons addressed the King, beseeching him to take measures to root out vice and immorality, and to give orders for the suppression of all books containing assaults on the doctrine of the Trinity, or on any other funda-

---

* Birch's "Tillotson," p. 427.   † Ib. p. 428.

mental article of faith. The same year an Act was passed prohibiting all such publications. Any person found writing, printing, publishing, or circulating any works, or preaching, against the doctrine of the Trinity, was condemned to lose nearly all the privileges of citizenship; he could neither sue nor be sued, and neither bequeath, nor receive property. He was disabled for ever from holding any public office, and he was to be imprisoned for three years without bail. The merciless severity of this Act appears to have excited no criticism and no remonstrance. Even the plain teaching of history was not once thought of. The history of the city where Servetus was burned was ignored. The men who had urged the passing of this law did not even dream of such a theological Nemesis as that their own direct ecclesiastical descendants should, in less than two generations, almost universally embrace the creed which they thus attempted violently to stamp out.

The future relations of the various Dissenting bodies to each other were, for a time, settled by the terms of concord established at the close of this controversy. The Quakers stood aloof from all intercourse with other denominations. There is no proof that the Baptists had, as yet, united with others in any public matters; the Presbyterians and Congregationalists were on terms of friendly intimacy with each other; and when interests common to Dissenters as such, required to be represented or defended, uniformly acted as one body. The theological creeds of the several parties were also clearly defined. It remained to determine in what relation they should stand to the Established Church. On this question there were the greatest differences, both of opinion and of action.

The principles of the Quakers prevented them from holding any religious communion with members of the State-Church, and the Baptists were equally opposed to it. Members of some Baptist churches were forbidden to enter, on any pretence whatever, the established places of worship; inter-marriage and social intercourse with Episcopalians were equally prohibited.* Of the practice of the Congregationalists there appears to be no record, but in all probability, it was milder than that of either the Quakers or the Baptists. The Presbyterians not only, in some instances, practised what was then termed, "Occasional Conformity," but publicly advocated it; but this was more characteristic of London than of the country. Many of their leaders, indeed, appear to have hesitated in taking any steps which might give fixity to the separation of the Presbyterians from the Church. When Edmund Calamy requested Howe to be present at his public ordination, Howe not only refused, but thought it necessary to take the advice of Lord Somers, as to the expediency of any such service taking place. Bates also, notwithstanding an admission to the effect that separation from the Church was not only justifiable, but necessary, as circumstances then stood, declined a similar request.† The older Presbyterians still looked on the Church with affection, and would have done nothing either to bring her into disrepute, or to separate themselves entirely from her communion.

Circumstances now arose, which compelled them to

---

* Robert Robinson's "Lecture on a Becoming Behaviour in Religious Assemblies." The above were Articles of Communion in the Baptist Church at Cambridge at this time.

† Calamy's "Own Life," i. 338—348.

defend their position. According to the Act of Uniformity, no person who was not a communicant of the Established Church could hold any muncipal office; but with the Presbyterian practice, a person could be a communicant, and yet be a Dissenter. In A.D. 1697, Sir Humphrey Edwin on being elected Lord Mayor of London, carried the regalia of his office to Pinners' Hall, which was then used by a Congregational church. The circumstance excited considerable irritation amongst Churchmen. It was described as a reproach to the city, and a crime against religion.* It was on this occasion that Daniel De Foe, for the second time, took up his pen to treat of an ecclesiastical question. De Foe was born of a Dissenting family, and had received a classical education at one of the best of the Dissenting academies. His ecclesiastical principles were Presbyterian, but he does not appear to have identified himself very closely with any particular congregation. As yet, he was a comparatively unknown man. He had, however, some years before, taken part in public questions. He had joined the Duke of Monmouth's rebellion, and had successfully exerted his influence to dissuade Dissenters from accepting James's offer of indulgence. He was noticed amongst the royal regiment of volunteer horse, composed for the most part of Dissenters, who went out to welcome William and Mary on their first state visit to the city.† Since that time he had been engaged, and had failed in business, and was now accountant to the Commissioners of glass duty. De Foe saw, in Sir Humphrey Edwin's conduct an inconsistency which was re-

---

* Dr. Nichols's "Apparet:" Calamy's Abridgement, i. p. 561.
† Oldmixon, iii. p. 36. Wilson's "De Foe," i. p. 189.

proachful to religion. Probably, he also saw, for his vision was constantly, and with singular accuracy, projecting itself into the future, that the pratice of occasional Conformity must, if persisted in, tend to the destruction of Nonconformity. He therefore published a remonstrance with Edwin,* in which, in the terse, vigorous and pungent style, which made him the most effective and the most celebrated political writer of his age, he pointed out the grave character of his act. De Foe set aside, altogether, the question whether Nonconformity was right, or whether it was wrong, but argued that when a man conformed he practically denied the lawfulness of his dissent; while at the same time, in dissenting, he was condemning the sinfulness of Conformity. If he could conscientiously commune with the Established Church, his conscience ought to allow him to become a member of that Church, and he was guilty of the sin of schism if he did not. De Foe examined the various reasons which might induce a person occasionally to conform. He might hold his act of communion to be a civil act only; but, inquired De Foe, How can you take it as a civil act in one place, and a religious act in another; is not this playing "bo-peep with God Almighty?" Or, a person might occasionally conform from patriotic motives, but the author plainly expressed his entire disbelief in the existence of persons who were willing to "damn their souls to serve their country;" and was of opinion that the power of God was omnipotent enough to protect a nation without the perpetration of any sin. In reply to the argument that it was not a sinful act, De

---

* " An Enquiry into the Occasional Conformity of Dissenters in Cases of Preferment." A.D. 1697.

Foe maintained that it was such in a Dissenter, or his dissent was sinful; and he expressed the opinion that no Church could lawfully separate from the Church of England, and yet allow its members to be occasional Conformists.

No notice appears to have been taken of this pamphlet on the occasion of its first publication, but three years afterwards, in A.D. 1701, another Dissenter, Sir Thomas Abney, a member of Howe's Church, was elected Lord Mayor. Having qualified himself for office by taking the Lord's Supper in an Established church, Sir Thomas afterwards communed with the members of Howe's congregation. De Foe, thereupon, republished his "Enquiry" with a preface dedicated to Howe, in which he asked Howe whether this practice of alternate communion was allowed by him or by Dissenters in general, and, if not, he conjured him by his tenderness for the weakness of others, by his regard to God's honour and the honour of the Church, to censure it, in order that the sincerity and purity of Protestant Dissenters might be vindicated. If it were allowed, he desired Howe to give his reasons in defence of the practice. Howe replied in a pamphlet, the publication of which all who venerate that great man's name, must regret.* De Foe had addressed Howe in terms of the utmost respect; Howe replied with insinuations and with abuse. His pamphlet abounded in personalities. He suggested that the writer of the "Enquiry" must be a Fifth Monarchy man, and openly stigmatized him as of "stingy, narrow spirit." Nor did he avoid gross

* "Some Considerations of a Preface to an Enquiry, etc." By John Howe. A.D. 1701.

misrepresentation, which, however, must have arisen from carelessness rather that from intention. It is strange, also, to notice that he did not give a direct reply to De Foe's question. He declined to say whether or not he approved of occasional Conformity, but instead, suggested a number of hypothetical cases in which a person might be justified in that practice. Howe's argument conveys and was evidently intended to convey, the impression that he considered the questions at issue between Church and Dissent as of minor importance. He closed it by remarking that if De Foe's judgment were true, that truth, accompanied by De Foe's temper, was much worse than any occasional Conformist's error. De Foe at once published a rejoinder,* in which, after remarking on the tone of Howe's reply, he assailed the position taken by Howe with the keenest logical acumen. Like many other controversialists, the two writers argued from different premises and with different objects, and would never have agreed. De Foe could not see how it was possible for a man to be conscientious in conforming, at the same time, to an Established Church, and to a Church which, on conscientious grounds, had separated from the Establishment. Logically, De Foe was right, but Howe did not try the position by the rules of logic. He tried it by the test of Christian sympathy, a sympathy which, in some cases, may be only another name for personal inclination or even for laxity and indifference, but may also be of a higher character. If De Foe, in his rejoinder, had tested Howe's arguments by Howe's own justification of

---

* "A Letter to Mr. Howe by way of Reply, etc." A.D. 1701.

Nonconformity, published twelve years before, he would have placed the divine in a painful position. The fact, however, that Howe did not openly state that he himself approved of occasional Conformity, while it is known that, privately, he approved of and defended it,* appears to be a sufficient indication that he did not feel his position to be logically tenable. With De Foe's second pamphlet the controversy on this subject was, for the present, closed, to be re-opened in a different and graver form by the Legislature itself in less than another year.

The tendency of public opinion towards the close of William the Third's reign, so far from being in favour of an increased measure of toleration, was favourable to a limitation of the liberty already enjoyed by Dissenters. By the death of Mary they had lost the protection of a Queen of large and liberal views, and of the most kindly feeling towards themselves. Tillotson and Stillingfleet were also dead; the Tories had obtained possession of power, and the clergy were advancing in their pretensions. The King, having had sufficient experience of the temper of Convocation in the year when the Comprehension scheme was under discussion, had not summoned that body to meet for business for ten years. In the interval, a claim was put forth to the effect that Convocation had a right not only to meet whenever the Houses of Parliament met, but to sit and transact business without the Royal license. This doctrine was boldly advocated in a "Letter to a Convocation Man," published anonymously, in A.D. 1694, but known to be from the pen of Dr. Binkes. Its novelty was only equalled by its

---

* Howe's "Letter to Boyse."   Roger's "Life of Howe," p. 295.

audacity. In the Act of Submission of A.D. 1532, Henry the Eighth had required the clergy to consent that no constitutions, canons, or ordinances of Convocation should be enacted or enforced without the King's consent, nor unless the King should first license the clergy to assemble, and give to their decisions his assent and authority.* In the next year, an Act was passed subjecting the clergy to fine and imprisonment if they assembled without the Royal writ. From that period, it had been the established law that a writ was necessary to meet; that another writ was necessary to allow of business; that after business had been transacted it could not take effect without the confirmation of the sovereign, and that even with the sovereign's own authority no canons could be made against the laws and customs of the land or the King's prerogative. The claim now advanced was, in effect, that the clergy were entitled to the same powers which they had enjoyed before the Reformation, and that, in fact, there neither was nor should be a Royal supremacy. The nature of this demand, which, if it had been acceded to, would have put the ecclesiastical laws and the religious liberties of Englishmen into the hands of the Jacobite clergy, was at once seen. The letter was replied to by Dr. Wake, afterwards Archbishop of Canterbury, in an elaborate work, in which the authority of the Crown was sustained with great learning and ability.‡ Wake, in return, was

* Fuller's History, v. p. 189. Before this period the Archbishop had been accustomed to summon the provincial Councils, for which no license was required.

† Lathbury's "History of Convocation," p. 110—111.

‡ "The Authority of Christian Princes over their Ecclesiastical Synods." A.D. 1697.

charged with surrendering the rights of the Church, and an endeavour was made to prove that the Act of Submission did not involve the Royal supremacy to the extent that had been supposed. Binkes was now silent, a far abler man having undertaken to defend the cause of the clergy. This was Dr. Francis Atterbury, a clever, learned, witty, but ambitious and unscrupulous clergyman, who was afterwards appointed by Queen Anne, Bishop of Rochester, and who was ultimately banished the kingdom for intriguing for the restoration of the Stuarts. Atterbury maintained that the Convocation had a perfect right to sit, and to make canons, without the permission of the sovereign, but he convinced few excepting the non-juring and Jacobite clergy of the accuracy or success of his arguments. So able a controversialist, however, could not remain unanswered. Bishop Burnet, Bishop Kennett, and a host of inferior writers took the field against him, and ultimately Wake, in a second work, summed up the whole case. But, while the upholders of the rights of the sovereigns of England were indisputably successful in maintaining their position in argument, the High Church party were equally successful in the main object for which this controversy was provoked. They did not destroy the King's prerogative, but they compelled him to summon a meeting of Convocation. This step was taken on the advice of his Tory ministry, and assented to by Tenison. Convocation met in the spring of 1701. The Lower House at once gave proof of their High Church spirit. It had always been assumed, up to this time, that the archbishop could prorogue both Houses, but the Lower House now refused to be prorogued by him, treating his authority as well as his acts with open contempt. They claimed to sit when, and as long, as they chose; they openly defied the episcopal bench, and proceeded, without asking for the Royal license, to transact business of the most important character. Their first work was of a nature the most congenial to their inclinations and their temper. Toland, a free-thinker, had published a book in disparagement of the divine nature of Christianity. This work was seized upon, extracts from it were selected, a so-called synodical censure of it was passed, and the proceedings reported to the Upper House. Such an assumption of independent authority could scarcely be overlooked. The bishops at once took legal advice concerning the power of the Lower House to perform such an act. The opinion of the lawyers, which was entirely against the possession of such a right, and hinted at the possibility of the penalty of the Act of Submission having been incurred, was communicated to Convocation by the archbishop, and the body again prorogued.

Similar scenes took place all through the summer. From the condemnation of Toland's book, the Lower House proceeded to deal with Bishop Burnet's Exposition of the Articles. They represented that it tended to introduce such a latitude and diversity of opinions as the Articles were framed to avoid; that it was opposed in many places to the received doctrine of the Church, and that it contained propositions which were dangerous to the Establishment. What were the passages complained of were not stated. Burnet asked that these representations might be received in order that he might reply to them; but it is obvious that if the bishops had consented to this step they would have acknowledged the right of the Lower House to make such a representation. In place of doing this they passed a series of resolutions, in which the power of the Lower House to censure any work was denied; their censure of the "Exposition of the Articles" denounced as defamatory and scandalous, and the author of that book formally thanked for his great service to the Church of England. After this, prorogation followed on prorogation, until, by the dissolution of Parliament, Convocation also was dissolved.* The new body was, however, possessed of no better temper than the old. From the first day of its meeting to the last it did little else but dispute concerning its rights and privileges. The death of the King put a brief termination to these scandalous and offensive proceedings.†

There was more in this memorable controversy than appeared upon the surface. Those who have read, with any attention, the works of the lower order of the clergy of King William's reign, will scarcely fail to have perceived that the doctrines which were advanced during the discussions which took place on the powers of Convocation and the relative authority of the Episcopacy, had a political as well as an ecclesiastical bearing. The bishops and the clergy belonged to different political parties. The former were, for the most part, ardent and steadfast adherents of the Revolution. They had, indeed, been selected for their known political sympathies. They were personally attached to the King, and they threw the whole weight of their influence into the measures which he was known to favour. The

* Lathbury's "History," cap. xi.
† These are Archbishop Tenison's own words. "Tenison's Life," 97—99.

clergy, on the other hand, were Tories. They hated equally the Revolution and its promoters. They despised every bishop who had been nominated to his see by the revolutionary King. Any ecclesiastical measure that was approved by Tillotson, Tenison, or Burnet was sure, on that account, to receive their opposition. They delighted to disparage every man who had received a single mark of favour from William. It was this feeling which gave its animus to the Convocation controversy. The clergy flouted the authority of the bishops, not because they were bishops, or because of their power as such, but because they were King William's bishops. While they treated Tenison with contempt, they reverenced every non-juror who had once held the episcopal office. If they had attached the supreme importance which they affected to attach to the questions at issue between the Upper and the Lower Houses, why did they not raise them when a Stuart was on the throne? By-and-by, there can be no doubt, this controversy became a sincere one. From writing as the clergy did, they came at last to believe what they wrote. Hence the controversy did not die with the death of William, but its temper was moderated. The incentive of hate to the reigning sovereign was lost, and for some time it seemed that their bigotry, and what they considered to be their loyalty, would be gratified by the return of the Stuarts to the throne. With such anticipations they could afford to let the question of their imaginary rights remain in comparative abeyance.

Anne was no sooner seated on the throne than it became evident that the liberties of Dissenters were in danger of serious restriction. The High Church tendencies of the Queen were well known, and it was confidently anticipated that she would view with favour the desires of the clergy to limit the operation of the Toleration Act. Dissenters were everywhere insulted; their ministers could scarcely walk the streets with safety; High Church ballads, all ending with the refrain of "Down with the Presbyterians" were composed and sung by drunken mobs under newly-erected Maypoles. "Queen Mary's bonfires" were hinted at for the effectual extirpation of obstinate schismatics; people talked of pulling down the Meeting-houses as places that should not be suffered to exist; and at Newcastle-under-Lyne they carried this desire into execution.* Two things, however, operated as a restraint on the indulgence of these intolerant passions. The first was the increased numerical power and social influence of Dissent. In the twelve years from A.D. 1688 to A.D. 1700, Dissenters had taken out licenses for no fewer than two thousand four hundred and eighteen places of worship.† De Foe, who knew as much as, if not more, of their condition than any other man, reckoned their number at this period at no fewer than two millions,‡ and states that they were the most numerous and the wealthiest section in the kingdom,§ but notwithstanding their great activity and the wide surface of the kingdom over which they had spread their network of Christian organizations, it is almost impossible to accept this estimate. The second circumstance in their

---

* Calamy's "Abridgment," i. 620; and "Own Life," i. 460. De Foe's "Christianity of the High Church," Ded.

† Parl. Return, 156. Sess. 1853.

‡ De Foe's "Two Great Questions," in the first series of the collection of his writings, p. 394.

§ "Christianity of the High Church." Ded.

favour was that they were known to approve of the renewal of hostilities with France, which, soon after the accession of Anne, declared in favour of the Pretender. The Queen herself, however, treated them with contempt. The first occasion that the three Denominations of Presbyterians, Congregationalists, and Baptists * united together for a common public purpose was on the accession of Anne to the throne, when a deputation, headed by Dr. Daniel Williams, waited upon her. Either their address displeased her, or she did not care to assume a courtesy which would not sincerely express her own feelings. She heard the deputation in silence. Not a word of thanks, nor a promise of protection escaped her lips. Since the time of James the First, the Dissenters had not been treated with such scant courtesy, and they must have left the royal presence with an increase of the cloudy apprehensions which a contemporary writer states to have generally prevailed amongst them.† In her first speech to Parliament, indeed, the Queen promised to protect the Dissenters so long as they conducted themselves peaceably towards the government, but she added that members of the Established Church would enjoy her favour. At the close of the session she deigned to be more distinct. She promised to preserve and maintain the Act of Toleration, but she again added, "My own principles must always keep me entirely firm to the interests and religion of the Church of England, and will incline me to countenance those who have the

---

* In this year, also, the body termed "Ministers of the Three Denominations," was formed. The committee consisted of four Presbyterian, three Congregational, and three Baptist ministers.—Ivimey, iii. 42.

† Calamy's "Own Life," i. 460.

truest zeal to support it."* This was nothing less than the offer of a royal premium upon High Churchism, and it is therefore scarcely to be wondered at that, from this time, High Churchism became the popular form of religion.

Neither the condition of political parties, nor the apparent tendency of public affairs, was calculated to dispel the apprehensions entertained by the Dissenters. Within two months of her accession to the throne, the Queen had dismissed from office nearly every statesman who had enjoyed the confidence and favour of William. The names of Halifax, Somers, and Orford, the great leaders of the Revolution, were struck from the Privy Council list. The conduct of public affairs was placed in the hands of Marlborough and Godolphin, both men of Tory sympathies but less extreme in their views than other members of their party. The House of Commons was "full of fury against the memory of the late King, and those who had been employed by him."† Its political sympathies were unmistakably evidenced by the election of Harley, once a Presbyterian and a Whig, and now a Tory Churchman, to the Speakership. Above any of these in influence, for, at this time, she commanded the Queen herself, was the wife of Marlborough, chief favourite at Court, who, during the early part of this reign, set up and pulled down men at her pleasure. This woman's politics were guided mainly by considerations of interest; but it happened that those interests were sometimes identical with those of the nation. Undoubtedly, she was no friend of the Jacobite

---

* Boyer's "Annals," vol. i.
† Burnet's "Own Times," p. 719.

party, and she saw that the fortunes of her husband and family could not be advanced by the return of the Stuarts or the promotion of extreme Toryism. Although she occupied this confidential position with a Tory Queen, the Countess of Marlborough was herself an ardent Whig. More than Somers or Halifax, she was the leader of the party, and so successfully, by means of Court intrigue, did she lead it, that she soon had the satisfaction of seeing a change in the administration of affairs.

Before this was brought about it was determined to make the Dissenters feel the effect of the death of their protector. The Church party raised a cry for the suppression of the Dissenting academies and for the repeal of the law which allowed occasional Conformists to hold public offices. A clergyman named Henry Sacheverell was chosen to discharge the preliminary work of inflaming the passions of the people. Sacheverell had qualifications which eminently fitted him for such a part. He was a man of hot and angry temperament, unscrupulous in his language, and fierce in his style of denunciation, but totally destitute of either learning, education, or refinement. He had all the bad qualities of a demagogue united to all the worst qualities of a bigot. He was what most men of his class are, both bold and cunning. His cunning taught him that he might rise to popularity, if not to eminence, by pandering to extreme Church prejudices, by preaching up the wrongs of the clergy, by denouncing, with holy horror, the schism of Dissent, and by warning the nation of the danger to be expected from the encouragement of men whose ancestors had rebelled against, and brought to the block, the "lawful King" and "martyred saint" and sovereign, the direct ancestor of the Royal lady who then sat on the throne. Sacheverell's first attempt in this direction was made in a sermon preached before the University of Oxford, on June 3, A.D. 1702.* In the slipshod style which characterized all his writings, Sacheverell referred to the Dissenters and their friends as enemies of the Commonwealth and State. "It is as unaccountable and amazing a contradiction to our reason," he cried, "as the greatest reproach and scandal upon our Church, however others may be seduced or misled, that any pretending to that sacred and inviolable character of being her true sons, pillars, and defenders, should turn such apostates and renegadoes to their oaths and professions, such false traitors to their trusts and offices, as to strike sail with a party that is such an open and avowed enemy to our communion, and against whom every man that wishes its welfare, ought to hang out the bloody flag and banner of defiance." In another sermon preached before the judges at assize, in the same city,† the same orator made formal complaint of Dissenting academies as being dangerous to the Church and State, and as "fountains of lewdness," from which were "spawned all descriptions of heterodox, lewd, and atheistical books;" their supporters were described as "worse monsters than Jews, Mahommedans, Socinians, or Papists;" and the State was asked to pass a law for the suppression of "such a growing mischief." Sacheverell was followed

* "The Political Union: a Discourse, showing the dependence of Government on Religion in general; and of the English Monarchy of the Church of England in particular."

† "The Nature and Mischief of Prejudice and Partiality."

by Samuel Wesley, a clergyman,* who attacked the educational institutions of Dissenters as being both immoral in their character and disloyal in their tendency. The last author was replied to with great force, and his character exposed by Mr. Samuel Palmer, a Dissenting minister of Southwark—a man in every way competent to such a task. The controversy between Wesley and Palmer extended through four years. Wesley was as unscrupulous and abusive as Sacheverell himself. The mildest words in which he could describe Dissenters were "villains," "hypocrites," and "murderers."† There can be no doubt that the success of the Dissenting academies had drawn away many from the Established Church as a religious institution, and that their natural tendency and effect were the perpetuation of an educated and learned ministry. But this was not the only grievance. It was asserted "that they endangered the success of the two national Universities." To prove this point Wesley explicitly refers to the numbers of nobility and gentry who would have sought their education at one or other of the great seats of learning, "had they not been intercepted by these sucking academies."‡ After stating the numbers who had been educated at

---

* "A Letter from a Country Divine, concerning the Education of Dissenters in their Private Academies in several parts of the Nation. Humbly offered to the consideration of the Grand Committee of Parliament for Religion." Wesley was father to the celebrated John Wesley.

† Those who may be curious to see the spirit in which Dissent was attacked, and the style of controversial writing which was deemed both allowable and respectable at this period, can scarcely do better than read the three pamphlets of Wesley. The title of the first has already been given; the second is entitled, "A Defence of a Letter" (A.D. 1704); the third, "A Reply to Mr. Palmer's Vindication" (A.D. 1707).

‡ "A Defence, &c.," p. 14.

certain well-known institutions, he adds that, on the whole, by a modest computation, "there must have been some thousands this way educated."* The reply to such an attack was very obvious. "It is the Church of England's own fault," said Palmer, "that we stand excluded from the public schools;" and he appealed both to the Universities and to the Colleges to remove the barrier which prevented Dissenters from taking advantage of the acknowledged benefits which they offered. It appears, from this writer, that Dissenters had made formal proposals for admission at Oxford and Cambridge. He states that they had expressed their willingness to be content with some of the inferior Colleges and Halls, and to submit to any civil or moral tests, and indignantly exclaims against the injustice of their exclusion.† Sacheverell met, at this point, with another antagonist, Mr. James Owen, who reminded him that from the reign of Queen Elizabeth to that of Charles the First, the degrees and preferments of the Universities were conferred without distinction of parties or opinions, and in reply to a taunt levelled at the ignorance of Dissenters, made the apt and pertinent remark that, while it was made one of the causes of prejudice and partiality, the Dissenter "was not allowed the benefit of a learned education to cure him of this vice." "He excludes them," said the author, "from the fountain of learning, nor will he allow them to drink water out of their own cisterns. He would have them punished for using the means of knowledge, and yet damns them for the prejudices of

---

* Ib., p. 15.
† Palmer's "Vindication," pp. 11, 12, A.D. 1705.

ignorance."* The right to participate in the advantages of the Universities, was, it will thus be seen, affirmed, as strongly by the generation of Dissenters who, by the operation of the Act of Uniformity, were the first to be excluded, as it has been by all their descendants.

Sacheverell's party, however, found in Daniel De Foe an abler and more astute opponent than was either Palmer or Owen. De Foe was now rising, with strong and rapid strides, to the height of his reputation as a political writer. Shortly before the death of William he had published the exquisite satire of the " True-born Englishman," in which those who were for ever carping at the King on account of his foreign birth were shown a not very flattering image of themselves. De Foe had previously enjoyed the friendship of the King, and by this service had laid him under a debt of gratitude. But De Foe's politics were not popular, and he took no pains to earn applause. If, amongst any people, he might have expected encouragement, it should have been amongst the Dissenters, for he was the only vigorous and constant advocate of what, at that time, was understood to be religious freedom. But, by the majority of Dissenters, De Foe was treated with undisguised contempt. Calamy sneeringly alludes to him as " a certain warm person, who thought himself well qualified for the management of any argument." † It was the policy of the clerical leaders of Dissent at this period not to advance any claims for further political concessions. Considering the threatening aspect of the dominant High Church party,

---

* Owen's "Moderation still a Virtue," pp. 98, 103, A.D. 1704.
† " Own Life," i. 464.

it is possible that this was a prudent attitude. The principal representatives of Dissent were in frequent communication with the members of the government and other parliamentary leaders, and, no doubt, shaped their public action according to the advice which they received. Excepting, therefore, in matters relating exclusively to ecclesiastical polity, they preserved a prudent, if not a dignified, quiet. If they prided themselves in anything, it was in being "moderate." When, at this very time, as well as afterwards, proposals were made to the Legislature for the abridgment of their liberties, this course was referred to as an argument in favour of their retention of the position which the law had already given to them. But it unfortunately happened, as under similar circumstances it has generally happened, that this argument was of no avail. However highly the statesmen of this period may have appreciated a quiet policy, and however sincere they may have been in advising and eulogizing it, they had no hesitation in sacrificing the Dissenters when party necessities made such a sacrifice desirable. So far, therefore, from anything having been gained by the adoption of a "moderate" course, much had been lost. The rights and principles which had been held back, or which had ceased to be actively urged, had lost ground. The fruit of "moderation" and quiet was retrogression and weakness. To the policy generally adopted in this reign, however prudent it may have seemed, and however conscientiously it may have been taken up, is, in part, to be attributed the rapid decline of Dissent in the immediately succeeding generations.

De Foe was no party to such a policy. If he was

conspicuous for the possession of one quality more than another, that quality was fearlessness. He was accused by persons of a more timid disposition of not being apt to consider consequences :* the fact is, he never considered immediate consequences. He seemed to be able to see past any present disadvantages that might arise from the recommendation or adoption of a particular course of action to what would be its ultimate issue. Temporary sacrifices, temporary unpopularity, or the excitement of temporary anger, weighed nothing with him. He had, in regard to ecclesiastical politics, what no other Dissenter of his day appears to have possessed, a firm and far-sighted policy—a policy which he carried out almost alone, at the cost of fortune, health, and reputation, but the wisdom, as well as the courage of which, posterity has gratefully vindicated.

De Foe met Sacheverell's furious denunciation of Dissent and apostrophe to the " bloody flag" of persecution by a satire so delicate that, for a time, it deceived those against whom it was directed into the belief that it was written on their own side; so keen and so severe that when the veil was once removed the desire for revenge against its author knew no bounds. " The Shortest Way with the Dissenters" belongs to the period in the history of English literature in which were produced the " Tale of a Tub," " Gulliver's Travels," and the " History of John Bull," and takes equal rank with either of those immortal satires. That, out of the circle of persons of literary pursuits, it is not so widely known and read as are the popular writings of Swift and

* Calamy, ib.

Arbuthnot, is owing to the fact that it takes the form of an ordinary and apparently grave political tract, instead of a humorous narrative. In politics, and especially in ecclesiastical politics, De Foe felt too deeply to allow the humorous to predominate over the serious. While he was not averse to pleasing the fancy, he was intent on convincing the reason. He was incapable, in his political writings, of subordinating his purpose to the instrument by which he chose to accomplish that purpose. Whenever, especially, he was engaged in attacking High Churchism, he was almost savagely earnest. A kind of Mohawk ferocity was a characteristic of most of the party writing of this age; and it was not an uncommon circumstance for people who were attacked by the pen to threaten a reply by the sword;* but De Foe rose above the ordinary level of party warfare. He saw, in the High Churchmanship of this reign, a power which threatened, if it was not resisted with all the vigour of which the mind was capable, to be fatal to the liberties of Englishmen; to undo, as was sometimes openly promised, the work of the Revolution, and arrest, perhaps, for generations, the progress of the people towards a more liberal government and a more religious life.

The author commences "The Shortest Way with the Dissenters" with a history of Dissent, in which its rebellious tendency and tyrannical character are described in exaggerated Sacheverellian style. The "purest Church in the world," he says, has borne with it, "with invincible patience," and a "fatal lenity." "Charity and love," he adds, "are her known doctrines." He then

* Both De Foe and Swift, as is well known, received frequent threats of assassination.

examines the reasons given by Dissenters for their continued toleration. They are numerous, but so were the Huguenots, and yet the French king disposed of them; but the more numerous they are the more are they dangerous, and the greater need there is to suppress them. If it be said that there is need of union in time of war, there is the greater need at such a time to take security against private enemies, and heaven, by depriving them of their "Dutch Sanctuary," had clearly made way for their destruction. The popular objection that the Queen had promised them toleration was worth nothing, for the promise was limited by the safety of the Church; and although there might be no immediate danger to that institutio, if the present opportunity was not taken it might be too late hereafter to do the work. "If ever," writes the author, in an admirable imitation of the High Church style, "you will establish the best Christian Church in the world; if ever you will suppress the spirit of enthusiasm; if ever you will free the nation from the viperous brood that have so long sucked the blood of their mother; if ever you will leave your posterity free from faction and rebellion, this is the time. This is the time to pull up this heretical weed of sedition that has so long disturbed the peace of our Church, and poisoned the good corn." Is it cruel, he inquires, to do this? "Is it cruel to kill a snake or a toad?" "I do not," he says, with mock charity, "prescribe fire and faggot, but they are to be rooted out of this nation." He proceeds to ridicule the laws imposing fines and imprisonment for not attending Church, and in sarcastic allusion to the "occasional Conformists," says, that they that will go to church to be chosen sheriffs and mayors would go to forty churches rather than be hanged. "If one severe law were made, and punctually executed, that whoever was found at a Conventicle should be banished the nation, and the preacher be hanged, we should soon see an end of the tale. They would all come to Church, and our age would make us one again." In his opinion Providence had given the country her present Queen, her present Parliament, her present Convocation, for the deliverance of the Church. After comparing the Church to Christ crucified between two thieves, "Let us," he concludes, "crucify the thieves. Let her foundations be established upon the destruction of her enemies, the doors of mercy being always kept open to the returning part of the deluded people. Let the obstinate be ruled with a rod of iron. Let all true sons of so holy and oppressed a mother, exasperated by her afflictions, harden their hearts against those who have oppressed her."

This work was no sooner issued from the press than it was caught up, and circulated with eager zeal by the High Church party. One clergyman, on receiving a copy of it from a friend, in expressing his thanks, wrote, "I join with that author in all he says, and have such a value for the book, that, next to the Holy Bible, and the sacred Comments, I take it for the most valuable piece I have. I pray God to put it into her Majesty's heart to put what is there proposed in execution."* De Foe himself says, that "the wisest Churchmen in the nation were deceived by this book.

* Wilson's "De Foe," ii. 86.

Those whose tempers fell in with the times hugged and embraced it; applauded the proposal, and filled their mouths with the arguments made use of therein." Some Dissenters even were taken aback, and from the popularity with which it was greeted, began to fear that they were in considerable danger. When, however, the fact came out that it was written by a Dissenter, with a view to expose the designs of the High Church party, and that it was nothing but a satire, a hot fury took possession of the men who had allowed their passions to cheat their judgments as to its real character and intention. In press and pulpit the author was now denounced as a malignant slanderer. The men who had been foremost in praise were now the most vehement in denunciation. Caught in a trap, their only resource was openly to disavow the doctrines which they had before enthusiastically approved. It was, they said, a base calumny on the Church, and no punishment could be too severe for the author. Hounded on by the rage of the clergy, the government undertook to ascertain who was the writer of the pamphlet, a task in which, by the Earl of Nottingham's perseverance, they quickly succeeded. A State prosecution against De Foe was immediately commenced. A proclamation was issued and a reward of fifty pounds offered for his apprehension. In this proclamation the "Shortest Way" is stigmatized as a scandalous and seditious pamphlet, and after the fashion of the "Hue and Cry," De Foe's personal appearance is minutely described. The House of Commons ordered the pamphlet to be burned in New Palace Yard by the common hangman. De Foe had, before this, prudently retired from the scene, but on learning that both his printer and publisher had been apprehended, he voluntarily surrendered himself. He then wrote a brief vindication of his work, and threw himself on the justice of the government. He was tried at the Old Bailey on February 24th, A.D. 1703. The Attorney-General, Sir Simon Harcourt, who prosecuted, appears to have treated him in the style in which State prisoners were treated before Jeffreys. De Foe frankly admitted his guilt, and was sentenced to a fine of two hundred marks, to stand three times in the pillory, to be imprisoned during the Queen's pleasure, and to find sureties for his good behaviour for three years. The leader of political Dissent was thus dealt with in the "shortest way," and his satire proved, by the sentence on himself, not to have been a libel.

It is to the disgrace of the majority of the Dissenters of that period, that, so far from defending or supporting De Foe, they did nothing but heap reproaches upon him. They affected to believe that he intended his work as a serious production, forgetting, as he well says, that he must then have designed to place his father, his wife, his six children, and himself in the same condition. He appears to have felt this conduct far more severely than he felt the effect of his sentence. For, although forsaken by his own people, the public, in place of treating him as a criminal, honoured him as a hero. When he appeared in the pillory they greeted him with shouts of applause; they hung what was intended to be the instrument of his disgrace with garlands of flowers, and plentifully supplied him with refreshments. De Foe himself, summoning all his moral courage to meet his position, turned it at once to advantage by composing a "Hymn to the Pillory," in which, in clever rhyme, he satirized his opponents and prosecutors, and vindicated his pamphlet. He occupied his whole time while in Newgate in publishing more pamphlets, and in collecting his works, until, after he had been in prison for more than a year, Harley put himself into communication with him, with a view to secure his literary services for the Ministry, and the Queen sent relief to his family, and set him free. It was during this imprisonment that De Foe established his "Review," a journal of politics and general information, published on an average about three times a week, written wholly by himself, and printed at his own risk. In the pages of the "Review" are, for the first time in English literature, to be seen the style and scope of the modern newspaper article. Questions of domestic and foreign politics, of education and morals, of arts and sciences, and trade and commerce, were treated with a fulness of information, sincerity of purpose, and vigour of style which, if the politics advocated had been popular, would have secured, even from the contemporaries of De Foe, as much respect and reward as they secured malignity and fear. De Foe came out of Newgate the scoff of the polite wits, but with the consciousness that after the controversy on the "Shortest Way," no "bloody flag" could, in his time, be reared in England. The High Church party had concentrated their vengeance on his single person. The conduct of the government in this case has been freely censured, and no words are strong enough to describe the arbitrary injustice with which they treated De Foe. But when the "Shortest Way" was written, they were not only

Tories, but at the mercy of the High Church majority in the House of Commons, and no government of Queen Anne's or any other reign were likely to sacrifice themselves for the sake of a Dissenter.

Between the publication of Sacheverell's sermon and De Foe's caustic reply, an attack was made on the liberties of Dissenters from another quarter. On November 4th, A.D. 1702, the members for the Universities of Oxford and Cambridge brought into the House of Commons a Bill for the prevention of occasional conformity. This measure was supported by the whole strength of the Tory and High Church party, and was carried through the Commons by an immense majority. The clergy successfully exerted themselves to inflame the passions of the people to their highest point in order to ensure the passing of the measure into law.* The Tory party, however, in prosecution this Bill, were not animated entirely by motives of religious intolerance. The "Occasional" Bill, from its first to its last introduction, was mainly a party measure. The Whigs, in many parts of the country, where the corporations returned members to Parliament, were, to a great extent, depended for their election on the Dissenting members of those corporations. On the fidelity of these members they could always rely. But, if the Occasional Bill were passed, no Dissenter could, in future, be a member of any corporation. The Whigs, accordingly, fought against the Bill with stubborn tenacity. The character, however, of the opposition to it, was as mixed

---

* "Among those who were hottest in this affair were the clergy, and a crowd of women of the lowest rank, inflamed, as it were, with a zeal for religion."—Cunningham's "Great Britain," i. 318.

as were the feelings which had led to its promotion. There were as sincere friends to religious liberty amongst the statesmen of the Whig party as there were sincere opponents to it amidst the Tories. Both parties, also, could raise the same cries of the welfare of the nation, and the welfare of the Church. The one party believed that the first could be secured only by excluding from its service the extreme adherents of the doctrine of resistance, and that the second would never be safe while Dissent was permitted to exist. The other party believed that the security of the State was best promoted by the good-will of all the people to the laws, and that the Church had gained, and would still gain, by preserving a mild and tolerant attitude to those who differed from her. In the Bill which passed the Commons there was much which might reasonably have suggested hesitation even to the warmest partisan of the Church. It prohibited any person who did not statedly commune in the Established Church from holding any civil, military, or naval office whatsoever. Not only every admiral, general, judge, alderman, town councillor or high officer of state, but every common soldier and sailor, every bailiff, and every cook and scullery maid in the Royal household was required to be a member of the Established Church. The bill further provided that if any person holding such an office should, at any time after receiving his appointment, attend any Conventicle or religious meeting other than one conducted according to the liturgy and practice of the Church of England, he should forfeit the sum of One hundred pounds, and Five pounds for every day that he continued in the execution of his office; and he was at the same time adjudged to be incapable, during the remainder of his life, of holding any public employment.*

The House of Lords, at this period, was not greatly affected by the prevailing High Church passion. It was, to a considerable extent, a house of William the Third's creation, and most of the bishops had owed their nomination to that liberal monarch. When, therefore, the Occasional Bill came before it, it proceeded to make modifications in some of its most offensive provisions, and to add to it clauses which were calculated to make its operation less extensive and less permanent. The Bill, in this amended shape, was sent down to the Commons, who at once requested a free conference with the other House. On the evening of this prolonged and celebrated meeting Dr. Calamy waited on Bishop Burnet, upon whom he urged the claims of the occasional Conformists with such apparent success that he concluded "it might answer very good ends for some of us sometimes to wait on great men." †

The conference between the two Houses was managed with great ability on both sides. It was opened by the representatives of the Commons, who denounced, in strong terms, the "scandalous practice" of occasional Conformity, and exposed, in vivid language, the dangers besetting the monarchy and the Church from the existence and encouragement of Dissent. This mode of argument was an unhappy one, for it threw upon the managers for the Lords the necessity of defending Dissent. The Lords had sent their ablest and most eminent men to manage this interview. The

---

* Boyer's "Annals," i. 173—177.   † "Own Life," i. 473, 474.

Duke of Devonshire represented the old landed aristocracy of the nation; Somers and Halifax represented the statesmen of the Revolution; and Bishop Burnet the episcopal bench. While the Lords admitted that it was a scandal to religion that persons should conform to the Church only for the sake of obtaining a place, they did not admit Dissent from the established religion to be such an evil as the Commons had represented it to be. They considered that Dissenters differed from Churchmen "only in some little forms," and that they should be charitably dealt with. They also argued that the principle of toleration had already produced such visibly good results, had, in fact, contributed so much to the security and reputation of the Established Church, and had so diminished the number of Dissenters, that it was unwise to trench upon it. Then then proceeded to vindicate the body from the charges of disloyalty and schism. The Commons had said that Dissenters had never wanted the will, when they had the power, to destroy the Church and State; this, replied the Lords, is "hard and untrue, since, in the last and greatest danger the Church was exposed to, they joined with her in all imaginable zeal and sincerity." The Commons had denounced separation from the Church to be schism, and, therefore, a spiritual sin; the managers of the Upper House replied that " the Lords cannot think the Dissenters can properly be called schismatics." With regard to one of the amendments, by which it was proposed to exempt workhouses from the operation of the Bill, the Lords somewhat satirically remarked that "it could never be conceived that the distribution of some Presbyterian bread to the poor, and Dissenting water-gruel to the sick could ever bring prejudice to the Church of England." Finally they advocated the practice of a charity such as the Almighty had both allowed and commanded,* and repeated that, owing to the exercise of such a charity Dissent was " visibly abating all over the nation," and that nothing but severity could prevent its final absorption into the Church. The Commons rejoined; but the Lords adhered to most of their amendments, and the bill accordingly fell through. For this issue the Dissenters were mainly indebted to Archbishop Tenison, who framed, and resolutely persisted in retaining, the Lords' amendments,† and to Bishop Burnet, who was one of the principal spokesmen in the conferences with the Commons. Burnet felt the gravity of the political issue involved. " Had the Bill passed," he says, " we had been all in confusion, and our enemies had had the advantage."‡ The Court strained its utmost to secure its success. The greatest number—a hundred and thirty—of peers that had ever, at that time, been brought together, met to decide upon it. The Queen's husband, Prince George of Denmark, although himself a Lutheran, and an occasional Conformist, was compelled to vote for it, while he exclaimed to one of its opponents, " My heart is vid you!" But even this vote and example failed to secure a majority, and the Court, at the end of the session, had to acknowledge itself defeated in the one measure which it had most desired to carry.

It was not to be expected, under such circumstances,

* Boyer's " Annals," i. 178—200 ; Chandler's " Debates," iii. *pass.*
† " Tenison's Life," p. 102.
‡ " Memorial to the Princess Sophia," p. 91.

that this question would be allowed to rest; but, during the close of one Parliament and the opening of another, a change had come over the temper of the Court. During the whole of the summer the Duchess of Marlborough had been intriguing for the restoration of the Whigs, and exerting her influence with the Duke to induce him to coalesce with that party.* When the Queen, in November, A.D. 1703, met the two Houses of the Legislature, the effect of this influence was immediately apparent. "I want words," she said, in the last paragraph of her speech, "to express to you my earnest desires of seeing all my subjects in perfect peace and union amongst themselves. Let me, therefore, desire for all that you would carefully avoid any heats or divisions that may disappoint me of that satisfaction, and give encouragement to the common enemies of our Church and State."† The Commons replied in words which merely echoed this wish; but the reply of the Lords was couched in the most emphatic and threatening language: "We, in the most solemn manner, assure your Majesty," they rejoined, "that we will not only avoid, but oppose whatsoever may tend to create any disquiet or dissension amongst your subjects."‡ All parties knew that this language referred to the Occasional Bill; but the fact that the Court seemed disposed to evade this question only served to inflame, to a greater height, the passions of those who had determined that it should pass. Accordingly, on the same month that the Parliament was opened, a new Bill was brought into the House of Commons. It was

---

* Coxe's "Life of Marlborough," cap. xviii.
† Boyer's "Annals," ii. 163. ‡ Ib. p. 166.

of a more moderate character, as regards penalties, than the former measure, but not less offensive in respect to its political tendency. Its most violent advocate was Sir John Pakington,* who, in supporting it, declaimed in furious language against Dissent and Dissenters. Its fate in the Upper House was, however, worse than the fate of the Bill of the previous year. Archbishop Tenison and Bishop Burnet led the majority of the bench of bishops to vote against it. Burnet, especially, distinguished himself by the warmth of his opposition ; but, although he opposed it because, he says, he had long looked on liberty of conscience as one of the rights of human nature antecedent to society, it is certain, if his speech has been correctly reported, that while he used his utmost power to throw out the Bill, he expressed himself as favourable to the exclusion of all Dissenters from public offices. He defended, that is to say, the practice of occasional conformity, because he judged it to be consistent with Christianity, and favourable to the progress of the Church. With regard to the latter point he repeated the argument which he had urged at the conference between the two Houses, in A. D. 1702. "Toleration," he said, "has not only set the Dissenters at ease, but has made the Church both stronger and safer, since God has so blessed our labours that we see the Dissenters lose as much strength as we gain by it. Their numbers are abated, by a moderate computation, at least a fourth part, if not a third." † The lay Lords spoke not less vigorously against the measure. On a division, the second reading was

---

* Ancestor of the present Conservative Member for Droitwich.
† Boyer's "Annals," ii. 179.

rejected by 70 to 59. In the majority were fourteen, and in the minority nine bishops. The Duke of Marlborough gave a silent vote in its favour, and used his influence to prevent the Bill becoming law. Both he and Godolphin had now become aware that the interest really at stake in this Bill was not the interest of the Church, but of the nation, and that it was impossible to dispense with the aid of Dissenters in securing a constitutional government.

By this decisive rejection of a measure which the majority of the Commons and nearly the whole of the clergy had resolved to pass, popular excitement was raised to its utmost pitch. The vote of the bishops drew down upon them unmitigated abuse.* They were denounced as traitors to the Church, and enemies to religion. The Queen and the Prince came in for their share of vituperation.† "I wish," writes Swift to Stella,‡ "you had been here for ten days, during the highest and warmest reign of party and faction that I ever knew or read of, upon the Bill against Occasional Conformity, which, two days ago, was, upon the first reading, rejected by the Lords. It was so universal that I observed the dogs in the streets were much more contumelious and quarrelsome than usual; and the very night before the Bill went up, a Committee of Whig and Tory cats had a very warm and loud debate upon the roof of our house. But why should we wonder at that, when the very ladies are split asunder into High Church and Low, and, out of zeal for religion, have hardly time

---

* As a specimen see Leslie's "Bishop of Salisbury's Proper Defence," A.D. 1704.
† Burnet's "Own Times." p. 741.   ‡ December 16, 1703.

to say their prayers. For the rest, the whole body of the clergy, with a great majority of the House of Commons, were violent for this Bill."

The controversy was now, for a time, transferred from the Legislature to the people. Clubs and societies were formed all over the kingdom to take measures for securing the success of the Bill when it should next be brought before Parliament, and the press teemed with pamphlets on both sides of the question. The Friends, the Baptists, and a large proportion of the Congregationalists, as they judged communion with the Church to be unlawful and unscriptural, took no part in the controversy; but it was otherwise with the Presbyterians, who occupied a high social position, were conspicuous for their wealth, and held many civil offices. It is not a little singular to find, amongst the reasons urged by this party for the continuance of occasional conformity, the argument which Burnet employed with such force in the House of Lords. Not satisfied with justifying the practice by the authority of ecclesiastical and political precedents, they gravely and earnestly argued that it should be allowed to continue because it strengthened the Established Church and depressed the Dissenting interest. They acknowledged the truth of the statements that occasional conformity had weakened them, and that, on account of the practice, their adherents were fast leaving their communion;* but with strange inconsistency and fatal blindness they still advocated it. De Foe alone, writing from Newgate, set forth the question on the only principles which a Nonconformist could

* "Moderation a Virtue," p. 29.

consistently urge. He condemned the practice, as he had done in his controversy with Howe, as both hypocritical in its character and injurious in its tendency, and maintained that no respectable Dissenter would be affected by the Bill. Taking the broad ground of religious equality, he denounced the intolerance which made either temporary or permanent Churchmanship a qualification for any public office. In answer to a violent pamphlet from the pen of Sir Humphrey Mackworth,* he showed that the Established Church of England was, in this respect, the most intolerant Church in Christendom.† He made the Church welcome to every man who could conform for a place or a salary; who could be bribed or bought, or frightened out of his Dissent; but, he asked, was it just that a Dissenter should be excluded, for any consideration, from places of profit, while he was compelled to serve in places of trouble; was it just that he should be pressed as a sailor, and he made incapable of preferment; that he should maintain his own clergy and the clergy of the Church, pay equal taxes, and yet not be thought worthy to be trusted to set a drunkard in the stocks? "We wonder" he cried, "that you will accept our money or our loans." He had no fear that Dissent would be endangered by the passing of the Act, for its foundation was lodged in God's especial providence; it would be strengthened by it, and its professors would learn to live like people under the power of those who hated them.‡ In none of De Foe's works is there so much passionate indignation

---

* " Peace at Home," A.D. 1703.
† " Peace without Union," A.D. 1703.
‡ " An Inquiry into Occasional Conformity," A.D. 1703.

as there is in this scornful rebuke of ecclesiastical intolerance and "politic Dissent." That the author did not stand alone in his views is evident from the fact that this pamphlet passed through four editions in less than a year.* He had also an able coadjutor in a Dissenting minister, named Stubbs, who roused the indignation of the moderate party by comparing them to a neuter gender in religion, and by calling upon them to choose, at once, between God and Baal.* No publication of this period, however, was of greater weight than one written by John Shute, afterwards Lord Barrington, in which the services of the Protestant Dissenters to the State, their necessary antipathy to an absolute Government, and the liberality of their principles, were stated with the greatest completeness. It being one of the stock arguments against Dissenters, that, on account of their supposed complicity with the execution of Charles the First, their toleration was incompatible with the existence of a monarchy, the author reprinted in his work the Vindication of the London Ministers, signed and published by fifty of their number, in which the trial of Charles was condemned, and the sentence upon him severely deprecated.‡

The Church party in the Commons met, in A.D. 1704, with a determination to carry matters with a high hand. The Occasional Bill, still more modified, was accordingly tacked to the Land-tax Bill, on the credit of

---

* Wilson's De Foe, ii. 137.

† "For God or Baal; or, No Neutrality in Religion. Preached against Occasional Nonconformity." Quoted in the "Interest of England in respect to Protestant Dissenters," pp. 58-9," A.D. 1703.

‡ "The Rights of Protestant Dissenters," A.D. 1704-5.

which Marlborough had just concluded a treaty with Prussia. It was taken for granted that the Peers would not reject a measure on the carriage of which the national faith had been pledged, and the success of the war depended. But the High Church party had, in the extravagance of their zeal, overreached themselves. They were deserted by their own friends, and the tack was rejected by 251 to 134 votes. This, however, did not dishearten them. The Bill, without the tack, was still persisted in, and again carried through the Commons. When it made its appearance in the Lords, Anne herself went down to hear the debate. Her presence had the effect of exciting the orators to unusual vehemence, even on this question; but it was understood that, at present, she did not desire that the Bill should pass. It was rejected by a majority of thirty-four, Marlborough and Godolphin both voting against it.* From this time the extreme Tories were nicknamed "Tackers;" their violence had made them unpopular; the Whigs were slowly rising to power, and the Occasional Conformity Bill slept the long sleep, for such a measure, of seven years.

This resolute and repeated attack against the civil rights of Dissenters had thus, owing to the exigencies of party, failed of its purpose. It was not, however, the only assault that was made upon them at this period. At no time was a more strenuous effort made to bring back, by the legitimate weapons of argument, the moderate Dissenters to the Church, than in the last years of King William's and the earlier years of Queen Anne's

* Chandler's Debates, A.D. 1704. Boyer's Annals, vol. iii.

reigns. The whole argument at issue, between the Church and the moderate party especially, was set forth on the part of Churchmen, with an ability of intellect, a fulness of learning, and a candour of spirit, which, at such a period, when the tempers of men had become softened by mutual charity, were likely to tell with successful force on the ranks of Dissent. There were many, and those the men of strongest brain and highest character, who had long been convinced that the best means to strengthen a church were those which were most in accordance with Christianity itself. Tillotson, Tenison, Burnet, Stillingfleet, and Patrick, were conscious that the attitude which the Established Church had hitherto assumed towards those who differed from her communion, had been a blunder as well as a crime. Persecution had only strengthened the persecuted. How was it possible that men, and especially good men, should be attracted towards a church which had always borne to them a forbidding aspect; which had been little more than an incarnation of Pagan vices, instead of Christian virtues ; and whose history had been signalized by repeated acts of the most deliberate oppression and cruelty? Instead, therefore, of invoking the vengeance of the civil magistrate, and instead of calling for more penal laws, the new order of Churchmen seriously prepared themselves to meet the Dissenters with their own weapons. In place of a collection of Acts of Parliament they published a " collection of Cases" which had been written to recover Dissenters to the Communion of the Church.* Here Sherlock,

---

* " A Collection of Cases," &c., A.D. 1698.

Dean of St. Paul's, Williams, Bishop of Chichester, and Freeman, Dean of Peterborough, discoursed of the terms of communion in things indifferent in religion; scrupulous consciences were attempted to be quieted, and their doubts satisfied by Sharpe, Archbishop of York; objections to the Book of Common Prayer were answered by Dr. Claget; Fowler, Bishop of Gloucester, undertook to show that the accordance, in certain particulars, of the Established Church with the Church of Rome, was no sufficient reason for Dissent; Hooper, Dean of Canterbury, vindicated his Church from the imputation of Romanism, and Tenison persuasively urged the interests of Protestantism as a reason why there should be no separation from the Established Protestant Church. These " Cases," twenty-three in number, are singularly free from many of the vices of theological controversy. They are characterized by great intelligence of treatment and fairness of argument. Of personal abuse, or the imputation of dishonesty in opponents, there is so little, that only a person who seeks for those blemishes could find them. The worst that can be said against all the writers is, that they are uniformly dull and prolix ; but that this was not considered a great fault, is evidenced by the fact that, whether caused by curiosity, interest, or by a desire to make proselytes, the Collection speedily passed through several editions. In conjunction with other circumstances, it is not at all improbable that these writings aided to thin the ranks of Dissent. Men who were already disposed to conform would at least find an excuse for taking the final step in the heavily-marshalled but friendly arguments of these exemplary controversialists.

The publication of Calamy's "Abridgment of the Life of Baxter" also gave occasion for a revival of the respective claims of Church and Dissent. Calamy, in one of the chapters of his work, had stated in plain and unexaggerated language, the reasons why Dissenters such as Baxter had separated from the ecclesiastical Establishment. His justification of this Dissent was received as an attack on the Church, and was answered with no little vehemence by a clergyman named Olyffe, and by Benjamin Hoadly, afterwards Bishop of Bangor.* Hoadly wrote with the hope of conquest animating his heart. He avowedly treated of those questions only which separated such men as Calamy from the Church; for their Dissent he judged to be more unaccountable than the separation of others. He thought it quite possible to convince these men of their error; for, he said, "there is somewhat both in the principles and the practice of these persons which suffers me not to think it altogether an hopeless attempt." Hoadly was the best specimen of Broad-churchmanship in his time; and if any writer could have succeeded in such an enterprise as the one he had undertaken, he would certainly have done so. The logical faculty in his intellectual constitution being subordinate to sentiment, he was a man of catholic principles respecting creeds; he held many views in common with Dissenters concerning the relative rights of peoples and sovereigns and Church and State, and was an open and fearless disputant. With all this he had utterly miscalculated the nature and character of moderate Dissent, and in at-

---

* "The Reasonableness of Conformity, A.D. 1703."

tacking Calamy had equally miscalculated the strength of his adversary.

Edmund Calamy now occupied the position of the principal representative of Dissent in the metropolis. It was his pride to consider that he was descended from "moderate" Dissenters, and to be a "moderate" Dissenter himself. His grandfather and his father belonged to the two thousand who were ejected by the Act of Uniformity of A.D. 1662; and their descendant adopted, with little alteration, the faith of his celebrated ancestors. "I had," he says, in the "Life" of himself, which has often been quoted in these pages, "moderation instilled into me from my very cradle."* When he had become celebrated for his preaching, Bishop Burnet consulted him as to the opinions, in ecclesiastical matters, of "the more moderate sort of Dissenters," "with whom," he remarks, "I was known to be most conversant."† Calamy's Dissent, however, was not less firm or conscientious because it was "moderate." The line which divided him, and perhaps the majority of Dissenters of this period, was not so broad as that which divided the Congregationalists, Baptists, and Friends, who were occasionally classified together under the title of "high Dissenters," from the ecclesiastical Establishment, but it was as distinctly marked. Being narrower it could be more easily stepped across, and accordingly most, if not all, of the secessions to the State Church were from the moderate or old Presbyterian ranks. But in the instances in which this Dissent was not merely hereditary or accidental, but conscientious, it was clung

---

* "Own Life," vol. i. 72.   † Ib. 470.

to with a tenacity quite as intense as that which characterized the more extreme sections. It may be difficult to explain why it should have been the case, but it is evident that the class to which Calamy belonged, considered their Dissent to be of a superior order to that of their brethren. Ecclesiastically, if not religiously, it was reckoned as of higher birth; it was more aristocratic in its pretensions; its adherents were more wealthy, and occupied a better social position; it stood nearer to the great, popular, and patronized Establishment than did the more unfashionable sects. There was, accordingly, the slightest tinge of Pharisaic pride in its attitude towards meaner brethren. The Congregationalists, Baptists, and Friends, might be good men, but they were not "moderate." Some of them questioned the scripturalness of a national establishment of religion, even of a national establishment of Presbyterianism: did it not follow that they were men of an inferior understanding and of a vulgar mind?

Calamy was the ablest and best representative of the last generation of Puritans. He appears, from the indications afforded in his "Own Life," to have been a man of courtly manners and affable address, shrewd in his dealings with men, and politic in his management of public affairs. He was one of a class who never allow their zeal to outrun their discretion. He was an eminently "safe" man. While, however, he was possessed, in a large degree, of the merely prudential virtues, he was not wanting in higher qualities. He was an active pastor, an unusually successful preacher, and a good and accurate scholar. The historical literature of Dissent is more indebted to him than it is to any other man. His "Life of Baxter," his Memorial of the two thousand ejected ministers; his defences of the character of the Puritans from the attacks of Archdeacon Echard and of Walker, and his "Own Life," are works which have laid, not merely English Dissenters, but all Englishmen under obligation to him. Nor was his own generation less indebted to him for the promptitude, vigour, and success with which he met Olyffe and Hoadly, in vindication of the principles of "moderate Nonconformity." The first portion of this work was published in the year 1703.* Hoadly was irritated by it, and immediately addressed "A Serious Admonition" to Calamy, which was followed by a treatise on the "Reasonableness of Conformity," and this by a defence of the "Reasonableness." Calamy also added two works to his first, the third of which was published in A.D. 1705. These works are remarkable for two characteristics. The positions sustained by the author are nothing but the old positions of the Puritans, in advance of which Calamy had not moved one step. The general ground taken was that the Established Church was unscriptural in its constitution and its ceremonies. But if this were the case, how could Calamy defend occasional conformity? The Presbyterians, in fact, pulled down their own arguments by their practice. When they observed conformity they did so on the plea that there was little difference between the two communions; when they justified their Dissent they did so because of the greatness of that difference. The second characteristic of Calamy's Defence is its masculine style. It is the first exposition of the reasons

---

* "Defence of Modern Nonconformity."

of Dissent written in modern English—the English of Addison and Pope, as distinguished from that of Shakespeare and Hooker.

But this mode of controversy did not satisfy the High Church zealots. Arguments which could not be enforced by a more effective weapon than reason were held by them in contempt. Having failed in all their appeals to the Legislature, they now raised the cry that the Church was in danger; not, it was insinuated, from Dissenters alone, but from the Crown itself. Anne's temporary desertion of them, in the case of the Occasional Conformity Bill, had stung them to the quick. One writer was found bold enough to put in print what the clergy talked only at home or at most in the coffee-houses. This was Dr. Drake, who, in a pamphlet entitled the "Memorial of the Church of England," attacked, with furious animosity, the Queen's ministers, the bishops, and all who had contributed to the failure of High Church tactics. The nation, remarked Drake, had for a long time abounded with sectaries; the sons of those who had overturned both Church and State, and who were heirs of their designs, yet remained in the country. The Church, the author went on to say, would be strong enough to encounter these men but for the treachery and supineness of its members. The head of the Church was inclined only to forgive and forget; she gave them comfortable speeches and kind assurances, while her prime minister gave them his countenance. The bishops were preaching indifference, and had extinguished the noble spirit which had animated their predecessors. Politicians were told that it was dangerous to rely too much on the apparent supineness of the clergy, or on their passive principles, for it was not to be expected that they would long bear to be used as they had been, or see the party in power courted at their expense, for the Church was in danger.* Here, at last, was found a cry which, like the war-whoop of an American Indian, was sufficient to excite the whole clerical race to do final battle. Every pulpit at once echoed with it. In the coffee-houses nothing was spoken of but the Church's danger. With such a cry the Whigs could be extinguished and the Dissenters exterminated. Drake's pamphlet was a repetition of De Foe's "Shortest Way" without its satire. Those who dreaded the consequences of its publication denounced it as a forgery. It was a second part of the "Shortest Way,"† and it was not written by a High Churchman. De Foe himself greeted its appearance with undisguised expressions of gratification. He publicly thanked the author for convincing the world that what he had said ironically was now declared to be true literally.‡ Reviewing the history of the High Church party from the accession of the Queen to the time of this publication, he showed that Drake's doctrines were the goals to which they had always tended.§ Pamphlet now followed pamphlet. The grand jury of Middlesex, Ashhurst the Presbyterian in the chair, made a presentation against it. By their order it was burned before the Royal Exchange, the Sheriff of London attending to witness the burning. ‖ This cere-

---

* "The Memorial of the Church of England," A.D. 1705.
† Leslie's "Rehearsal," No. 98.   ‡ Review, ii. 266—270.
§ "The High Church Legion," A.D. 1705.
‖ Boyer's "Annals," iv. 174—177.

mony, a stupid relic of the *auto dà fe*, was almost as frequently witnessed in the "Augustan age" of Queen Anne as it had been in that of Queen Elizabeth. What a revolution in thought had occurred between the two periods may be seen by the burning of the "memorial." Drake, in Elizabeth's days, would have been made a bishop, and Calamy and his books would probably have shared the fate of Penry and his works. But the Presbyterian could now preach within ear-shot of the Queen's palace, while the High Church bigot saw his pamphlet condemned to the greatest public ignominy. The fact might have suggested, both to High Churchmen and to Presbyterians, that burning books did not, as they seemed to think, annihilate thoughts.

The Legislature which had been so zealous in prosecuting De Foe could scarcely ignore Dr. Drake. On December the 5th, A.D. 1705, on the motion of Lord Halifax, the House of Lords took into its consideration the alleged danger of the Established Church. The debate was led by the Earl of Rochester, who stated his belief that such danger existed. He ascribed it to the Act of Security in Scotland, which, while it established Presbyterianism as the national religion, had not tolerated Episcopacy; but this, as it was subsequently pointed out, was not a correct description of the ecclesiastical condition of Scotland, for Episcopacy, although not endowed, was tolerated in the same sense that Dissent was tolerated in England. Another reason assigned by the speaker was that the Occasional Bill had not passed; and this, indeed, was the exciting cause of the cry. The Earl of Halifax, in deriding the affected anxiety of Churchmen, called attention to the fact that, soon after the accession of William the Third to the throne, the cry of the Church in danger began, and that it had been continued all through that sovereign's reign. The suggestion conveyed by this remark was, no doubt, sufficiently obvious to those who heard it. It was, that a Church of England, framed according to the ideal of the High Church party, could not co-exist with a constitutional government, and that its old pretensions were opposed to those rights of the subject which it was the design of the Revolution to establish. The Bishop of London recognized this suggestion, by immediately adding that, in the doctrines contained in a sermon which had been recently preached before the Corporation of London, by Hoadly, in which the right of resistance to a bad government was sustained with all the boldness of which Hoadly was so capable, he saw a source of danger to the Church. Burnet, with his quick and ready wit, aptly retorted on his brother bishop for this unfortunate observation. He recollected that Compton, since his appointment to the Episcopal office, was the bishop who, himself, had taken arms against James, by joining the revolutionary standard at Nottingham. "His lordship," therefore, remarked Burnet, "ought to be the last man to complain of that sermon, for, if its doctrine was not good, he did not know what defence his lordship could make to his appearing in arms." Sharp, Archbishop of York, now pointed out another source of danger. Drawing an arrow from Sacheverell's quiver, he gravely suggested that the greatest danger was to be apprehended from the increase of Dissenters, and particularly from the many academies which they had established. The archbishop followed up this attack by moving, almost in Sacheverell's words, that the judges be consulted as to what laws were in force against such seminaries, and by what means they could be suppressed Sharp found in Lord Wharton an ironical seconder. Wharton's memory was as apt and faithful as Burnet's. He remembered that Sharp himself had had his two sons educated at a Dissenting academy. "I second the motion," he cried "for a noble lord in this House has had both his sons educated at one of these institutions." Three Liberal bishops—Patrick, of Ely, Hooper, of Bath and Wells, and Hough, of Lichfield and Coventry—next followed. The last spoke plainly what was in the thoughts of the majority who were present. "If," he said, "a source of danger existed anywhere, it was to be found in the clergy, and the clergy only." This closed the debate and it was then formally resolved, "That the Church of England, which was rescued from the extremest danger by King William the Third, of glorious memory, is now, by God's blessing, in a most safe and flourishing condition, and whosoever goes about to suggest and insinuate that the Church is in danger under her Majesty's administration, is an enemy to the Queen, the Church, and the kingdom." This resolution was at once communicated to the Commons, when the van of the High Church party again led the attack on Dissent. Bromley, who had brought in the Occasional Bill, dwelt on the increase of Presbyterian schools and seminaries; Pakington, with equal lugubriousness, enlarged on the increase of Presbyterian conventicles; but words which had told with effect when used against Dissenters only, were comparatively powerless when the honour of the Crown was, by a happy coincidence, identified with their liberties. The Commons, therefore, sustained the resolution of the Lords by a majority of fifty-two.* The next step was the issue of a proclamation by the Queen, which recited that several persons, endeavouring to foment animosities, and to cover designs which they dared not publicly own, had "falsely, seditiously, and maliciously" suggested the Church to be in danger. Order, therefore, was given to all judges, justices, magistrates, sheriffs, mayors, and bailiffs, to "apprehend, prosecute, and punish" such persons. Again, the High Church party suffered defeat, and again was supplied fresh stimulus to take, on the earliest occasion that might offer, their revenge on the Dissenters.

One of the most characteristic illustrations in English history of the manner in which it has been sought to place the interests of the Established Church before the general interests of the nation, occurred in the following year. No measure of supreme importance, whether for a good or for an evil purpose, has ever been brought before the nation, which has not, to some extent, been affected by a consideration of its probable influence on the fortunes of the Church. The broad stream of English history, whether flowing in peace or in turbulence, has had its course mainly directed by minds in which care for the public welfare has been entirely subordinated to a desire for the predominance of the particular ecclesiastical institution which the State had linked to its own fortunes. It had been, for many years, the desire of the most ardent patriots and

---

* "Parliamentary History," vi. 479—507.

greatest statesmen, to bring about a legislative union between England and Scotland. In the year 1706-7, owing partly to the management of Lord Barrington and De Foe, who had been sent to Scotland for the purpose, the northern Parliament had agreed to the proposed terms of this union. On the 10th January, therefore, in this year, a bill was introduced into the House of Lords for sanctioning the union. No manner of objection but one was offered to this great measure. It was acknowledged that it would tend to preserve and increase peaceful relations between the two kingdoms; it was acknowledged that trade would be largely augmented, and that the security of the Protestant succession to the Crown would be greatly strengthened, if not finally secured, by the Act; but was it not possible that the presence of Presbyterian Peers and Commoners in the Parliament of Great Britain would tend to endanger the safety and supremacy of the Church of England? The clergy at once took alarm. The Lower House of Convocation, which was then sitting, appointed committees to consider the subject. It was well known of what nature the report of those committees would be, and it was stated that the Lower House intended to address the Commons against the measure. Anne, therefore, took the decisive step of proroguing this body for three weeks.* During this interval, the measure underwent discussion in the legislature, in which its sole opponents were the members of the ultra-Church party. Amongst these, the Earl of Nottingham, Lords North and Grey,

---

* Lathbury's "History," p. 402. Burnet's "Own Times," p. 806. Tindal's Continuation, iii. 794.

Lord Haversham, and the Bishop of Bath and Wells, spoke against it. It was urged that there would be danger to the Church in union with a country in which Presbyterianism was established by law;* that it might result in the bishops being turned out of the House of Lords;† that it would be generally of the most dangerous consequence to the Church,‡ and that Scotch members should be prevented from voting on any ecclesiastical matters.§ The bill, however, passed. When Convocation again met, it met with a feeling of exasperation which led the Lower House beyond the bounds of loyalty. They at once drew up a representation, protesting that no such arbitrary course had been adopted by the Crown since the Act of Submission of Henry the Eighth. The records were searched, and it was found that there were several precedents for such a step. This act of the clergy was too much even for Anne, who, herself, wrote to state that they had invaded her supremacy. Her message was received with studious contempt, and was followed by another royal prorogation.‖ The Dissenters, on the other hand, showed their gratification with the measure by preaching sermons in its honour on the day appointed for a public thanksgiving, and by presenting, through the medium of the Dissenting ministers of the three denominations, a special address of congratulation to the Queen.¶

With Marlborough and Godolphin, united with the

---

* Earl of Nottingham's Speech, Jan. 10.
† Lord Haversham's Speech, Feb 3.
‡ Lords North and Grey's Speech, ib.
§ Bishop of Bath and Wells' Speech, ib.
‖ Lathbury's "History," pp. 402, 403.
¶ This address is in Calamy's "Own Life," vol. ii. pp. 63, 64. Note.

leading members of the Whig party in power, the Legislature was, for two years, free from the compulsion to debate ecclesiastical affairs. Such a condition of quiet was, however, ill-suited to the designs of the High Church party. In the autumn of the year 1709, Sacheverell sounded, from the pulpit of St. Paul's cathedral, the first blast of a new war. In a sermon on the "Perils of False Brethren both in Church and State," preached before the lord mayor and aldermen of London, on the anniversary of the Gunpowder Plot, Sacheverell boldly attacked the doctrines of the Revolution, the course of legislation which had been pursued since that time, the men who had conducted the national affairs, and the liberties still enjoyed by Dissenters. The doctrine especially attacked was that of the right of resistance; the "false brethren" were the Whigs and the Dissenters, and those who, by their active connivance or from apathy, allowed the Whigs to govern and the Dissenters to be tolerated. He affirmed that the great security of government was the belief of the subject's obligation to an absolute and unconditional obedience to the supreme power, and the utter illegality of resistance upon any pretence whatsoever. The opposite doctrine was characterized as a "damnable position," and equivalent to "rebellion and high treason." He raked, from the dung-pits of the worst and lowest style of ecclesiastical controversy, every word which could depreciate the motives or the character of Dissenters. He charged them with committing "the most abominable impieties," and with justifying "murder, sacrilege, and rebellion, by texts of Scripture;" they were filthy "dreamers, and despisers of dominion;" in their seminaries "atheism, deism, Lutheranism, Socinianism, with all the hellish principles of fanaticism, regicide, and anarchy, were taught;" they were "monsters and vipers," "sanctified hypocrites," "unhallowed, loathsome, and detestable;" "miscreants, begot in rebellion, born in sedition, and nursed up in faction." The Bishops of the Church were called upon to "thunder out their ecclesiastical anathemas" against them, and all true Churchmen were exhorted to have no fellowship with their works of darkness.*

The proper way to have treated such a man as this would have been, either to have left him alone or to have sent him to a madhouse; but, unhappily, Godolphin was stung to personal resentment against Sacheverell by a contemptuous comparison of him, in this sermon, to Ben Jonson's character of "Volpone."† It was therefore decided to impeach Sacheverell before the House of Lords, for "high crimes and misdemeanors." The trial began on the 27th February, A.D. 1709-10. No state-trial since the impeachment of the seven bishops had created such an excitement. A special court was erected in Westminster Hall, and there, on the first morning, the Lords, accompanied by the judges, the masters in Chancery, the peers' eldest sons and peers minor, the heralds, and other officers of the House, proceeded in state.‡ The Commons, in Committee of the whole House, were accommodated with seats within the bar. The articles of impeachment

---

* "Perils amongst False Brethren," A.D. 1709, *pass.*

† Swift's "Memoirs relating to the Change of Ministry."

‡ "The Tryal of Dr. Henry Sacheverell," &c. Published by order of the House of Peers, A.D. 1710.

charged Sacheverell with maintaining that the Revolution had been brought about by odious and unjustifiable means; that the toleration which had been approved by the legislature was unwarrantable, and that those who defended the liberty of conscience granted by it were " false brethren;" that the Church was in a condition of peril under her Majesty's administration; that the administration tended to the destruction of the constitution; and that the Queen and her ministers were chargeable with general bad conduct of the affairs of the nation. Sacheverell denied the accuracy of the whole of these charges.

In the ten days during which the subsequent proceedings lasted, the populace became mad with enthusiasm for Sacheverell, and with rage against his opponents. The man himself, who was scorned by those who were making him their tool;* who had not one of the qualities even of an able preacher, and who lived on the garbage of the popular passions, suddenly found himself exalted into a hero, with a fame as celebrated, in his own country, as that of Marlborough himself. The mob, as he went every morning to the trial, surrounded his coach by thousands. His progress to and fro was as that of a conqueror. The women begged to kiss his hands; every one who passed was commanded to shout "High Church and Sacheverell for ever!" or he was at once knocked down, his head cleft open, † or otherwise brutally maltreated. The Queen, who did not care to disguise her personal sympathy for Sacheverell, as she

---

* " Duchess of Marlborough's Account,"p. 247.

† Burnet's "Own Times," p. 849. " Complete History of Europe," p. 709, p. 358.

went every day to the Lords' to hear the arguments, met with a reception scarcely second to Sacheverell's own. "God bless your Majesty!" cried the insane mob "we hope your Majesty is for High Church and Dr. Sacheverell." One of the Queen's chaplains was indiscreet enough publicly to pray for his impeached brother clergyman; while all of them stood round him at the trial to give him their encouragement. The clergy almost to a man, expressed their sympathy with him.* The feelings of the mob were expressed in still more decisive manner than in shouts. Sacheverell's enemies were their enemies, and the men whom he had denounced were to be punished. Accordingly, the Congregational meeting-house of Daniel Burgess, near Lincoln's Inn, was pulled down, and the pulpit and pews burnt, to cries of "High Church and Sacheverell." A bonfire was made of Earle's meeting-house, in Drury Lane, and of other churches; Salters' Hall, Mr. Shower's church, Hoadly's church and Burnet's house, were threatened with a similar fate; but before this could be accomplished the military made their appearance, a few ringleaders were apprehended, and the people dispersed.†

The arguments of those who conducted the prosecution of Sacheverell, and of those members of the House of Lords who were in favour of his condemnation, were pointed mainly towards a proof of the constitutional legality and moral obligation of the doctrine of resistance. The fact was, that if that doctrine was

---

* "Parliamentary History," vi. 830.

† Burnet's "Own Times," p. 849, 850. Calamy's "Own Life," ii. 228. "Parliamentary History," vi. 630. Perry's "History of the Church of England," iii. 222.

denied, the Revolution and the governments which
had succeeded it stood condemned both in law and
moral equity. The weight of testimony, brought from
English history and from judicial decisions in favour of
this doctrine was overwhelming, but there was a point
at which Sacheverell's counsel could break the force of
much of this evidence. They clearly enough established
the fact that many of the greatest divines in the Church,
and many English judges and statesmen, had condemned it as equally contrary to divine law and to
the rights of English sovereigns. These men had not
even been prosecuted : why, therefore, should Sacheverell be condemned? But Sacheverell had attacked
an existing government which had been founded
on that doctrine, the sovereign herself owing her
throne to its practical application. References were frequently made, in the course of the speeches, to the conduct of the clergy. The boldest speaker on this subject
was the Duke of Argyle, who remarked that "the
clergy had in all ages delivered up the rights and liberties of the people." * " These proceedings of clergymen," said the Bishop of Oxford, "are of that dangerous tendency and consequence that if some effectual
stop be not put to them, they will put an effectual
end to our constitution."† The Lords, on March 20th,
by a vote of sixty-nine to fifty-two, found Sacheverell
guilty, and on March 23rd condemned him to suspension from his office for three years, and his sermon
preached at Derby and the sermon preached at St.
Paul's to be burned by the common hangman.‡

* " Parliamentary History," vi 846.   † Ib.
‡ " Tryal of Sacheverell," p. 326.

Such a sentence, after such a trial, was equivalent to an acquittal, and so all men treated it. If those who had pushed the prosecution forward had not before had doubts of the wisdom of their proceeding, they must have been convinced of it by the manner in which Sacheverell was received by the nation. This inflated bigot, as soon as his trial was over, made a procession through England. The University of Oxford received him with honours; at Banbury, the mayor and corporation went out to meet him; at Warwick, he was welcomed by a body of horsemen headed by the mayor and aldermen; at Shrewsbury, five thousand horsemen met him on his way to the town, and gave him their escort; at Bridgewater, the road he was to travel was lined for miles with people from all the surrounding country, the hedges were decorated with flowers, and four thousand horse and three thousand foot constituted themselves his body-guard; at Ludlow, riding into the town on a white palfrey, he was received with sounding trumpets and flying colours.* The Dissenters, as a matter of course, felt the vengeance of the excited mobs. At Wrexham, among other places, the effigies of the Dissenting ministers were burnt; at the same town, an effigy of Dr. Daniel Williams was buried, and an effigy of Hoadly scourged, pilloried, and then drowned.† When Sacheverell's period of suspension had expired, bells were rung, bonfires were lit, and illuminations made all over the kingdom to celebrate the happy event. On the Sunday following he preached a sermon at St. Saviour's Southwark, in which he compared his

---

* Boyer's "Annals," vol. ix.   † Wilson's "Life of De Foe," iii. 109, 110.

sufferings with those of Christ.* He was next called upon to preach before the House of Commons. The Queen rewarded him with the benefice of St. Andrew's, Holborn, one of the most valuable in the metropolis. But in the possession of a good income, and in the enjoyment of the social advantages of a high clerical position, Sacheverell's zeal expired. The world, after his promotion, heard little more from his lips of the dangers of the Church and the nation. He had, however, done enough for one man and one life to satisfy the highest ambition. Under the influence excited by his prosecution, the Whigs were hurled from power; and a vulgar sermon, preached by a comparatively illiterate man, changed the Government of the country, the fortunes of generals and statesmen, and the destinies of the nations of Europe.†

If any in the nation were, at this time, in danger, it was the Dissenters. Although they were still almost as active as before in opening new places of worship, they were, as has been seen from the statements made in the discussions on occasional conformity, losing ground in two directions. Many of their ministers were seceding to the Established Church, and, in some parts of the

* "Parliamentary History," ix. 1208.
† "The trial of Dr. Sacheverell had raised or discovered such a spirit in all parts, that the ministers could very safely leave the electors to themselves."—Swift's "Memoirs relating to the Change in the Queen's Ministry," Works, ii. 196.
"He (Sacheverell) hates the new ministry mortally, and they hate him and pretend to despise him too. They will not allow him to have been the occasion of the late change; at least some of them will not, but my lord keeper owned it to me the other day."—Swift's "Journal to Stella," Aug. 23, 1711. The accession of this ministry to power led to the peace of Utrecht.

country at least, there was a considerable decrease in their numbers. The causes of this decrease have already been hinted at; but in addition to the mild attitude of the liberal Church party, the practice of occasional conformity, and the absence of a sufficiently energetic assertion of their civil rights, there were other circumstances which, undoubtedly, had great influence in contributing to their depression. The first of these was the loss by death of all the great leaders who had been ejected by the Bartholomew Act. Few of the younger generation of Dissenters, in the latter part of the reign of Queen Anne, could have known anything of Baxter, Bates, Howe, Owen, Kiffin, Knollys, or Fox, but from their works or from the lips of their fathers. Personal attachment to these men kept many in the ranks of Dissent, who stayed no longer than life stayed with their old pastors. The frown of the Court could have had no less influence in deterring men from connecting themselves with any of the Free Churches. The only congregation at this time in London, with which a comparatively considerable proportion of the aristocracy was still connected, was Edmund Calamy's, in Westminster, and this proportion was rapidly decreasing.* It is difficult to say whether the general withdrawal of Dissenters from other circles of society, which began at this period, had much effect upon their numbers; but it certainly decreased, as it has ever since done, their moral influence.

* The Bedford family, who had formerly attended Manton's ministry, transferred themselves on his death to that of Mr. Cotton, of Dyot Street, Bloomsbury. Cotton was chaplain in the family of the dowager ladies Robert and James Russell; Lady Clinton also attended his ministry. Wilson, iv. 385.

To a great degree, this withdrawal was compulsory. It was a necessary result of their exclusion from the best places of education, and of the general tone of public opinion. But it was not necessary that Dissenters should have withdrawn themselves also from intercourse with literary persons. With a few remarkable exceptions, however, it was apparently the opinion of the generality of ministers now rising that it was most undesirable for religious persons to read any but technically religious books. The strictness of Puritanism without its strength or its piety, was beginning to reign. With the death of the ejected two thousand and their contemporaries the intercourse of Dissenters, excepting for purposes of trade, with the "outer world," almost ceased. Shakespeare's plays were forbidden writings, and Bacon was a "profane" and unknown author. The "Spectator" was probably unknown to nine-tenths of the members of the Free Churches. Any person reading the memoirs, diaries and letters of this reign, might naturally imagine himself to be reading of two totally different periods of English history. He would scarcely gather, from any work written by a Dissenter, that such men as Addison, Steele, or Pope, had lived at the same time as themselves.* He would infer, from the controversial writings of the great essayists, and from certain references in contemporary correspondence, that a class of people called Dissenters existed at the period when the writers were in existence,

---

* I am aware that Watts contributed to the "Spectator;" that Grove, the head master of the Taunton Academy, was a frequent contributor to the same periodical, and that Hughes, the friend of Addison, Pope, and Watts, also wrote for the "Spectator," "Tatler," and "Guardian;" but these instances were exceptional.

but who they were he could not even guess. On the part of Dissenters this unwise and unnatural estrangement came at last to be taken as a matter of course. It grew into a habit, and had almost the influence of a holy tradition. Narrow as they were good, men did not consider that few things could be more unfortunate for a nation than for its purest religion to be divorced from its best literature. As was plainly enough proved, also, during and immediately after the trial of Sacheverell, Dissent was as unpopular with the lower as it was with the upper classes of society. Debased and ignorant to the last degree, the labourers and mechanics of Queen Anne's reign were, in matters of belief, if their attachment to the Church may be correctly described by a word which implies thought and reason, under the natural control of the squires and the clergy. They followed the religion which the Queen, the aristocracy, and the local gentry followed, and which they had been taught, from their births, was the only respectable religion.

The principal representatives of the Presbyterian ministry at this period were Dr. Daniel Williams, of New Broad Street, Dr. Edmund Calamy, of Westminster, William Tong, of Salters' Hall, John Shower, of Old Jewry, Dr. John Evans, Dr. Grosvenor, of Crosby Square, and Dr. Wright, of Blackfriars. The characters and labours of Williams and Calamy have already been noticed. Tong, before he was chosen as minister of Salter's Hall, had preached with great success at Chester, Knutsford, and Coventry, in the neighbourhood of which, by his evangelistic work, he had laid the foundation of many other churches. His election to the Salters' Hall Church, where he succeeded Nathaniel Taylor, whom Doddridge has described as the "Dissenting South," elevated him to the pastorate of the principal Presbyterian and one of the wealthiest, if not the wealthiest, Dissenting congregation in London. He was a man of large learning and culture, and of exquisitely graceful manners. He is remembered, now, principally by his memoir of Matthew Henry, who succeeded him at Chester. Shower, as a preacher, excelled in pathos, and was remarkable for his gift of prayer. His publications consist exclusively of sermons, the majority of them preached on occasion of the deaths of eminent persons.* Dr. Evans was, at this time, co-pastor with Daniel Williams, and was now, probably, occupied in collecting the materials for a History of Nonconformity, which, he not living to finish, was afterwards taken up by Daniel Neal. From his vigilance, activity, and energy, and peculiar adaptation for public work, Dr. Evans was engaged in all the affairs of the Dissenters of his time.† To such a man, at a period when Dissent was attacked from all sides, more labour than reputation must have been gained; but Dr. Evans was also one of the most effective preachers and useful writers of his denomination. At Crosby Square, where Charnock had formerly been pastor, Dr. Benjamin Grosvenor preached. Grosvenor had originally been connected with the Baptists, and was a member of Keach's Church, but upon his return from his academical studies, joined the Presbyterians. His acute intellect, his cheerful temperament, his graceful elocution, and his devotional spirit soon raised him to the highest position

---

* Ib. ii. 308—320.
† Wilson's "Dissenting Churches," ii. 212—220; Harris's "Funeral Sermon," A.D. 1730.

amongst the Dissenting ministers of the metropolis. He was a favourite lecturer at Salters' Hall and at the Weigh-house, and one of the best historical students of his day. Dr. Grosvenor's ministry extended over fifty years, from the end of King William's to the end of George the Second's reign.*

In Matthew Sylvester's old Church in Blackfriars Dr. Samuel Wright preached. Wright's Church was one of the places of worship which was nearly destroyed by Sacheverell's mob. The people afterwards removed to Carter Lane. Wright's eminence as a preacher was such that Herring, afterwards Archbishop of Canterbury, in order to learn elocution, frequently attended his ministry. The Presbyterians could also, in London, number several eminent laymen. They were largely represented in the Courts of the Aldermen and Common Council of the City. Sir Thomas Abney, in whose house Watts became a guest for nearly forty years, was the most conspicuous of these. The family of the Ashursts had also, as it has always had, its representative in the Free Churches of the metropolis. Of all the members, however, of the Presbyterian body, De Foe was the most eminent; but he took more interest in the public relations of Dissent than he did in its internal organization.

Foremost among the country ministers of this period was Matthew Henry, of Chester, son of Philip Henry, a man whose holy character dated almost from his birth. Matthew Henry was the founder of the Chester Church. No man more exemplified the graces of Christianity than he. In devotion to his ministerial work he equalled

---

* Crosby's "History," iv. 203. Wilson's "Dissenting Churches," i. 344—351. Barker's Funeral Sermon.

his father; the fervency of his preaching excelled that of any other person; and his "Life of Philip Henry" and his Commentary on the Scriptures have earned for him the highest name amongst Nonconformist divines. Henry removed in A.D. 1712 to Hackney, to take the pastorate of the Church formerly presided over by Bates, and died two years afterwards. "Great," said Dr. Daniel Williams, in his funeral sermon for Henry, "was his acceptance, though his lot was to be in an age wherein the office is so despised, that the same qualifications which commend all others can scarce preserve a minister from contempt." His death, says the same author, was the subject of "universal mourning."*

There died, in the year 1710, another person whose name is intimately identified with the history of the Free Churches. This was Lady Hewley, wife of Sir John Hewley, of York. During her lifetime this eminently pious and benevolent woman was a chief supporter of the Presbyterian congregations in the north of England. Her personal charity to ministers seemed to know no limit. In the year 1704, Lady Hewley executed a deed conveying valuable landed property to trustees for the use of "poor godly preachers of Christ's Gospel;" for the support of the Gospel in poor places, and for exhibitions, or scholarships, in aid of the education of young men for the ministry.† Although she was a Presbyterian she placed no sectarian limit on the application either of this or of her other charities. She was what

---

* Tong's "Life of Matthew Henry." Williams's Works, ii. 459.

† "History, Opinions, and Present Legal Position of the English Presbyterians," pp. 114, 115, A.D. 1834. Wilson's Historical Inquiry," pp. 250, 251.

in these days would be termed an orthodox Christian, or a moderate Calvinist. Whether she would have bequeathed such property, under such a catholic and open trust, if she could have known that a large proportion of the funds derived therefrom would ultimately be applied to purposes which the Presbyterians of her day would have characterized by every evil name, may be honestly questioned.

Amongst the Congregational Ministers of London, in the reign of Queen Anne, the name of Isaac Watts stands pre-eminent. On the day of the death of William III., Watts, then twenty-seven years of age, had been chosen as successor to Dr. Chauncey, of Mark Lane. It was no slight honour for any man to stand in the pulpit which had been occupied by Caryl, Owen, and Clarkson; and few of those who chose him, although he had been their assistant pastor for four years, could have anticipated that they had selected a minister who was destined to shed a lustre on their church equal to that which it had received from the pastorate of Owen himself. Isaac Watts had been born and cradled in Nonconformity. His father, a deacon in the Congregational Church at Southampton, was imprisoned for six months for his attachment to Nonconformist principles, and he drew nourishment from his mother's breast while she sat on the steps of the gaol in which her husband was confined. His genius for poetical composition seems to have been inbred, for as soon as he could write he wrote in verse. In A.D. 1705 he published his "Lyric Poems," and two years afterwards the "Hymns and Spiritual Songs." With the exception of an Essay on Uncharitableness, and a Sermon, these were, as yet, all the works by which he was publicly known; but they were sufficient to rank him amongst the most eloquent of preachers and the most original of Christian poets. The poetry of the Christian Church in England, until Watts published his Hymns, was unaccountably inferior to all the other means of Christian worship. More sublime discourses have never been preached than had been preached since the establishment of the Reformation. From Hooper, Latimer, and Cartwright, to Bunyan, Charnock, South and Howe, there had been a succession of orators of the highest order of Christian eloquence. Prayer seemed to be a Divine gift to the Puritans of both ages. They were men who wrestled with God, with strong cries and tears, and who wrestled until they prevailed. But of Christian song, as an art, they knew little or nothing. Excepting in the mountains and woods, it had, indeed, been dangerous, until thirty years ago, to exercise it. They did sing, but only a rough and uncouth doggrel. Sternhold and Hopkins, Tate and Brady, with their limping lines, and poverty-stricken thought, were the Churchman's necessary choice, and the scarcely superior Patrick and Bunyan,—for Bunyan the hymn-writer was not equal to Bunyan the preacher and dreamer—the almost sole refuge of the Nonconformist. Some of the finest ore of Christian poetry had been wrought into the happiest verse in the ancient and the mediæval churches, but much of it had been lost, and little of what had been left was known. What is most remarkable is that the hymns of Protestant Germany should, apparently, have been equally unknown. The early Reformers of Queen Elizabeth's reign, during their exile in the towns of Germany and Switzerland, must have become well acquainted with these hymns. The Presbyterians and Congregationalists of James II.'s reign, some of whom were educated at the German Universities, and many of whom had resided and travelled for some years on the Continent, must also have been familiar with them; but no translation of them was either imagined or attempted. But for the enjoyment and the culture of pure devotional poetry a period of comparative rest from the struggle for mere existence is required. Many of Luther's Hymns are religious war-songs, and, like the songs sung by the minstrels to the Plantagenet Crusaders, were written to nerve Christian warriors to fight against the enemies of Christian freedom. Excepting at the time of the Commonwealth, no such religious war had taken place in England, but the Puritans of the Commonwealth drew their inspiration from the Book of Judges and the Psalms. The songs of Miriam and Deborah, and the wrathful imprecations of David, well served their need. But now that rest had been felt and enjoyed, and comparative peace had come upon the churches, there arose a half-unconscious desire for better words of praise. No sooner, accordingly, did Watts's Hymns appear than they were eagerly sought for and joyfully used. They were like showers of rain on the parched earth; and from nearly all the free Christian Churches of England and America a new harvest of praise to God at once arose.

Dr. Johnson, who never commended when he could detract, and who grudged to acknowledge the existence of any virtue or ability in a Dissenter, has made some remarks on the devotional poetry of Watts, which, on the whole, are scarcely just or truthful. "As a poet," says the great critic, "had he been only a poet, he would probably have stood high among the authors with whom he is now associated. For his judgment was exact, and he noted beauties and faults with very nice discernment. His ear was well tuned, and his diction was elegant and copious. But his devotional poetry is, like that of others, unsatisfactory. The paucity of its topics enforces perpetual repetition, and the sanctity of the matter rejects the ornaments of figurative diction. It is sufficient for Watts to have done better than others what no man has done well."* Johnson probably read the poetry of Watts with a High Churchman's habit of thought. Its range, to him, was narrow, because it did not include many subjects which, in his public devotions, his mind had been accustomed to dwell upon. It made no reference to saints' or to "holy" days; it did not commemorate the death of the Royal martyr or the failure of the Gunpowder Plot. It was confined to the praise of the attributes and the work of the Almighty, and to the various phases of Christian experience. The feelings of the Christian man in all their infinite variety it was impossible for one person to express. Johnson's complaint that Watts's devotional poetry is deficient in sprightliness is more correct, and he might have added that it was also deficient in that almost feminine softness which, since his time, has been prized as a favourite characteristic of Christian poetry. But it was equally deficient in the coarse voluptuousness which, in the eyes of a large class of worshippers, is the chief merit of devotional song. If his imagination had ever associated together the ideas of Divine and of gross physical love,

* "Lives of the Poets," art. "Watts."

Watts would have shrunk with horror from expressing them. His fancy was as chaste as it was lofty, and was ever held in check by a profound and awful reverence for the character of the Almighty God. His errors are, for the most part, errors of style and execution. He had not the musical ear or the delicate critical judgment of Addison. His verse is often faulty in its rhythm, and careless and inaccurate in its rhyme. From its mixed vigour and tameness of thought and expression, it is singularly unequal. But, compared with everything of their kind that had gone before, his Hymns must have seemed like the addition of a new sense to the Christian worshipper.

The reputation of Watts as a poet has overshadowed his reputation as a preacher, as a man of letters, and as a philosopher; but, amongst his contemporaries, he was renowned for the latter qualities. He had, probably, the best elocution of any preacher of his generation; his sermons, while they are weighty with thought, and, as religious addresses, scrupulously faithful to the consciences of his hearers, indicate the possession of a very high order of imaginative power. It appears to have surprised even men of ability equal to his own that he could trust mainly to his extemporary power for the delivering of his discourses.* His Nonconformity, like that of nearly all his contemporaries, was, if moderate, thorough; and, as will be seen, he took an active interest in the questions which related to the religious liberties of the people. His scholarship and his acquaintance with men of letters of all descriptions did much to redeem Dissent from the charge of narrowness and littleness.

* Johnson's Lives, ib.

He was, as yet, unknown as a philosopher, and it was not until he had attained his greatest fame that, with a child's innocent heart, he wrote those " Divine and Moral Songs," which have since, to millions of the Anglo-Saxon race, been amongst the most precious of all the memories of child-life.

The position of Watts in the history of the Free Churches of England is one of peculiar interest. He is the link which unites the later Puritans to the founders of Methodism. As a young man, he was the intimate associate of Howe. Richard Cromwell also, after visiting the deathbed of the great chaplain of the great Protector, admitted him to the friendship of his old age, and to no house was Watts a more frequent visitor than to his. Cromwell's celebrated, but eccentric granddaughter, Mrs. Bendish, was a member of Watts's congregation; and Whitfield, when at the commencement of his evangelistic work, sought Watts's advice. He was a witness to the decline and extinction of Puritanism. In the generation which followed, while the Free Churches were gradually settling on a new foundation, he opposed to his utmost the united torrents of scepticism and irreligion. He lived also to see the beginning of a general revival of personal piety, to the marvellous effects of which the Free Churches of the nineteenth century owe, in greatest measure, their high character and their great numerical success.*

In the old Congregational Church in Silver Street, of

---

* For the foundation of these remarks on Dr. Watts, I am chiefly indebted to Mr. Milner's most interesting " Life," published in A.D. 1834, and, after this, to Gibbon's " Life," to Johnson's " Life," and to the Leeds edition of his works.

which Philip Nye, of the Westminster Assembly, was the first pastor, there preached a man somewhat younger in years than Watts, but destined, in his own sphere, to achieve an equally honourable, if not an equally famous, reputation. This was Daniel Neal, who, some years later, published the " History of the Puritans."* Excepting, however, as a useful and laborious preacher, Neal, at this time, was unknown. Both Watts† and Neal, as well as Dr. Evans, were educated by Thomas Rowe, the pastor of the Congregational Church at Haberdashers' Hall, and one of the most eminent tutors who have ever been connected with this body. Rowe, however, at the time of which we write, had been dead for four or five years. At New Court, Carey Street, Lincoln's Inn Fields, ministered Daniel Burgess, the wit and humourist of the Congregational denomination. Burgess combined, in some measure, the characteristic qualities of Latimer and Rowland Hill. His church was the resort of the players of Drury Lane Theatre, who, if they went in sport, must often have left in pain. Burgess, we are told, seeing so many of this profession present at his church, would often address them personally, and his ministry amongst them was so successful that many became exemplary Christians.‡ The Fetter Lane Church, another of the oldest Congregational Churches in London, was presided over by Thomas Bradbury, a man of great pulpit power, remarkable animal vivacity, and one of the

---

* It is somewhat singular that the historian of the Puritans should have been succeeded in the same pulpit by the two joint historians of Dissent, Dr. Bogue and Dr. Bennett.

† Watts, in his " Lyric Poems," has an ode addressed to Rowe—
"I love thy gentle influence, Rowe."

‡ Wilson's " Dissenting Churches," iii. 497.

most courageous defenders of the liberties of Dissenters. Bradbury almost equalled De Foe in his public denunciations of High Churchism, and his attachment to the doctrines of the Revolution was second only to his attachment to the doctrines of Christianity. If Sacheverell could preach sermons on one side of the question, Bradbury did not hesitate to preach sermons on the other side. Politics were a part of his religion, and the government of Queen Anne had no more dangerous or implacable foe than Bradbury. It is credibly stated that the Queen, who called him "the bold Bradbury," to purchase his silence, sent Harley to him with the offer of a bishopric. He was often mobbed, and once threatened with assassination, but lived, after a ministry of upwards of sixty years, to the end of George the Second's reign.* During his lifetime more than a hundred and fifty of his sermons were published.†

Matthew Clarke, of Miles' Lane Church, was another well-known preacher, remarkable for his high character, his reverent spirit, and his hospitable disposition. The epitaph on his tomb, in Bunhill Fields, is one of Watts's most elaborate efforts of this description.‡ Dr. Jabez Earle, who had been the pastor of the Weigh-House Church until A.D. 1707, was now removed to Hanover Street, Long Acre, where he remained, for more than sixty years, as one of the ablest divines of the Congregational denomination.§ In the country the most emi-

---

* No juster epitaph was ever written than that which appears on Bradbury's tomb in Bunhill Fields,—that great and holy burying-place of nearly all the eminent Dissenters of two centuries.
† Wilson's "Dissenting Churches," iii. 504—535.
‡ Ib. i. 471—491.
§ Ib. i. 169, iii. 508.

nent minister of this body was Timothy Jollie, the master of the Sheffield Academy for ministers, and one of the most successful of all its pastors.* Sir John Hartopp, in whose family Watts had been a tutor, and whose name is familiar to all who know Watts's poetical works, was the principal layman in the Congregational denomination. He was a man of unflinching integrity and courage—a standard-bearer of Nonconformity when to bear that standard was to brave certain punishment.

At the head of the Baptist denomination stood Joseph Stennett, son of Edward Stennett, his successor in the pastorate of the Seventh-day Baptist Church in Curriers' Hall, and the father and grandfather of two equally celebrated ministers of the same denomination. Joseph Stennett, although belonging to a religious body which was assumed to neglect human learning, was one of the greatest scholars who at that time adorned the pulpits of the Free Churches of the metropolis. His acquaintance with Hebrew and with historical literature was almost unrivalled. A polished preacher, possessed of an eloquence which flowed so smoothly from his lips that it was compared by his contemporaries to a silver stream which ran along without bush or shore to intercept it,† of winning manners and gentle address combined with the most inflexible adherence to principle, it is not surprising that he occupied an position inferior to that of no other minister. He represented the denomination in all public affairs; he was chosen as the spokesman of the electors of the City of London when, on an important occasion, they wished to make known their wishes to

* Wilson's "Dissenting Churches," i. 345. Note.
† Gibbon's "Life of Watts," p. 154.

their members, and was selected by the Tory government as the only man who could influence his denomination in their favour in the political crisis which ensued on the conclusion of the peace with France. On that occasion, two peers were deputed to seek an interview with Stennett, in order that the London Baptists might be induced to give an expression of their approval of the political conduct of the government. He was told that if they would comply it would secure them not only the esteem of Majesty, but any favour which they could reasonably expect. Stennett unequivocally refused to use his influence for the desired object, and Dr. Williams, on behalf of the Presbyterians, taking the same course, both were warmly thanked by the leaders of the Whig party.* Stennett had engaged to write a history of the denomination, but did not live to complete it. John Piggott probably stood next to Stennett in public estimation. He was the founder of the Baptist Church in Little Wild Street, † which, under the pastorates of Dr. Joseph and Dr. Samuel Stennett, subsequently became the principal Baptist Church in the metropolis. Not inferior to either of these men in learning was William Collins, of Petty France, one of the authors of the Confession of the faith of the Particular Baptists. Collins, however, had died in A.D. 1702.‡ To Dr. John Gale, the pastor of the Barbican Church, who, from his high literary culture, was the intimate associate of the most eminent scholars, the Baptists were indebted for a reply to Wall's "History of

---

* "Life of Stennett." Wilson's "Dissenting Churches," ii. 595—605. Ivimey's "History," iii. 24—69. Crosby's "History," iv. 319—326.

† Ivimey, iv. 565—567. ‡ Ib. 332—338.

Infant Baptism." It is probably to Gale that the subsequent tendency of the General Baptists to Unitarianism is, in part, to be traced. On the subject of the Trinity, Gale held opinions which, at least, were "latitudinarian."* No reference to the Baptists of this period would be complete without some commemoration of the labours of William Mitchell and David Crossley, the founders of the denomination in Lancashire and Yorkshire. Both these men were comparatively uneducated, but were of equally ardent religious temperament. They began, in the reign of Charles II., to preach to the people in the townships around Halifax and Whalley. In the year 1705, when Mitchell died, they had founded no fewer than twenty churches. Crossley afterwards came to London, and was guilty of some moral delinquency, but lived to redeem his character. †

The Baptist Churches of London were now organized into an association, which had been formed in the year 1704. Two subjects, especially, occupied the early attention of this body, viz., the ordination and the education of ministers. It was resolved that ordination, either to the office of an elder or a deacon, by imposition of hands, was "an ordinance of Jesus Christ still in force," ‡ and it was earnestly recommended that every church should contribute to a fund for the better education of persons who were fitted for the ministry. It was the custom of the Baptist ministers in Queen Anne's reign to meet once a month at Deering's Coffee House, in Finch Lane, to consult concerning public measures. The public posi-

---

* Ivimey, iv. 212—215.
† Hunter's "Life of Heywood," pp. 280—281. Ivimey, iv. 361—363.
‡ Ivimey, iii. 57.

tion of this denomination in the metropolis was, at this period, equal, if not superior, to that of the Congregationalists.

The Quakers continued throughout the whole of this reign in the active prosecution of their evangelistic work. Year after year they continued to bear their testimony against the maintenance of religious institutions by physical force. Their resistance to church-rates excited the Lower House of Convocation to pray for a more speedy method of recovering this charge.* It was seldom, in fact, that it could be recovered in any manner from the members of this body, who unhesitatingly went to prison rather than pay what they deemed to be an unrighteous and unscriptural demand. In every "Epistle" written at this period reference is made to the numerous imprisonments of Friends on this account. "The chief sufferings," says the Epistle of the year 1703, "Friends at present remain under are those of tithes, and those called Church-rates; on which accounts five have died prisoners, seventeen have been discharged, and forty-three remain prisoners, since last year's accounts. And we find the value of what our Friends have suffered on these accounts, this last year, amounts unto about £4,200. And several Friends are under prosecution in the Exchequer and Ecclesiastical Courts, on the said accounts. However, we desire and hope such severities will not weaken the faith of any, nor discourage them from maintaining their Christian testimony in these and all other parts thereof."† The power which was sus-

* Lathbury's "History of Convocation," p. 384.
† "Yearly Epistles," i. 105.

tained by such methods was plainly stigmatized as the power of "Antichrist," * and the members of the body were exhorted to continue faithful in their "ancient testimony" against it.† The Quakers were now entering, unconsciously to themselves, on the trial of their denomination. The generation then living were the first hereditary Quakers. In what manner the principle of hereditary succession would ultimately affect the numbers and the spiritual character of the body remained to be seen. As yet there were no indications of weakness or declension. The Society was kept in vigorous life by the missionary spirit of its members. Like George Fox, the preachers of the denomination travelled throughout the length and breadth of the land, and in such a sense, that the Quakers may be justly described as the founders of the first home missionary organization.

With respect to their civil and political position, there was an entire absence in all these parties, whether Presbyterian, Congregational, Baptist, or Quaker, of any aggressive spirit. They were thankful if they could retain what they already held. They were, in fact, too profuse in their expressions of gratitude to the Queen for being allowed the very limited toleration which was accorded to them. Every year they waited on her Majesty to thank her for her protection. When Marlborough gained a victory, when peace was made, when the union with Scotland was effected, advantage was taken of the occasion to present additional addresses, in which the same thankfulness was expressed. The

---

* "Yearly Epistles," p. 127, A.D. 1710.   † Ib. 135, A.D. 1713.

Quakers were not behind the other Dissenters, and, to her face, extolled the Queen for her great goodness.* All this time it was well known that Anne, had she dared, would have withdrawn every liberty from Dissenters, and had given her heartiest support to any government which would propose to legislate according to the old Stuart pattern. Every favour which royalty could confer on the Church she had conferred; every act which could propitiate the good-will of the clergy she had carefully set herself to perform. In A.D. 1704, at Burnet's suggestion, she had relinquished her right to the "First Fruits," thus presenting the clergy, out of her own revenues, with a sum equal to about £17,000 per annum. This sum, denominated "Queen Anne's Bounty," has, ever since that period, been applied to the augmentation of the livings of the poorer clergy. In A.D. 1711, in compliance with an address from Convocation, she sent a message to the House of Commons, suggesting the erection of fifty new churches in the metropolis; and accordingly, in May of that year, the House voted the sum of £370,000 for that purpose. † All her promotions had been of those who were notorious for their High Church zeal, for their hatred of Dissent, and for their opposition to the doctrine of constitutional government. She could overcome, as in the case of Swift, her most violent personal antipathies in order to reward men who had well served the Tory party. During the whole of her reign she never quite gave up the hope

* Most of the addresses of this period are in Ivimey and Calamy : the addresses of the Quakers are in Sewell's "History." Dr. Watts, following the prevailing fashion, addressed an eulogistic ode to the Queen, which, however, he afterwards retracted.

† Boyer's "Annals," A.D. 1711, p. 374.

of seeing "the Pretender" on the throne of England. She hated even to hear the name of her Hanoverian successor, and, as far as prudence would allow, guided her domestic policy, or allowed it to be guided, in harmony, not with the interests of her country, but with the traditions of her family. Nothing would have pleased her better than to see the Church governed by a second Laud, and the State ruled by a second Strafford. But there was one hindrance to the success of such a policy. This was the political power possessed by the Dissenters, and the success which was attending the educational efforts of that body. If the kingdom was to be governed on Tory principles, it was necessary that the corporations should be cleared of all these men, and that they should be deprived of the power of educating the rising generation. Both these steps were resolved upon.

In A.D. 1711—the year in which the Church received its grant from parliament—the Occasional Conformity Bill was again introduced into the legislature. Its avowed object, which was openly stated in the preamble of the measure, was the better security of the Church of England. It was therefore provided that no person who did not conform to the Church should be capable of holding any civil or military office; that if, after his admission to such an office, any person should be found in a conventicle or in any religious meeting consisting of more than ten persons, other than one conducted according to the rites and ceremonies of the Established Church, he should forfeit the sum of forty pounds and be disabled for the future from holding any offices. This Bill was supported both by Whigs and Tories. It was the price paid for a coalition. The Whigs could not regain power without the active aid of the Earl of Nottingham, and Nottingham would not join them unless they consented to pass the Occasional Conformity Bill.* For this the Dissenters were unscrupulously sacrificed. The Bill was introduced by Nottingham on December 15th, passed without opposition, through all its stages, in three days, and received the Royal assent on the eighth day after its introduction. What could be done to prevent its success was done. De Foe inveighed against it; Shower addressed Lord Oxford personally on the subject; application was made to every politician of influence to oppose it; but the bargain had been struck, and, as though they were beneath contempt, the Whigs ignored the Dissenters' services, and the Tories exulted in their disgrace.

Three courses were now open to those Dissenters who were immediately affected by this measure. They could conform; they could cease to attend the public worship of their own body, and commune sufficiently often to save their places; or they could relinquish their offices, and agitate for a repeal of the law. There is no authentic record that many adopted the first course. Dr. Williams, as soon as the Act had passed, delivered an address on the duties of Dissenters at this new crisis in their history. With mournful indignation he dwelt on the temper of the Church and the ingratitude of public men; but, in his judgment, there was no alternative but for all who held office to resign their posts.† The third

---

* Wilson's "De Foe," iii. 238. Coxe's "Life of Marlborough," Cap. cv. Calamy's "Own Life," ii. 243.

† "An Enquiry into the duty of Protestant Dissenters." Works, ii. p. 407.

course was advised by De Foe, who counselled Dissenters of all classes to form a federative union, and to act independently of parties and persons. "Alas, poor people!" he cried, "when are ye to open your eyes?" Their supineness excited in him a feeling of angry contempt. "Now is the time for them," he said, "to stand upon their own legs, and be truly independent; they will soon make circumstances recover, and the figure they make differ from anything they ever made before."* This would have been unquestionably the wiser policy, for statesmen are no exception to the rest of mankind in estimating people at the value which they put upon themselves. The Dissenters, as a body, chose, however, to take counsel of their prudence, by adopting the second line of policy. This was the case with Sir Thomas Abney and Sir John Fryer, aldermen of London, with the mayors of several country corporations and with justices of the peace, who decided to hold their offices and to cease their attendance at any public place of worship. The conduct of this class is stated to have been decided by the representations of the leaders of the Whig party and the Resident of Brunswick, who pledged their word that, on the death of the Queen, and the accession of the House of Hanover to the throne, the law should be repealed. Sir Thomas Abney, amongst others, ceased attendance at any public place of worship for seven years, Dr. Watts acting during the whole of that time as his private chaplain.† This course met, however, with severest condemnation from some of the Presbyterian ministers, who stigmatized it as a gross

---

* "Present State of Parties."
† Calamy's "Own Life," ii. 245, 246. Milner's "Life of Watts."

dereliction of duty, as a desertion of the brethren who continued in public communion, and as a virtual condemnation of those who had suffered for the Dissenting interest.*

Nor did the studious moderation of this course meet the reward which it certainly deserved. The Act was found to have failed, to a great extent, of its principal purpose. It had not materially injured Dissent, and it was necessary, if the schemes of certain politicians were to succeed, that Dissent should not only be weakened, but, if possible, extinguished. Amongst the statesmen of this period there was more than one who had conceived the bold design of destroying the Protestant succession. At the head of these were Francis Atterbury, Bishop of Rochester, and Henry St. John, Viscount Bolingbroke, who had been appointed Secretary of State to the last Tory ministry of this reign,—a ministry formed of Jacobite materials, and which no sooner entered on office than it began to make arrangements for securing the Pretender's succession to the Crown. While Dissent, in any form, existed, it was felt to be impossible to count on the result of such an engagement.† Whoever might turn traitors to the Constitution, it was very well known that the Pretender would find his strongest and most persistent opponents in this party. Bolingbroke therefore resolved to strike at the roots of Dissent. Accordingly, on May 12th, A.D. 1714, a Bill, popularly termed the "Schism Bill," was introduced into the House of Commons. By this measure it was provided that no person should keep any public or private school, or teach or instruct, as

* Williams's "Enquiry." Works, ii. 454.
† Chamberlin's "Queen Anne," p. 495.

tutor or schoolmaster, who had not subscribed a declaration to conform to the Established Church, and obtained, from the bishop of the diocese in which he resided, a license to teach. No license was to be granted unless the applicant could produce a certificate that he had received the Sacrament according to the rites of the Church, for a year previous. If he taught without such a license he was, on conviction, to be imprisoned without bail.

Sectarian hate scarcely ever gave birth to a more scandalous proposal than that of the Schism Bill. While its precise object was to destroy Dissent, and, by destroying it, to bring in the Pretender, its actual effect would have been the extinction of the best means of religious education to be obtained at that time in England. It was a proposal to sacrifice the intelligence and religion of the people at the shrine of the Established Church. Its first blow would, of course, have fallen on the institutions established for the training of ministers. The Presbyterians had academies for this purpose at Hoxton, Taunton, and Shrewsbury; the Congregationalists at Plasterers' Hall, while throughout the country, at Bridgewater, Tiverton, Tewkesbury, Colyton, Carmarthen, Bridgenorth, and other towns, many ministers of the denomination had established private academies for ministerial education. The Baptist institution connected with the Broadmead Church at Bristol, and the Quakers' schools, would also have been extinguished. Besides these, private schools for the middle classes existed in every large town. The rapid increase and successful career of these institutions had been a source of alarm for many years. They had furnished a stimulus to the zeal of High Churchmen in the matter of Occasional Conformity, for the sight of a Dissenting academy inflamed the passions of men of the Sacheverell order almost to madness. The members of the Established Church, by the formation of the Society for the Promotion of Christian Knowledge, had done a little to overtake the ignorance of the people; but the Dissenters had, nearly a quarter of a century before, set them the example. The first school for the poor established in England was founded in A.D. 1687, in connexion with Nathaniel Vincent's church in Southwark. To the honour of the founders it was of an unsectarian character. Children, it was stipulated, should be received into it "without distinction of parties, the general good being intended."* In the year 1714, in the debates on the Bill now under review, Lord Cowper stated that the schools in many country towns were chiefly supported by Dissenters, who educated Churchmen with themselves.† In the charity schools founded by the Christian Knowledge Society, all children were required to be taught the formularies of the Established Church, and were taught, besides, to hate the existing government.‡ There was, in fact, a systematic attempt to train the children in the principles of

* Toulmin's "History," p. 430. Milner's Watts, p. 430.
† "Parliamentary History," *in loco*.
‡ Dr. Watts, in his "Essay towards the Encouragement of Charity Schools, particularly among Protestant Dissenters," published A.D. 1728, remarks, "Many others were formed by persons of the Established Church, to which several Dissenters subscribed largely; but at last they found, by sufficient experience, that the children were brought up, in too many of these schools, in principles of disaffection to the present government, in bigoted zeal for the word Church, and with a violent enmity and malicious spirit of persecution against all whom they were taught to call Presbyterians, though from many of their hands they received their bread and clothing. It was time then for the Dissenters to withdraw that charity which was so much abused."—*Works*, i. p. 527.

Jacobitism.* With the Dissenters' schools closed, and all other educational institutions in the hands of the High Church clergy, the re-establishment of the Stuart dynasty would have been a matter of comparative ease.

The introduction of this bill excited the gravest alarm, and the Dissenters at once took active measures to prevent its being passed. Statements were written and circulated amongst members of both houses of the legislature; Calamy addressed the bishops in a series of pungent queries; and meetings were held from day to day in the City, the Temple, and at Westminster, to concert measures of opposition;† but no time was given for agitation. It was carried in the Commons, after hot debates, by two hundred and thirty-seven to one hundred and twenty-six votes, the Bill being read three times in one day. In the Upper House, Lord Cowper, Lord Halifax, and Lord Wharton led a vigorous and almost successful opposition to it. The argument used in its favour was that it was necessary for the security of the Church. "Dissenters," said the Bishop of London, "have made the Bill necessary by their endeavours to propagate their schism, and to draw their children to their schools and academies." Lord Wharton appears to have made the ablest speech against it. He remarked that such a measure was but an indifferent return for the benefit the public had received from these schools, in which the greatest men had been educated —men who had made a glorious peace for England, who had paid the debts of the nation, and who had extended

---

* This was animadverted upon with great severity by Wake, Archbishop of Canterbury, in 1716, and also by Gibson, Bishop of London.

† Calamy's " Own Life," ii 282—285.

its commerce.* Three divisions were taken on the Bill. In the first it was carried by fifty-nine to fifty-four votes ; in the second by fifty-seven to fifty-one; and in the third and final struggle, when both parties brought their whole forces together, by seventy-seven to seventy-two.†

The Queen had, from the first, given the Schism Bill her heartiest encouragement. She signed it on the 25th of June. On Sunday, the 1st of August, it was to have been put in operation. On the morning of that day Thomas Bradbury, the Congregational minister of Fetter Lane, was walking through Smithfield, when he met Bishop Burnet. Burnet called to him from his carriage, and inquired why he seemed so troubled? "I am thinking," replied Bradbury, "whether I shall have the constancy and resolution of that noble company of martyrs whose ashes are deposited in this place; for I most assuredly expect to see similar times of violence and persecution, and that I shall be called to suffer in a like cause." The bishop, endeavouring to calm him, informed Bradbury that the Queen had been given over by her physicians, and was expected every hour to die, and that he himself was then on his way to Court. He offered to send a messenger to Bradbury to give him the earliest intelligence of the Queen's death, and arranged that, if the messenger should find Bradbury in his pulpit, he should go into the gallery of Fetter Lane Chapel, and drop a handkerchief. The Queen died on the same morning; and while Bradbury was preaching the messenger arrived, and dropped his handkerchief

* Calamy ii. 287.   ‡ "Parliamentary History."

from the front gallery. The preacher made no reference to the event in his sermon, but in the succeeding prayer he offered public thanks for the delivery of the nation, and implored the Divine blessing on King George I. and the House of Hanover. He then asked the congregation to sing the eighty-ninth Psalm. It is reported that, shortly after, Bradbury preached from the text, "Go, see now this accursed woman, and bury her; for she is a king's daughter." He often, in after life, made reference to the fact that the first public proclamation of the accession of the house of Hanover to the throne was made from the pulpit of the Congregational Church in Fetter Lane.*

With the decease of Anne the Schism Act became a dead letter. No attempt was made to enforce it. The High Church party had lost their chief strength, and the last law for the limitation of religious liberty in England had been passed. Through the fiat of the Almighty, the legacy which the revolutionary King and his statesmen had left to the country was preserved nearly intact. Henceforward, the struggle was to be, not for the preservation, but for the extension of freedom.

Almost simultaneously with the death of the Queen, three men who had devoted all their great abilities to the cause of a free and constitutional government, also dropped from the page of ecclesiastical history. Tenison and Burnet lived barely long enough to see George I. ascend the throne. They both died full of years, and every generation which has succeeded them has cast its chaplet of honour on their tombs. De Foe, at the same

* Wilson's "Dissenting Churches," iii. p. 513.

period, relinquished his political labours. Hated more than any man of his time by the Tories and Jacobites, whose chief literary employment was to load him with abuse, he at last incurred the almost equal hatred of the Whigs. The cause of this was his opposition to their foreign policy, and his exposure of their desertion of the Dissenters; or rather, as he stigmatized it, "the barbarity" of their treatment. The members of his own ecclesiastical party were scarcely less displeased with him for his bold rebukes of their timidity and of their continued adhesion to the men who had betrayed them. In a strain of mournful eloquence he wrote, in one of the last numbers of his "Review:" "And now I live under universal contempt, which contempt I have learned to contemn, and have an uninterupted joy in my soul; not at being contemned, but that no crime can be laid to my charge to make that contempt my due." Of the Dissenters themselves and his relation to them, he wrote at the same time, "It is impossible for the Dissenters in this nation to provoke me to be an enemy to their interests. . . . Not that I am insensible of being ill-treated by them, or that I make any court to their persons. When any party of men have not a clear view of their own interests, he that will serve them, and knows the way to do it, must be certain not to please them, and must be able to see them revile and reproach him, and use him in the worst manner imaginable, without being moved. I remember the time when the same people treated me in the same manner upon the book called 'The Shortest Way,' and nothing but suffering for them would ever open their eyes. He that cleared up my integrity then, can do it again by the same method, and I leave it to Him."* He warned them again of the folly of looking to politicians for their liberties, instead of to themselves and their own exertions. In a subsequent " Appeal to Honour and Justice," he reviewed the course of his own political life from the time when, thirty years before, he had joined the standard of the Duke of Monmouth, and had cautioned Dissenters not to listen to the promises of James. This vindication is written with an affecting earnestness, which shows how much he felt the reproaches of his friends. His life, he said, had been one of " sorrow and fatigue;" but he was desirous that his children should not be disturbed in the inheritance of their father's character. This was one of the last of his political publications. The "Review" was discontinued in the place where it had been begun—in Newgate—where a second imprisonment for a second political "libel" was awarded to him. The remainder of his life, as all know, was devoted to writing works on political economy and on education, and to that marvellous series of fictions of which "Robinson Crusoe" was the forerunner. It is scarcely surprising that the Dissenters of his own day did not understand such a man. De Foe lived many generations before his time. The character of his mind and work belong more to the nineteenth than to the seventeenth century. He was too inventive and enterprising; too original and bold; too broad, too political, and too versatile for men of "the Old Dissent." They never, therefore, understood him. And now, happily, he could lay down his political work, for religious liberty was to become a watchword given from a King's mouth.

* Wilson's " Life of De Foe," iii. pp. 294, 295.

CHAPTER IV.

FROM THE SCHISM ACT TO THE ORGANIZATION OF THE DISSENTING DEPUTIES.

A.D. 1714 TO A.D. 1732.

THE history of the Free Churches of England during the reign of George I.—a period which is nearly conterminous with the time to be reviewed in the present division of this work—is the history of that decline in religion which immediately preceded the rise of Methodism. It commenced with a popular outbreak against the government and the Dissenters. George was a Lutheran in religion, but on coming to the throne expressed his firm purpose to maintain the Churches of England and Scotland as by law established. At the same time he remarked that, in his opinion, this could be effectually done without impairing the toleration, which was so agreeable to Christian charity, allowed by law to Protestant Dissenters.* The three denominations, in common with others, presented an address on the occasion. Nearly one hundred ministers, all clad in their black Genevan cloaks, were present. "What have we here?" asked a nobleman—"a funeral?" On which Bradbury replied: "No, my lord! a resurrection."† Dr. Daniel Williams, for the last time in his

---

* "Parliamentary History." † "Monthly Repository," 1820, p. 316.

life, headed the deputation. Their address was excusably egotistic. The deputation referred to their adherence, against all temptations and dangers, to the revolutionary settlement. "Our zeal," they went on to state, "has been proved to be very conspicuous by those noble patriots who now surround your throne." They expressed their determination to uphold the government against all pretenders whatsoever, and thanked the King for his declaration in their favour—a declaration which both relieved them from anxiety and gave them grounds of hope for future protection and favour. The King expressed his pleasure at receiving the address, and assured the ministers that they might depend on his protection.* The coronation of George was accompanied by tumults, riots, and murder, in several towns. In A.D. 1715 the Pretender was proclaimed as King James III. The cries of the "Church in Danger," "High Church and Sacheverell," and "No Presbyterianism," were now again heard. The Pretender's adherents, as though the question at issue were one of Church and Dissent—as, indeed, to some extent, it was—began at once to demolish the meeting-houses. At Oxford—then, as now, the headquarters of High-Churchism—the places of worship belonging to the Presbyterians, Baptists, and Quakers were destroyed; the Baptist chapel at Wrexham, the Presbyterian church at Nuneaton, several churches in the county of Stafford and in other parts of England, shared the same fate.† The whole of the Dissenters, during this rebellion, rallied round the Hanoverian

---

* Calamy's "Own Life," ii. pp. 299, 300.

† Calamy, ii. 313. Ivimey, iii. 121. Gough's "History of the Quakers," iv. 165.

dynasty. At Newcastle-on-Tyne a corps of seven hundred keelmen, mostly Dissenters, were embodied for defence.* At Chowbent, in Lancashire, the Dissenting minister, Mr. Wood, rallied together four hundred Dissenters, armed and equipped at his own expense, and took them to join the standard at Preston—an act of loyalty which, owing to the penalties attendant on the Occasional Conformity Act, was obliged to be condoned by a special Act of Parliament.† The Dissenters, as soon as this rebellion had been quelled, waited on the King, the spokesman being, for the first time, a member of the Baptist denomination, Mr. Nathaniel Hodges.‡ They referred at length, in their address, to the treatment they had received, adding, with truth, that whenever there had been a design to introduce Popery and arbitrary power in England, the Protestant Dissenters had generally been the first to be attacked.§ The King, in reply, expressed his concern at the "unchristian and barbarous treatment" which they had received, and promised compensation.§ "Unchristian and barbarous" were words that had never before fallen from a King in description of acts committed by Churchmen against Dissenters; and there need be no wonder at the general feeling of peace and satisfaction which ensued.

* Belsham's "History of Great Britain," iii. p. 36.

† George i. c. 39. The losses of Dissenters on this occasion were represented to the House of Commons, and two years afterwards, but with great difficulty, the sum of five thousand pounds was obtained in reparation of the damages which had been sustained.

‡ Crosby, iv. 126. This circumstance gave occasion to a writer in the "Weekly Journal" to ridicule the "mean occupations" of "that dipping set of people." Hodges was afterwards knighted, and was, I think, the first Baptist who received that honour.

§ "Gazette," May 17, A.D. 1715.

For the first time in the history of the Free Churches, an endeavour was now made to obtain an exact return of their number and distribution. This was effected, after great labour, by Daniel Neal, than whom, for such a task, no man, whether in respect to ability or to honesty, was more competent. Neal gives the total number of the Free Churches in England and Wales, in the years 1715 and 1716, at eleven hundred and fifty.*

* Neal thought it necessary to distinguish only Baptists and Pœdobaptists. His List, with his own classification, was as follows :

	Total.	Baptists.		Total.	Bapt.
Bedfordshire	23	22	Somersetshire	55	12
Berkshire	26	10	Suffolk	34	0
Buckinghamshire	17	7	Surrey	20	4
Cambridgeshire	23	5	Sussex	16	1
Cheshire	21	4	Staffordshire	16	2
Cornwall	12	0	Warwickshire	18	4
Cumberland	19	2	Wiltshire	20	4
Derbyshire	28	9	Westmoreland	5	9
Devonshire	61	6	Worcestershire	18	8
Dorsetshire	35	5	Yorkshire	48	0
Durham	9	0		—	—
Essex	52	8	Totals	1107	247
Gloucester	51	16			
Hants	32	9	WALES.		
Herefordshire	8	1	North Wales—		
Hertfordshire	26	10	Anglesea		1
Huntingdonshire	31	1	Carnarvonshire		1
Kent	52	27	Denbigh		3
Lancashire	47	4	Merioneth		1
Leicestershire	33	9	Montgomery		2
Lincolnshire	22	3	Flint		1
Middlesex	91	26	South Wales—		
Monmouthshire	8	2	Brecknock		3
Norfolk	20	4	Cardigan		3
Northamptonshire	40	22	Carmarthen		9
Northumberland	27	0	Glamorgan		7
Nottinghamshire	8	1	Pembroke		8
Oxfordshire	14	3	Radnorshire		4
Rutland	6	3			—
Shropshire	15	2			43

But there is evidence that his list, although no doubt substantially accurate, is not correct in all particulars. Neal states that there were no Baptist churches in Yorkshire at this period; but it is certain that Mitchell and Crossley had founded, before this, more than four in the two counties of Yorkshire and Lancashire. There was a prejudice, at this time, as at the time of the Rothwell controversy, against recognizing any assembly as a church which was not presided over by a regularly ordained pastor; and not many Baptist churches, in the early part of the eighteenth century, could boast of such men.* The Quakers also are evidently omitted from the whole list, and in Yorkshire alone they had founded, before this period, eighty permanent churches.† If Neal's list is absolutely correct, more than half of the churches for which licenses had been taken out between A.D. 1688 and A.D. 1710 were extinct in A.D. 1715. It is possible that this was the case, for subsequent statistical inquiries tended to confirm Neal's general accuracy as regards the three denominations. Taking the list as it stands, it is curious to observe the numerical relations of the different orders of Free Churches. All but one of the twenty-three Free Churches of Bedfordshire were Baptist. These were the fruits of Bunyan's labours; but it would seem that the body had not sufficient heart-power to send its faith to the extremities of the kingdom. There was not, apparently, a single Baptist church in Cornwall, Durham, Northumberland, or

---

* I am aware that no existing Baptist church in Yorkshire can trace its origin to this date, and it is therefore possible that Mitchell and Crossley's labours were ultimately fruitless.

† Parl. Paper, 156, September, 1853.

Westmoreland. The position of this denomination in the agricultural counties of Dorset, Hereford, Huntingdon, Lincoln, Monmouth, Sussex, Suffolk, and Wiltshire was almost equally low. In Suffolk, indeed, there was no Baptist church whatever. There were no counties where Baptists and Pædobaptists were equally divided, but the list indicates a predominance of Baptist over Congregational Churches in the metropolis, for it is known that there were more than fifty Presbyterian places of worship in London at this period. On the whole, however, Neal's list, while it does not bear out the language of those who appeared to consider Dissenters to be a majority in the kingdom, shows the great power of the voluntary principle in religion. As the result of little more than thirty years' toleration, and under the greatest discouragements, more than fifteen hundred places of worship had been opened and kept open.

The Quakers were the first to take advantage of the new spirit in the conduct of public affairs. By the Act of William the Third, they had been allowed to make an affirmation instead of an oath. This Act was, however, limited to a term of years, in order that it might be seen whether it would work consistently with the public interests and the administration of justice. As this term was now on the point of expiring, application was made for its extension. A Bill was therefore brought into the House of Commons, and, in a few days, an Act was passed giving the Quakers this right in perpetuity. At the same time the operation of the law was extended, for a brief period, to Scotland and the Colonies.* The rapidity

---

* Sewell's "History," ii. 469.

and ease with which this measure was conducted through the legislature were bright omens of a more tolerant system of law.

It now remained to be seen whether the Whig party would redeem their promises, and several writers began to remind them of their engagements. In A.D. 1715 there appeared the first claim, from the new government, for a full toleration. This was made in a pamphlet entitled "The Case of the Protestant Dissenters in England fairly stated," the author of which reviewed the history of the Test and Corporation, the Occasional Conformity, and the Schism Acts, and demanded their repeal as well in the interests of the House of Hanover as of the Dissenters themselves.* The next year Calamy wrote in favour of the repeal of the Occasional Conformity Act.† With his habitual caution he did not take the initiative in this without the instigation of several members of Parliament, and when he wrote he asked merely for the repeal of the law which bore most harshly on Presbyterians. Others at once followed his example. At the commencement of the year 1717 the agitation took a shape as systematic in form as it was formidable in character. Members of the House of Commons, indignant at the injustice which had been done to Dissenters, and at the delay which had taken place in fulfilling the promises made to them, met together, and at last, on the 20th March, summoned a meeting, which was attended by more than two hundred members, at the Rose Tavern, Temple Bar, to consider the subject. This large and influential assembly was addressed by

---

* Calamy, ii. 344. † Ib. 369.

Lord Molesworth, Sir Richard Steele, and Mr. Jessop, who reminded it that the Dissenters suffered from their disabilities solely in consequence of their zeal for the Protestant succession; and urged that such friends of the Government should be placed in a capacity to serve it. They had reason to believe, they added, that the King himself was favourable to the object. It was stated, in reply, that, as a matter of fact, the Court was apprehensive of the opposition of the House of Lords. The meeting was then adjourned. On assembling again, a few days afterwards, it was authoritatively stated that the obstacles to the introduction of a Bill were now removed, and it was therefore resolved to prepare a measure for the full relief of Dissenters.*

Hoadly, who had now been promoted to the bishopric of Bangor, threw the weight of his powerful intellect into the same scale. In a sermon on the "Nature of the Kingdom or Church of Christ," preached before the King on the 31st March, A.D. 1717, the general doctrine of which will presently come under review, Hoadly attacked all the laws which limited the civil rights of any classes of Christians. The Church of Christ, he maintained, could not be protected or encouraged by human laws and penalties. It was "something," he said, in another work, "of quite another nature than anything that can be supported by the acts and statutes and laws framed in the different nations of the world; and something which is best and most effectually preserved according to the will of Christ, by methods agreeable to the spirit of the Gospel."† Six months afterwards the

---

* Tindal's "Continuation," vii. 96, 97. Fifth edition.
† Hoadly's "Rights of Subjects," p. 172.

King indicated the state of his own feelings in a passage of his speech on opening Parliament, in which William the Third's customary language was adopted almost word for word. "I could heartily wish," he said, "that at a time when the common enemies of our religion are, by all manner of artifices, endeavouring to undermine and weaken it both at home and abroad; all those who are friends to our present happy Establishment might unanimously concur in some proper method for the further strengthening the Protestant interest, of which as the Church of England in the great bulwark, so will she reap the principal benefit of every advantage accruing by the union and mutual charity of all Protestants."* This significant language, coupled with the address of the House of Lords in reply, which echoed the King's sentiments in his own words, indicated that, in the judgment of the Crown and its ministers, the time had arrived when all the disabilities of the Dissenters might be removed.

Protected by a powerful party in Parliament, and with the certainty of success attending their efforts, the Dissenters now boldly took the field. Meetings were held all over the country,† and it was resolved to demand the repeal, not only of the Occasional and Schism Acts, but of the Test and Corporation laws. On December 13th, A.D. 1718, Earl Stanhope, who had become principal Secretary of State, brought in a Bill for " strengthening the Protestant interest " by a repeal of portions of the Occasional Conformity Act, of the Schism Act, and of some clauses in the Test and Cor-

* "Parliamentary History," vii. 502.
† Tindal's "Continuation," vii. 224.

poration Acts. The Earl, in moving the second reading of the Bill, enlarged on the equity, reasonableness, and advantage of restoring Dissenters to their natural rights, and on the probable effects of such a measure, which, he said, would strengthen the Protestant interest, and be of advantage to the Established Church. The end, in his judgment, would be that the Archbishop of Canterbury would become the patriarch of all the Protestant clergy. The authors and supporters of the Acts fought for their preservation with all the strength and eagerness with which a parent will fight for the lives of his offspring. They said that it would "pluck the Church of its best feathers;" that it would invest her enemies with power; that they were the "main bulwark of our excellent constitution in Church and State," and that to repeal them would be to break the articles of union with Scotland. No man was more vehement in his opposition than the old Earl of Nottingham, who, in William the Third's reign, had, by his own influence, prevented the repeal of the Test and Corporation laws, and who was himself the author of the Occasional Conformity Act. The debate was then adjourned for five days. On the 18th December the Bill was read a second time without opposition, but on the motion for going into committee the Earl of Nottingham again raised the standard of opposition. No bishop had yet spoken upon it, and accordingly an appeal was made to the episcopal body for an expression of their opinions. Wake, Archbishop of Canterbury, the successor of Tenison and the opponent of Atterbury, at once responded to the appeal by intimating that he should vote against the measure. In his judgment, also, the Acts proposed to be repealed "were the main bulwarks and supporters of the Established Church." Dawes, Archbishop of York, took the same side, and urged the danger of trusting the open and avowed enemies of the Church with power and authority. Next rose Hoadly, who, in a speech characterized by an eloquent statement of the principles of Christian liberty, said that if Dissenters were ever to be drawn over to the Church it must be by "gentle means." All religious tests, he affirmed, were an abridgment of the natural rights of men, an injury to the State, and a scandal to religion. The laws proposed to be repealed were persecuting laws, and could no more be justified than could the persecution by heathens of the early Christians. The power, he went on to say, of which the clergy seemed so fond, he had learned, from reason and from the Gospel, must be kept within due bounds, and not be allowed to entrench upon the rights and liberties of fellow-creatures, and fellow-countrymen. An endeavour was made by Smalridge, Bishop of Bristol, to break the force of Hoadly's speech, but he was ably replied to by Willis, Bishop of Gloucester, and Gibson, Bishop of Lincoln. The Earl of Nottingham now again rose, and warned the House that Dissenters were "an obstinate set of people, never to be satisfied." In wise governments, said Dr. Robinson, Bishop of London, who followed, "all offices and places of trust are in the hands of those of the National Church." Atterbury next took up the argument, and dwelt on the hardships which Dissenters were bringing on the Church. Next to Hoadly's, however, the speech of the debate was White Kennet's, Bishop of Peterborough, who said that it was the promotion, by the clergy, of arbitrary measures and persecutions which, in Charles the First's reign, had brought contempt upon themselves and ruin on the Church and State. In ridicule of the cry of "Church in danger," he said that, while raised for sinister designs, it merely made "a mighty noise in the mouths of silly women and children." The debate lasted until six in the evening, and was then adjourned to the 19th December. Twenty-six speakers, on this occasion, recapitulated the old arguments, and the Bill was then put to the vote, when it was declared to be carried by eighty-six to sixty-eight. The next day, on going through committee, the clauses relating to the Test and Corporation Acts were withdrawn, and the Bill passed the third reading by fifty-five to thirty-three. It was brought into the Commons on December 24th, and on the 7th January in the next year was debated for eight hours and a half.* On a division it was carried by two hundred and forty-three to two hundred and two. It was attempted to introduce a clause, the object of which was to exclude Unitarians from the benefit of the Act, but the amendment to this effect was negatived, and it finally passed through committee by two hundred and twenty-one to one hundred and seventy votes.†

If the world had not had some previous experience of the inconstancy of public opinion, and the influence exercised on the fortunes of public measures by a knowledge of the views which are popular with courts, some astonishment might be expressed at the contrast afforded by the divisions on this measure with those on the two

* Owing, it is said, to the exclusion of all strangers excepting the Prince of Wales and some peers, no report of this debate is in existence.

† "Parliamentary History," vii. 567, 590.

Acts which it repealed. But, with the accession of George, and the increasing security of his government, the Church and Tory party were driven from a contest for perpetual supremacy to a struggle for existence. They had seen some of their most eminent members beheaded for rebellion; Oxford, the favourite minister of Anne, was in the Tower awaiting his impeachment for high treason, and Atterbury, their episcopal leader, was about to be indicted for the same offence. The opinion of the English people was slowly deciding in favour of a constitutional government, and a constitutional government meant, in George the First's mind, equal liberties for all, and no distinction whatever between Churchmen and Dissenters.

It appears to have been owing, in some measure, to the want of firmness in Dissenters themselves that they did not, at this time, obtain the repeal of the Test and Corporation Acts. The King was known to be in favour of their repeal, but is reported to have observed to Lord Barrington, who was considered to represent the public interests of Dissenters, that he was assured, by his ministers, that this point could not be carried, and he was persuaded that the Dissenters would not insist on an act which might be prejudical to himself.* The authority for this assurance was Lord Sunderland, who had informed the King that to attempt a repeal of the Test would ruin the whole Bill. At the same time assurances were given that it should soon be repealed.† The Dissenters, in fact, were sacrificed, as had been the case in former periods of their history, to what was said to be the

* Belsham's "Great Britain," iii. 132.
† Tindal's Continuation," vii. 244.

general good of the nation. As on previous occasions, they willingly and cheerfully accepted their position, and, as on previous occasions, the promises made to them were forgotten almost as soon as they were made. But they do not seem to have inquired why they, and they only, were perpetually sacrificed ostensibly for national, but often for mere party; purposes. They never asked how it was that such rare self-abnegation was not expected from the Church. They appear to have considered that it was one object of their existence to be occasionally offered up on the altar of patriotism. But in George the First's case there was, undoubtedly, some excuse for their willing resignation of claims which had long been recognized as both appropriate and just. The King was known to entertain a high respect for them, and a warm appreciation of their past services. His sincerity could not, for a moment, be doubted; and when he made the withdrawal of their claims a matter of personal favour to himself, it would have been difficult, and apparently ungracious, to refuse it. And they could not have suspected that, by the course which they then took, they were fastening the Test and Corporation Acts on the necks of their descendants to the third and fourth generations.

The human mind seldom or never becomes enlarged in one direction only. Growth in respect to the laws of civil polity is sure to be accompanied by a similar growth in respect to the laws of ecclesiastical polity. Sacerdotalism in religion and Absolutism in politics, have generally risen and fallen together. While, therefore, the principles of toleration were receiving a practical recognition from the Government, the exorbitant claims of the Church and its clergy were being dealt with in an equally effective manner. Hoadly's sermon on the "Nature of the Kingdom or Church of Christ," which has been already referred to, soon attracted the attention of the Lower House of Convocation. It could scarcely, indeed, in any age, have passed without criticism, for its doctrines were opposed to all the doctrines relating to the mutual relations of the Church and the State on which the ecclesiastical government of England is founded. Taking as his text the significant declaration of the Saviour that His kingdom was not of this world, Hoadly proceeded to show that the Church of Christ was a kingdom of which only He himself was King. He was the sole Lawgiver to His subjects; He had left behind Him no visible human authority; no vicegerents who could supply His place; no interpretations upon which His subjects were absolutely to depend, and no judges over the consciences or the religion of His people. If any pretended to possess such an authority they usurped Christ's office, or ruled in their own kingdom, and not in His. The Church itself he defined to be the number of men, whether small or great, whether dispersed or united, who were truly and sincerely subjects to Jesus Christ alone in matters relating to the favour of God and their eternal salvation. The laws of this kingdom, Hoadly went on to say, had no tendency to the exaltation of some in worldly pomp and dignity, or to their absolute dominion over the faith and religious conduct of others of His subjects, or to the erecting of any sort of temporal kingdom, under the covert and name of a spiritual one. Its rewards and penalties were not the rewards and penalties of this world; and if they could be, sincerity and hypocrisy, force and persuasion, a willing choice and a terrified heart were become the same things, and truth and falsehood stood in need of the same methods to propagate them. If an angel from heaven were to give any account of His kingdom contrary to what Christ himself had given, it ought, added the Bishop, to have neither weight nor authority with Christians.

It must be doubtful whether Hoadly, in laying down such broad principles relating to the spirituality of the kingdom of Christ, saw to what extent those principles would apply. His audience, probably, understood him to be preaching a sermon against the Test and Corporation Laws and the claims of the High Church party, but Hoadly's language, which was used by one who knew the full and exact value of words, has, obviously, a far broader reach than this. Is it possible that, at this time, Hoadly, flushed with the prosperity of the Liberal party, and the decline of High-Churchism, had sketched for himself the career of a second Cranmer, and that he preached this sermon as a tentative step in the direction of the further reformation of the English Church? He, unquestionably, had a full and clear conception of the gross inconsistency of a church which claimed to be Christian, being patronized, supported, and controlled by the State. He saw the totally unscriptural character of what was known as "Church authority," and he recognized the fact that human law has no right to limit the claims of the individual conscience. His sermon was, in fact, a proclamation of the unchristian character of the church of which he himself was a bishop. It can hardly be imagined that he made such a proclamation without thought of its exact nature, but it is more than probable that he had not reflected on all the consequences of the step he had taken, and that he did not sufficiently know himself. If, at any time, he had indulged in the great design of purifying the Church by separating it from all which separated it, in character, from the kingdom of Christ, he abandoned it. In the worry of personal controversies, and the succession of elevation after elevation upon the episcopal bench, Hoadly, if he ever felt it, lost the zeal of a Church reformer. He continued, throughout his life, the dreaded opponent of all who, whether in civil or ecclesiastical politics, or in theology, were disposed to advance the pretensions of collective authority in preference to individual right, and in this sense he reformed the Church of England, but the precise reform sketched in his celebrated sermon he took no steps to carry into execution. What he did was to break the neck of Church power. For years subsequent to the publication of this sermon, one of the greatest ecclesiastical controversies that had ever been waged in England, took place. Hoadly was necessarily the principal disputant, and he did not cease from the warfare, until, by sheer weight and force of brain, he had shattered all the defences which ambition and tradition had erected around the usurped authority of the Church.*

The doctrines embodied in Hoadly's sermon con-

* I have read no more, and perhaps less, than some other writers have read of the "Bangorian Controversy." It extends certainly beyond a hundred pamphlets, and any one who would thoroughly digest these would do a great service to ecclesiastical literature. I do not think that the practical influence of the controversy, in the direction indicated in the text, has ever been sufficiently recognized.

tained a declaration of principles which were utterly opposed to the constitution in Church and State. In less than a month from its publication, the Lower House of Convocation accordingly made a representation concerning it to the Upper House. They connected with the sermon another publication of Hoadly's, entitled "A Preservative against the Principles and Practices of the Non-jurors both in Church and State," in which Hoadly had attacked, at the same time, the sacerdotal claims of the priesthood and the doctrines of the Jacobites. They complained that Hoadly appeared to deny the authority of the Church to judge, censure or punish offenders in the affairs of conscience and eternal salvation; to affirm that all such exercises of authority had been an invasion and an usurpation upon Christ's kingdom; that such doctrines tended to breed in the minds of the people a disregard to those who were appointed to rule over them; that he put all religious communions on an equal footing, and that he left God alone to be judge of the conscience. If, said the Lower House, these doctrines be admitted, "there is evidently an end of all Church authority to oblige any to external communion, and of all power that one man can have over another in matters of religion;" "there are in the Church no governors left; in the State, none who may intermeddle in the affairs of religion." They charged Hoadly with undermining the constitution of the Church and impeaching the supremacy of the King, and besought the Upper House to "vindicate the honour of God and religion," and to "assert the prerogative given to all godly princes in Holy Scripture."* The Upper House

* Wilkin's "Concilia," iv. 672, 676.

had, however, no opportunity of replying to the representation. Convocation was immediately prorogued, and no further license was given to it to proceed with synodical business. The extravagant pretensions which it had put forward, and the mischievous character of its proceedings, had become offensive to the State. So fast had been the growth of the minds of men, since Jacobitism, by the safe accession of the Hanoverian dynasty, had lost every hope of success, that it was already an anachronism in the constitution. For a hundred and fifty years the representation against Hoadly was its last official act. Church power, as it had hitherto existed in England, became a thing of past history only. As it had thriven, so it perished, with absolutism.

There was no class in England which did not feel relief from the final removal of the weights which had been placed on the free movement of human thought. In no direction was this more visible than in theology. Men everywhere felt that they were at liberty to think for themselves. The natural and immediate result of this feeling was Latitudinarianism. In many minds an enforced respect to authority gave place either to a license of reason, or to an indifference respecting absolute truth. Others, who were not wanting in natural reverence, tried anew the doctrines of the Christian religion, and rejected at once all such as did not, to them, seem to be in accordance with the Scriptures alone, or with the unaided and undirected human reason. To this movement, as natural as it was inevitable, is to be attributed the apparently sudden growth, at this period, of Unitarianism in England. Hitherto the distinguishing doctrines of the Unitarians, although they had been actively propagated, had not, as far as can be seen, greatly influenced the religious opinions of the people. But there were many men, eminent either for great power of thought or for an enlarged benevolence, who had become more or less imbued with the spirit of Unitarian theology. The philosophy of one age is generally the theology of the next. Locke had made the philosophy of the then living generation, and its tendency was in favour of the Arian form of Unitarianism. He was accordingly denounced by the orthodox and claimed by the Unitarians themselves. Stillingfleet's death is said to have been hastened by Locke's treatment of him in the Trinitarian controversy, and it is certain that the great philosopher succeeded in defeating the great theologian on his own ground. On the Trinitarian side, the whole of the argument was so managed as to prove, if anything was proved, the existence of three Gods. The defenders of the received belief lost themselves in a maze of metaphysical subtleties, and seldom did more than give an advantage to their opponents. In his "Reasonableness of Christianity," Locke again offended, and was again denounced, Watts, charitable as he was, accusing him of darkening the glory of the Gospel and debasing Christianity.* Locke himself, however, in a vindication, denied that there was one word of Socinianism in his work. Whatever he may have thought, he did not, either by act or word, formally identify himself with Unitarianism, but the general influence of his writings was

* All that can be said in favour of Locke's Unitarianism has been said by Mr. Wallace, in his "Anti-trinitarian Biography," Vol. iii. Art. Locke. It is one of the questions on which there must always be some difference of opinion.

unquestionably in its favour. If Sir Isaac Newton, as has been claimed, was also an Unitarian, he had not the moral courage to state the fact in his lifetime.* In the Established Church the elements of this doctrine could be very distinctly traced. Men who had subscribed the Thirty-nine Articles, who used the Book of Common Prayer, and who repeated the Athanasian Creed, did not hesitate to express their disbelief in the Trinity. Early in this generation one of the authors of the Unitarian tracts had written as follows:—" We place not religion in worshipping God by ourselves, or after a particular form of manner, but in a right faith, and a just and charitable conversation. We approve of known forms of praising and praying to God; as also in administering Baptism, the Lord's Supper, Marriage, and the other religious offices; we like well of the discipline of the Church by Bishops and parochial ministers; and we have an esteem for the eminent learning and exemplary piety of the Nonconforming clergy. For these reasons we communicate with that Church as far as we can, and contribute our interests to favour her against all others who would take the chair." † Such conduct laid them open to merited rebuke from their opponents. They were charged with cowardice and with dishonesty; ‡ but at present they did not choose to reveal themselves. When, however, a divine such as Dr. Samuel Clarke did not hesitate to argue in favour of the inferiority of the second person of the Trinity, and to defend his continuance in the Established Church by laying down, as a rule of sub-

* Wallace, iii. Art. Newton.
† " The Trinitarian Scheme of Religion," p. 28. A.D. 1692.
‡ Edwards's " Socinian Creed," p. 185. A.D. 1697.

scription, that any person might reasonably subscribe to any formularies or confessions whenever he could, in any sense at all, reconcile them with Scripture,* inferior men need scarcely have hesitated to take, openly, the same ground. It must, however, be said that there had been plain warnings of the dangers of such a confession of faith. William Whiston, Professor of Mathematics in Cambridge University, had embraced Arianism, and was expelled the University and censured by Convocation. Samuel Clarke incurred the same censure; and although such acts were not now followed by any civil punishments, they placed a man under the ban of a large and influential section of society. Punishment by public opinion is felt quite as acutely by a man of sensitive mind as is a grosser form of punishment by a man of sensitive body; and the clergy of the Established Church, as well as the clergy out of the Established Church, have always known how most effectively to administer it. In the days of which we write it was certainly more profitable, so far as this world is concerned, for a man to live in open violation of the whole of the moral law than for him to deny the truth of the Athanasian creed. A large proportion of the clergy did the former, and held their benefices without let, hindrance, or opprobrium. Convocation did not dream of censuring them; but if a Whiston, a Clarke, or a Hoadly—men of unstained life and transparently honest nature—gave to an old truth a new form, or departed from the lines laid down by law on which the thoughts of the Established clergy were to travel, a hoot of execration arose against him. Some excuse, therefore,

* Clarke's "Scripture Doctrine of the Trinity," Perry's History, iii. 305.

although no justification, can be found for those persons who held the Unitarian creed remaining in the Church. One thing, at least, they lacked, without which an unpopular opinion has little prospect of becoming popular—. a fearless courage. They loved their creed sufficiently to advocate it in private, but they loved their benefices more.

Of open and avowed Unitarians the most conspicuous was Thomas Emlyn, a man of devout temperament and considerable ability, who had been virtually excomunicated from the Presbyterian communion. Emlyn had been educated in Doolittle's academy, and had been pastor of a small Dissenting congregation in Lowestoft. He ascribed his change of views on the subject of the Trinity to reading Sherlock and Howe's defence of that doctrine which, he considered, tended only to polytheism. Afterwards, he went to Dublin, to take the pastorate of the Church formerly presided over by Dr. Daniel Williams. He did not, however, announce his change of views, which was privately discovered by a member of his congregation. He then said that if such views were obnoxious to his congregation he would immediately resign. The Dublin ministers, however, met before this resignation could be arranged, and agreed that he should not be allowed to preach again. His congregation thought it desirable that there should be only a temporary cessation of his ministry. The ministers, however, decided that he should preach neither in Ireland nor in England during the interval—an assumption of authority which Emlyn boldly refused to recognize. Two messengers, one a Presbyterian, the other a Congregationalist, were forthwith despatched to London to warn the ministers of those denominations of Emlyn's heterodoxy, and of their decision respecting him. "If," said Emlyn, upon this, "the Presbyterians and Independents claim such power as this, not only to reject from their own communion, but to depose from their office such pastors of other churches as conscientiously differ from them in opinion, and to extend this to other kingdoms, forbidding them to preach there also, I think they have a mighty conceit of their own large dominion, and discover a very ridiculous ambition. I wonder who gave them this sovereign deposing power over their brethren." Emlyn now published a statement of his belief. On his return to Dublin, soon after this, in February, A.D. 1702, at the instance of a Baptist of the name of Caleb Thomas, he was arrested for writing against the Trinity, tried, found guilty, sentenced to pay a fine of a thousand pounds, and to lie in gaol until the fine was paid, the Chief Justice telling him that the pillory was his due, and that, if he had been in Spain or Portugal, he would have been burned. The fine was subsequently reduced,* and Emlyn came to reside in England, where he lived on terms of friendship with Whiston and Clarke.†

* The Archbishop of Armagh, as Queen's Almoner, claimed a shilling in the pound on this fine, and refused to take it on the reduced amount. "I thought," writes Emlyn, "that the Church was to be as merciful as the State; but I was mistaken herein."

† Wallace's "Anti-trinitarian Biography," iii. Art. "Emlyn." This persecution called forth a sarcastic rebuke from Hoadly, who, in a preface to Steele's "Account of the State of the Roman Catholic Religion throughout the World," published in A.D. 1717, wrote, "Sometimes we of the Established Church can manage a prosecution (for I must not call it persecution) ourselves, without calling in any other help. But I must do the Dissenting Protestants the justice to say, that they have shown themselves, upon occasion, very ready to assist us in so pious and Christian a work as bringing heretics to their right mind; being themselves but very lately come from experiencing the convincing and enlightening faculty of a dungeon or a fine.

Amongst Dissenters, Unitarianism had also made some progress. It is probable that the Baptists had never been entirely free from this taint. The Dutch Anabaptists of Henry VIII. and Elizabeth's reigns were all Arians, and the General Baptist denomination was scarcely formed before a charge of heterodoxy on this subject was brought against one of its principal members. Gale, the pastor of the Barbican church, who was now living, was an able opponent of Trinitarian views, and other ministers had discovered an equal tendency to speculation on this, to some minds, dangerously attractive question. It is not possible, however, to trace the existence of Unitarianism, amongst the General Baptists, to their theological creed. Arminianism does not necessarily or naturally lead to either the Arian or the Socinian form of Unitarian doctrine. The connection of this body with Unitarianism was accidental, and may be traced, in the first instance, to the existence of the Dutch Anabaptists, and, in the second instance—as is the case with all creeds—to the personal influence and the writings of one or two men of unusual mental and moral power. Such a man was Dr. John Gale. Neither the Particular Baptists nor the Congregationalists evinced any tendency towards anti-Trinitarian opinions. Both these bodies professed a higher order of Calvinism than was professed by any other Nonconformist communions; but that Calvinism is, in itself, no effectual protection against the inroads of Unitarianism, has been sufficiently proved by the experiences of New England and

...... The Nonconformists accused him (Emlyn), and Conformists condemned him, the secular power was called in, and the cause ended in an imprisonment and a very great fine ; two methods of conviction about which the Gospel is silent."

Geneva. Why these two denominations should have been free from the tendency which was affecting all other bodies may partly be explained by the fact that, with the exception of Watts, neither of them contained a man of eminently speculative mind; and Watts himself, when, after this period, he became involved in the vortex of this discussion, no sooner touched it than he also fell from the orthodox standard. The Presbyterians, however, shared equally with, if not to a greater extent than, the General Baptists, the characteristic tendency of theological thought. They were men, for the most part, of larger reading than other Nonconformists, and the writings of Whiston and Clarke had found their way amongst them.*

While this movement of thought was taking place, a circumstance occurred which gave to it a sudden impulse as well as a wide, if a factitious popularity. There were in the city of Exeter, four Presbyterian churches. Amongst the ministers of these churches there was one, James Peirce, formerly a member of Matthew Mead's congregation, who was suspected of holding anti-Trinitarian views. Peirce had already made himself well known and highly respected by the Dissenters of England for his vigorous and able defences of Nonconformity against the attacks of two clergymen of the Established Church—Snape and

---

* Peirce, of Exeter, writes:—"The common vogue of this people is that there was nothing of this doctrine in the city before my coming into it; that I was the first who brought it amongst them; and abundance of reproaches and untoward wishes have been bestowed upon me for this cause. But there is no truth in this report. Dr. Clarke, Mr. Whiston, and other writers, who differ from the common notion, had been read here before my coming." "Western Inquisition," p. 11. Both Peirce and Hallet became Unitarians by the perusal of Clarke's works.

Nichols. The most elaborate of these defences was written in Latin for circulation amongst the Protestant Churches of Europe.* In this work Peirce compared the constitution of the Established Church, its forms and ceremonials, its ritual, and the origin and administration of its revenues, with the practices which prevailed in the early ages of Christianity. This work became, in a brief period, the most popular defence of Nonconformity, and was one of two subsequently recommended by Doddridge for the education of Nonconformists.

Peirce is described by Calamy, who had no sympathy with his doctrines, as a minister of good repute, and courted and beloved by his people.† He appears also to have been a man of great reading, honest judgment, of an eminently candid mind, and Christian spirit. Although he held the anti-Trinitarian doctrine, he did not think it necessary to preach it, but, for consistency's sake, he omitted from his services all phrases which implied the equal divinity of the three persons of the Trinity. A brother minister, however, in the course of a private conversation, finding that Peirce did not hold the orthodox view, repeated the conversation to another minister, Mr. Lavington, of Exeter, who, in his turn, felt it to be his duty to proclaim that fact amongst the people. All Exeter soon rang with the information. In Peirce's own pulpit, during his temporary absence from the city, another minister charged some of the Dissenters of Exeter with "damnable heresies, denying the Lord that bought them." Peirce was then

* "A Vindication of the Dissenters: In answer to Dr. William Nichols' Defence of the Doctrine and Discipline of the Church of England, etc." By James Peirce. A.D. 1718.
† Calamy's "Own Life," ii. pp. 403, 405.

requested by three members of his congregation, to preach a sermon on the nature of the satisfaction of Christ, which he did, and which appears to have pleased the majority of the people. Charges of heterodoxy, however, are not quickly abandoned, and, when it was found that Peirce did not stand alone in his views, the Committee of Dissenters, who, by a local arrangement, were charged with the management of the temporal affairs of the four Exeter churches, and in whom the property was vested, resolved to take up the matter. They accordingly appointed a deputation to wait upon each of the ministers, with a request that they should assert the eternity of the Son of God. Peirce could have no objection to do this, and therefore replied that he would say anything which was to be found in the Scriptures, but nothing beyond. Most of the people were now satisfied. Meantime the question was carried to London, and brought back in enlarged dimensions. At a conference of Western ministers it was proposed that another clearance should be made by another test, and this was carried by a large majority. Each minister at once declared what he believed on this subject in his own words. Peirce's declaration was, " I am not of the opinion of Sabellius, Arius, Socinus, or Sherlock. I believe there is but one God, and can be no more ; I believe the Son and Holy Ghost to be divine persons, but subordinate to the Father, and the unity of God is, I think, to be resolved into the Father's being the fountain of the Divinity of the Son and Spirit." Mr. Hallett, of Exeter, another of the Presbyterian ministers who was also a suspected man, closed his declaration by quoting Baxter's words, " Two things have set the church on fire, and been the plagues of it above a thousand years ; first, by enlarging our creed and making more fundamentals than God ever made ; secondly, composing, and so imposing, our creeds and confessions in our own words and phrases." Some ministers denied the right of any body of men to demand their opinions, and refused to make any declaration. The official record of the result was, " It is the general sense of the assembly that there is but one living and true God, and that Father, Son, and Holy Ghost are the one God" " which," says Peirce, "was the sense of about two to one of the assembly." Official proceedings and records of this character have not been celebrated for settling private opinions or for quieting public controversies ; and the result of the deliberations of the Western ministers was no exception to the usual rule. From this time scarcely any question was debated throughout the West of England but the question of the Trinity. It was discussed in families, preached about from the pulpit, written about in pamphlets, and the local journals teemed with intelligence of what was being said and done. In this condition the Exeter Committee again addressed themselves to the ministers for another declaration of their real opinions. This, however, did not satisfy the people, and it was resolved to make an appeal to London for advice.

The London ministers had already been informed of the nature and progress of this controversy. Those who obeyed the summons addressed to them by their brethren, more than a hundred and fifty in number, met, therefore, fully prepared to discuss it. But some of the most eminent of the ministers declined to have anything to do with the matter. They rightly judged that it could only end in divisions amongst themselves, and they also doubted their competency, as Dissenters, to form a court for the adjudication of such a question. Amongst those who refused to meet were Calamy, Watts, and Neal—certainly the three most eminent men belonging to the Presbyterian and Congregational denominations. The wisdom of their course was made apparent almost as soon as the assembly met. The meeting was summoned at Salters' Hall on February 19th, A.D. 1718-19, and it was the general opinion that a letter of advice to the brethren at Exeter should be drawn up and forwarded to them. It was thereupon proposed by Bradbury, at the unanimous direction of the Congregational ministers, and, after hot and angry debates, pressed to a division, that every minister then present should, as a witness to his own faith, subscribe the first Article of the Established Church on the doctrine of the Trinity, and the answers to the fifth and sixth questions in the Catechism of the Westminster Assembly. This motion was opposed mainly on the ground that it was an imposition of a human creed, and that to impose such a creed was inconsistent with the principles of Protestant Dissent. On being put from the chair the motion was rejected by seventy-three to sixty-nine votes, or, as was subsequently said, "the Bible carried it by four."* On this vote taking place the minority left the conference, and resolved themselves into a distinct body. Two assemblies now met. The first, or non-subscribing assembly, was presided over by

* Nearly all the Congregationalists voted with the minority; the Baptists were divided by ten to nine.

Dr. Joshua Oldfield, minister of the Presbyterian church in Maid Lane, Globe Alley, close to the spot where the Globe Theatre formerly stood. Oldfield was a man of great learning and sound judgment, and one of the most eminent of the tutors connected with the Presbyterian body. Amongst the members of this assembly were John Evans, Benjamin Grosvenor, Dr. Gale, Samuel Chandler, Dr. Avery, Nathaniel Lardner, William Jacomb, and Daniel Burgess. The majority of this assembly were Presbyterians, but it included a few Congregationalists and Baptists. The second, or subscribing assembly, was presided over by Thomas Bradbury. It included nearly all the Congregational ministers of the metropolis, and a majority of the Nonconformist pastors actually exercising the pastoral office. Amongst the most eminent were William Tong, Jabez Earle, and Daniel Mayo. The two assemblies forwarded separate addresses to Exeter, each address containing "Advices for Peace." The Non-subscribing ministers completed their paper on March 10th. They expressed, in this paper, their opinion that there were errors of doctrine sufficiently important to warrant and oblige a congregation to withdraw from the minister; that the people are the sole judges as to what these errors are; that the Bible only is the rule of faith; that no man should be condemned because he would not consent to human creeds; that no man should be charged with holding the consequences of his opinions if he disclaimed those consequences; and that, if agreement could not be arrived at, there should be quiet withdrawal without the censure of any person withdrawing. Accompanying the advices, the non-subscribing ministers forwarded a letter disclaiming their right to judge the matter at issue, as well as all sympathy with Arian doctrine. Following the letter was a statement of reasons for not subscribing, at the Salters' Hall conference, the paper relating to the Trinity. Amongst the reasons alleged were—that there was no necessity for clearing themselves from suspicion as to their orthodoxy; that it would have been taking a side against one of the Exeter parties; that no declarations, in other words than those of Scripture, could serve the cause of peace or truth; that the subscription insisted on was beyond what even the legislature required; that it would have been paying an unwarrantable regard to the Assembly's Catechism; that it would have been contrary to the principles of Protestantism, of the nature of an imposition, and a surrender of their Christian liberty. They observed, in conclusion, that they were of opinion that if such a demand were complied with, no one could tell where it would stop. These documents were published with the signatures of seventy-three ministers.

In the following month (April 7th, A.D. 1719) the subscribing assembly forwarded their "advices for peace." It was prefaced with a declaration of faith in the Trinity expressed in the words of the first Article of the Established Church and the answers on that subject in the Assembly's Catechism. These were signed by forty-eight London and eleven country ministers, and eighteen other ordained or licensed preachers. Great pains and some pressure, it is said, were used to obtain these signatures. In the accompanying advices the rights of the people are stated in almost the same language as that used by the non-subscribers; the opinion is then expressed that, in such cases, neighbouring ministers might be called in for counsel; that it was proper that a minister should be called upon for a declaration of the faith, when that faith was suspected; that if the attempts at union and agreement should fail, the people and the minister should quietly withdraw from each other, and that the denial of the doctrine of the Trinity was an error contrary to the Scriptures and to the faith of the Reformed Churches.

If these proceedings had terminated at this point, although they were already the subject of scandal throughout the country, no very great harm perhaps would have been done. But the non-subscribing ministers had published their documents under the title of "A True Relation;" the subscribing ministers therefore saw fit to publish theirs' under the title of an "Authentic Account," and to these followed an "Impartial Statement." "Proceedings," "Accounts," "Animadversions," "Defences," and "Letters," now followed each other in rapid succession. The London prints opened their columns to both parties. Each side defended itself and attacked the other with a virulence and an animosity which disgraced equally their characters and their manners. Charges of deliberate lying and the gravest accusations respecting personal character were made and retorted without stint or measure. It must be said, however, that the non-subscribing party showed themselves, in their manner of conducting the controversy, far superior to their brethren. The subscribers were led by "the bold Bradbury," whose zealous and fiery temper communicated itself to nearly all his party. Bradbury himself wrote the most violent of the whole series of pamphlets. The best controversialist was

Peirce, who wrote, throughout, with a grave moderation of style and a charity of tone which his orthodox brethren might well have copied.

It unfortunately happened, for both the parties to Salters' Hall dispute, that their letters of advices were delivered just too late to be of any service. While the London ministers were disputing, the Exeter people had taken the matter into their own hands. The trustees, after consulting with seven neighbouring ministers, and without bringing the question before the church or congregation, took upon themselves to lock Peirce out of his chapel. Peirce remonstrated that the people should determine this, but received the reply that, as there might be a majority in his favour, it was resolved not to consult them, and that he and his brother minister Hallett might preach at another meeting. Liberty to do this was, however, denied, and Peirce's friends, to the number of three hundred, subsequently built for him a new place of worship. The London advices were delivered after Peirce had been locked out.*

From this time Unitarianism spread with unexampled rapidity. It was unfortunate for the orthodox party

---

* I have endeavoured to state the history of this controversy with absolute accuracy, but some of the narratives are so contradictory that, on some points, I may have failed to do so. The principal authorities which I have consulted are Peirce's "Case," "Western Inquisition," "Defence," "Justification," and "Reply;" the Exeter peoples' "Account of the Reasons of their withdrawal from Peirce's and Hallett's Ministry;" the "Non-subscribing Ministers' True Relation," the Subscribing Ministers' "Authentic Account," "The Synod," Bradbury's "Answer to the Reproaches," Easty's "Propositions," the Non-subscribing Ministers' "Reply to Subscribing Ministers' Reasons," Calamy's "Own Life," and Murch's "Western Churches." The whole of the pamphlets in this controversy are perhaps seventy in number, and the greater portion, if not all, are to be found in Dr. Williams's library.

that their cause, both in London and in the West, had
become identified with an act of personal injustice, and
something like synodical tyranny. It is impossible,
however, to throw the whole blame of this transaction
on one party. Peirce himself cannot escape the charge
of want of ingenuousness. When his faith was questioned
the most honourable course for him to have pursued
would have been to offer to resign his charge. The act
of the trustees was probably as illegal as it was harsh,
for no trust-deeds of that time contained any specification of doctrines. The injustice to which he had been
subjected rankled in Peirce's breast until his death, and,
courteous although he was in print, he scarcely ever
forgave those who had inflicted it upon him. For their
part, while they had succeeded in one object, that of
removing Peirce from his place of worship, they had
utterly failed in another and a greater. They contrived
to make the doctrine of Unitarianism popular, and they
lived to see nearly every Nonconformist church in
Exeter, and some of the principal churches in Devonshire and Somersetshire, lapse from the orthodox
standard. The Presbyterian churches of London,
Lancashire, and Cheshire became similarly infected.
In less than half a century the doctrines of the great
founders of Presbyterianism could scarcely be heard from
any Presbyterian pulpit in England. The denomination
vanished as suddenly as it had arisen, and, excepting in
literature, has left little visible trace of the greatness of
its power.

The Unitarians became, from this period, a distinct
and separate denomination in England. Hitherto it had
been their desire as well as their practice to worship

with other persons. They held the opinion that differences in matters of doctrine, even a difference on the question of the Trinity, should not separate Christian believers. They had the expectation that, in the course of time, the churches with which they were connected would be brought round to their own views. They do not seem to have perceived that their position, in this respect, was a false, if not a dishonest one. But the variations in the degrees in which they differed from the orthodox standard were so numerous that it is almost impossible to define what, at this period, Unitarianism was. Locke rejected the accusations both of Arianism and of Socinianism. Watts wrote against both these doctrines, and Peirce openly, and no doubt sincerely, stated that he belonged neither to the school of Arius nor Socinus. Yet all these rejected, in different degrees, the doctrine of the Trinity as stated in the Athanasian Creed. Whether it would have been wise and prudent not to have forced the more moderate section of the Unitarian party, to which Peirce belonged, from all ecclesiastical association with existing churches must be doubtful. Those, certainly, who remained in communion with the Established Church did not succeed in altering the doctrine of that Church. On the other hand, no notice of their existence was taken by many congregations, and a large number of those congregations subsequently became Unitarian. Their creed was, in fact, neither suppressed by the excision of those who held it, nor by tacit connivance in their presence. It was a development of thought,—the first form which rationalism took after mental freedom had been finally secured.

Some good came even from the Salters' Hall disputes.

While the Bangorian controversy was exciting attention to the fictitious nature of the claims of the sacerdotal party in the Established Church, the Salters' Hall controversy was exciting, amongst Dissenters, an equal amount of attention to the mischievous character and influence of the imposition of human creeds. On this question there was little difference of opinion between the subscribers and the non-subscribers. Both parties rejected the principle of such an imposition, but disagreed as to whether the declaration concerning the doctrine of the Trinity could be correctly indicated by that title. While, therefore, the non-subscribers vigorously attacked the system of creeds, the subscribers maintained that such attacks were wholly uncalled for. None, after this controversy, ventured to suggest the framing of any system of doctrine which bore the smallest likeness to a human creed. The authority of all past compositions of this nature was gone.

The lull which succeeded to these exciting controversies extended over the lifetime of a generation. Religion, whether in the Established Church or out of it, never made less progress than it did after the cessation of the Bangorian and Salters' Hall disputes. If, as was undoubtedly the case, breadth of thought and charity of sentiment increased, and were, to some extent, settled into the mental habit of the nation, religious activity did not increase. The churches were characterized by a cold indifferentism. The zeal of Puritanism was almost as unknown as it was unimitated. It seems to have been impossible for the Christian men of this generation to fight with the old force of Christianity while they were being fitted into a new armour of thought.

Everything was changing, and until the change was completed, and they had accommodated themselves to it, they seemed half paralyzed. When the old dogmas of church authority were exploded, the Episcopalians scarcely knew what to do. The great buttress of their whole system was gone. The edifice had not been maintained with extraordinary success, as a religious institution, under the best of circumstances: would it now bear the smallest extension? They had also to meet Protestant Dissenters who were free to say anything that they pleased. There was no possibility of putting Watts in Newgate as Delaune and De Foe had been put. Not merely gibbets, racks, and thumbscrews, but even the pillory was gone, and gone for ever. Men who would have liked a return of such days saw themselves frowned upon at Court, and, as a result, sneered at by the people. Church questions dropped, one after another, from public view, and, for the most part, men were glad to be rid of them. Full liberty of thought had been obtained, and it can scarcely be a matter of surprise that they were thankful to rest in order to enjoy it.

On the part of the Dissenters this quiet, and, indeed, worse than quiet condition, was, for other reasons, equally natural. They had fought the last great battle for toleration, and God had given them the victory. They were sure, now, that they might exist, and they appear to have been grateful simply to enjoy, for almost the first time, a security that was disturbed neither by threats nor by apprehensions. Their old enemy was virtually extinct; they were on good terms with governments and ministers, and none of the Georgian bishops were at all likely to make them martyrs. They existed by the side of a wholly different Church from that to which they had lately been accustomed. In their judgment, therefore, the warfare against that Church was over. They went to their little meeting-houses; heard their preachers; paid them, perhaps, as well as they could, and were satisfied. They admired the bishops from a respectful distance, and were very fond of quoting Hoadly. If they thought much of the deadness, ignorance, and corruption that were around them, they never thought of removing it. It must have seemed, indeed, too great to be removed. The early part of the Georgian era was not characterized, in any form or section, by intensity. Intensity had, for a time, done its work, and was now giving place to breadth. When breadth should be matured, intensity might come again to build on a new and a better foundation than the old.

Nothing that required great exertion or great sacrifice was either attempted or done during this period. The Quakers, with their habitual moral boldness and sagacity, were the only people who sought and obtained an enlarged degree of liberty. Penn, who had been, for the greater portion of their existence, their parliamentary agent, negotiating, on their behalf, terms with monarchs, ministers, and members of parliament, had died in the year 1718; but the Society was not therefore left without a similar representative. Joseph Wyeth and Thomas Story were selected to take the initiative in the delicate work which was now required to be done. The form of Affirmation which had been imposed by the statute of William III. in place of an oath, for the use of Quakers in courts of law, did not, it would appear, meet the approval of some members of the body. It contained the words, "In the presence of Almighty God," which, it was objected, made it equivalent to an oath. It was therefore resolved to move for a new form of affirmation. Wyeth, who was well known to the King, addressed a letter on the subject to his Majesty, and secured his concurrence in their wishes. Story, who had frequently appeared, on public occasions, at Court, waited on the Earl of Sunderland, principal Secretary of State, and, from his interview, had reasons for believing that the Government would support them. Next, with painstaking assiduity, the two primates were visited, and interest made with members of both houses of the legislature.* Everything being prepared for the successful passage of the measure, a petition, signed by a hundred and thirty-two persons, was presented to the House of Commons on December 14th, A.D. 1721. The petition represented that, in consequence of the scruples of certain members of the Society, many " had fallen under great hardships by imprisonment or loss of their property, they not being able to answer in courts of equity, take probates of wills, prove debts on commission of bankruptcies, verify their entries on the leather or candle acts, take up their freedoms in corporations, be admitted to their polls on their freeholds, or give evidence on behalf of others not of their persuasion;" and they prayed that a Bill might be brought in for granting such a form of affirmation as might remove their difficulties. This was accordingly done, and the Bill passed through all its stages on the ninth of the following month. On the same day it was introduced

---

* Gough's "History of the Quakers," part iv. 180—183.

into the House of Lords, where it was opposed by Atterbury, who remarked that he did not know why such a distinguished indulgence should be allowed to men who were "hardly Christians." The Earl of Iley replied that they were Christians by Act of Parliament, at least, inasmuch as they were included under the Toleration Act; to which Atterbury angrily rejoined that to call Quakers Christians by Act of Parliament was a reflection on Christianity itself. The first reading took place with no further opposition; but when, on January 15th, the motion for the second reading was made, Atterbury again endeavoured to prove that Quakers could not claim to be Christians. After a lively debate, the Bill was carried by sixty-four to fourteen votes. Four days afterwards the House was to have gone into committee, when a petition against the measure, from some of the London clergy, was presented by Dawes, Archbishop of York. The clergy alleged that if the Bill should pass, their tithes would be in danger; that society would be injured if justice were to be administered without an appeal to God; that the enemies of Christianity would triumph when they saw such consideration made by a Christian legislature to "a set of men" who renounced the divine institutions of Christ; and that it might tend to the increase of Quakerism. The Archbishop moved that the petition be received and read. A hot and angry debate took place on this motion. Fourteen peers—seven on each side—argued the question; the Government firmly opposed the reception of such a document, and it was ultimately decided to reject it. Sunderland then expressed the opinion that a committee should be appointed to inquire into its authors and promoters, for it was nothing but a libel. The question that the petition be rejected was again put, and carried by sixty to twenty-four, several peers, headed by the Archbishop of York, entering their protest against the decision. The Bill was then suspended, but, on the fifth of March following, the protest of the peers was ordered to be expunged from the records of the House. On the 18th of June the Bill finally passed by fifty-two to twenty-one votes, Wake, Archbishop of Canterbury, and Potter, Bishop of Oxford, signing a vehement protest against it.*

Nothing could more clearly indicate the change in the spirit of Government and in the opinions of the people than the history of this measure. It was enough that it received, in the first instance, the opposition of the High Church clergy, and that Atterbury, now about to be impeached for high treason and be banished the kingdom, appeared as its principal opponent, for it to pass by the most commanding majorities. If the Presbyterians had been possessed of anything like the courage and persistency of the Quakers, they could, no doubt, at this time, have procured, with ease, the repeal of the Test and Corporation laws. While, however, they enjoyed the liberty of occasional conformity, and could thus qualify for office by partaking of the Sacrament according to the rites of the Established Church—joining the Church, that is to say, for half-an-hour every year and protesting against it during the remainder of their twelve months of office, they appeared to think that they had secured all that was needful and honourable.

The indifference of Dissenters with respect to their

* "Parliamentary History," vii.

civil rights has, however, another explanation. In the next year they received a substantial mark of the royal favour. Daniel Burgess, secretary to the Princess of Wales, and, as it supposed, son to the minister of that name, is reported to have suggested to Lord Townsend that a grant from the royal purse would be highly esteemed by the Nonconformist bodies. Townsend, we are told, took the advice of Sir Robert Walpole, Chancellor of the Exchequer, and Walpole concurring, the subject was mentioned to the King. George the First, whose disposition was as generous as was his creed, immediately ordered £500 to be paid out of the Treasury for the benefit of the widows of Dissenting ministers. This grant, upon application, was afterwards increased to nearly £1,000 per annum, payable half yearly.* Such, at least, is the public history of the origin of the "Regium Donum," but its private history is scarcely so simple. It was, in fact, a bribe to the Dissenting ministers from the statesman who declared that "every man had his price." All of them were not satisfied that the promises which they had received had been so scandalously ignored. In order to quiet them, and, at the same time to keep them in subjection, Walpole requested to meet their principal representatives. He informed these that he wished to relieve them from their disabilities, but that the time for doing so had not yet arrived. He was the greatest friend that they had, and as a proof of his goodwill he offered them the royal bounty. "Pray," said the wily minister, "receive this for the use and comfort of the widows of Dissenting ministers, till the administration can more effectually

* Calamy's "Own Life," ii. 465.

serve your cause."* The ministers accepted the money, which was privately distributed by nine of their number. It was not, however, taken without some grave doubts as to what would be the opinion of posterity with respect to those who consented to receive and distribute it. In the fear that this secret bounty might subsequently "come to be inconveniently known," Calamy, who was one of its first distributors, attempts, in his diary, an elaborate justification of the act. It had become in his own lifetime, he says, "more known than was ever to have been desired ;" but he reminds those who might afterwards hear of the circumstance that, according to Burnet, Charles II. gave similar bounties to many of the Presbyterian ministers of his reign. It is true that Baxter would not touch the money, and that he sent it back ; but most of those to whom it was offered took it. "The Court," adds Burnet, "hired them to be silent, and the greatest part of them were so, and very compliant." "But," says Calamy, "there was in the reign of George I. nothing to be silent about, unless it was the continuance upon the Dissenters of the hardships they were under, of which they often complained." He remembers also that Dr. Owen received a thousand guineas from Charles II. for distribution amongst Dissenters ; but he also remembers that Owen was severely blamed for receiving it. Daniel Williams, however, for refusing the offer of a similar amount, was censured for not accepting it. Calamy then asks why the Dissenters of England might not as thankfully receive such help

---

* These facts are taken from an article in the "London Magazine" for 1774, said to have been written by the well-known Congregational minister and tutor, Dr. Mayo. Calamy, ii. 466, note.

as the Presbyterians of Ireland, to whom, in A.D. 1690, William III. ordered a royal grant, although even they were condemned for taking it?* The fear of the grant becoming publicly known is, however, a sufficient proof that Calamy himself was not satisfied with his own excuses. No one can imagine that there was an open and direct bargain between the Court and the Dissenters, but there can be as little doubt that if the latter accepted it as a free gratuity the former considered it to be a bribe. And it had all the demoralizing effects of a bribe. For more than a century and a quarter the "Regium Donum" continued to be a source of weakness, strife, discontent, and reproach. It destroyed the self-respect of those who received it; it subjected its distributors to the odium of their more independent brethren, and it has never ceased to be a subject of taunt from the controversial advocates of an endowed religion.

The necessitous circumstances of many widows of Dissenting ministers, as well as of many of the ministers themselves, was, at this period, attracting the attention of all denominations of Dissenters. The Presbyterians and the Congregationalists established funds for their relief, with very liberal rules for their administration. In A.D. 1717 the Particular Baptists resolved to establish a similar fund. In the preliminary paper of proposals which was issued, the reason for this organization is stated to be the "great decay" of the Baptist interest in some parts of England, and the difficulty they experienced in keeping up the public worship of God "with any tolerable reputation in other parts; the great want

* Calamy, ii. 468, 472.

and credibility of the books of the Bible were denied. Like the Unitarian, the Deistic controversy arose from the release of the human mind from the fetters of authority, and, in its essence, was only an extension of the spirit of free-inquiry. It was a challenge of the human intellect to the ability of the Christian Church to prove, by reason, the foundations of the Christian faith. The Unitarians had denied the fact of the necessity of an expiatory sacrifice for sin in the form in which the doctrine of the Atonement had hitherto been stated; the Deists denied that the Almighty had, at any time, revealed a religion to mankind. They did not deny the existence of a natural religion in the heart and conscience of man, but they did deny the historical foundation, the necessity, and, to a great extent, the beneficial influence, of Christianity. The books of the Bible were, to these men, either forgeries, or impositions, or both; and they challenged the Church to prove the contrary. As early as the beginning of the previous century, Lord Herbert of Cherbury had announced and defended similar views; and Thomas Hobbes, of Malmesbury, had succeeded him. Mr. Charles Blount followed. The tendency of the works of all these writers was simply to eliminate Christianity, except as an amusing system of morals, from the authentic history of the world. In A.D. 1701, Toland had been censured by Convocation for his book entitled "Christianity not Mysterious." Toland, however, was scarcely a Deist, and considered himself to be a Christian. The design of his work was to prove that there was nothing in the Christian religion either contrary to, or above, reason. He systematically depreciated, however, the genuineness of the books of the New Testament, comparing them, in their character, to the spurious gospels which had made their appearance in the early history of Christianity. In A.D. 1711, Lord Shaftesbury took the same side by the publication of a work entitled "Characteristics." In this work the state of the world under the heathen and the Christian administrations was compared, and judgment given in favour of the former. In the most polished style, and with the most caustic irony, Shaftesbury ridiculed the characteristics of the Christian religion. The "saving of souls," he exclaimed, "is now the heroic passion of exalted spirits." He denounced the doctrine of future rewards and punishments as equally unphilosophical in character and demoralizing in tendency, producing a narrowness of spirit, a neglect of the public good, and a selfishness of aim "which was observable in devout persons of almost all religious persuasions."* Shaftesbury, however, was careful to distinguish between himself as a thinker and as a citizen. He proclaimed, accordingly, with sarcastic solemnity, that he accepted the Christian religion "as by law established," and was steadily "orthodox" in his adhesion to it. Taking the ordinary ground of State-Churchmen, he remarked that he considered it, indeed, "immoral and profane" to doubt the truth of any religion whatever to which the State had given its sanction. He also accepted the Scriptures, although their text was not authentic, as "witty and humorous" books; but the scheme of the Christian religion, as a whole, he considered to be an invention of the clergy for their own aggrandizement. The highest morality, he conceived, was the pursuit

* "Characteristics," ii. 58.

and credibility of the books of the Bible were denied. Like the Unitarian, the Deistic controversy arose from the release of the human mind from the fetters of authority, and, in its essence, was only an extension of the spirit of free-inquiry. It was a challenge of the human intellect to the ability of the Christian Church to prove, by reason, the foundations of the Christian faith. The Unitarians had denied the fact of the necessity of an expiatory sacrifice for sin in the form in which the doctrine of the Atonement had hitherto been stated; the Deists denied that the Almighty had, at any time, revealed a religion to mankind. They did not deny the existence of a natural religion in the heart and conscience of man, but they did deny the historical foundation, the necessity, and, to a great extent, the beneficial influence, of Christianity. The books of the Bible were, to these men, either forgeries, or impositions, or both; and they challenged the Church to prove the contrary. As early as the beginning of the previous century, Lord Herbert of Cherbury had announced and defended similar views; and Thomas Hobbes, of Malmesbury, had succeeded him. Mr. Charles Blount followed. The tendency of the works of all these writers was simply to eliminate Christianity, except as an amusing system of morals, from the authentic history of the world. In A.D. 1701, Toland had been censured by Convocation for his book entitled "Christianity not Mysterious." Toland, however, was scarcely a Deist, and considered himself to be a Christian. The design of his work was to prove that there was nothing in the Christian religion either contrary to, or above, reason. He systematically depreciated, however, the genuineness of the books of the New Testament, comparing them, in their character, to the spurious gospels which had made their appearance in the early history of Christianity. In A.D. 1711, Lord Shaftesbury took the same side by the publication of a work entitled "Characteristics." In this work the state of the world under the heathen and the Christian administrations was compared, and judgment given in favour of the former. In the most polished style, and with the most caustic irony, Shaftesbury ridiculed the characteristics of the Christian religion. The "saving of souls," he exclaimed, "is now the heroic passion of exalted spirits." He denounced the doctrine of future rewards and punishments as equally unphilosophical in character and demoralizing in tendency, producing a narrowness of spirit, a neglect of the public good, and a selfishness of aim "which was observable in devout persons of almost all religious persuasions."* Shaftesbury, however, was careful to distinguish between himself as a thinker and as a citizen. He proclaimed, accordingly, with sarcastic solemnity, that he accepted the Christian religion "as by law established," and was steadily "orthodox" in his adhesion to it. Taking the ordinary ground of State-Churchmen, he remarked that he considered it, indeed, "immoral and profane" to doubt the truth of any religion whatever to which the State had given its sanction. He also accepted the Scriptures, although their text was not authentic, as "witty and humorous" books; but the scheme of the Christian religion, as a whole, he considered to be an invention of the clergy for their own aggrandizement. The highest morality, he conceived, was the pursuit

* "Characteristics," ii. 58.

of virtue for its own sake, and its perfection must always be owing to the belief of a God.*

Contemporary with Shaftesbury was Anthony Collins, author of a "Discourse of Free-thinking," of an "Essay concerning the Use of Reason," and of a "Discourse on the Grounds and Reasons of the Christian Religion." Collins, in these works, boldly attacked the sacred writings, charging them with gross textual errors, and putting the foundation of Christianity, not on the actual life and work of the Saviour, but on prophetical fulfilments only.† Another Free-thinker soon followed. This was Thomas Woolston, who selected, as his ground of attack on the Christian religion the narratives concerning the miracles of Jesus Christ. In six discourses, published between A.D. 1727 and 1729, Woolston maintained that these miracles never really took place; that they were merely allegorical representations; and that the supposed life of Christ himself was also nothing more than an allegory. The Gospel narratives he denounced as absurd and incredible, and the Resurrection as a myth.‡

No sooner was the last of Woolston's discourses published than another author appeared, who argued that Christianity was, after all, nothing but a hashup of the "Law of Nature." Dr. Tindal, who elaborated this theory, considered that the Christian religion, or such portions of it, at least, as were really historical, if any were, was an entirely supererogatory performance. The God of nature, in his creation of man, had given him all that was needful for his spiritual

---

* Leland's "View of Deistical Writers," Letters v. vi.
† Ib. Letter vii.   ‡ Ib. Letter viii.

existence, and any external revelation was therefore unnecessary.*

The personal character of those who made these bold and repeated assaults on the bases of the Christian religion, rendered their writings more influential and dangerous than would otherwise have been the case. They were, for the most part, men of great intellectual ability and of high attainments. They were not only virtuous men, but they considered their system to be more favourable than the Christian religion to the cultivation of all human virtue and dignity. Their doctrines found thousands of willing believers. Amongst the wits and rakes Deism became a fashionable creed. Society then witnessed, on a small scale, what would be the effect of the withdrawal of the sanctions of the Christian religion from human life. All the best Christian thought of the nation was accordingly employed to make good the defences of the Gospel. Accepting issue on the ground selected by the impugners of the received doctrines, both Church and Dissenting writers undertook to prove the entire reasonableness of the Christian faith. They were quite willing that it should be brought to the bar of that intellect and judgment which the Creator had given to man. "Those amongst us," said Gibson, the learned Bishop of London, "who have laboured, of late years, to set up reason against revelation, would make it pass for an established truth that if you will embrace revelation you must of course quit your reason, which, if it were true, would doubtless be a strong prejudice against revelation. But so far is this from being true, that it is universally acknowledged that revelation itself is to

* "Christianity as Old as the Creation," A.D. 1730.

stand or fall by the test of reason, or, in other words, according as reason finds the evidences of its coming from God to be or not to be sufficient and conclusive, and the matter of it to contradict or not contradict the natural notions which reason gives us of the being and attributes of God."* "Our religion," said Dr. Rogers, the Boyle lecturer, "desires no other favour than a sober and dispassionate examination. It submits its grounds and reasons to an unprejudiced trial, and hopes to approve itself to the conviction of any equitable inquirer." † "If in revelation," said Bishop Butler, "there be found any passages the seeming meaning of which is contrary to natural religion, we may most certainly conclude such seeming meaning not to be the real one." ‡ Dr. James Foster, the successor of Gale at the Barbican Baptist chapel, held similar language. "The faculty of reason," he remarks, "which God hath implanted in mankind, however it may have been abused and neglected in times past, will, whenever they began to exercise it aright, enable them to judge of all these things." ǁ The Deists themselves acknowledged the candour with which they were met. Collins said, publicly, that many of the replies to him were " written with a temper, moderation and politeness, unusual in theological controversies, and becoming good, pious, and learned men;" that the authors allowed the subject to

* "Second Pastoral Letter," A.D. 1730.
† "Boyle Lectures," A.D. 1727, p. 59.
‡ "Analogy of Religion," part ii. chap. 1.
ǁ "Truth and Excellency of the Christian Religion," A.D. 1731. I am indebted to Mr. Pattison's Essay on the "Tendencies of Religious Thought in England, 1680-1750," for the suggestion of the above quotations.

" depend only on the force of the argument, appeal only to the reason of men for a determination, and disclaim all force and other application to the passions and weakness of men, to support and maintain the notions they advance."* With one exception, none dreamed of putting law in force to punish the authors of these works. Woolston was indicted, under the Blasphemy Act, for the publication of his Discourses, and was condemned to a year's imprisonment and a fine of a hundred pounds, but no person expressed a stronger condemnation of such a resort to force for the purpose of putting down opinion than Woolston's ablest antagonist, Nathaniel Lardner. In the preface to a " Vindication of the Miracles of the Saviour," Lardner remarked that if men were permitted to propose their objections to Christianity no one need be in pain for the event. All force, he said, on the minds of men in matters of belief, was contrary to the spirit of Christianity; and severity, instead of doing good, had always done harm.†

The most popular reply to the deistical arguments was from the pen of Sherlock, Bishop of Bangor, the old opponent of Dissenters, who selected, for attack, Woolston's discourses. Throwing the argument for the Resurrection of the Saviour into the form of a legal trial, Sherlock wrote a book,‡ which, if coarse and familiar in its language, largely influenced public opinion, and, probably because it was coarse and familiar, passed rapidly through fourteen editions. Nathaniel Lardner, then a young Presbyterian minister in Poor Jewry Lane,

---
* " Scheme of Literal Prophecy Considered." Preface, p. 4.
† Kippis's " Life of Lardner," p. 15—18.
‡ " Trial of the Witnesses of Jesus Christ," A.D. 1730.

conceived the design of an exhaustive work on the Credibility of the Gospel History, and published, in A.D. 1727, the first part of that great performance, which occupied thirty years of one of the most laborious of human lives. Lardner also defended the Miracles from Woolston's attack, in which he was followed by Dr. Zachary Pearce, of St. Martin's, London, and Smallbrooke, Bishop of St. David's. Dr. Waterland, an eminent Church scholar, replied to Tindal. Dr. James Foster surveyed the whole argument. Balguy, in "A Letter to a Deist" (A.D. 1729), sustained the beneficial influence of Christianity on moral virtue in reply to Shaftesbury. Woolston met with no fewer than twenty adversaries, the most conspicuous of whom, amongst Dissenters, were Dr. William Harris, of the Poor Jewry Church,[*] and Mr. Hallett, of Exeter. Watts also took the field. Next to Sherlock, however, the most popular of the opponents of Deism was Dr. James Foster, who, at this time, and for many years subsequently, occupied the most prominent position amongst the preachers of the metropolis. Foster had been educated for the Dissenting ministry by Hallett, of Exeter, and had imbibed from his tutor, and probably also from Peirce, who held him in high estimation, anti-Trinitarian views. As early as the year 1720 he had published an essay to prove that the doctrine of the Trinity was not one of the fundamentals of Christianity. At the same time he vindicated the Resurrection of the Saviour in a sermon preached in reply to the objections of the Deists. The

---

[*] Dr. Harris, who was one of the most accomplished scholars and one of the greatest masters of the English language of his time, made a magnificent collection of works on Christian polemics, the whole of which he left, by will, to Dr. Williams's library.

reading of Gale's work on Infant Baptism induced him to forsake the Presbyterians and to undergo adult immersion. He was subsequently elected successor to Gale, and while in charge of the Barbican Church commenced a Sunday evening lecture at the Old Jewry. Few, if any, of the Dissenting churches of this period held evening services, and Foster's lectures commanded a great and varied audience. This, however, was entirely due to the eminent and unrivalled abilities of the lecturer. Possessed of the finest elocutionary powers, a clear reasoner, chaste in his style, happy in his choice of language, combining energy with simplicity and dignity with pathos, with a voice that charmed the ear and a manner that added expressiveness to every sentence which he uttered, he both surprised and enchanted all who heard him. "Here," says the friend who preached his funeral sermon, "was a confluence of persons of every rank, station, and quality; wits, free-thinkers, and clergy, who, while they gratified their curiosity, had their prepossessions shaken, and their prejudices loosened."* Pope, who did not spare even more eminent men, has handed Foster's name down to all posterity:—

> Let modest Foster, if he will, excell
> Ten Metropolitans in preaching well.

Until Edward Irving's ministry, probably no preacher for nearly a hundred years, enjoyed such marked popularity as this famed General Baptist minister. Subsequently, the Deistical controversy gave rise to the great work of Bishop Warburton on the "Divine Legation of

* Wilson's "Dissenting Churches," ii. 270, 282. Dr. Fleming's Funeral Sermon, p. 15.

Moses," and of Bishop Butler on the "Analogy of Natural and Revealed Religion;" but these works belong to the generation succeeding that of the most conspicuous early Deists.

With such an exhibition of power and of scholarship arrayed against it, it is not surprising that Deism, as an intellectual theory, was quickly beaten from the field of controversy, and it is not more surprising that practical and vital religion did not gain from its defeat. The apologists of Christianity, in fact, were, to a great extent, drawn aside by the controversy in which they were engaged, from the principal work of preachers of the religion of Jesus Christ. They built up, with masterly ability, and acknowledged success, the external defences of their faith; they proved, beyond cavil, the superiority of the Christian religion as a moral agent, but they did little more than this. They strangely forgot the internal evidences of the truth of Christianity. Whether Shaftesbury's sneer had or had not told upon them, they neglected, to a lamentable extent, one of the chief means of "saving souls." They fell into a habit of treating Christianity as an intellectual creed, as a system of morals, and a means of virtue. In no age, probably, have so few appeals to the spiritual affections of men been made as were made during the age of Deism. As few persons are moral from considerations of reason and prudence alone, and as none can be religious without the strongest feelings of the heart going forth towards their Maker and Redeemer, it followed that the Christian preachers exercised little influence on either the morals or the religion of the people. Christianity, as an intellectual belief, was enlightened and steadied, but faith as a vital power scarcely ever existed in less degree. Preaching, if accurate and polished, was cold and heartless. Foster's sermons are the best illustrations of the most popular Christian oratory of the Deistic period. Foster was an Addison in the pulpit, but he expressed even less of Christian affectionateness than the moral essayist. Amongst, however, the most eminent of preachers and writers, Watts was one who carefully guarded himself against this danger. In three sermons on the "Inward Witness of Christianity, or an evidence of the truth of the Gospel from its Divine effects," Watts proclaimed the superior character of the testimony derived from the conscience and experience of man to that of any external evidence. He warned the Christian world against a religion which consisted in merely correct morals and a correct theology, "while devotion freezes at the heart;" and he vindicated zeal in the ministry of the word from the ridicule of an age which pretended to "nothing but calm reasoning." But even Watts was careful to abjure the charge of "enthusiasm," and appealed to "common sense and reason" in defence of preaching characterized by the "movements of a sacred passion," and by a living fire.* It must be said, however, in honour of the Christian apologists of this generation, that the special work which was given them to do they did with conscientious care and unrivalled success; with such care and such success, indeed, that all subsequent labourers in the same field have done little more than to add, here and there, small outworks to their great system of fortifications.

---

* "Three Sermons," &c., Dedication, A.D. 1730.

As it is impossible for Nonconformity, in the circumstances in which it has been placed in England, to live and extend without the possession, by its adherents, of an unusual measure of personal piety and of the spirit of self-sacrifice, its comparative decline, under the influences of the [age of reason, was very natural. Calamy mentions no fewer than twenty-five ministers, amongst whom were Joseph Butler, afterwards Bishop of Durham, and author of the "Analogy," and Thomas Secker, afterwards Archbishop of Canterbury, who seceded to the Church. Amongst the number of those who conformed were eighteen of the non-subscribing ministers in the Salters' Hall controversy, who resented the imposition of one tenet, but who had no hesitation to subscribe to the "six hundred," which are reported to be contained in the thirty-nine Articles of religion.*

In London, and the neighbourhood within the bills of mortality, it appeared that between A.D. 1695 and A.D. 1730, one church only had been erected, but that, by enlargements, increased accommodation had been made for four thousand persons. Twelve of the old congregations had been dissolved and ten new congregations

---

* Calamy says:—"Some of those who had before gone over from us to the Church had been scandalous, but it was otherwise with those who now conformed. They were generally persons of sobriety and unblemished character, and might therefore be received and caressed by those whom they fell in with, with a better grace." Calamy observes that many of those who had left Dissent were soured in spirit by the change, and discovered "enmity and contempt with respect to those whose company they quitted." He adds, "It was easy to be observed and much taken notice of, that most that conformed about this time, complained much of a spirit of imposition working among the Dissenters, which discovered itself in the proceedings at Salters' Hall, and on other occasions, when the debates about the Trinity grew warm."—"Own Life," ii. 503, 506.

organized; fourteen had increased, fifteen had declined, and twenty remained in about the same state. The Presbyterians are described as being almost equally divided between Calvinists, Arminians, and Baxterians, but principally moderate Calvinists; the Congregationalists as all Calvinists, and the Baptists as divided between Arminians and Calvinists, with the addition of three Socinians, of whom Foster was one. The Congregationalists are described as being greatly deficient in unity and sympathy with each other.*

While the fact of this declension was generally acknowledged, there were considerable differences of opinion concerning its causes. The first writer who directed attention to it, and who, himself, afterwards conformed to the Established Church, assigned it to the ignorance of Dissenters of their own principles, and to

---

* Palmer MS. in Dr. Williams's library. The numbers of the churches of the different denominations were :—

PRESBYTERIANS 44	Calvinists	19
	Arminians	13
	Baxterians	12
INDEPENDENTS - 33	Calvinists	27
	Doubtful	1
	Antinomian	3
	Disorderly	2
BAPTISTS - - - 26	Seventh Day—	
	Calvinists	1
	Arminian	1
	Particular—	
	Calvinists	7
	Antinomian	9
	General—	
	Arminian	5
	Socinian	3

The Palmer MS., from which these particulars are taken, is one of the most valuable records of the state of Nonconformity in the last century. Its author is said to have come from Northampton to London, but no one has been able to fix his identity. It contains an account of the state and condition of every church, and is written with great care, but perhaps too great freedom. The substance of the MS. was reprinted, seventy years ago, in the "Protestant Dissenters' Magazine."

the bad management of their affairs. Amongst the proofs of the latter, he adduced, especially, the want of culture in ministers, which, he asserts, had lost them many "gentlemen."* The reply to this pamphlet proceeded from the pen of a young minister at Northampton, who had recently engaged in a work which was designed to remove any occasion for the last charge. This was Philip Doddridge. Doddridge was then twenty-eight years of age. He had been educated at St. Albans, by Dr. Samuel Clarke, and pressed by his tutor to devote himself to the ministry. Calling for advice and assistance on Dr. Calamy, he met, from the fashionable and stately Presbyterian, only a frigid reception. "I waited," he says, "upon Dr. Edmund Calamy to beg his advice and assistance that I might be brought up a minister, which has always been my great desire. He gave me no encouragement in it, but advised me to turn my thoughts to something else. It was with great concern that I received such advice; but I desire to follow providence, and not force it."† Providence led him, and in A.D. 1723 Doddridge was settled as pastor of the Congregational Church at the village of Kibworth. From Kibworth he removed to Harborough, where, under the urgent solicitation of Watts and of the ministers of the neighbourhood, he established an institution for the training of students for the ministry. In A.D. 1729 he removed to Northampton, taking his pupils with him. His gentleness of manner, his devotion of spirit, his extreme charity and conscientiousness, and the

---

* "An Inquiry into the Causes of the Decay of the Dissenting Interest," A.D. 1730.

† Orton's "Life of Doddridge," Works, i. 21.

breadth and thoroughness of his learning, had already signalized him in the eyes of those who most intimately knew him, as a man who was capable of great and varied service. His reply to Gough was his first publication. In it he ardently identified himself with the "Dissenting cause," which, he was persuaded, was "founded on reason and truth," and that the honour of God, and the public good, and the interests of liberty and serious piety, were nearly concerned in its support. He agreed with Gough as to the necessity of teaching the principles of Dissent, and the injury which had been received from unscriptural impositions and uncharitable contentions. He was of opinion that more practical religion was to be found in the free than in Established places of worship, and that it was a religious reverence for the divine authority which was their main support. Concurrently with this, he urged that preachers should study the character and temper of the populace, and not neglect the common people, who already constituted the bulk of the Dissenting interest. He apprehended that it would never be worth the while of Dissenters to neglect the populace in order to bring over gentlemen who had forsaken them. He would rather, he remarked, have honest and godly mechanics or day-labourers in the congregations than any who would be likely to leave them from "delicacy of taste." It was evident, in his judgment, that some of those who had quitted Dissent had been influenced by merely secular views, and particularly by marrying into the Church— a custom which had given it a "fatal blow." Notwithstanding this, he vindicated the utmost simplicity in preaching, and was of opinion that any other style would accomplish the ruin of Dissent. Such a style of preaching had been accompanied with a great increase in the number of Dissenters in his neighbourhood, who would be surprised to hear of an inquiry into causes of decay.* Another writer immediately followed Doddridge. He acknowledged that the decline of Dissent, so far as the conformity of some of its ministers was concerned, was plain; that all were of opinion that there was a general decay; and that one of the causes of it was that very belief—people being ashamed to continue in a " sinking cause." If, in local cases, it was declining, the circumstance was to be attributed to, amongst other things, the fact that it was not apparently the social or commercial interest of a man to be a Dissenter, and that Dissenters too often sent their children to Church schools.†

Before this discussion was concluded the Dissenters had resolved that one mark of their civil inferiority should, if possible, be removed. In November, A.D. 1732, two meetings were held at the Silver Street Chapel to consider the advisability of applying to the legislature for a repeal of the Test and Corporation Acts. At the first of these meetings a general committee was appointed. At the second it was resolved that every church of the Presbyterian, Congregational, and Baptist denominations, within ten miles of the metropolis, should be requested to appoint two deputies. On the 29th December in the same year the first General Assembly of the Deputies was held. In consequence of

---

* " Free Thoughts on the Most Probable Means of Reviving the Dissenting Interest," A.D. 1730.

† " Some Observations on the Present State of the Dissenting Interest," A.D. 1731.

the report presented to this body by the committee appointed at the previous meetings, in which it was stated that, upon consulting the ministers of State and others, there seemed to be no possibility that any application which might then be made to Parliament would be successful, it was determined not to take immediate action on the subject, but the committee and the deputies were confirmed in their appointments.* At last, therefore, there seemed to be some probability that the civil rights of Dissenters would receive something like adequate attention from themselves. An organization was now established which, if not so extensive as the one which De Foe had suggested, gave indication of increased self-respect and increased firmness of purpose. For the first time in their history the Dissenters resolved to take, with respect to the laws by which they were injured, and ultimately with respect also to the social disability and oppression which naturally grew out of those laws, an aggressive attitude. If they had not yet lost faith in the promises of politicians, they had resolved, as De Foe had advised them, to act, in some measure, for themselves.

* "A Sketch of the History and Proceedings of the Deputies," etc., pp. 1—2, A.D. 1813. This was just previous to the General Election of 1734, and Walpole, to obtain the support of the Dissenters, gave them promise of future support. Belsham's "Great Britain," vol. iii. 481. Tindal's "Continuation."

CHAPTER V.

FROM THE ORGANIZATION OF THE DISSENTING DEPUTIES TO THE ESTABLISHMENT OF METHODISM.

A.D. 1732—A.D. 1744.

AFTER the General Election of A.D. 1734, when the whole strength of the Dissenters was exerted to keep Sir Robert Walpole's ministry in power, application was again made to that statesman for the repeal of the Test and Corporation Acts. Walpole's conduct on this, as on a subsequent occasion, must be judged by what is known of the general character of the man. He was unscrupulous, he was tenacious of power, and he was equally tenacious of popularity. Personally, he had no objection to the repeal of these Acts, but, as a politician, he declined to identify his government with any motion to such an effect. He knew, and frankly acknowledged, his obligations to Dissenters, and also the obligation which the Crown was under to them,* but he dreaded to raise again the cry of "the Church in danger." He remembered how that cry had been sufficient, in a former reign, to cast out one of the strongest ministries, and almost to endanger the Hanoverian suc-

* Coxe's "Walpole," i. 476.

cession; and he shrank from the probability of its renewal. This is the most reasonable explanation of his conduct. He would have served the Dissenters if he could have done so consistently with his own political interests, but, as it was, he announced his intention to oppose them. For the first time, therefore, the Dissenters acted independently of the Government. They did what they could to ensure success, but knew beforehand that they would be beaten. A Bill was drawn up and committed to the hands of Mr. Plumer, member for Hertfordshire, who moved it on the 12th March, A.D. 1735-6. Mr. Plumer did equal justice to his subject, both in matter and manner. His statement was convincing, his argument conciliatory, and he was well supported in debate. When, however, Walpole himself rose, and, while doing justice to the services and the public spirit of Dissenters, expressed his opinion that the motion was ill-timed, and that the Government must resist it, its fate was settled. On a division it was lost by 251 to 123.[*]

It is remarkable that where the general body of Dissenters failed, the Quakers, immediately afterwards, although on another question, should again have almost commanded success. The prosecutions of this body for tithes and church-rates were so frequent, and entailed so much suffering, that they had become anxious to facilitate the processes of law by which they were convicted. Since the Act of William III. providing for the recovery of these charges in a summary way, eleven hundred and eighty members of this society had been prosecuted in the superior courts, more than three

---

[*] "Parliamentary History."

hundred had been imprisoned, and several had died in prison.* Nothing could exceed the severity with which the law on this subject was administered, or the personal hardship which was inflicted upon those who opposed it. For debts of a few shillings, which were not disputed, costs to the amount of scores of pounds were incurred, followed, in several instances, by forfeiture of all goods, and by loss of personal liberty. It was therefore determined to make a representation of their sufferings. In an address presented to Parliament, they pointed out that these prosecutions were an evasion of the Act for the summary recovery of rates, and asked that their prosecutors might, in future, be restrained from making the process of recovery so expensive and ruinous. A bill was accordingly brought in, providing that when a tithe or rate was not litigated, the warrant of two justices of the peace should be sufficient for the levy of a distress. Walpole gave his hearty support to this Bill, and, in doing so, roused once more the very cry which, as a statesman, he most dreaded to hear. No sooner was it before the House, than "the Church in danger" resounded throughout the land. Gibson, Bishop of London, led the way; and in the "Country Parson's Plea against the Quakers' Bill for tithes," endeavoured to prove that if the way of recovering these dues was made less ruinous than it was, the opposition to the payment would increase. Other pamphlets followed; circulars were sent to the clergy throughout the country to petition against the measure, and it was resolved to ask permission to appear by counsel before the

* Gough's "History," iv. 279. These and other particulars were separately published and brought before Parliament in the year 1736.

House against it. This unusual liberty was accorded to both sides; but the power of the Government, although not until the measure had been debated for several days and considerably modified, was sufficient to procure its passage. It finally passed the House by 164 to 48 votes. In the Lords it was met by every species of resistance. Arguments against its merits having failed, the plea was at last put forward that the measure had been rendered so imperfect by its manipulation in the Commons' committee, that it was not fit to be passed, and that there was no time left to amend it. On this ground it was rejected by 54 to 35 votes, the majority including fifteen bishops. No man was more irritated by this result than Walpole. It was not the habit of this minister to give the support of the Government to measures which were likely to fail, and he had fully reckoned on his ability to carry this Bill. His mortification at his defeat is represented to have been extreme,* and he visited upon the author of it all the punishment which a minister of state knows so well how to inflict. Gibson was deposed from the position of confidential adviser of the Crown on ecclesiastical questions, and received no further promotion. The elation of the clergy, however, was as great as was the humiliation of the minister. Those of London and Salisbury voted special addresses of thanks to their bishops for the zeal and success with which they had opposed the measure. Those of London expressed their gratitude for the vigilance with which the "legal rights of the clergy had been maintained;" and those of Salisbury came forward to manifest their " grateful sense of their preservation from that strange and un-

* Coxe's "Walpole," i. 478.

heard-of infringement of their rights," and for the defence of "their just and indisputable privileges." * The "rights" of the clergy meant, in this instance, the right not to tithes or other dues, but to punish, with the greatest punishment next to that of death, those who, without compulsion, refused to pay them. Their "privileges" meant, simply, the privilege of persecution. All that the Bill, had it been passed, would have accomplished, would have been to cheapen the process of recovery; but it was scarcely in the nature of ecclesiastical pride and hate to lessen any of the disadvantages of Dissent.

It was probably in consequence of the mortifying defeat which he experienced on this occasion that when Walpole was next applied to by the Deputies to use his influence to relieve them from the tests, he gave an abrupt and unqualified refusal to assist them. A deputation, headed by Dr. Chandler, waited on the minister, and, reminding him of his repeated promises, solicited his influence in their behalf. He made, says his biographer, the usual answer, that, whatever were his private inclinations, the attempt was improper, for the time had not yet arrived. "You have so repeatedly returned this answer," said Chandler, "that I trust you will give me leave to ask when the time will come?" "If you require a specific answer," said Walpole, "I will give it you in a word—Never!" † In spite, however, of the discouragement given by these words, it was resolved, in A.D. 1738-9, again to bring the subject before the Legislature. The Deputies prepared for their work with systematic care and vigour. Early in the year a paper of reasons in favour of the rights of Dissenters was issued, and a copy

* Gough, iv. 287.   † Coxe's "Walpole," i. 608.

put into the hands of every member of the House of Commons. On March 30th a Bill was brought in. No particulars of the debate which followed are reported, but its issue was even more unfavourable than on the previous occasion. The Bill was rejected by a hundred and eighty-eight to eighty-nine votes. This result did not, however, immediately discourage its friends. The committee of the Deputies met soon after the rejection of the measure, and reported themselves to be satisfied, if not with the issue, at least with the character of the debate. Measures were at once taken to extend, by correspondence, the power of the Deputies in the country. Letters were sent into every county, and a general meeting of Dissenters from all parts of England summoned for the following year. It is to be presumed that this meeting, if it was ever held, advised the Deputies to discontinue their exertions. Nothing more was done, and the subject was allowed to sleep for half a century.* During this long period the Deputies were occupied in defending, often at great expense, the civil and ecclesiastical rights of Dissenters throughout the kingdom. If a clergyman refused to bury the child of a Dissenter, they put the law in motion to compel him to do so; if Dissenting chapels were unjustly taxed, they resisted the claims that were made; if ignorant or intolerant Justices refused to register places of worship, they served them with a mandamus from the Court of Queen's Bench to compel them to discharge their duty; they successfully resisted demands for clerical fees and for clerical charges made for services that had never been rendered; they protected the rights of Dissenters in respect to charity

* "History and Proceedings," etc., pp. 7—12.

schools, and saw to the legal observance of trust deeds. In a very brief period their vigilance gave them such power that a check was effectually put upon the inroads of intolerance. Much of their success was unquestionably due to the character and energy of their chairman, Dr. Benjamin Avery, a physician of London, who occupied the post of chairman and treasurer for not fewer than twenty-eight years—from A.D. 1736 to A.D. 1764.*

In the year 1742 a case occurred which tested the consistency of the Baptist denomination in respect to occasional conformity to the Established Church. A Mr. Baskerville, member of the Baptist Church in Unicorn Yard, had been elected to the common council of the city of London, and had qualified himself for his office by receiving the sacrament according to the rites of the Church. Being immediately remonstrated with, he defended the course which he had taken, and resented what he deemed to be an interference with his own rights of conscience and of private judgment. The church at once took the advice of the London Baptist Board on the course which they should pursue towards him. At a meeting of the Board the question was proposed whether a person ought to be continued in the fellowship of the church who had received the sacrament in the Church of England to qualify himself for an office when he did not incur any penalty if he refused to accept the office. The Board unanimously decided that it was absolutely unlawful for any member of a "Gospel Church" to communicate with the Established Church on any consideration whatever. The matter was then submitted

* "Sketch of the History," etc., *pass.*

to the churches individually, who agreed, without exception, that such a person ought not to be continued in the fellowship of the church. At a subsequent meeting of ministers and deputies of all the churches, an address to the Unicorn Yard Church was agreed upon. In this address, after making an allusion to the bad example which would have been set had any sanction been given to the practice of occasional conformity, and referring, with grief, to the indulgence and growth of it amongst other Dissenting denominations, the assembly proceeded to state the grounds of their decision. They reminded the church that their forefathers had separated from the National Establishment on principle, and because they would not submit to any religious constitution which was not strictly regulated by the Word of God. They would submit to no ordinance or duty that was enjoined by a human authority which invaded the rights of conscience and the prerogatives of God; they did not hesitate for an instant to refuse to commune with a church the very frame of which was contrary to the appointment of the Lord and His Apostles, that had sprung from human policy and power alone, that assumed to itself an arbitrary right of imposing prescriptions on the consciences of men, and that harboured in its bosom multitudes of people of the most corrupt principles and the most profligate lives. These men had been faithful to blood in their testimony: if we, therefore, said the Assembly, submit to a wicked prostitution of the holy Supper for the sake of mere worldly honour or lucrative employment, we should be unworthy of the character of our ancestry, we should be exposing our profession to ridicule, we should be esteemed hypocrites, and we should draw down the righteous indignation of Heaven upon our inconsistency. The church was therefore exhorted to watch against all corruption, and to put away from it the root of bitterness. In the next year, Mr. Baskerville repeating his offence, he was formally adjudged, after another expostulation, to be no longer a member of the church.* This decisive course saved the London Baptists from any repetition of this practice.

It was at this period that the names of three young clergymen, who, for a year or two past, had been holding extraordinary religious services in the metropolis and other towns, were becoming the subject of the familiar but prejudiced talk of all religious circles. The first of these was John Wesley. If, in early life, any one man more than another had been carefully nurtured in Church principles, John Wesley had been so nurtured. Both his paternal and his maternal grandfathers had been ejected by the Act of Uniformity of A.D. 1662. His father, however, had not only conformed to the Church, but was one of the most bitter, unscrupulous, and malignant opponents of Dissent. His mother, the daughter of Dr. Samuel Annesley, had also conformed. The father appears to have been a man of no more than average piety, but the mother was a woman of high principle, deep religious feeling, consistent life, and unusual intelligence. To her the Wesley family probably owed the remarkable religious and intellectual gifts with which all its members, in greater or less degree, were endowed. It is possible to trace the secret of many of John Wesley's higher characteristics, and of some of his inconsistencies, to the influences which were brought to

* Ivimey, iii. 228—233.

bear upon him in early life. Saved, when an infant, as though by a miracle, from perishing in the flames which consumed his father's house, he was led to consider himself consecrated for some great work. His mother, in consequence of it, was especially careful of the soul of this saved child. In early life he saw, in his father's family, that conflict between Church principles and Christian duty which he himself was afterwards to illustrate on the grandest scale of any Churchman or Christian. When his father was from home, his mother insisted on taking his place as a Christian teacher and exhorter. She held public religious services, at which she read sermons and prayed with and advised the people. Her husband took alarm, first at what he considered to be the unfitness of such a proceeding in a woman, and, secondly, at the invasion of Church authority which was involved in such acts. In reply to the first, Susanna Wesley fell back on her responsibility as a Christian. She, as well as he, had a stewardship to administer; and she cared nothing for unfitness. "If," she said, "I am unfaithful to Him or to you, how shall I answer unto Him, when He shall command me to render an account of my stewardship?"* In her further answer, as to its "looking particular," there is to be seen a projection of one of the principles which guided John Wesley through his life. "I grant it does," she said ; "and so does almost everything that is serious, or that may any way advance the glory of God or the salvation of souls, if it be performed out of a pulpit, or in the way of common conversation ; because in our corrupt age the utmost care and diligence has been used to banish all discourse of God, or spiritual

* Southey's "Life of Wesley," chap. i.

concerns, out of society—as if religion were never to appear out of the closet, and we were to be ashamed of nothing so much as confessing ourselves to be Christians."* In reply to the second objection, that she was invading the authority of the Church, she did not do what many would have done, namely, question and deny the claims of that authority, but simply pointed to the good that had been and was being effected. Exactly the same character was in her, in this respect also, that was in John Wesley. She would not yield to her husband's desire that she should discontinue her services. "Send me," she replied, "your positive command, in such full and express terms as may absolve me from guilt and punishment for neglecting this opportunity of doing good, when you and I shall appear before the great and awful tribunal of our Lord Jesus Christ." From his mother also he derived a taste for works of Christian asceticism and mysticism. Law's "Serious Call" and à Kempis's "Imitation" were two of her favourite books, and those two books became his almost constant companions. Add to this, that supernatural noises were constantly heard in his father's house, and that they were credited, by all the members of the family, as supernatural, and Wesley's subsequent tendency to superstition may also, in part, be accounted for. The child was, in nearly all instances, the father of the man : even his earliest acquired mental weaknesses were destined to be a source of influence.

Wesley, when he went from his father's house to Oxford, went with somewhat chaotic religious impulses. He said, a few years after, of this period, as he said,

* Southey's " Life of Wesley," chap. i.

after that, of the subsequent period, that he did not then know God, and that he had no true faith. When the first course of his residence at the University was nearly completed, he became strongly influenced by religious feelings. With his brother Charles and a few other members of the University, he gave up his life to visiting the poor, the sick, and the imprisoned. He read deeply and prayerfully in the Bible, and read with it, again, Law, à Kempis, and Taylor's "Holy Living and Dying." He fasted long and often, prayed by day and night, lived by strict "method," and became a Christian ascetic, with a strong inclination for a retired and meditative life. But although he and his friends were sneered at throughout the University as the "Holy Club," as "Methodists," and as everything else that was deemed to be contemptible in that school of the prophets of the Established Church, they gained too much from their work for themselves and their fellow-men to swerve from it. Nor were they men, in other respects, who could be put down by coarse jokes or contemptuous tongues. Wesley was a man as learned and as cultured as any amongst them. He was a good classical critic, he had almost a natural capacity for logic, he had been elected to the Greek chair, and was moderator of the classes. His religious devotion adorned his academical position, and his academical position adorned his religion. Charles Wesley was younger by five years, but was giving equal promise of ability and eminence. To the "Holy Club" was soon joined another, and an equally powerful spirit. This was George Whitefield, who went from the position of a beer-drawer in Bristol to that of a "poor scholar" at the University. The "Imitation" had fallen, also, into his hands, and after a depth of despair almost equal to that of Bunyan, he, too, had taken hold of God and his Christ. It is singular how both Wesley and Whitefield went through, in their earliest religious experiences, the same process, not of mental conflict, but of physical discipline. Whitefield fasted twice a-week for thirty-six hours; went, like David, to his closet for prayer, seven times a-day, and devoted the whole of Lent to the most laborious religious exercises. He, too, afterwards looked back upon this time as upon a time of spiritual ignorance. When he went to Oxford, before he became acquainted with the Wesleys, the "Serious Call" fell into his hands. It intensified equally his religious feelings and his ascetic inclinations. Soon afterwards he joined the " Holy Club," and became, next to John Wesley, its most devoted member.*

Wesley's call to Georgia to be a missionary amongst the Indians probably saved him from becoming the leader of a "Ritualistic" party in the eighteenth century. He went there with a noble and self-sacrificing purpose, but with all the ecclesiastical tendencies of a High Churchman, combined with a somewhat superstitious faith in what may be described as Christian magic. Instances of the latter are to be found in the whole of his journals. The first occurs on the voyage to Georgia. A woman who thought that she was dying, wished to receive the communion. "At the hour of her receiving," says Wesley, "she began to recover, and in a few days was entirely out of danger." † One of his first acts of minis-

---

* Philip's " Life and Times of Whitefield," chap. i.
† "Journal," Nov. 10, 1736.

terial duty in Georgia was to baptize an infant. "The child was ill then," remarks Wesley; "but recovered from that hour."* His visit to America was a failure, and his rigid and priestly adherence to the rubrics of the Established Church, which brought upon him a law-suit, ultimately compelled him to return to England. From the Moravians on board the ship which took him out he had, however, learned one doctrine, the disclosure of which came upon him with surprise. Having occasion to consult Mr. Spangenberg, one of their pastors, he was asked, "Have you the witness within yourself? Does the spirit of God bear witness with your spirit that you are a child of God?" Wesley says he was surprised, and did not know what to answer. "Do you know Jesus Christ?" continued the pastor. Wesley could only say that he knew He was the Saviour of the world. "But do you know that He has saved you?" The reply was simply an expression of a hope that He had died to save him. "Do you know yourself?" asked Spangenberg. "I do," replied Wesley; but he adds, "I fear they were vain words." †

Further acquaintance with the Moravians in London and in Germany strengthened Wesley's views in this direction. He saw that the Gospel to be preached was a Gospel which offered free pardon to all sinners; which proclaimed the necessity of a new birth, and which gave prominence to the doctrines of justification by faith and the witness of the Spirit. His heart grew within him as he thought of the happiness which man might enjoy, and of the salvation of which he might partake, if the Gospel were but preached to him as it

* "Journal," Feb. 21, 1736-7. † Ib. Feb. 7.

might be preached. And to such preaching he determined to devote himself.

Much, however, as John Wesley's name has been identified, and justly so, with the great religious awakening which followed from his preaching, and from that of his followers, it is to Whitefield that the origin of the movement is more especially due. It was not Wesley, but Whitefield, who first awoke the people from the sleep of spiritual death; and it was not Wesley, but Whitefield, who first broke the bonds of ecclesiastical conventionalisms and laws. This occurred while the Wesleys were in Georgia. Whitefield was ordained in A.D. 1736. His first sermon, preached immediately afterwards in Bristol, was reported to have "driven fifteen persons mad," which simply meant that it roused several from a state of religious indifference to an intense and awful anxiety. When he next visited Bristol, in A.D. 1737, crowds of all denominations went to hear him. It was the same in London, at Gloucester, and everywhere that he went. Young as he was—not twenty-three years of age—he was now sought for from all parts of the kingdom. He preached several times in a week, and people went miles in order to hear him. When he left Bristol he was escorted out of the city by a multitude of horsemen and other persons. The beginning of the revival he himself traces to a sermon preached by himself in this year, "on the nature and necessity of our regeneration or new birth in Christ Jesus." "This sermon," he remarks, "under God, began the awakening at Gloucester, Bristol, and London."* From this time he consecrated himself to

* Andrew's "George Whitefield," p. 27.

the work of an evangelist. He preached nine times a
week, and in London people rose before daybreak in
order to be able to hear him, and, with lanterns in their
hands, might be seen threading their way from all parts
of the metropolis to the place where he was to preach.
This had not lasted three months before the clergy
began to oppose him. He was emptying their dull
churches, and was consequently assailed as a "spiritual
pickpocket." Pulpits were now refused to him. To
add to his bad odour, he was accused of visiting Dissenters—a charge which was true; for many Dissenters
opened their houses to him, and welcomed him as their
guest. The people, however, shared in none of the
jealousy of their Church leaders. When, at Wesley's
solicitation, he was about to leave for Georgia, "they
pressed," he says, "more eagerly and affectionately
than ever upon me. All ranks gave vent to their
feelings. Thousands and thousands of prayers were
put up for me; they would run and stop me in the
alleys of the churches, hug me in their arms, and follow
me with wistful looks."

Returning from Georgia for priest's orders, after an
absence of a few months from England, Whitefield found
the churches of the metropolis more than ever closed
to him. He was violating the diocesan and parochial
systems, by expounding the Scriptures from house to
house. He was doing good not according to ecclesiastical law. He was saving souls in a manner of which
a beneficed clergyman could not approve. The result
was, that the greatest preacher in England could scarcely
find a church in all London in which to preach. From
similar motives, every church in Bristol was now closed

to him. He took refuge in the prison chapel, but from this also he was soon cast out. A man who did not respect the parochial system was not considered fit to preach, even to condemned felons. Whether souls were saved or whether they were damned was, to the clergy of those days, a matter of entire indifference, so long as their own privileges could be maintained intact. Whitefield, who, although a reverent son of the Church of England, thought less of the decrees of councils and of canons than Wesley, at once made up his mind as to what he should do. He waited on the Chancellor of the Diocese of Bristol, who asked him why he preached without the Bishop's license? Whitefield replied, that he thought that custom had grown obsolete. The Chancellor, he adds, then read over to him that part of the Ordination Service which precludes any minister preaching in a private house, and demanded of him what he had to say to that? Whitefield's reply had a terrible force. "There is a canon," he said, "which forbids all clergymen to frequent taverns and play at cards; why is that not put into execution?" The Chancellor answered that if complaint were made on that point, he would attend to it; and then said, "I am resolved, sir, if you preach or expound anywhere in this diocese till you have a license, I will first suspend you, and then excommunicate you."* But the Chancellor, in this instance, spoke without considering his diocesan, who gave Whitefield the necessary authority.

It was immediately after this that, for the first time, Whitefield engaged in field preaching. He determined

* "Whitefield's "Journal," A.D. 1739.

to carry the Gospel to the savage and heathen colliers of Kingswood. "Finding," he says, "that the pulpits are denied me, and the poor colliers are ready to perish for lack of knowledge, I went to them, and preached on a mount to upwards of two hundred. Blessed be God that the ice is broken, and I have now taken the field. I thought it might be doing a service to my Creator, who had a mountain for His pulpit, and the heavens for His sounding-board, and who, when the Gospel was refused by the Jews, sent His servants into the highways and hedges." When Whitefield next preached to the colliers of Kingswood he had an audience of ten thousand. His preaching was followed by marvellous results. He could see the tears coursing down their blackened cheeks as he spoke, and hundreds, according to his own statement, were soon brought under deep conviction. Whitefield's way was now open to him, and he preached wherever he could find space or standing room. At Bristol his audiences rose from five and ten to twenty thousand persons—more than all the churches together could contain. He preached once at Gloucester, but only once, for the churches of the city were immediately closed to him. From Gloucester he went to Wales, and, accompanied by Howel Harris, the founder of Welsh Methodism, preached throughout every part of the principality. Here, as in England, the churches were shut against him, but the people flocked by tens of thousands to hear his voice. It was the same in the country districts of England, which he afterwards visited. At Basingstoke, the landlord of the inn turned him out of his house, and the mayor forbad him to preach. There, however, he preached twice—once in a field, and once on the racecourse; for the man who had bearded the Chancellor of his diocese was scarcely likely to be frightened by the opposition of a country mayor. In very few places which he afterwards visited was he allowed the use of the church. One of the cities to which he went was Oxford, where he was received with the characteristic wisdom and charity of the University authorities. The Vice-Chancellor sent for him. " Have you, sir," he inquired, " a name in my book here ?" " Yes," said Whitefield, " but I intend to take it out soon." " Yes," replied the Vice-Chancellor, " and you had better take yourself out too, or otherwise I will lay you by the heels. What do you mean, going about alienating the people's affections from their proper pastors ? If you ever come again in this manner, I will lay you first by the heels, and then these (referring to Whitefield's friends) shall follow." It is satisfactory to find that Whitefield did not meet with a similar reception from Doddridge, upon whom he called at Northampton, after leaving Oxford. Doddridge received him with both kindness and courtesy. He, at least, was not afraid of his people's affections being alienated by the most powerful preaching of the Gospel of Jesus Christ. At Hertford, Whitefield was compelled to go to the common to preach; at Hitchin, the churchwardens ordered the church-bells to be rung, so that his voice, as he stood under the shadow of the church in the market-place, might be drowned. After this he returned to London, and began his memorable mission at Moorfields, which then contained the refuse of the metropolis. Here, and on Kennington Common, his audience consisted of as many as forty thousand persons.* Everywhere his voice was a two-edged sword, and for the first time for generations men could understand the Divine interrogation, " Is not my word like a fire, saith the Lord, and like a hammer that breaketh the rock in pieces ?" From London, Whitefield once more sailed to Georgia. He remained there but a few months ; but he did not leave America until he had preached in all the principal cities, breaking, in the new world as in the old, the sleep of soul in thousands of men.

It was after Whitefield had first met the colliers of Kingswood that he addressed a letter to Wesley, beseeching him to go down and preach to the people. Wesley was still holding affectionate intercourse with the Moravians. A "Society," formed to a great extent on the plan of modern Methodist class-meetings, existed in Fetter Lane. Here Wesley attended "love-feasts," which lasted all through the night ; here he enjoyed "penitential" seasons ; and here he was wrought up to a state of the highest devotional rhapsody. His preaching now began to be attended by those physical manifestations which have often accompanied revivals of religion. Strong men and women cried aloud, before assembled congregations, in the agony of their spirit : when the pains of hell gat hold upon them, they roared and shrieked in suffering. Fits were frequent amongst those who heard. By-and-by,—sometimes in a few hours or even minutes,—agony would give way to joy, terror to peace, the fear of hell to the possession of heaven below, the service of the devil to an assured acceptance with God. Such phenomena, believed, at that time, to have been unprecedented, drew down on the

* Whitefield's Journal," A.D. 1739. Andrew's " Whitefield," cap. iv.

preaching of the Wesleys a not unnatural opprobrium. They were contrary to all that had hitherto been experienced of the operations of the Spirit of God on the soul of man. Good Christians were scandalized. Wesley, however, accepted their defence; and, whatever may be thought of all such abnormal manifestations, his reply must be held, to a certain extent, to be conclusive. "You deny," he writes to his brother Samuel, "that God does now work these effects; at least, that He works them in such a manner. I affirm both, because I have heard these facts with my ears and seen them with my eyes. I have seen (as far as it can be seen) many persons changed in a moment from the spirit of horror, fear, and despair, to the spirit of hope, joy, and peace; and from sinful desires, till then reigning over them, to a pure desire of doing the will of God. These are matters of fact, whereof I have been, and almost daily am, eye or ear witness. Upon the same evidence (as to the suddenness and reality of the change), I believe or know this, touching visions and dreams. I know several persons in whom this great change from the power of Satan unto God was wrought either in sleep or during a strong representation to the eye of their mind of Christ, either on the cross or in glory. This is the fact; let any judge of it as they please. But that such a change was thus wrought appears, not from their shedding tears only, or sighing, or groaning, but from the whole tenor of their life, till then in many ways wicked, from that time holy, just, and good. I will show you him that was a lion till then, and is now a lamb; he that was a drunkard, but now exemplarily sober; the whoremonger that was, who now abhors the very lusts of the flesh. These are my living arguments of what I assert, that God now, as aforetime, gives remission of sins; and the gift of the Holy Ghost, which may be called visions. If it be not so, I am found a false witness; but, however, I do and will testify the things I have both seen and heard."* It is needless to say that Wesley might have obtained an explanation of all these extravagances without assigning them to the method of divine agency. But the ecstatic temperament in himself, which was communicated, by a natural law, to those whom he addressed, enabled him not only to see, in all these manifestations, the finger of God, but to rejoice in them. He liked excitement, he liked mystery, he liked the marvellous, and he believed with the utmost credulity, in the superhuman, or all that appeared to be so.

Such was the man who was about to follow Whitefield to Bristol; but Wesley hesitated to take this step without consulting his oracles. He wished to know the will of God respecting the matter, and, in order to ascertain it, resorted to his favourite practice of Bibliomancy. He opened the Bible once, and the text on which he stumbled was not of good omen; he opened it again, and it was worse; a third and fourth time, and it was worse still. Then he consulted the Fetter Lane Society, who had recourse to the lot, and the lot decided that he should go. Immediately afterwards, the Bible was opened in several places, and every text indicated, as had been the case with Wesley himself, personal damage to Wesley if he accepted the invitation. The little society accordingly came to the conclusion that the

* "Journal."

journey would be fatal, and Charles besought to go and die with him. But Wesley accepted the issue of the lot as the appointment of the Lord, and went.

Whitefield must have been intimately acquainted with Wesley's ecclesiastical prejudices and weaknesses, and he adopted the best method of overcoming them. He preached himself in the open air, before Wesley, and then left his coadjutor to his own course. Wesley says, "I could scarce reconcile myself at first to this strange way of preaching in the fields, of which he set me an example on Sunday; having been all my lifetime (till very lately) so tenacious of every point relating to decency and order, that I should have thought the saving of souls almost a sin, if it had not been done in a church."* How reluctant he was to follow Whitefield's example, may be gathered from an entry made four days after this: "I submitted," he says, "to be more vile, and proclaimed in the highways the glad tidings of salvation." "More vile!" Nothing could more clearly indicate, than does this expression, the rooted ecclesiasticism of Wesley's character, the utter abasement which he experienced in doing anything that appeared to be unclerical, or inconsistent with the established conventionalisms of a priest in orders. But as the churches were one after another closed to him, as they had been to Whitefield and to himself in London, and as the sheriff soon prohibited his preaching even to the prisoners in gaol, he appears to have thought little more of the vileness of proclaiming the Gospel in the open air.

From this time Methodism became an established

* "Journal," March 29, A.D. 1739.

institution. In the year 1739, the first Methodist "meeting-house" in England was built at Kingswood, and the first Methodist meeting-house opened in England, opened at the Foundry, in Moorfields. Wesley called the congregations who used these places of worship, "societies." These societies were divided into "bands" and "class-meetings," in which spiritual exercises were indulged, and the devotional feelings cultured. Wesley's idea at this time, and for many years afterwards, was merely to revive the state of religion in the Church; but he knew enough of the condition of society in England, and of human nature, to be aware that unless those who had been brought under the awakening influence of the Gospel met together, and assisted each other in keeping alive the fire which had been lit in their hearts, it must, in many instances, seriously diminish, if not altogether die out. His societies, however, differed in no respect whatever from Dissenting churches, excepting that their members did not, at first, everywhere build places of worship, and did not celebrate the Lord's Supper, or have the separate administration of baptism. But both Whitefield and Wesley were at this time Dissenters in a degree. They had openly and deliberately broken an essential law in the Church's constitution. How many more laws they might break, was simply a question of time, circumstance, and conscience.

It was during Whitefield's residence in America that the first breach was made between himself and Wesley. Whitefield was a Calvinist, and he had heard from England, to his intense surprise, that Wesley was preaching against the Calvinistic doctrines. When they had separated from each other at Oxford, there was no difference of opinion between the two friends on doctrinal questions. But Wesley, in the meanwhile, had come under Moravian influences, and from the Moravian had gone to the Arminian creed. With all the ardour of a new disciple, he was not satisfied with expounding the doctrines of that creed, but made it a practice to denounce all the characteristic tenets of Calvinism. Whitefield, accordingly, wrote to Wesley, expostulating against his conduct. There was no intolerance in Whitefield's disposition; of the two men he had by far the finer human nature. He did not, therefore, denounce Wesley's new creed; he simply said, "I differ from your notion about not committing sin, and your denying the doctrine of election and final perseverance. I dread coming to England unless you are resolved to oppose these truths with less warmth. I dread your coming over to America, because the work of God is carried on here by doctrines quite opposed to those you hold." He besought him with painful earnestness, not to preach as he had been preaching. "For Christ's sake, dear sir," he wrote, "if possible, never preach against election in your sermons; no one can say that I have mentioned it in public discourses, whatever my private sentiments may be. For Christ's sake, let us not be divided amongst ourselves; nothing will so much prevent a division as your being silent on this head."* Next, he expressed regret at Wesley's doctrine of sinless perfection, and, with somewhat unnecessary irony, his contempt of Wesley's superstitious practice of casting lots. But Wesley would not be silent, and he would not give up

* Andrew's "Whitefield," 117, 118.

casting lots. Whitefield therefore again took up his pen, and in terms of anguish thus addressed his brother in the Gospel: "For Christ's sake, be not rash; give yourself to reading; study the covenant of grace; down with your carnal reasoning; be a little child; and then instead of pawning your salvation, as you have done in a late hymn-book—if the doctrine of universal redemption be not true, instead of talking of sinless perfection, as you have done in the preface to that hymn-book, and making man's salvation to depend on his own free will, as you have done in this sermon; you will compose a hymn of praise of sovereign distinguishing love, you will caution believers against striving to work a perfection out of their own hearts, and print another sermon the reverse of this, and entitle it Free Grace Indeed; free, because not free to all; but free, because God may withhold or give it to whom and when He pleases. God knows my heart; nothing but a simple regard to the honour of Christ has forced this letter from me. I love and honour you for His sake; and when I come to judgment, I will thank you before men and angels for what you have, under God, done to my soul."* This letter getting, unfortunately, into print, Wesley took it with him to the Foundry, at Moorfields, where it was being circulated, and, before the whole congregation, tore it into pieces.

When Whitefield, in the year 1741, returned again to London, he was received with no diminution of affection by the Wesleys. He found, however, or imagined he found, that the preaching of the two brothers had seriously damaged his reputation. "Many," he writes,

* Southey's "Wesley," chap. xi.

"very many of my spiritual children, who, at my last departure from England, would have plucked out their own eyes to have given me, are so prejudiced by the dear Messrs. Wesley's dressing up the doctrine of election in such horrible colours, that they will neither hear, see, nor give me the least assistance; yea, some of them send threatening letters that God will speedily destroy me."* What is termed an explanation followed, when Whitefield said that the Wesleys and himself preached two different Gospels; that he could not hold out the right hand of fellowship to them; and that they must part. From this time the Methodist movement was divided into two lines: Whitefield preached Calvinism, and the Wesleys Arminianism, and both were equally successful in turning men from darkness to light, and from the power of Satan to the salvation of God. The personal friendship of the men was, however, soon renewed, and each helped the other in the work he had in hand.

The three years which Whitefield now spent in England were the years of probably the greatest revival of religion that had been known since Christianity was first preached. His first work, after separating from the Wesleys, was to go to Scotland. Presbyterian sectarianism stood, for a time, in his way. The Erskines had invited him, but would not hear of his preaching in any other pulpits but those of their own section of Presbyterianism. "Why?" asked Whitefield. "Because," said Ralph Erskine, "we are the Lord's people." "I then," says Whitefield, "asked, were there no other Lord's people but themselves; and, supposing all others

* Southey's "Wesley," chap. xi.

were the devil's people, they certainly had more need to be preached to, and therefore I was more determined to go into the highways and hedges; and that if the Pope himself would lend me his pulpit, I would gladly proclaim the righteousness of Christ therein."* Whitefield, in fact, always preferred the "highways and hedges." "Field preaching," he remarked, "is my plan. I cannot join so in any particular place. Every one hath his proper gift." While, therefore, the presbytery was quarrelling about him, he took himself out of the hearing of their wrangles, and would have nothing to do with their solemn league and covenant. But his success amongst the people was as great as it had been in England. His audiences numbered tens of thousands; and hundreds, as the result of his preaching, appear to have undergone a change of heart. He is next found, in the year 1742, preaching at Moorfields Fair, an act which none but a man with the courage of a lion and the faith of a saint would have attempted. At six o'clock in the morning of Whit-Monday, "getting," as he says, "the start of the devil," he preached to ten thousand people. In the afternoon this number was doubled. The fair was now at its height, but large numbers left the shows to hear him. The result was that he was pelted with rotten eggs, stones, and dead cats; but he preached to the end, and announced that he would return in the evening. A merry-andrew, whose show had been forsaken, came, on this occasion, to lash him with a whip, but did not succeed in doing any harm. Other attempts to stop his preaching also failed. When the service was over,

* Whitefield's "Journal," A.D. 1739.

Whitefield returned with a pocket full of notes from persons brought under concern. He therefore visited the fair again, when he experienced, in addition to the former peltings, the greatest of all indignities by a man who, in the wantonness of beastliness, mounted a tree near the pulpit, and exposed his person to the whole congregation. Even this, however, did not disconcert the preacher, and he left the ground with unprecedented proofs of the triumph of the Gospel over sin. Once more, during these years, he visited Scotland, where he was the principal agent in the great revival at Cambuslang; and once more he went through England and Wales, meeting, in many places, with an intense spirit of opposition, but in others with a glad and fervent reception. At Hampton, near Bristol, his presence occasioned a riot; at Axminster, the church bells were set in motion to stop him, and a clergyman asked him by what authority he preached; at Kidderminster, the bells were also rung; and at Plymouth, he was nearly assassinated. From this town he left again for America.

The labours of the Wesleys during this period were not less incessant or arduous than those of Whitefield; nor was the opposition to them less disgraceful. One or two clergymen had identified themselves with their work, and they were treated, notwithstanding their comparative obscurity, as the leaders of the movement themselves were treated. They were spoken of by the clergy at large "as if the devil, not God, had sent them." Some repulsed them from the Lord's table; others stirred up the people against them, representing them, even in their public discourses, as "Felons not fit to live,"* "Papists," "Heretics," "Traitors," "Conspirators against their King and country." The converts of these men encountered the same measure of obloquy. "They drove some of them," says Wesley, "from the Lord's table, to which, until now they had no desire to approach. They preached all manner of evil concerning them, openly cursing them in the name of the Lord."† The opposition to Wesley himself was more violent. At Epworth, where his father was incumbent for forty years, and where Wesley himself was born, he was refused the use of the church, and, by the drunken successor of Samuel Wesley, denied the Sacrament because he was "not fit." The greatest opposition, however, was encountered in the Midland districts. At Wednesbury, Eggiston, the clergyman, incited the people to a riot, during which every Methodist—man and woman—who could be found was beaten, stoned, and pelted, and their houses dismantled. At Walsall, the mob, says Wesley, "roared at him like the roaring of the sea, and demanded his life." At Falmouth, his house was beset by an innumerable multitude, who wished to drag him out. But Wesley's courage and presence of mind never once deserted him. He would walk straight into the midst of the furious mob, ask what he had done to harm them, and at once begin to pray or preach. The worst and the most violent retreated before him. No men, indeed, ever possessed greater moral power than Wesley and Whitefield. Their looks were sufficient to quail the angriest mobs. As though a Divine presence manifested itself,

* Wesley's "Further Appeal." Coke's Life of Wesley," p. 218.
† Ib.   ‡ "Journal," July 4, A.D. 1744.

men fell back before them, and allowed them to have their course.

The history of Charles Wesley's labours is a similar history of personal zeal, and, to a considerable extent, of popular and official opposition. Although not so good a preacher as his brother John or as Whitefield, and although extremely uncertain in the command of his power, he produced the same effect upon the people. His first great tour was in the north of England, on his way to which he preached in almost every town. At Walsall he was attacked by the mob and stoned; but, although hit several times, and twice dismounted from the steps of the market-place, where he was standing, he continued his service to the end, and then passed unhurt through the multitude. At Sheffield, to use his own language, "Hell from beneath was moved to oppose us." Here, too, he was stoned, and several of the missiles struck him in the face. The riot in this town raged throughout the night, and the meeting-house was pulled down by the mob to the foundations. Charles, who was even a higher Churchman than his brother, states that this riot was occasioned by sermons preached against the Methodists by the clergy of Sheffield.* The following day the rioters broke the windows of his lodging. His next tour was throughout the West of England and Cornwall. At Devizes, the curate led a mob against him, who played the fire-engine into his house, and broke the windows. Two influential Dissenters assisted on this occasion.† At St. Ives, the meeting-house in which he preached was gutted by the miners, who, with clubs, in their hands, threatened him

* Stevens's "History of Methodism," i. 191.   † Southey's "Life," cap. 14.

with instant death if he preached again. This mob was headed by the town-clerk. At Poole, the churchwardens led the mob to where Charles Wesley was preaching, and drove him and his congregation from the parish.* None of these things, however, hindered him. The more they were opposed, the more these men saw the necessity for their work. Opposition did nothing but increase their zeal. "Crucify him!" cried the mob of Wednesbury at John Wesley; and there was not one of the three great evangelists who would not have braved even crucifixion in the discharge of his work.

In almost every large town in England the leaders of Methodism had now made many converts. Whitefield had neither the inclination nor the natural faculty for organizing, either into societies or churches, those who had been influenced by his preaching. John Wesley, however, had both the inclination and the faculty. Few men, in any age, have exceeded him in the skill of organization or the wisdom of administration. He resolved, first, on the formation of societies. He met, at this point, with the objection that he was creating a schism. His answer to this, to himself at least, was conclusive. He acknowledged that if by schism was meant only "gathering people out of buildings called churches," he was creating a schism; but if it meant dividing Christians from Christians, it was not; for his converts were not Christians before they joined the societies, and they did not separate from Christians, unless, indeed, drunkards, swearers, liars, and cheats were Christians.

* The vestry-books of Poole contain, to this day, a statement of the expenses incurred at an inn for drink to the mob and its leader, for driving out the Methodists. Smith's "History of Methodism," ii. 2.

All that he did was to form those who were Christians into classes, appointing leaders to those classes, who were to watch over the conduct of every member. Over all the classes he exercised a personal superintendence, giving every consistent member a ticket or certificate of his satisfaction with his personal godliness. At the weekly meetings of the classes mutual confessions of sins and statements of religious experiences were appointed, and once a quarter a "love-feast" was held.*

Societies being established, the question of preachers came next to be considered. Wesley had always thought that preachers would be supplied from the pulpits of the Established Church, but in this he was disappointed. There was no resource, therefore, but to use laymen for this service. Charles Wesley opposed this step with all his influence, and Wesley himself accepted the necessity with the greatest reluctance. At first the laymen were allowed only to read the Scriptures, but reading soon led to expounding, and expounding to preaching. The first who, in regular connection with the Society, preached, was a man named Thomas Maxfield, a member of the Moorfields Society. Wesley was absent from London at this time, but as soon as he heard that Maxfield was preaching he came up in great anger. He was met by his mother. "Thomas Maxfield has turned preacher, I find," said Wesley. Susanna Wesley—who had preached herself—replied, "John, you know what my sentiments have been; you cannot suspect me of favouring readily anything of this kind; but take care what you do with respect to that young man, for he is as surely called of God to preach as you are. Examine

* Coke's "Life of Wesley," 228—230.

what have been the fruits of his preaching, and judge for yourself." Wesley did so, and then exclaimed, "It is the Lord, let him do what seemeth him good." After Maxfield others arose, some of them men of great natural genius and remarkable spiritual power. Amongst them John Nelson, a Yorkshire mason, holds the first place. Nelson was almost as abundant in labour and in suffering as the Wesleys, and his influence over the working classes, especially in Cornwall, was equal to that of Wesley himself. Nelson, also, met at the hands of the clergy and the worse part of the people the same reception as Whitefield and the Wesleys. His house at Bristol was pulled down; at Nottingham, squibs were thrown in his face; at Grimsby, the rector headed a mob to the beat of the town drum, and, after supplying them with beer, called upon them to "fight for the Church." Fighting for the Church meant the demolition of the house in which Nelson was residing, and its windows were forthwith pulled to pieces and the furniture destroyed.* The preaching of Nelson was of an extraordinary character. Thorough Yorkshire common sense, homely wit, and intense pathos were its characteristics. The drummer of Grimsby, who had been hired by the rector to beat down Nelson's preaching on the day after the riot, was one of the witnesses of its power. After beating for three quarters of an hour, he stood and listened, and soon the tears of penitence were seen rolling down his cheeks. Men who went to mob the mason-preacher, left him in agonies of remorse. Not even Whitefield possessed more power over the common people. Without Nelson, and similar lay preachers, Methodism could not have been sustained

* Nelson's "Journal," p. 92.

as it was. The seeds which the leaders of the movement sowed, were by these men carefully matured. The few grew into many; here and there societies were added to those already existing, all, in course of time, to grow into regularly constituted Christian Churches.

The organization of Methodism thus gradually assuming shape and completeness, required but one addition to assimilate it to the conventional forms of established ecclesiastical governments. This addition was made in the year 1744. On the 25th of June in that year, Wesley summoned a conference of the clergymen and lay preachers who had identified themselves with the new movement. Six clergymen, and at least four lay preachers attended. Wesley had many objects in summoning this conference. One was to classify the various societies into circuits; another, to settle questions of government and discipline; and a third, to come to an agreement respecting doctrine. The first and second were easily affected; the third was discussed at considerable length, but as all the men were of a catholic spirit, and recognized the Christianity of every Christian, whatever might be his creed, the conference made no shipwreck upon dogmatism. It was decided that the truth of the Gospel was very near both to Calvinism and to Arminianism, even "within a hair's breadth;" so that it was altogether foolish and sinful, because they did not quite agree with either one or the other, to run away from them as far as possible.* One of the questions asked at the conference was, "Are we not Dissenters?" The answer was, "No. Although we call sinners to repentance in all places of God's dominion; and although

* Coke's "Life of Wesley," p. 275.

we frequently use extemporary prayer, and unite together in a religious society, yet we are not Dissenters in the only sense which our law acknowledges—namely, those who renounce the service of the Church. We do not, we dare not separate from it. We are not seceders, nor do we bear any resemblance to them. We set out upon quite opposite principles. The seceders laid the very foundation of their work in judging and condemning others. We laid the foundation of our work in judging and condemning ourselves. They begin everywhere with showing their hearers how fallen the Church and ministers are: we begin everywhere with showing our hearers how fallen they are themselves."* The refined self-righteousness with which the self-righteousness of others was thus condemned was consistent with the weaker side of John Wesley's character. When occasion served, as in defending his work from the charge of schism, he could show how "fallen" the Church and ministers were, in language which condemned them, by implication, to destruction.

The character and the labours of this conference formed an era of Methodism. A body had been constituted which assumed to itself the direction of all the affairs of the societies, determined their doctrines, and assigned to the officers their duties and the mode in which they should be discharged. Wesley had summoned to this conference those only whom he chose to summon. He had thus kept it, and under the circumstances, no doubt wisely, in his own hands. But he had also established a precedent, and that precedent he took care, in after times, systematically to follow.

* Coke's "Life of Wesley," p. 287.

The opposition and the success which attended the Methodist movement were due to various, and in some respects opposite, causes. The Wesleys, throughout their lives, wished to walk in harmony with the Church of which they were ordained members, yet from that very Church they encountered the most malignant persecution. All ranks of the clerical order, from the bishops downwards, opposed them. One who had held intimate intercourse with the bishops of the Establishment remarks that he had been an ear-witness of the treatment which the Methodists received from that body, and that, in their common discourse, their language was not only below Episcopal dignity, but even inconsistent with common decency—an example which was followed through every rank down to the country curate.* John Wesley's own opinion of the difference between himself and the other clergy of his Church related to two questions: first, of doctrine, and, secondly, of the parochial system. He maintained that his doctrine was entirely consistent with the articles and homilies of the Church; but that, with regard to the clergy generally, he differed from them in five points. They, he said, confounded justification with sanctification, whereas he believed justification to be necessarily antecedent to sanctification; they spoke of being justified by works, whereas he believed that the death and righteousness of Christ were the sole causes of justification; they spoke of good works as a condition of justification, while he believed that there could be no good works previously to a man's being justified; they spoke of sanctification as if it were an outward thing: he believed it to be an

* Archdeacon Blackburne's Works, i. 312.

inward thing—namely, the life of God in the soul of man, a participation in the divine nature, the renewal of the heart after the manner of Him that created mankind; they also spoke of the new birth as an outward thing, as if it were no more than baptism: "I," he said, "believe it to be an inward thing, a change from inward wickedness to inward goodness, an entire change of our inward nature from the image of the devil (wherein we are born) to the image of God—a change from the love of the creature to the love of the Creator, from earthly and sensual to heavenly and holy affections—in a word, a change from the tempers of the spirits of darkness to those of the angels of God in heaven." "There is, therefore," he added, "a wide, essential, fundamental, irreconcileable difference between us; so that if they speak the truth as it is in Jesus, I am found a false witness before God; but if I teach the way of God in truth, they are blind leaders of the blind."* If Wesley's description, in this case, was correctly drawn, as no doubt it was, there need be no wonder at the state of religion and morals at this period. For, according to his authority, the clergy could have had no notion whatever of what religion really was. Not only could they not have felt its power in their own hearts, but they could not have had a proper intellectual knowledge of it. And, if they had, they dared not have preached it, for their preaching would have condemned their own lives. Both the bishops and the clergy of this period were habitually non-resident; pluralities had increased to a shameful degree, and the lives of country incumbents were often openly immoral. Whitefield and the Wesleys were a

* "Journal," Sept. 13, 1739.

living rebuke to all this class. Their preaching tended to expose their real character, and to bring them into contempt. The vast numbers who listened to them, and the many who were converted through their instrumentality, would know, perfectly well, that their own parish ministers could have had no practical acquaintance with religion. Hence, one reason of the opposition which they encountered. The clergy dreaded the exposure of their real character. The new preachers virtually pronounced them to be either grossly ignorant or grossly hypocritical. They therefore stood on their defence, and, in return, proclaimed the Methodists to be nothing better, and probably worse, than enthusiasts and fanatics.*

But this was not the only reason for the treatment which the leaders of the Methodist movement experienced. They were Chuchmen, but they were not, in all things, obedient sons of the Church. A friend once, naturally enough, asked Wesley how it was that he assembled Christians who were none of his charge to sing psalms and pray, and hear the Scriptures expounded, and how he could justify doing this in other men's parishes ? Wesley replied, "I know no other rule, whether of faith or practice, than the Holy Scriptures. But on scriptural principles, I do not think it hard to justify what I do. God, in Scripture, commands me, according to my power, to instruct the ignorant, reform the wicked, confirm the virtuous. Man forbids me to do this in another man's parish; that is, in effect, to do it at all,

---

* The state of the clergy at this period has been most faithfully described by a recent Church historian, the Rev. G. G. Perry, in his "History of the Church of England," vol. iii. cap. xlii. Southey's description, in his eighth chapter of the "Life of Wesley," is almost too well known to need reference.

seeing that I have now no parish of my own, nor probably ever shall. Whom, then, shall I hear—God or man? Suffer me now to tell you my principles in this matter. I look upon all the world as my parish; thus far, I mean, that in whatever part of it I am, I judge it meet, right, and my bounden duty, to declare unto all that are willing to hear, the glad tidings of salvation."* This was good Christianity, but it was clearly not, nor is it now, Church of Englandism. It is Dissent, and Dissent of the oldest form. The clergy were at least enlightened enough to be aware of this. The new preachers were invading their rights, and the invasion was resented. It is not necessary to ascribe a bad motive for this resentment. Whatever the clergy did not believe, they did believe in the constitution of the Established Church, and they had a moral, as well as a legal, right to protest against brother clergymen invading their parishes. They were less to blame in this than their system; and if that system was so very bad, why did the Wesleys so constantly tell their hearers to attend their parish churches, and insist on the members of their societies partaking of the Lord's Supper according to the rites of the Church?

Another cause of opposition is to be found in the general condition of the people. If the clergy were ignorant and debased, the people were more so. It has been justly remarked, by an acute and philosophical writer, that the preaching of Wesley and Whitefield was a test of what the people had been previously taught or allowed to rejoice in as Christian truth, under the tuition of their great religious guardian, the National Church; and, carrying with them this quality of a test, how were

* "Journal," June 11th, 1739.

those men received? They were generally received on account of the import of what they said, still more than from their zealous manner of saying it, with as strong an impression of novelty and strangeness as any of our voyagers and travellers of discovery have been by the barbarous tribes who had never before seen civilized men.* To the mass of the people, indeed, religion was almost unknown. Their morals were, for the most part, more degraded than those of beasts. Drunkenness was not merely not frowned upon: it was fashionable. "I remember," said Dr. Johnson, "when all the decent people in Lichfield got drunk every night, and were not thought the worse for it." † The people of Wales and Cornwall were little better than heathens—uninstructed by the clergy, whom they seldom saw, and who gave them no good example when they were seen, and so ignorant as to have scarcely the knowledge of a God. Such a people were ready enough to join in a riot against the Methodist leaders. Under the same guidance they would have joined in a riot against anyone and anything. The hatred of the clergy to the leaders was an intelligent hatred; but that of the lower classes was an ignorant and brutish passion. When they listened, and came to understand or to feel what was being said to them, and why it was being said, they received the preachers with raptures and went out by thousands to welcome them. Their great human hearts then drank eagerly of the message of salvation. Before Whitefield and the Wesleys went amongst them they were like a Sahara. No sooner did the rain of the Gospel descend upon them

---

* Foster's "Essay on the Evils of Popular Ignorance."
† Boswell's "Johnson," i. 340.

than the desert became like unto a garden, and brought forth fruit unto perfection.

The attitude of the Dissenters toward the new movement was, for the most part, one of calm observation. Their congregations were unquestionably in need of a revival of religion. The decay of piety was deplored on all sides. Joseph Stennett, the principal minister amongst the Baptists of this period, has left a vivid picture of the times in which he lived. Infidelity, he remarks, was making an amazing progress; the Gospel was being reduced to only a few lectures on morality; practical iniquity was keeping pace with the corruptions of doctrine, and there was nothing but a melancholy prospect to all the friends of true religion.* The whole land, he publicly declared, was corrupted with blasphemy and profaneness, with drunkenness and lewdness, with fraud and perjury. Those who had separated themselves in profession, from the positively wicked, were filling up the cup of national guilt; ordinances were despised and neglected, religious conversation was changed for fashionable and vicious entertainments, and family religion was laid aside.† It might have been supposed that, under such circumstances, the advent of the Methodist leaders would have been eagerly welcomed; but there was more than one cause of hindrance to this. The scenes which took place during the preaching of Whitefield and the Wesleys induced many persons to hesitate in acknowledging their mission. The Wesleys also were bitter opponents of Dissent. Charles, who was always "harping on the Established

---

* "The Christian Strife." A Sermon, etc., A.D. 1738.
† "Rabshakeh's Retreat." A Sermon, etc., A.D. 1745.

Church," remarked that he would sooner see his children Roman Catholics than Protestant Dissenters. He applied, publicly, in one of his sermons, the shipwreck of Paul to the difficulty of being saved out of the Church of England.* Charity for sinners he had to a large extent, but no charity whatever for any Christian who was not a member of his own church. It was impossible for Dissenters to receive such a man with the good feeling which a less sectarian course would have excited. There was no such difficulty, however, with Whitefield. Whitefield often avowed his attachment to the Church, but he was as far removed from a bigot as any man of his time. "I exhort all," he wrote to Howel Harris, "to go where they can profit most. I preach what I believe to be the truth, and then leave it to the Spirit of God to make the application."† While, therefore, the Wesleys were received with coolness by the Dissenters, Whitefield often met from them the warmest welcome. When he was driven from preaching near the church at Kidderminster, the Baptist chapel was opened for him. He took counsel of Watts, and held friendly intercourse with Doddridge. "I have lately," wrote James Hervey, one of the Oxford "Holy Club," and a well-known writer, "seen that excellent minister of the blessed Jesus, Mr. Whitefield: I dined, supped, and spent the evening with him at Northampton, in company with Dr. Doddridge."‡ Doddridge also lent Whitefield his chapel. No coarse disparagement of the labours of these men is to be found in the writings of any of the Dissenters of this period. When Methodism was

* Everett's "Life of Adam Clarke, i. 83.
† Andrew's "Life of Whitefield," p. 147.   ‡ Ibid. p. 240.

better known, and its results well attested, they gladly acknowledged the good which it had effected.

The causes of the success of the new movement need not be sought from afar. It is mainly to be attributed, as a matter of instrumentality, to the remarkable characters of those who conducted it. Its origination was owing to Whitefield. He was not the first of the "Holy Club," but he was the first who adopted aggression as a principle of Christian effort. The earnestness of John Wesley would, no doubt, have compelled him, in course of time, to have had recourse to open-air preaching as a means, and as the only means, of reaching the people; but Wesley, with all his enthusiasm, was a man of cautious and deliberate judgment, and, unless Whitefield had set the example, would have hesitated, for some time, in taking the first step in such an innovation on the established order of his Church. Whitefield had no caution. He was the impersonation of religious ardour. The preaching of the Gospel was, to him, not a duty merely, but a divine passion. This passion gave to it a character such as has been possessed by no other Christian orator. It was not that his sentences were well constructed, his periods well balanced, his emphasis accurate, and his language forcible: some of these desirable but minor qualifications he did not possess in an equal degree with other great orators. But the man himself gave to every word which he uttered a character which no other man could give. Baptized by the Spirit of God; his whole heart yearning for the recovery of lost souls as a mother yearns for the return of a prodigal son; alive, from intense experience, both to the horrors of sin and the delights of holiness, he

pleaded his Saviour's cause with a love for Him and
those with whom he pleaded, which made him seem, for
a time, like one possessed. He was endowed with most
of the attributes of a great public speaker. Though not
high in stature, and, in the first years of his work, of
slight and delicate frame, his exquisitely musical voice
could be distinguished at a mile's distance, and by
every one of forty thousand persons in the open air.
In gesture and action he equalled the most distinguished professors of the dramatic art, and his oratory
was as spontaneous as it was powerful. Although he
often preached sixteen times a week, he was never known,
after his earliest efforts, to study a sermon. His printed
sermons are loose, and, to some extent, inaccurate in
style, and no adequate conception of his genius can be
obtained from them. His most impassioned bursts of
eloquence came, and seemed to come, as an inspiration.
Numerous anecdotes of his power over his audiences have
been preserved by those who heard him. They wept as
he wept, and visibly trembled with terror when he
described the judgments of the Almighty. So vivid
were his descriptions, and so dramatic his action, that he
would make a whole congregation look around as though
seeking the things which he described. His greatest
weaknesses were irritability and hastiness. He was
not, like Wesley, a wholly self-controlled man. But he
was a warmer-hearted and a more generous man than
Wesley, and he had the most catholic and unselfish
temper of any of the Methodist leaders. Not, however,
by any natural gift did he acquire his marvellous power
over the human heart. He spent whole nights in prayer;
and although he invariably rose at four in the morning,

he would often, in the course of the night, get up to read and pray.

But if Whitefield gave to the new movement its first and greatest impulse, John Wesley was, unquestionably, its head and leader. Young though all these men were, their characters were fixed and formed when they commenced their work. The intensity of their religious experience had given to them a maturity which other men scarcely acquire when they reach to middle life. What John Wesley was at thirty he was, with scarcely any change, at eighty years of age. With an intellect keen, clear, and logical; a judgment whose balance was almost perfect; a will as strong as steel; cool and self-possessed, yet ardent and even enthusiastic, and an able administrator, he was, above all men, qualified to be the founder and the organizer of a new religious sect. But he added other and still greater qualities to these. He was a man capable of the most rapt devotional feelings; he possessed a conscience that never swerved from its sense of right; personal self-denial and self-sacrifice he counted as nothing; what would have been privation to others, was a rule of his life; hunger and thirst he endured with indifference; work which would have killed stronger men in a few months, brought to him no sense of weariness. Through all he felt himself to be upborne by the Divine arm, and he cared for nothing so long as he was doing his Master's will. In most respects Wesley was an entirely different preacher from Whitefield. The characteristic difference consisted in the fact that Whitefield was mainly a preacher to the passions, and Wesley to the consciences, of men. Whitefield aroused the half-dead soul by appealing to its fear, and hope, and love; Wesley, by stating the Divine claims, and the corresponding human obligations. Whitefield would make men feel, Wesley would prove them, to be in the wrong. The style of their addresses was as different as was the substance. Whitefield was loose, inconsequential, dramatic, and declamatory; Wesley was chaste, accurate, and logical. There was a difference, also, of tone. Whitefield had the finer human feelings and the more tender affections; Wesley the greater intellectual power and moral force. Whitefield could not have been a bigot; Wesley never wholly freed himself from an ecclesiasticism which, while it cannot be confounded with bigotry, is nearly allied to it. The Spirit of God, however, possessed in perhaps an equal degree, both of these great but very different men. The same audiences heard them with equal delight and equal profit. They had sought perfect spiritual character, and spiritual power was given to them in greater measure than it had ever been given to any men since the first day of Pentecost.

Charles Wesley was, in all respects but one, the inferior of both these men. He was narrow, exclusive, and priestly. He could preach occasionally, if not often, with marvellous power and unction; but as a speaker he was extremely unequal. On one day his sermon would be instinct with eloquent thought and moving pathos; on another, it would be dry, cold, spiritless, and childish. He was, however, of great assistance to his brother, although sometimes, from his priestly dogmas, of greater hindrance. Apart from his brother, Charles Wesley would probably have been known only as a learned, zealous, spiritual, and active clergyman, of great intellectual capability and great poetic power, but he would never have performed the work which he did, and never have enjoyed the reputation which has actually followed him. It was at the beginning of the Methodist movement, that, in conjunction with his brother, he published his first hymns. Here he far excelled both of his coadjutors; and in depth and warmth of devotional feeling has excelled most other Christian hymnologists.

Such were the men who, excepting for the most part by the common people, were now everywhere spoken against. Yet they were successful. But, apart from their characters, one especial cause of success attended them. The Arminianism of the Wesleys and the Calvinism of Whitefield divided the men from each other for a brief season, but none ever lived who were more tolerant of theological differences. In the first year or two of his preaching, Wesley could not leave the doctrines of election and reprobation alone, but afterwards he preached few formally theological discourses. It was his boast, in later life, that the Methodist societies were founded on a more liberal basis than any Christian church. "They do not impose," he said, "any opinions whatever. People might hold particular or general redemption, absolute or conditional decrees. They think and let think." * "Look all around you," he added, at another period; "you cannot be admitted into the Church, or society of the Presbyterians, Anabaptists, Quakers, or any others, unless you hold the same opinions with them, and adhere to the same mode

* "Works," vii. 321.

of worship. The Méthodists alone do not insist on your holding this or that opinion. . .. . Now I do not know any other religious society, either ancient or modern, wherein such liberty of conscience is now allowed, or has been allowed, since the age of the apostles. Here is our glorying, and a glorying peculiar to us." It was so; and none amongst the secondary causes of their success contributed to it more than this spirit.

The spiritual influence of the Methodist leaders was not, however, confined to the lower classes. Through the influence of the Countess of Huntingdon they were brought into immediate contact with a large section of the aristocracy. This celebrated lady, after having been a frequent attendant, with her husband, on the preaching of the Wesleys and Whitefield, took Whitefield under her especial patronage. Defying all ecclesiastical order, she engaged the preacher to hold services in her own residence, which the nobility were invited to attend. They accepted the invitation in great numbers. Amongst those who heard him were the Earl of Chesterfield, Viscount Bolingbroke, the Duke of Argyle, the Earl of Aberdeen, the Duchess of Montagu, Lord Lyttelton, the Duke of Kingston, Mr. Pitt, and most of those who formed the Court of the Prince of Wales.* With some of these Whitefield maintained an affectionate intercourse through life, and was of eminent use to them. To his preaching and the work of the Countess, may be ascribed the revival of religion in the aristocracy as well as in the common people.

Few women have ever deserved a noble fame so fully

* Life and Times of Selina, Countess of Huntingdon," vol. i. cap. vii.

as the widowed Countess who had undertaken to bring the claims of religion, urged by the most eloquent and powerful of preachers, before the members of her own section of society. Herself of high lineage, and intimately connected by marriage with the most conspicuous noble families, she had an opportunity of religious service of which she took advantage to the utmost extent. Although the tone of thought amongst the aristocracy was especially unfavourable to the culture of the religious character, and extraordinary piety was generally identified with extraordinary ignorance and fanaticism, the Countess lost, by her fidelity and zeal, little, if any, of her social influence. She might be smiled at, and be made the butt of a few town wits, but the strength, thoroughness, and sincerity of her character generally secured for her the utmost respect. Her most intimate friends were women of her own circle and family. Next to these ranked Whitefield, the few clergy of the Established Church, such as Romaine, Venn, and Howel Harris, who were classed with the Methodist party, some of the lay preachers, and, amongst Dissenters, Dr. Doddridge, who was her constant correspondent and frequent guest. She adopted Whitefield rather than either, or both of the Wesleys, because Whitefield was a Calvinist. She could not, indeed, have worked long with John Wesley, for she had many of the intellectual characteristics of the founder of Arminian Methodism. Her faculty of organization was almost equal, and her strength of will quite equal to that of Wesley's own. She saw, with Wesley, that organization was necessary to the permanence of the results which were being produced by the new preaching. She had wealth, influence, capacity, and time to frame this organization, and she framed it. She founded colleges—Trevecca and Cheshunt,—she built places of worship, she appointed ministers and she sent out evangelists, and, although in different respects, aided in founding two denominations—the Calvinistic Methodist of Wales, and the Countess of Huntingdon's Connexion in England. The latter, owing to many influences, has since become almost identified with the Congregational body. Like Wesley, the Countess had no intention of leaving the Established Church, but she had more moral courage than Wesley in respect to Church laws and ordinances. She saw no difference of species between a layman and a clergyman, and she saw no reason why, when Christians met together, they should not celebrate the Lord's Supper. Her societies, therefore, became organized for all religious and ecclesiastical purposes much more quickly than those which Wesley directed. Wesley warded the pain of separation from himself; the Countess felt it in her lifetime. When it came, in the shape of a legal decision which compelled her to certify her buildings under the Toleration Act, she exclaimed, "I am to be cast out of the Church now, only for what I have been doing these forty years—speaking and living for Jesus Christ."* How was it that she did not remember that almost all religious earnestness, from that of early Puritanism, had met with a similar fate? How could she have expected to escape?

When the early Methodists appeared, religious life was dying out of England. Even Dissent seemed to have lost its spiritual force, and, with it, its power of aggression. It had, apparently, almost done the work

* Stevens's "History of Methodism," ii. 100.

which had been committed it to do. In its first period it had fought for spiritual liberty, and had won that hardest of all human battles. In its second period it had saved the country from arbitrary power. Statesmen and people, ecclesiastics and laymen, had now been brought round to a practical recognition of its service to the politics, the intellect, and the conscience of the nation. Through it, the English people had grown to a broader type of thought than it would have been possible for them otherwise to have possessed; for the doctrines of political liberty, of resistance to arbitrary power, and of the rights of conscience, were either the characteristic doctrines of Dissenters, or they were the natural consequences of them. But it seemed impossible to make any farther advance. The obstacle to this was to be removed by the infusion of a new religious life into the churches. For, in proportion as men and nations grow in religious, do they grow in political liberty. Neither is the offspring of indifference, but of belief. When, and not until that time, the churches had been baptized anew by the Spirit of God, did they once more seek for the extension of civil freedom and religious equality. The power to attain this is ultimately to be traced to the Methodist movement.

CHAPTER VI.

THE REVIVAL OF RELIGION IN WALES.

REFERENCE has more than once been made, in the course of this History, to the state of religion in the Principality of Wales, and the efforts of several godly and zealous men to effect some improvement in the moral and spiritual condition of the remarkable people who have inhabited that portion of the British Islands. Like Ireland, Wales had suffered not only from the fact of its being a conquered country, but from its being inhabited by a race alien to the origin and the language of the conquerors. Probably no people placed in similar circumstances had so steadily or so successfully preserved their national characteristics as the people of Wales. It may be said that, for centuries, the land only—the bare earth on which they had lived—was kept in subjugation, for the spirit of the nation had undergone no change. They were never effectually conquered by Imperial Rome; they never, as members of the ancient British Church, bowed the neck to Papal Rome. The strong hand of the Normans was employed for two centuries before the native government was set aside; and when, at last, the last Welsh prince was defeated, all the civil rights of the conquerors were made the rights also of the conquered.

After the Reformation, so far as religion was concerned, the Welsh, also like the Irish, were treated with a studied and contemptuous neglect. Their ecclesiastical revenues were, to a great extent, appropriated to the augmentation of the revenues of the Church of England or bestowed upon English laymen. Englishmen, to whom the Welsh language was as unknown as Syriac or Sanscrit, were appointed to bishoprics, rectories, vicarages, and even curacies. These men necessarily ministered to fractions only of the people. But they were, for the most part, incapable of giving any spiritual instruction, for in morals they were as licentious as in religion they were ignorant. Towards the end of the sixteenth century, John Penry, the martyred apostle of Wales, described the clergy as "unlearned dolts," "drunkards" and "adulterers." At that time, a Bishop of St. Asaph held, in addition to the revenues of his see, sixteen livings in commendam, and only three incumbents in all the diocese resided upon their livings.* "Ye bishops of Wales," cried Penry, "seeing, you yourselves know, and all Wales knoweth, that you have admitted into this sacred foundation rogues, vagabonds gadding about the country under the name of scholars; spendthrifts and starving men, that made the ministry their last refuge: seeing you permit such to be in the ministry as are known adulterers, known thieves, roisterers, most abominable swearers, even the men of whom Job speaketh, who are more vile than the earth, do you not say that the Lord's service is not to be regarded?"†

* Strype's Annals. Quoted in Rees's "Nonconformity in Wales," p. 5.
† "Penry's Exhortation," A.D. 1588, ib. p. 7.

In the middle of the seventeenth century, the Rev. Rees Pritchard, Vicar of Llandovery, said that it would be difficult to decide whether the clergyman, the farmer, the labourer, the artizan, the bailiff, the judge, or the nobleman was the most daring in iniquity.* The picture of the state of the nation nearly a hundred years later was drawn in almost equally dark colours. The Rev. Thomas Charles, of Bala, thus describes it:—" In those days the land was dark indeed. Hardly any of the lower ranks could read at all. The morals of the country were very corrupt; and in this respect there was no difference between gentle and simple, layman and clergyman; gluttony, drunkenness, and licentiousness, prevailed throughout the whole country. Nor were the operations of the Church at all calculated to repress these evils. From the pulpit the name of the Redeemer was hardly ever heard; nor was much mention made of the natural sinfulness of man, nor of the influence of the Spirit. Every Sabbath there was what was called 'Achwaren-gamp;' a sort of sport in which all the young men of the neighbourhood had a trial of strength, and the people assembled from the surrounding country to see the feats. In every corner of the town some sport or other went on till the light of the Sabbath day had faded."†

During this long period a few men had, like the prophets of Judah, lifted up their voices for their God. Besides Penry in the reign of Elizabeth, and Vavaseur Powell, in the time of the Commonwealth, three Welsh clergymen, William Wroth, rector of Llanvaches, Rees

* Pritchard's " Welshman's Candle," ib.
† " The Trysorfa," A.D. 1799. Quoted in Philip's " Life of Whitefield."

Pritchard, vicar of Llandovery, and Walter Cradock, stood conspicuous as shining lights in the spiritual darkness in which the nation was enveloped. Wroth was born in A.D. 1570, and was almost the first preaching incumbent in Wales.* From a man of gay and frivolous temperament he had suddenly become absorbed in the importance of the Divine message to mankind. His natural eloquence, his fervour of address, and his unwearied zeal soon made his name known throughout his native country. But he was guilty of ecclesiastical irregularities. When his church would not hold the people who went to hear him he preached in the churchyard, for which offence he was called to account by his diocesan, who angrily inquired of him how he dared to violate the rules of the Church? Wroth, it is said, replied, with tears in his eyes, by calling the bishop's attention to the spiritual ignorance of the people and the necessity of employing every means to remove it, a reply which, for the time, availed. But he added to this offence the crime of refusing to read the "Book of Sports." Dragged afterwards, by Laud, before the Court of High Commission, he was summarily deprived of his benefice. Such a man was not likely to suffer mere ecclesiastical regulations or Episcopal prohibitions to influence his conduct. He still, therefore, continued to preach from house to house, and from town to town, and in A.D. 1638 founded, at Llanvaches, a Church on the Congregational model. He died in four years afterwards, leaving a reputation eminent for its sanctity, a title, "the blessed apostle of South Wales," of the highest spiritual rank,

* Johnes's "Essay on the causes which have produced Dissent from the Established Church in the Principality of Wales," p. 6.

and a work which time can never destroy nor his countrymen forget.

Rees Pritchard, or, as he was more familiarly styled, "Vicar Pritchard," was, if equally eminent in piety, not so unfortunate in respect to his ecclesiastical relationships. It happened that the Earl of Essex, when in his minority, resided near Llandovery, where Pritchard was born, and to his protection the vicar probably owed his immunity from persecution. His popularity was not less than that of Wroth. Vast multitudes went to hear him preach, and even the Cathedral of St. David's was not large enough to contain the hearers. Pritchard therefore preached in the open air, and, as in Wroth's case, a charge was immediately preferred against him in the Ecclesiastical Court. He escaped punishment, but did not relinquish his labours. The tradition of Pritchard's labours has descended from generation to generation of his countrymen, amongst whom his name, at the end of more than two centuries, is still held in veneration: But he established other claims upon their gratitude than those belonging to a zealous preacher of the Gospel. He was the "Welsh Watts." His religious poetry is one of the most prized inheritances of his nation. No book in the Welsh language, it is said, excepting the Bible, has had so extensive a circulation; and, at one time, wherever the Holy Scriptures were to be found, there also was to be found the volume of "Pritchard's Poems."*

Walter Cradock, who was born in the early part of the seventeenth century, was a disciple of Wroth's, and imbibed from his spiritual teacher something of his zeal

* Johnes's "Essay," &c., pp. 12, 15. Rees's "Nonconformity," pp. 30, 36.

and his independence. But these qualities were, at that time, an offence in the eyes of the ecclesiastical authorities. For refusing to read the "Book of Sports," he was ejected by the Bishop of Llandaff, in A.D. 1633, from his first curacy, at Cardiff. From thence he went to Wrexham, where his eloquence drew crowds from the country around to hear him, and where his labours effected a signal reformation in the manners of the people. But before he had been there a year he was driven away. He is found, after this, at Llanvaire, from whence he made evangelistic excursions through all the neighbouring counties of North Wales. In the time of the Commonwealth, he became a Congregationalist, and zealously defended the right of private judgment.* A hundred years after his death, the aged people amongst the Dissenters of the principality still talked of Walter Cradock.†

Excepting these men, scarcely any appeared until just before the rise of Methodism to enlighten the people concerning the Divine revelation to mankind, and these—the forerunners of Welsh Dissent—were frowned upon by all the ecclesiastical authorities. In common with both the earlier and the later Puritans, they were compelled to break through established rules, or to see the people die in their sins; and the judgment of those who were set over them was, that it was better that people should die in their sins than that one iota of the canon law, or the smallest of the rubrics should be broken. The success and the popularity of Wroth, Pritchard, and Cradock, apart from their religious characters, were partly

* Rees's "Nonconformity," pp. 51, 59.
† Thomas's History of the Baptist Associations in Wales, p. 3.

due to the fact, that they were eminently representative Welshmen. The English incumbents, and their English curates, had they been, what they were not, fit men to preach a pure religion, could never have touched the hearts of the people. One of their own nation was needed to speak and to plead with them; and, as it has ever been since Christianity was first revealed, no sooner was it placed before them than thousands joyfully accepted it. It is not, however, necessary to suppose that the spiritual rulers of the people were altogether averse to their becoming a religious people. For the most part, they simply cared nothing about them. They, no doubt, recognized the fact that those who actually became subject to religious influences did not appear to possess that attachment to the Church, as by law established, which they preferred them to possess even at the risk of their personal salvation. But, on the other hand, they thought lightly of the doctrine of a new heart, and a new life. If the people had been "baptized," what more could they require? Men like Wroth, Pritchard, and Cradock, were considered enthusiasts, who were dangerous to the peaceable, if stagnant, order of things. If the religious sentiment should grow, there would be an end of non-resident Bishops living upon the proceeds of dozens of livings, and of non-resident incumbents who never saw their parishioners. The State was equally indifferent, and was not animated by any loftier principles, than the hierarchy. If it had been, it would never have suffered the appointment of English prelates to Welsh dioceses, and never have overlooked the scandalous neglect of their duties of which the ecclesiastical officers of the Crown were habitually guilty. It would, at least, have seen that men fit for their peculiar work were sent to discharge that work. The native Welsh, or ancient British race, has always been marked by three characteristics,—an ardent imagination, and warmth and activity of feeling. No people are more susceptible to the beauties of poetry or the charms of popular oratory, and none are more easily moved by appeals to the religious affections. Nor is the sentiment of nationality more deeply fixed, or more universally distributed amongst any of the Celtic race—where this sentiment seems to last longer than in any other race—than it is amongst the descendants of the earliest inhabitants of Britain. To this people, preachers, such as they were, were sent, who could have had no feelings in common with their parishioners. A warm and highly imaginative race was expected, if anything whatever was expected, to be influenced by the comparatively cold, hard, and matter of fact manner of the ordinary Englishman. A race who had stored up in their memories the traditions of centuries of an independent national life, was expected to be influenced by men who despised the very name of Welshmen, and altogether ignored the national tongue. What wonder if such a people ultimately turned, almost as a whole nation, from a Church which had treated them, from the year of its birth, as aliens and outcasts, rather than as brethren and sons?*

In the early part of the eighteenth century another clergyman arose, whose labours were probably of even greater practical benefit to his countrymen than those of

* The causes of dissent in Wales have been most exhaustively treated by two Churchmen, the Rev. A. J. Johnes, in the "Essay" which has already been quoted in the text, and by Sir Thomas Phillips, in his very comprehensive work on "Wales."

any of his predecessors. This was the Rev. Griffith Jones, incumbent of Llandeilo and Llandouror. To this eminent man belongs the honour of establishing, long before Bell and Lancaster were born, a system of popular day-school education in Wales. Finding his own parishioners deficient in information upon the ordinary subjects of Christian doctrine and conduct, he founded a school for their benefit. The advantage of such an institution soon being made evident, he thought of the great good which would result if "a well organized system of schools" was established throughout Wales. Aided by contributions from friends, he began to put into execution such a scheme. His plan was to engage travelling schoolmasters, who should visit town after town, stopping in each as long as their services were required, and revisiting them from time to time. In order to procure proper teachers, he founded a teachers' seminary, to which he would admit none but apparently religious persons, the majority of whom, it appears, were Nonconformists. In A.D. 1741, or about ten years after their establishment, a hundred and seventy-eight of these schools had been conducted during the year. The result was soon apparent. Intelligence improved, manners became more civilized, and churches were better attended. Twenty years after this, when death put an end to the labours of this devoted and active philanthropist, the number of schools which had been established, at different times, and in various places in Wales, amounted to three thousand four hundred and ninety-five, and the number of scholars taught to more than a hundred and fifty thousand, or at least a third of the whole population of Wales. By far the larger number of the scholars in these "circulating schools" were adults, who lamented, with tears, that they "had not had an opportunity of learning forty or fifty years sooner." When Griffith Jones died he left, as has been well said, " in the religious regeneration, and the religious gratitude, of a nation of mountaineers, a memorial, which will be envied most by those who are at once the proudest and the humblest of mankind." His work, however, met with much clerical opposition, and the bishops of Wales did not give him the least countenance.*

In the early period of the patriotic labours of this man, a young preacher, of the name of Howel Harris, a native of Trevecca, appeared amongst the people. Harris had been to the University of Oxford, but had left it in consequence of the immorality of the place. Having been refused orders, because he had preached as a layman, he began, on his return home, to address the people in the open air and in private houses. "After my return" (which was in A.D. 1725), he says, "I was occupied in going from house to house, until I had visited the greatest part of my native parish, together with those of neighbouring ones. The people now began to assemble by vast numbers, so that the houses wherein we met could not contain them. The Word was attended with such power that many on the spot cried out to God for pardon of their sins. Family worship was set up in many houses, and the churches, as far as I had gone, were crowded, and likewise the Lord's table. It was now high time for the enemy to make a stand in another manner; therefore he not only influenced the populace to revile and persecute me, but

* Johnes's "Essay," pp. 15, 25.

caused the magistrates and clergy to bestir themselves—
the former to threaten me, and such as would receive
me to their houses, with fines ; while the latter showed
their indignation, and used their endeavours to discourage me by other means. By this time I gained
acquaintance with several Dissenters, who kindly received me to their houses." In order to maintain the
work which he had thus commenced, Harris proceeded
to establish religious societies. "This," he says, "was
before any other society of the kind was established in
England or Wales, the English Methodists not being yet
heard of." There can be no doubt, in fact, that as the
system of popular education was established in Wales
before it was established in England, so also the system
of religious "societies" was established in Wales by
Howel Harris before it was established in England by
John Wesley.

When Howel Harris commenced his work, Dissent in
Wales existed only in the most insignificant proportions.
The number of Dissenting congregations in the whole
principality and the county of Monmouth, in the year
1715, was about one hundred and ten, and the actual
attendants not much more than twenty-five thousand
persons.* Of these the majority were Congregationalists
and Presbyterians; the rest belonged to the Baptists
and the Society of Friends. Most of these Churches
had sprung from the labours of Wroth, Pritchard, and
Cradock. There is a vague tradition that a Baptist
Church existed at Olchon in the year 1633, and such
traditions have usually some sort of fact for their basis;
but the first Baptist Church, the origin of which can be

* Rees's "Nonconformity," etc.," pp. 292, 293.

clearly ascertained, was founded at Ilston, near Swansea, in the year 1649. The pastor of this Church, John Myles, was the first who maintained, in Wales, the practice of unmixed communion.* In A.D. 1736 there were only twelve Baptist Churches in the Principality, and five years later only fifteen.† In the few Churches connected with the various bodies of Dissenters there was an earnest religious life, but they exercised comparatively little influence upon the character of the nation at large. Before the rise of Methodism—that is to say, before the preaching of Howel Harris—the Churches were " little attended by the great mass of the people," and ".indifference to all religion prevailed as widely as Dissent" has since prevailed.‡ Harris himself says that, with the generality of the people, public worship being over, the remaining part of the Sunday was spent in indulging in the prevailing corruptions of nature; that all family worship was laid aside, except among some of the Dissenters, "while an universal deluge of swearing, lying, reviling, drunkenness, fighting, and gaming had overspread the country, and that the clergy themselves were evidently not in earnest in their work."§

The labours of Harris soon excited not only the attention of his own people, but the notice of the Methodist party in England. Whitefield put himself in communication with him; Wesley went to Wales and saw him, and the Countess of Huntingdon also visited him. He now extended his labours; and all through Wales his voice was heard as that of a prophet crying in the

* Thomas's " History," etc., p. 5.   † Ib., pp. 43, 45.
‡ Morgan's " Life of Howel Harris," p. 12.
§ Johnes's " Essay," pp. 26, 27.

wilderness. He met, in many places, with the same treatment that the founders of Methodism in England received. He was mobbed, stoned, and often in danger of his life. At Machynlleth, where he was assailed by a mob, headed by the local attorney and the parish clergyman, a pistol was fired at him, and he was driven with sticks and stones from the town. At Newport the stones flew about his head, and he was considerably injured. At Caerleon he was pelted with dung, eggs, and dirt. At Monmouth a dead dog, in addition to other missiles, was flung at him. Near Bala the incumbent rushed upon him with an uplifted club; the mob threatened him with death, and he was beaten and trampled upon until he was almost senseless. In Carnarvonshire he heard himself denounced by the chancellor of the diocese as a minister of the devil; and when the chancellor called upon the people to rise up against such a man, he was hunted from the church and the town.* Mr. Perrott, the curate of Bedwelly and Mynyddislyn, wrote to him as follows:—"I am surprised at the liberty you take of coming to my curacies. . . . You must recede, or else yourself and the person or persons that have invited or sent for you, must expect that just resentment due for unlawful practices."† But in almost all places that he visited his preaching was successful. By-and-by some clergymen took part with him, and a band was organized, resembling, in some manner, Wesley's band in England.

Writing in A.D. 1749, Harris relates that every day for seven years, in all weathers, and generally out of doors, he had preached three or four, and frequently

* "Stevens's History," ii. 72, 75.   † Rees's "Nonconformity, etc.," p. 366.

five times, travelling from place to place, from ten to thirty miles a day. Although he had not received orders in the Established Church, he strenuously adhered to its communion. He says that, for this, he was blamed by people of all denominations, and when he found some of his converts becoming Dissenters he thought it his duty " to declare against them." What he, in common with the leaders of the English Methodists, desired was that all those who were influenced by his preaching should remain members of the Established Church, but the progress of events effectually frustrated this intention. If the necessity for greater freedom of religious action than could be obtained in the Church had not compelled the disciples of Harris and of his coadjutors to separate from it, the animosity which was felt towards them by its rulers, and which found expression in almost every Charge which came from their pens, would have been sufficient to cause an alienation, at first of temper, and ultimately of formal communion. The conduct of Harris was undoubtedly inconsistent. He was a law unto himself, or rather his conscience sat in judgment on the ecclesiastical regulations of the Church of which he was a member, and unhesitatingly rejected those which stood in his path as a preacher of the Gospel. This was actual Dissent, and accordingly Welsh, like English Methodism, terminated in secession from the religion established by law.

It was not long before Harris found coadjutors. Amongst these William Williams, of Penty-Celyn, stood eminent. He had been a licensed curate, but having committed the grave offence of preaching in other parishes than his own, was refused orders. Thenceforward he devoted himself to itinerant preaching; and in A.D. 1716 took the bold step of administering the communion in a Welsh Methodist chapel. It is stated that in the course of his journeys Williams travelled a distance equal to four times the circumference of the earth. He was a man of an intense devotional spirit, united to an ardent poetical feeling. He, also, adhered to the Established communion.

Contemporary with Williams was Daniel Rowlands, of Nant-cwnlle and Llangeitho, who, after preaching thirty years, was ultimately (about A.D. 1763) ejected from the Church for preaching in unconsecrated places, and for visiting other parishes than his own. The ministry of Rowlands appears to have been one of almost unsurpassed power. The church at Llanddewi-hefi, which he served with his curacies, would contain three thousand persons, and was filled in every part. The strength of feeling and the degree of personal attachment to himself, which he excited, is indicated by the fact that persons would follow him from one church to another on the Sunday, and return home without having taken food from Sunday morning until Monday morning. After his ejection, Rowlands preached in a large place of worship built for him at Llangeitho, which became the centre of an extraordinary religious influence. Here, thousands, from every part of Wales, were accustomed to resort, some persons travelling sixty and even a hundred miles in order to hear him. The description of these remarkable assemblages, given in the life of the Rev. Thomas Charles, of Bala, is not unlike that which the Psalmist of Judah has given of the pilgrimage to Jerusalem. "From twenty to thirty travelled together, or in two companies, some on foot and some on horseback, both men and women. Those on foot started early on Saturday, and took a shorter course over the mountains, without any support except the food they brought with them, and their drink was pure water from the mountain springs. After hearing one or two sermons from Rowlands they returned home again, fully satisfied and abundantly repaid for all the toil of their journey."* Every county in the Principality was represented at these meetings. Llangeitho, in those days, took a position somewhat similar to that occupied by the cathedrals in the early period of English ecclesiastical history. There, the new order of preachers met every month, and from it, as a centre, they went forth to evangelize the country. One, who was equal to Rowlands, and who subsequently took the place of Rowlands both in the estimation and affection of his countrymen, and in public influence, the Rev. Thomas Charles, of Bala, wrote that "his gifts and the power which accompanied his ministry were such that no hearers in the present age can form any adequate idea of them; there is no one who has not heard him that can imagine anything equal to what they were."†

The external results of the labours of these men was the organization of numerous religious societies, the parents of the Welsh Calvinistic Churches throughout the whole of North and South Wales. In A.D. 1747, their first meeting-house was erected at Builth, in Breconshire. In the next year two more were erected in Carmarthenshire. After that they rapidly increased. In A.D. 1767 the Countess of Huntingdon founded a

* Sir Thomas Phillips' "Wales," p. 142.   † Ib. p. 146.

college at Trevecca, for the education of students, some of whom took orders in the Established Church, and became indentified with the rising Evangelical party, while others remained in the Countess of Huntingdon's "Connexion," or ministered to Congregational Churches. A Methodist Association, at which Whitefield was present, was held for the first time in Wales in the year 1743, when rules were laid down for the government of the body. From that period similar associations have been periodically held. In the same year, Rowlands is stated to have had three thousand communicants in Cardiganshire, and Howel Harris two thousand in Pembrokeshire.* Differences between Rowlands and Harris impeded the progress of Methodism for some time after this, and theological controversies had the same effect on other religious bodies, but the general progress of religion, resulting from the labours of these eminent, although discarded members of the Established Church, was without precedent. The whole aspect of the nation was changed. Religious societies sprung up in every part of the land. Dissenting churches rapidly increased in number. An effectual check was given to all amusements of an immoral tendency. The habitually warm temperament of the people began to flow, in greater and greater volume, in the channel of religious feeling. But when the early leaders of Welsh Methodism had died, no provision for a permanent organization of the forces which they had created had been made. Howel Harris died in A.D. 1773, Rowlands died in the same year, and Williams in A.D. 1791. As the founders of Calvinistic Methodism in Wales, Harris and Rowlands performed

* Johnes's Essay," p. 36.

the greatest work which the Almighty has given to men to perform. They began the regeneration of a whole people who, until they and their fellow-labourers appeared, were sunk in almost heathen darkness. The good which they effected they effected against the will and in spite of the prohibitions of their own Church, which, as in England, and not in relation to the Methodists alone, had again exhibited herself in what was still her characteristic attitude, as the opponent of all sincere religious life, and all active religious work. But whatever credit may attach to a communion from the zeal of individual members is to be attached, in this instance, to the Established Church in Wales. Although she disowned and expelled the men who were regenerating their country, their personal attachment to her was never lessened. It is impossible to say whether their spiritual power and success would have been greater if they had possessed less of this feeling. Their communion with the Church, and their constant professions of attachment to it, probably contributed, in the first instance, to their personal influence. It gave them, for a time, free access to churches, and gained them the ear of Churchmen. It is possible that, afterwards, its influence was not beneficial. For, when parish ministers could not address their people in the only language with which they were acquainted; when these ministers seldom even appeared in their parishes, and when their lives, if not always scandalous, were not such as to adorn an ordinary religious profession, the urgent advice to remain in the Church, if it were followed, was not calculated to conduce to the personal piety of the people. To supplement the deficiencies of the Church, or rather to supply that for which it ostensibly existed, the numerous Methodist Societies were formed. These possessed the soul, while the Church itself was only the skeleton of the community. The work of the pioneers of Welsh Methodism stopped short of the assurance of permanent success. This was obtained in the next generation, by persons whose individual sympathies were naturally freer than those of men who had been born and nurtured in the Church.

CHAPTER VII.

FROM THE ESTABLISHMENT OF METHODISM TO THE SECOND AGITATION FOR THE REPEAL OF THE TEST AND CORPORATION ACTS.

A.D. 1744—A.D. 1793.

THE Methodist controversy was not the only controversy which attracted public attention at this period. Once more the relative merits of the Established Church and of Dissent, which every generation, from the time of the first Separatists, has discussed anew, were brought under consideration. The literature of this question received, from the active and inquiring intellect which characterized the nation during the greater portion of George the Second's reign, more important additions than had been made to it since the time of the later Puritans. The new controversy arose from a publication by Dr. Watts. When the causes of the decay of the Dissenting interest were under discussion, Watts wrote a solemn and impassioned appeal to Dissenters to live in a manner which should be worthy of the principles which they professed, and the position which they occupied.* He considered that these were eminently favourable to a religious life, and that therefore Dissenters were under special obligations to adorn the Christian profession. Their religious

* "An Humble Attempt towards the Revival of Practical Religion among Christians." A.D. 1731.

advantages he considered to be numerous and important. They, for instance, were in no danger, such as Churchmen were in, of mistaking baptism for inward and real regeneration; they were freed from the impositions and incumbrances of human ceremonies in Divine worship; they were not confined to set forms of prayer; they could not only worship God in their ordinary way, but they could choose their own ministers; the communion of their Church was kept more pure and free from unworthy and scandalous members, and their conduct was strictly observed, and their behaviour watched with a narrow and severe eye. The real reason why they dissented from the National Church, was that they might make better improvements in religion than if they continued in her communion. What is this, he inquired, that we mean by asserting the right and freedom of conscience in our separation, but more effectually to promote the kingdom of God amongst men, to do more honour to the name of Christ in His institutions, and better to carry on the work of the salvation of souls? As was the case with the disciples when they followed after Jesus, so, he remarked, it was and would be generally the case with all honest and sincere persons in their religious separation from any Established Church. What advantage did they derive if it were not that they hoped to advance in godliness? To be an irreligious Dissenter he counted as a degree of folly that wanted a name, for such a man got nothing by his profession but reproach and contempt in this world, and damnation in the next.

Notwithstanding that Watts was careful to eschew ecclesiastical controversy in this work, he could not avoid frequent reference to the points of difference between the ecclesiastical constitutions of the Established and of the Dissenting communities. He also plainly stated his conviction of the unscripturalness of any National Church. "Christ," he said, "has not established any such church on earth. God alone is the Lord of the conscience, and He has appointed His Son Jesus to be King and Ruler of His Church." The whole question of a Civil Establishment of religion he subsequently discussed in another publication.* In this, one of the most careful of all his writings, he laid down the proposition that the civil government, in its proper aims and designs, had no object beyond the benefit of men in this world, nor did the things of religion nor the affairs of a future state come within its cognizance. No civil ruler, he held, had any right to require or command the people to profess or practise his own religion, nor to levy tithes or other compulsory dues for its support. The usurpation of the civil power in things sacred, or of the ecclesiastical power in things civil, had, he said, produced nothing but infinite confusion, persecution, hypocrisy, slavery of soul and body, fraud and violence of every kind. With his characteristic speculativeness of intellect, however, Watts proceeded to inquire whether a certain establishment of a national religion was not within the sphere of the civil government. He held that it was; that every government should make an acknowledgment of the existence of a God; that it should impose oaths; that it should employ public teachers of

---

* "An Essay on Civil Power in Things Sacred; or an Inquiry after an Established Religion, consistent with the just liberties of mankind and practicable under every form of Civil Government." A.D. 1739.

the same right of resistance which they had in any other case.* Doddridge, in this instance, was guilty of the fallacy which Paley subsequently held, namely, of resolving a question of right and wrong into a question of majorities and minorities. Not merely a majority in a question, but every man, has an equal right to justice. Not merely a majority, but every man, has an equal claim to the protection of his conscience and his property. If Doddridge had formally argued this question from an exclusively scriptural point of view, he might have expressed himself with more hesitation upon it, but it does not appear to have been one to which he attached a paramount importance. Persecution he could not but hate; but, providing it were sufficiently "large," he might even have joined an Established Church.

But the two principal representatives of the Free Churches were not the only persons whose thoughts were directed to this topic. By the failure of the old arguments in support of Church authority, which had been exploded during the Bangorian controversy, Churchmen were being driven to find new defences for the establishment of their religion. Formerly, it had been sufficient to urge that they belonged to the Church of the successors of the Apostles, and had therefore inherited peculiar gifts, and were entitled to peculiar privileges; but this style of argument was no longer of any avail amongst intelligent men. It might be accepted amongst the bucolic tenants of bucolic country gentlemen—men who considered that Charles II. had been an anointed king, and who still had a profound reverence for the services and the reputation of the great Dr. Sacheverell,—

* "Lectures on Ethics." Works, iv. 503, 504.

but within the confines of intelligent Christian civilization it was received with a smile and a shrug of contempt. It was necessary, therefore, to justify the connection between the Episcopalian Church and the State by another theory. This work was accomplished by a clergyman who afterwards became one of the most eminent of all the bishops of the Establishment. In the year 1736, the Rev. William Warburton, incumbent of Brant-Broughton, published a treatise on the "Alliance between Church and State." Warburton is entitled to the credit of framing a new and ingenious theory of this alliance. Treating the Church and the State as two separate and independent powers, he argued, from the analogy of civil government, that when the Church entered into an alliance with the State she necessarily sacrificed her independence. In return for this, she received peculiar privileges and a public endowment for her ministers. This was her benefit; but the State was equally benefited, for the Church exerted her influence and authority on the side of public virtue and social order. The advantages of a public endowment were defended by Warburton at great length. He considered it rendered the clergy independent of the people, and did not subject them to the temptation of pandering to their passions. When Selden denied the divine authority of English tithes, he was compelled to recant his opinions, but Warburton equally abandoned that basis of ecclesiastical taxation. He considered it to be merely an eligible and convenient method of providing for the maintenance of the clergy, and he therefore approved of it. He defended the presence of "superior members" of the Church in the legislature of the nation as being a just concession to the

the same right of resistance which they had in any other case.* Doddridge, in this instance, was guilty of the fallacy which Paley subsequently held, namely, of resolving a question of right and wrong into a question of majorities and minorities. Not merely a majority in a question, but every man, has an equal right to justice. Not merely a majority, but every man, has an equal claim to the protection of his conscience and his property. If Doddridge had formally argued this question from an exclusively scriptural point of view, he might have expressed himself with more hesitation upon it, but it does not appear to have been one to which he attached a paramount importance. Persecution he could not but hate; but, providing it were sufficiently "large," he might even have joined an Established Church.

But the two principal representatives of the Free Churches were not the only persons whose thoughts were directed to this topic. By the failure of the old arguments in support of Church authority, which had been exploded during the Bangorian controversy, Churchmen were being driven to find new defences for the establishment of their religion. Formerly, it had been sufficient to urge that they belonged to the Church of the successors of the Apostles, and had therefore inherited peculiar gifts, and were entitled to peculiar privileges; but this style of argument was no longer of any avail amongst intelligent men. It might be accepted amongst the bucolic tenants of bucolic country gentlemen—men who considered that Charles II. had been an anointed king, and who still had a profound reverence for the services and the reputation of the great Dr. Sacheverell,—

* "Lectures on Ethics." Works, iv. 503, 504.

but within the confines of intelligent Christian civilization it was received with a smile and a shrug of contempt. It was necessary, therefore, to justify the connection between the Episcopalian Church and the State by another theory. This work was accomplished by a clergyman who afterwards became one of the most eminent of all the bishops of the Establishment. In the year 1736, the Rev. William Warburton, incumbent of Brant-Broughton, published a treatise on the "Alliance between Church and State." Warburton is entitled to the credit of framing a new and ingenious theory of this alliance. Treating the Church and the State as two separate and independent powers, he argued, from the analogy of civil government, that when the Church entered into an alliance with the State she necessarily sacrificed her independence. In return for this, she received peculiar privileges and a public endowment for her ministers. This was her benefit; but the State was equally benefited, for the Church exerted her influence and authority on the side of public virtue and social order. The advantages of a public endowment were defended by Warburton at great length. He considered it rendered the clergy independent of the people, and did not subject them to the temptation of pandering to their passions. When Selden denied the divine authority of English tithes, he was compelled to recant his opinions, but Warburton equally abandoned that basis of ecclesiastical taxation. He considered it to be merely an eligible and convenient method of providing for the maintenance of the clergy, and he therefore approved of it. He defended the presence of "superior members" of the Church in the legislature of the nation as being a just concession to the reasonable expectations of a church which had surrendered to the State her own independence and authority. Starting with these primary principles, he proceeded to inquire what religion should be selected for such an alliance, and replied that, from motives of policy, it should be the strongest. Such an alliance could, however, subsist only so long as the selected church might maintain its relative superiority over other sects. When that superiority should cease to exist, it would be the duty of the State to select the body which had taken the place of the other. In any case, other religious societies should have free toleration; but not so as to injure the established religion, and there should therefore be "tests." Dissenters, he argued, ought not to complain of being compelled to support the established religion, because it was maintained not for the promulgation of any particular religious opinions, but for the benefit of the State, of which they themselves were members.

Warburton's theory was evidently constructed to suit the actual position of the English Church. It is the lowest theory of an established religion that could be framed. It ignores the difference between truth and error, and justifies the State in propagating one as well as the other. It degrades the clergy to the rank of a body of police, and the Church to a mere office of Government. How far such a connection was consistent with the nature of religion, or how much it would be likely to hinder the design of the founders of Christianity, or whether it must not misrepresent the character of the Gospel, Warburton never inquired. He wrote his book, avowedly, in the interests, not of the Church, but of the State. The subject was, with him, not a religious, but a political one. That Warburton did not stand alone in this idea is proved by the sudden popularity of his treatise, and by Bishop Horsley's criticism upon it—that it was an admirable specimen of scientific reasoning applied to a "political" subject.*

While Warburton's work, singularly enough, excited no public controversy, and provoked only one public reply, Watts's "Humble Attempt" was vigorously assailed. In a series of letters † especially addressed to "a gentleman dissenting from the Church of England," the Rev. John White, vicar of Ospring, attacked the argument of Watts that the principles of Dissent and the position of Dissenters were more favourable to the growth of piety than those of Churchmen. After denying the fact, the author proceeded to the proof of the contrary position. He then examined the reasons of Dissent, going over the principal grounds of the old controversy on this subject. White's "Letters," written, as they were, in a pointed and popular style, went quickly through several editions. They found, however, an opponent far more able and astute in controversy than White himself. This was Micaiah Towgood, a Presbyterian minister of Crediton. Towgood replied to the whole of White's letters. His work, which for three generations remained the standard work on this subject, and which has been more frequently reprinted, both in England and America, than any other publication of the kind, derives its chief merit from the prominence which it gives to the unscriptural character of

---

* Watson's "Life of Warburton," p. 57.
† "Three Letters to a Gentleman Dissenting from the Church of England." By John White, B.D., A.D. 1743.

the constitution of the Established Church. For the manner in which it exposed the subjection and dependence of the Church on the State, and the inconsistency of such a position with the rights of the Church, and in which it contrasted the character of a Christian with the character of the Established Church as such, this work had, for nearly a hundred years, no equal. Previous writers had confined their arguments mainly to a discussion of liturgies, rites, ceremonies, and other incidental characteristics of the State Establishment. Towgood, making less of, but not undervaluing, these points, boldly attacked the foundations on which the Church rested. He denounced it for having surrendered its Christian liberty, for being not an "ally," but a mere creature of the State. He exposed its ambitious and persecuting spirit. Subjection in religious matters, he held, was due to Christ alone, and civil governors had no right to intermeddle with them. He agreed that with the alteration of what was unscriptural in its character, Dissenters would be glad to return to the Church. They bore it, he said, no enmity. They wished it prosperity and peace, and the glory of being formed according to the perfect plan of the primitive Apostolic Church. They wished to see it established upon a broad and catholic foundation, Jesus Christ himself being its only Lawgiver and King. As for the Church as it was, he denied that it was any essential part of the British constitution, or that it and the State must fall together. He asked any one to annihilate, in his imagination, its present form; to suppose that its clergy, liturgy, articles, canons, ceremonies, and rites, were entirely vanished from the land; its immense revenues applied to the ease of taxation, and the payment of public debts, and the preachers to be paid only by voluntary contributions—where, he inquired, would be the essential loss to the State? Would the monarchy be overthrown, the courts of judicature shut up, parliaments no more meet, commerce and trade be brought to stagnation—because what people called their "Church" was no more?* This was the boldest suggestion that had yet been made on this subject. The author did not enlarge upon it, but left it to bring forth fruit in succeeding generations. White added five other publications on this subject, continuing the controversy to the year 1751, but he never grappled with Towgood's leading argument in proof of the natural freedom of the Christian Church from State control. Towgood himself lived until nearly the close of the century in which he wrote, dying in A.D. 1791, at the great age of ninety-one. Though a keen controversialist he was a man of singular modesty, and he was satisfied, to the end of his life, with the pastorate of a country congregation.† The earlier editions of his answers to White were all published anonymously. His ministerial activity, his devoutness, and his public spirit, were acknowledged by all his contemporaries. His service in vindication of the principles of the Free Churches has made his name one of the most eminent and honourable in their literature.

Those persons who have the most clear conception of the proper functions of the State, are also those who will be found to obey, with the greatest willingness, such

---

* "The Dissenting Gentleman's Answer to the Reverend Mr. White's Letters," etc. A.D. 1746, 1747, 1748.

† Manning's "Life and Writings of Towgood." A.D. 1792.

laws of the State as are in harmony with the everlasting principles of justice. That the growing perception of the injustice involved in the connection between the Church and the State did not tend to alienate the Dissenters from the established Government was apparent in the rebellion of A.D. 1745. While the Jacobites and High-Churchmen received the news of the Pretender's landing with satisfaction and delight, Dissenters of all classes at once rallied in defence of the Crown. As soon as the news of the event was received, the Committee of the Dissenting Deputies passed a resolution recommending the whole body of Dissenters throughout the kingdom to join with others of his Majesty's subjects in support of the Government. They next despatched a circular letter throughout the country, expressing their earnest desire that in view of the dangerous situation of public affairs, Dissenters would act in the most zealous manner.* This appeal was responded to with enthusiastic alacrity. Armed associations of Dissenters were formed in all parts of the kingdom;† chapels were converted into parade grounds;‡ and ministers became voluntary recruiting officers. Doddridge was especially active in furthering this movement. He addressed letters to his friends, went personally amongst his own people in Northampton, encouraging them to enlist, and printed a private address to the soldiers of one of the regiments of foot, afterwards engaged in the battle of Culloden, encouraging them in their duty.§ The Dissenting pulpits resounded with

---

* "Sketch of the History," &c., p. 21, 22. † Ib.
‡ "History of the Baptist Chapel in Little Wild Street," p. 36. Ivimey, iii. 239.
§ Orton's "Life of Doddridge," p. 208.

the call to arms, and the king was addressed to assure him that, whoever besides might fail him, he might rely with confidence on the loyalty of the Protestant Dissenters.* Even the Quakers could not refrain from giving an expression of their active sympathy with the Government. Their principles forbade them to incite men to shed blood; but they contributed to the health of the regiments under the command of the Duke of Cumberland, by supplying all the soldiers with flannel for their winter campaign.† The reward which the Dissenters received for this service, apart from the earnest thanks of the king, consisted in their inclusion in the Act of Indemnity, and in the royal pardon for the rebels who had taken up arms against the Government. In accepting commissions in the volunteer army, they had incurred the penalties of the Test Act. As in the rebellion of A.D. 1715, so in this more serious crisis, they had broken the letter of the law in order to save the Crown and Government. Those who would have sacrificed both for the sake of increased ecclesiastical predominance, were still too powerful to prevent the test from being taken off.‡

* Ivimey, iii. 238.
† "Journey along with the Army of the Duke of Cumberland," p. 14.
‡ The manner in which the Dissenters were treated on these occasions was severely commented upon by Fox, in his speech in favour of the repeal of the Test Act, on March 2nd, A.D. 1790. The great orator said that "a candid examination of the history of Great Britain would, in his opinion, be favourable to the Dissenters. In the rebellions in 1715 and 1745, this country was extremely indebted to their exertions. During those rebellious periods they had acted with the spirit and fidelity of British subjects, zealous and vigilant in defence of the Constitution; at both these periods they stood forward the champions of British liberty, and obtained an eminent share in repelling the foes of the House of Hanover. Their exertions then were so magnanimous that he had no scruple to assert that to their endeavours we owed the preservation of Church and State. What was the

From this time, and for many years, the life of the Free Churches flowed with smooth, and unless disturbed by death, with almost unruffled course. The first amongst eminent men to drop from their living ranks was Watts, who died in A.D. 1748. For a long period this ablest of their representatives had been in feeble and declining health, but his intellect, until very lately, had been in ceaseless activity. Judging from his writings, it would seem to have been the noble ambition of this man to render the utmost service of which he was capable in the instruction and guidance of the human mind in all its spheres of action; and in all its spheres he was one of the few men competent both to instruct and to guide. As a mental philosopher he ranked next to Locke. Had he written only his "Logic," his essay on the "Improvement of the Mind," his "Philosophical Essays," his essay on the "Freedom of the Will," and on the "Civil Power in Religion," his name would have occupied a high and honourable place amongst the philosophical writers of his country. But he rendered greater service than this. At a time when infidelity was making the boldest assaults on the grounds of the Christian faith, he was one of the first to stand forward in defence of revealed religion and

---

reward they obtained? We generously granted them a pardon for their noble exploits, by passing an act of indemnity in their favour. Gentlemen should recollect that, at the times alluded to, the High Churchmen did not display such gallantry, for many appeared perplexed and pusillanimous. Hence, the superior glory of the Dissenters, who, regardless of every danger, had boldly stood forth in defence of the rights and liberties of the kingdom. The Dissenters, regardless of the foolish Acts existing against them, drew their swords in defence of their fellow-subjects, and made the scale immediately preponderate in our favour. The Church, as a very liberal encouragement for their achievements, adopted the plan already described, by passing an act of indemnity or pardon for the henious crime of defending the Constitution."—*Parliamentary History.*

scriptural truth. Unlike many men, however, he was as capable of pressing the Gospel on the hearts and consciences of men as on the intellect alone. He believed that the Christian should be characteristically a whole man, with his affections going out in deep and spontaneous feeling towards his Maker, his Redeemer, and his fellow-men, his conduct being guided by a devout and cultivated intellect, and an enlightened conscience. His sermons and practical writings, therefore, while they indicated a strong and polished mind, and an accurate taste, were full of chastened feeling and of close application to the conscience. Having added to his Hymns a metrical version of the Psalms of David, he had given the church a collection of poetry for its assistance in public worship, which, with all the great additions that have since been made to that department of religious and poetical composition, has been rivalled by no other single writer. Nor was he satisfied to serve only the grown man and Christian. He therefore added, to his Divine Songs for children, books for the guidance of their education in religion, and in the most familiar of the arts and sciences. Having thus, in nearly fifty years of active life, given to his own and succeeding generations the fulness of the strength of a mind of the highest order of Christian excellence and aim, he died, at the age of sixty-four, an humble and devout death. He chose to rest where so many of the confessors of the Free Churches had rested, and was therefore, in the presence of an immense concourse of spectators, buried in Bunhill Fields. Those who attended his funeral must have felt a gratitude for his work such as can be excited by but few men. The poorest as well as the richest in intellectual gifts, the oldest Christian as well as the youngest child, might have been almost equally indebted to him. As Dissenters, they owed to him especial gratitude. In vindication of their principles he had done no more than many had done, but he had, in one conspicuous manner, given strength to the Free Churches. Although of high literary renown, and brought into constant contact with the most eminent scholars in the Established Church, he had remained inflexible in his principles as a Congregational Dissenter. It was a fashion for vulgar writers in that, as it has been in more than one subsequent age, to identify Dissent with vulgarity of manners and narrowness of mind. In Watts, at least, it was seen that a man might belong to one of the most democratic sections of Dissent and write in favour of the separation of the Church from the State, and yet be a cultured scholar and a Christian gentleman.

After Watts's death the most eminent position amongst Dissenting ministers was occupied by Doddridge. Doddridge had now been about twenty years at Northampton. He had not been allowed to assume the office of tutor without opposition. He was summoned by a clergyman for non-compliance with the provisions of the Test Act respecting Dissenting teachers, but the prosecution was stopped by order of George II., who declared that he would have no persecution for conscience' sake during his reign.* His life, since that period, had been one of singular industry and usefulness. He was the model Christian pastor and minister, and the most eminently successful tutor who had ever been connected with the Free Churches. Doddridge's, how-

* Orton's "Life of Doddridge." Works, i. 149.

ever, was not a seminary intended only for the education of young men for the ministry: he received into it any who would go there,—noblemen's and gentlemen's sons, and persons of all religious persuasions, whether Episcopalian, Presbyterian, Unitarian, Baptist, or Congregationalist. He incurred some censure from his stricter brethren for this, and was to some extent beset by what he terms "Orthodox spies," in consequence; but he chose not to relinquish his system. He was consequently accused, during his lifetime, as most eminent men of his class are, by the envious and the less eminent, of looseness of theology. The fact that an Unitarian went to his seminary, was allowed to remain there as an Unitarian, was not dishonourably interfered with by his tutor, and, when he left, was an Unitarian still, was considered to indicate the possession of a laxity of sense of duty on the tutor's part. But Doddridge could not have done what would have pleased such men. He was not above all things, but he valued highly the reputation of being a gentleman and a man of honour, and therefore his orthodoxy was suspected. Those who, wherever the Anglo-Saxon language is spoken, have read and sung his hymns; those who have been brought to the feet of their Saviour by his "Rise and Progress of Religion in the Soul;" those whose Christian affections have been warmed, and whose judgments have been enlightened by his "Family Expositor," may well wonder how such a man could have been even suspected by the worst minded of all his contemporaries. But Doddridge, while he held fast to the Gospel of Jesus Christ as the "anchor of his soul," held intercourse with some whom others denounced. Whitefield, as has

been seen, was one of these; but Warburton, who had written a massive book to prove that Moses and the Israelites knew nothing of the doctrine of a future state, was another, and Doddridge, with Warburton's consent, had written, in a popular publication, a commendatory review of this work. Gentleness, goodness, and love were in his heart wherever he went, and if he erred it was from excess of the amiability of his disposition. This, however, as is natural, so far from interfering with his duty, stimulated him towards its performance. He preached constantly, and lectured before his pupils on almost every subject of human study. The accounts which have come down to us from his own pen, and from the description of his pupils, of the range and method of his teaching, give a high impression of the breadth and thoroughness of his intellectual culture. His academy took the highest rank amongst all similar institutions. Doddridge's preaching was experimental and practical rather than formally dogmatic. His theological creed is to be found interwoven in all his sermons and writings, but he evidently cared less for creeds than for a Christian life. One of his greatest services to religion in his own neighbourhood was the institution at Kettering, in the year 1741, of an association for the reformation of religion and for evangelistic purposes in Northampton. A special object of this association, it is worth noticing, was the propagation of Christianity in heathen lands.*
To this movement, and to the great impulse which Doddridge's own zeal gave to all forms of religious activity

---

* "The Evil and Danger of Neglecting the Souls of Men." Dedication. Works, iii. 229.

in Northamptonshire, is probably to be attributed the generally high, consistent, and bold character of Dissent in the midland counties. This admirable man died at Lisbon in the year 1751. The expenses of the journey thither, taken with a forlorn hope of recruiting a constitution which, for years, had been slowly undermined by excess of zeal, were defrayed by the Countess of Huntingdon and her Church friends, and his widow found means of subsistence from the same source. With the death of Watts and Doddridge the leadership of Dissent passed from the Congregational body. No man was left who was in any manner competent to take their places.

The comparative inaction which followed on the death of Doddridge was broken only by a legal controversy with the City of London concerning the compulsory liability of Dissenters to serve the office of sheriff. This case is interesting for the protection which it secured for Dissenters against the arbitrary claims of the Corporation, and for the interpretation which it gave of their rights under the Toleration Act. In A.D. 1742, a Mr. Robert Grosvenor had been elected to the office of sheriff, but, on refusing to qualify for the office by taking the sacrament according to the rites of the Established Church, was cited by the Corporation before the Court of Queen's Bench. The defence of his case was undertaken by the Committee of Deputies, and the Court decided against the claim. To meet, as it judged, any future case of this kind, the Corporation, in A.D. 1748, passed a bye-law, imposing a fine of four hundred pounds and twenty marks upon every person who should decline standing for the office after he had been nominated to it, and of six hundred pounds upon every person who, after having been elected, should refuse to serve. The fines thus obtained were to be appropriated towards the building of a new Mansion House. The scheme was worthy of the lowest type of commercial chicanery, and the Corporation of London must have sunk infinite degrees below its ancient spirit for it to have been entertained for an hour. Had there been occasion for a Pym or an Eliot to have taken refuge in the metropolis at this period, they, too, would probably have been sold to the Government, and the proceeds devoted to the erection of the Mansion House. It was carried into operation with all the cunning and greed by which it is possible—but which, in the case of the City of London, it had not hitherto been common—for such a body to be distinguished. Whenever a sheriff was required to be elected, a Dissenter was immediately nominated. One after another declined to serve, and was at once mulcted of the fine. This system had gone on for six years, during which the fines had produced more than fifteen thousand pounds, when, in A.D. 1754, a spirit of resistance was raised. In that year three Dissenters, Messrs. Sheafe, Streatfield, and Evans, were successively elected to office. On consulting the Deputies they were advised to refuse service, and to resist the payment of the fine. The Corporation at once commenced proceedings against them in the Sheriffs' Court. The case against Mr. Streatfield fell to the ground, inasmuch as he was proved to be out of the jurisdiction of the Court. In the year 1757, after prolonged delays, judgment was given against Mr. Sheafe and Mr. Evans, who then appealed to the Court of Hustings—now abolished—of which the Recorder of the city was the sole judge. The Recorder hving confirmed the judgment of the Sheriffs' Court, Mr. Sheafe and Mr. Evans sued for a special commission, consisting of five judges, who, with one exception, reversed, in 1762, the decisions of the Courts below. The Corporation then brought a writ of error before the House of Lords, but before the case could be tried there, Mr. Evans, by the death of Mr. Sheafe, was left sole defendant. The case was argued at great length before the Lords on the 21st and 22nd of January, A.D. 1767. On the 3rd and 4th of February following, six out of seven judges gave judgment in favour of Mr. Evans. The decision of the Lords was then delivered by Lord Mansfield, who, in the highest strain of eloquence, expressed his abhorrence of the persecution which Dissenters had suffered, and vindicated the principles of English law with respect to religious liberty. Of the attempt of the Corporation, to make two laws—one to render men incapable of serving office, and another to punish them for not serving, " If," he said, " they accept, punish them; if they refuse, punish them; if they say ' Yes,' punish them; if they say ' No,' punish them. My Lords, this is a most exquisite dilemma, from which there is no escaping : it is a trap a man cannot get out of; it is as bad a persecution as that of Procrustes: if they are too short, stretch them; if they are too long, lop them." " The law of the Corporation," he went on to remark, " was made in some year of the reign of the late king—I forget which; but it was made about the time of the building of the Mansion House. . . Were I to deliver my own suspicion, it would be, that they did not so much wish for their (the Dissenters') services as for their fines. Dissenters have been appointed to the office—one who was blind, another who was bed-ridden; not, I suppose, on account of their being fit and able to serve the office." He proceeded to state his belief that they chose them because they were incapable of serving. In his vindication of the principles of religious liberty, the judge remarked that it was now no crime for a man to say he was a Dissenter; nor was it any crime for him not to take the sacrament according to the rites of the Church of England. "There is no usage or custom," he went on to say, "independent of positive law, which makes nonconformity a crime. Conscience is not controllable by human laws, nor amenable to human tribunals. Prosecutions, or attempts to enforce conscience, will never produce conviction; and are only calculated to make hypocrites or martyrs. My Lords, there never was a single instance from the Saxon times down to our own, in which a man was ever punished for erroneous opinions concerning rites or modes of worship, but upon some positive law. The common law of England, which is only common reason or usage, knows of no prosecution for mere opinions. For atheism, blasphemy, and reviling of the Christian religion, there have been instances of persons prosecuted and punished upon the common law, but bare nonconformity is no sin by the common law; and all positive laws inflicting any pains or penalties for nonconformity to the established rites and modes, are repealed by the Act of Toleration; and dissenters are thereby exempted from all ecclesiastical censures. What bloodshed and confusion have been occasioned from the reign of Henry IV., when the first penal statutes were enacted, down to the Revolution, in this kingdom, by laws made to enforce conscience. There is nothing certainly more unreasonable, more inconsistent with the rights of human nature, more contrary to the spirit and precepts of the Christian religion, more iniquitous and unjust, more impolitic, than persecution. It is against natural religion, revealed religion, and sound policy."* With this denunciation the Corporation was ignominiously dismissed. The end of the thirteen years' prosecution found the defendant, Mr. Evans, dying, but he was sufficiently conscious to express the satisfaction which the judgment gave him. To his firmness, supported by the Dissenting Deputies, is owing the fact that Church and Tory corporations, all through the kingdom, had not the legal ability to use their power for the oppression of their Nonconformist neighbours.

When this cause was decided, George III. had been king for nearly seven years. By the death of his predecessor, the Dissenters had lost a firm and sincere friend to their liberties. George the Second's attachment to the principles of constitutional freedom was almost the only redeeming feature in that monarch's character. He had inherited the traditions of the Revolution, and would allow neither civil nor ecclesiastical politicians to sway his mind in opposition to them. It was one of the happiest circumstances for English freedom, that the two sovereigns who succeeded to Anne were not natives of England. Had they been so, the probability is, that they would have succumbed to the influences of the territorial aristocracy and of the Church, whose predominant dispositions were in favour of a more or less arbitrary

* "History and Proceedings of the Deputies," 25, 38.

system of government. As regards civil liberty, the first two Georges were constitutional from interest as well as from principle. Their maintenance of the doctrines of the Revolution was necessary to the establishment of their dynasty, and it was not until the suppression of the rebellion of A.D. 1745, that the Hanoverian dynasty was finally secured from every prospect of successful assault. George III., if he escaped some of the vices, inherited, unfortunately, none of the virtues of his grandfather. His political position was secure, and, so far as English parties were concerned, he had nothing to do but to hand it down in undisturbed safety, to his children and his children's children. The Jacobites had cast their last die; they had lost all hope of changing the succession to the Crown; but the spirit of Jacobitism yet remained. Instead, however, of making a party, they adopted a wiser course; they allied themselves to the extreme section of the Tories. In George III. they found a man after their own heart. Ignorant, in consequence of the shameful manner in which he had been educated, to almost the last degree; bigoted and prejudiced as a sacerdotal priest; more obstinate than a mule, and more jealous of his prerogative than a workhouse official, he was born and bred to favour a high Tory and High Church system of government. His one governing principle of action was the governing principle of all weak and obstinate men who have no natural moral force. "I will be master," was his self-assumed motto, and any one who would let him be master was sure of his favour and patronage. Notwithstanding an early moral failing, he had, and sustained, a good domestic character, the character of a respectable ploughman. He would have made a good overseer of the poor in his time, when that office was executed somewhat after the manner of a slave-driver; but by disposition, intellect, and education, he was the less fitted for a king than almost any man who ever sat on a throne. Such a person the High Church party, however, could work with. Their leading idea was the same—to promote and sustain prescriptive power, whether just or unjust, whether adapted to a nation's welfare—as it sometimes is—or injurious to her best interests and her legitimate prosperity and influence, as was the case with England during the whole of the reign of this narrow-minded, selfish, and therefore unfortunate monarch.

The state of the Church in the earlier portion of George III.'s reign was what it had been for the last thirty or forty years,—as respects the bishops and the clergy, one of scandalous indifference to the claims of religion, as well as to the claims of ecclesiastical duty. Pluralities and non-residence were universal,* and none rose to condemn them. Wesley and his fellow-labourers were still the object of sarcasm and scoff, and vital religion was almost as little known amongst the clergy as it was amongst the people whom they taught. Yet there were men eminent for their great intellectual ability in the Established Church. Foremost amongst them was Joseph Butler, Bishop of Durham, whose "Analogy of Natural and Revealed Religion" had placed him amongst the greatest of all theological writers. Butler, however, in the proportion that he excelled in his own department of thought, failed in other departments.

* Perry's "History of Church of England," pp. 398—399.

The work by which his name has been immortalized will always remain one of the masterpieces of human reasoning, and the greatest of all the intellectual defences of the Christian religion. As a preacher, however, Butler partook of the tendency of the times in which he lived. His theology was broad and liberal in tone; but, in common with many men of his school, and with most men of his peculiar intellectual culture, he preached with little religious feeling. His sermons are cold and colourless essays, as deficient in spiritual as they are superior in intellectual power. But no man, by his natural and acquired strength of mind, and his unequalled service to the literature of Christian evidences, ever adorned the Episcopal bench in a greater degree than Joseph Butler.

Next to Butler, but of later period, was William Warburton. Warburton, after the publication of his "Alliance," attracted more attention than any other ecclesiastic. The extraordinary extent of his reading, and his brawny power of brain, are certified in his "Divine Legation of Moses," and in his many controversial works; but he wrote scarcely a single work in which he did not degrade himself by his coarse and vituperative abuse of every person who happened to differ from him. Not to agree, to the minutest and most unimportant point, in all that he said, was to be paraded through the literary world as "an ass" and "a fool."* To oppose him was to be "a wretch," "a rogue," and "a scoundrel." Warburton was one of the bishops who led the opinion of the

---

* See Watson's "Life of Warburton," cap. xxxiii., for specimens of this style.

Church respecting the Methodists. Whitefield was, in his view, "quite mad."* John Wesley did nothing but "turn fools into madmen," and was himself "a hypocrite."† "What think you," he asks a friend, "of our new set of fanatics called the Methodists?"‡ Warburton wrote against Wesley's doctrine of grace.§ His friend Hurd, afterwards himself made a bishop, prophesied that the discourse would, "like Pascal's Letters, and for the same reason—the singular merit of the composition—be read when the sect that gave occasion to it is forgotten, or, rather, the sect will find immortality in this discourse."|| This work is now never read, and its only importance is derived from the fact that it was written against the great and successful body of the Methodists. If, amongst other bishops, Lowth, by his learning and his wit, served to redeem the character of the bench, Lawrence Sterne, by his profligate life and coarse if humorous writings, dragged down the reputation of the clergy. Archbishop Secker, who filled the primate's chair, was inferior in ability to any of these. He was possessed of some learning, which he used to its fullest extent in ecclesiastical controversies, but as a preacher he was scarcely respectable.

Archdeacon Blackburne, at this time, scandalized the Church by writing against its doctrines, orders, and ceremonies, and yet remaining within its borders. Blackburne had the dexterous force and the

* Ib. p. 524.   † Ib. p. 535.   ‡ Ib. p. 523.
§ "The Doctrine of Grace; or, the Office and Operations of the Holy Spirit Vindicated from the Insults of Infidelity and the Abuse of Fanaticism," A.D. 1762.
|| Watson's "Life," p. 539.

happy directness of style which are necessary to the successful controversialist, and he would have wielded his powers with a moral as well as an intellectual success, if he had supported his doctrines by his practice. But when he, a Church dignitary, proceeded to denounce all creeds and confessions of faith,* to assert the right of private liberty in theological matters, and to hold up his Church to scorn and opprobrium, men, however they might acknowledge the accuracy of his judgment and the truth of his criticism, saw that he lacked the necessary evidence of moral sincerity. His works are an armoury of sharp and polished weapons of attack against the Established Church; but Blackburne himself should have been the last man to invent or to use them. But anything, and almost any man excepting one of great spiritual earnestness, could have been borne with at a period when all that was expected of a bishop was that he should be sufficiently obsequious to the Crown and its ministers, and of a clergyman, that he did not turn a Methodist. Justice Blackstone, who made a point, at this time, of hearing the most celebrated preachers in London, states that, in all his visits to the churches, he did not hear a sermon that had more Christianity in it than a speech of Cicero's, and that it would have been impossible for him to tell whether the preacher was a Mohammedan or a Christian.† Scattered through England were a few "Methodist" clergy, the founders of the Evangelical party in the Established Church, who laboured incessantly for the advancement of religion; but they were outnumbered by thousands, and frowned upon by all who were in

* In "The Confessional," A.D. 1766.   † *Christian Observer*, 1858.

authority. Of these clergy Fletcher of Madeley, Venn of Huddersfield, Grimshaw of Haworth, Romaine of Blackfriars, and Berridge of Everton, were the chief. Hervey, the author of "Theron and Aspasia," had died in A.D. 1758. To Fletcher, Methodism in the Church owed more than it did to any excepting its original founders. Fervour of feeling, holiness of spirit, and simplicity of character were combined in him in degrees that have seldom been equalled in any other man. Venn made Huddersfield the centre of the most untiring evangelistic labours; and Grimshaw, of Haworth—that Haworth which the three daughters of a succeeding incumbent have made more celebrated than it was made even by Grimshaw—brought thousands of Yorkshiremen to hear him preach the new Gospel. Romaine was the Evangelical preacher of the metropolis, proclaiming the "doctrines of grace" with a power that had seldom been equalled. But of all the founders of the Evangelical party, Berridge, of Everton, was the most conspicuous. He was the only one whose preaching produced the abnormal and painful physical effects which often accompanied the preaching of the Wesleys and Whitefield. His evangelistic powers were surpassed only by the three apostles of the early movement. Everton, in his time, was a place where thousands from all the country round about crowded to hear its extraordinary preacher and to share in the wonderful revival of religion of which it was the centre. Berridge's eccentricity probably contributed in no small degree to his personal popularity. He was possessed of a rough and knotty wit, which he used unsparingly in his public addresses, as well as in private intercourse. But he was far removed from vulgarity. None of these men were, in any sense, vulgar men, unless, as it undoubtedly was at that time, vulgar to be pious, and to yearn for the salvation of souls.

Out of the Church, Methodism was increasing with marvellous rapidity. Its preachers, going through the length and breadth of the land with an energy and rapidity that had never before been seen in the history of Christianity in England, left, wherever they went, new friends and converts. All these did not, however, formally identify themselves with the Wesleyan societies. The continued opposition of the clergy had aroused in many minds a corresponding spirit of opposition to the Established Church. Lay preachers began to assert their right to administer the sacraments, and members began to secede to one or other of the Free Churches. In this crisis it was resolved to bring the relations of the Methodists towards the Church before the Conference. This was done in A.D. 1755, and after three days' debate, which was attended by sixty-three preachers, it was resolved that, whether it was lawful or not, it was not expedient to separate from the Church.* This decision was arrived at mainly, no doubt, through the personal influence of John and Charles Wesley. It is easy to understand Wesley's position with respect to the Establishment. He was rapidly seceding from his former Church views; he had given up apostolical succession and the divine origin of Episcopacy; he had scorned the authority of ecclesiastical law, but it would have been inconsistent with his original purpose to leave

* Wesley's "Journal," A.D. 1755.

his Church. That purpose had been to arouse the sense of religion within her own borders, and Wesley believed that if his societies once separated themselves from her—once became sectarians—they would have no influence whatever upon her future character. He went on, hoping against hope that the clergy would one day join him, and that, though their union, the Church itself would become one vast Methodist organization; but none of these hopes were ever realized. As Methodism grew, it receded further and further from the Establishment, until it became necessary formally to separate from it. Nor did Wesley, in another sense, succeed. The revival of religion which ultimately took place in the Church was in the direction of Whitefield's, and not of Wesley's theology. The forerunners of the Evangelical party were Calvinists, and more closely associated with the Countess of Huntingdon than with Wesley. But, while still determined to remain a member of the Church, Wesley candidly avowed that he "could not answer" the arguments of those Methodists who advocated secession.* But this determination need not have excited bitter feelings towards the Free Churches. Yet, when the Baptists drew away some of his members, he could not restrain the expression of his indignation; while Charles, to whom Christian charity was almost an unknown feeling, railed against them as the "cavilling, contentious sect, always watching to steal away our children,"†—the very charge which the Church herself brought against John and Charles Wesley.

* "Letter to the Rev. Mr. Walker," printed in the "Arminian Magazine," A.D. 1779.
† Jackson's "Charles Wesley," cap. 20.

The decision of this Conference modified, in no degree whatever, the feelings of the clergy, and had probably a most injurious influence upon the spread of Methodism itself.*

The Congregationalists possessed, at this period, no man of a very high order of genius, but many who were more or less eminent for their scholarship and their abilities. Amongst these Dr. Thomas Gibbons, pastor of the Haberdashers' Hall Church, and one of the tutors of the Mile End Academy, occupied a conspicuous position. He was one of the most active preachers of the metropolis and the author of a great variety of published works. His name is best known in connection with his intimacy with Watts, of whom he was the earliest biographer. It was probably from this intimacy that he conceived the purpose of writing a volume of hymns, a few of which are to be found in most modern selections.† At Pinners' Hall preached Dr. Caleb Fleming, almost the only Congregational minister in the metropolis who held Unitarian views. Fleming was most conspicuous as an advocate of these opinions; but few men did greater service in his generation than he, in writing against the civil establishment of religion. He was the only Dissenter who replied to Warburton's

* I cannot avoid quoting the criticism of the able historian of Methodism, Dr. Abel Stevens, whose work is the most exact and comprehensive of all the histories of this movement, on the decisions of the Conference of A.D. 1755 :—" Had Methodism," he says, " taken a more independent stand at this early period, when it had so many intolerable provocations from the Establishment, and the popular mind so little ground of sympathy with the clergy, it is the opinion of not a few wise men that it might, before this time, have largely superseded the Anglican hierarchy, and done much more than it has for the unscriptural connection of the Church and State." —" History," i. 399.

† Wilson's " Dissenting Churches," iii. 178—183.

"Alliance," and probably the first who publicly assigned the increase of infidelity and of Romanism to the existence of an Established Church.* For more than forty-five years he maintained, with undiminished ardour, the cause of religious liberty. Dr. John Guise, of New Broad Street, one of Doddridge's most intimate friends, was, "though dead, yet living." He is still known as the popular author of a carefully composed paraphrase of the New Testament, and was a man greatly honoured and loved by his people. In his latter days he became blind, having suddenly become so while leading the devotions of his congregation, but he continued preaching while health remained, and, it was said, with greater spiritual power than he had ever before shown. Guise's successor at New Broad Street, Dr. Stafford, occupied also a respectable position as a metropolitan minister.

In the pulpit of Owen and Watts, was Dr. Samuel Morton Savage, a man of equal learning and power, and one of the professors at the Hoxton Academy. Dr. David Jennings was professor in the same academy. At Jewin Street Joseph Hart, a man of remarkable religious experience, and one of the most popular ministers for the brief period of his ministerial life, was pastor. Hart is well known as the author of a volume of rather sensational hymns, abounding in extravagant expressions, but which are still prized by a certain class of religious people. Although he entered the Christian ministry at forty-eight years of age, and died eight years afterwards, he had become so known and esteemed that his funeral at Bunhill Fields was attended by no

* Ib. ii. 232, 243.

fewer than twenty thousand persons.* The Weighhouse Church was presided over by Dr. William Longford, a useful and ingenious, rather than powerful preacher, who was assisted by the more eminent Samuel Palmer, afterwards of Hackney, who subsequently became one of the most eminent Congregational ministers of London.†

The names of a few country ministers of this denomination obtained a deserved eminence amongst their contemporaries. Dr. Addington, of Harborough, and Kibworth, the successor of David Some, and, some years afterwards, pastor of Miles' Lane Church, London, was an admirable specimen of a devoted country minister. An impressive preacher, and a diligent and conscientious pastor, he belonged to the large class of ministers of the Free Churches, who, in country districts at that time, kept alive the flame of religion and adorned the profession of Christianity. Such a man also was Benjamin Fawcett, of Kidderminster, one of the successors of Baxter, and who, in thirty-five years' ministry, almost equalled Baxter in labour and in diligence. And another was Darracott, of Wellington, a man of refined manners, who attained the rare success, for such a man, of great spiritual influence amongst the poor of an agricultural district. The Rev. Job Orton, of Shrewsbury, the friend and biographer of Doddridge, was another of the best known and most highly respected Congregational ministers in the Midland Counties. Doddridge wrote of him, "Not merely my happiness, but that of the public, in him, is beyond all my hopes." Educated at Northampton, and preaching statedly there for Dod-

* Ib. iii. 343, 347.   † Ib. i. 183, 187.

dridge, he obtained that intimate knowledge of the great divine which no other man could have obtained. It was natural that he should have been invited to succeed Doddridge, but he declined to remove from Shrewsbury. His publications on religious subjects—nearly all of a practical character—were very numerous, and to his suggestion the " Nonconformist Memorial " is owing. As far as can be ascertained, he was the only minister who commemorated the centenary of the Ejectment of A.D. 1662. His personal manners were rough, and his habits eccentric, but Dr. Kiffin states that he was the most striking preacher he ever heard.* None of these were what would be considered great men. The Congregationalists were now more eminent for teaching than for pulpit power. With considerable foresight, they had engaged their ablest men for their educational institutions. Such were Drs. Jennings and Savage, and Walker, Gibbons, and John Conder, the three last of the Mile End—afterwards the Homerton academy—under whose tutorship many of the ablest ministers of the succeeding generations were educated. Dr. Ashworth, of Daventry, whither Doddridge's academy had been removed after his death, was of equal if not greater eminence.

For theological scholarship, however, no minister amongst the Congregationalists could compare with Dr. John Gill, one of the ablest divines which the Baptist denomination has ever produced. Gill was elected pastor of the Baptist Church at Horselydown in the year 1720, and continued in that position for more than fifty-one years. As a biblical commentator and a theological controversialist few persons have surpassed this able man.

* Biog. Brit., Art. Orton. *Protestant Dissenters' Magazine*, May, 1795.

With a mind enriched with all the stores of biblical learning, and a brain of singular strength and capacity, he was able to do great service in behalf of the principles to which he was attached. His " Exposition of the Scriptures" is a work which can never lose all its value, and his Defences of Calvinism and Adult Baptism are, as they deserve to be, works of the highest authority in his own denomination. Gill did, for the dogmas of Calvinism, a work which was more needed in his day than it has since been. Never were they so positively unpopular, or viewed with so much indifference, as in the middle of the eighteenth century. Gill brought to their defence the mind of a refined scholar, as well as the heart of a Christian. He showed that they could at least be defended by powerful reasoning, and that they were not to be driven from the belief of men either by the sneer of the Deist or the shrug of the latitudinarian. His style, however, was not equal to his learning, and one of his own denomination has characterized his works as a " continent of mud."*

In Gill's church at Horselydown was a schoolmaster and deacon, named Thomas Crosby, who deserves mention as the first historian of the Baptists. Crosby wrote his work mainly to supply the deficiencies of Neal's History. The charge against Neal, that he had not done justice to the Baptists, must be acknowledged to have been correct, and Crosby's design was therefore a laudable one. He has furnished subsequent writers with many materials which would probably have perished but for his care, and his zeal and industry are unquestionable ; but, beyond this, his history is destitute of every literary excellence.

* Robert Hall. Works i. 125: ed. 1832.

The name of Stennett had been connected with Baptist Church history for nearly a hundred years : the third of the name—Samuel Stennett—was now preaching at Little Wild Street. Not less eminent than his father and grandfather, he lived to adorn the Christian ministry, and add, by his genius and his character, strength and stability to all the Free Churches. Samuel Stennett was, after Bunyan, the first Christian hymnologist amongst the Baptists. There is now scarcely any selection of hymns which does not contain some of his productions. In Eagle Street, Dr. Andrew Gifford, one of the greatest antiquarians of the eighteenth century, preached. From his remarkable acquaintance with literature, and especially with numismatics, Gifford was chosen, in A.D. 1717, to the post of assistant-librarian of the British Museum. He was one of Whitefield's most intimate friends. Gifford, like Gill, belonged to the strictest school of Calvin, and was an eminent favourite with the earliest Evangelical ministers, such as Romaine and Toplady.*

Just rising into prominence was a man of very different order from any of these—Robert Robinson, of Chesterton. For boldness, versatility, vivacity, and wit, this remarkable man had no equal amongst his brethren. These qualities do not always consist with prudence, and Robinson was not a prudent man. But he was intensely sincere, and one of the most ardent lovers and teachers of Christian and civil liberty who ever lived. Hierarchies, priests, and the superstitions and traditions by which these characteristics of corrupt churches are mainly sustained, found, in Robinson, a vigorous and persistent

* Ivimey, iii. 591, 613.

enemy. He had something of the spirit which animated De Foe, united to a finer but to a more irregularly developed intellect. Robinson began his church life as a Calvinistic Baptist, but subsequently lapsed—without, however, ceasing his pastorate—to anti-Trinitarian views. His writings are wanting in coherence, but they contain some of the most vigorous thought, expressed in vigorous language, to be found in ecclesiastical literature. His " Arcana," and his " History and Mystery of Good Friday," are the best of his works; his unfinished " History of the Baptists" is a strange and unsuccessful medley.*

Amongst the General Baptists there were few who had retained the theological principles of the founders of that body. A large majority had embraced Unitarian views; but in A.D. 1770 a " New General Baptist Association" was formed, which adopted for its creed the characteristic principles, which, at one time, had distinguished the denomination. The principal founder of this Association was Dan Taylor, a man of naturally vigorous and able intellect, whose earliest religious impressions were due to the Methodists. Taylor's views on the subject of Baptism changing, he joined the General Baptist Association in Lincolnshire, and was pastor of the Church at Wadsworth, in that county. Disapproving of the theological views of most of his brethren in the ministry, Taylor, in conjunction with William Thompson, of Boston, and nine ministers from the churches in Leicestershire and the neighbouring counties, established a new association. The distinctive creed of the new body

* Dyer's Life of Robinson. Robinson's Works.

was contained in the small compass of six articles, which declared the natural depravity of man; the obligations of the moral law; the divinity of Christ, and the universal design of his atonement; the promise of salvation for all who exercise faith; the necessity of regeneration by the Holy Spirit, and the obligation, upon repentance, of baptism by immersion.* This creed especially guarded the new Association, by its third article, both from the Unitarians and from the Particular Baptists. Taylor subsequently removed to London, where he became pastor of the General Baptist Church in Virginia Street, Ratcliffe Highway, and was the recognized leader of the denomination. He was held in high estimation, both for his abilities and for his character, by all bodies of Christians. In a controversy on the nature of human inability with the more celebrated Andrew Fuller, he gave a remarkable illustration of his power as a theological reasoner.

But neither the Baptists nor the Congregationalists, nor both combined, could at this period compare, for mental power, and public service to civil and religious freedom, with the Unitarian Presbyterians. The history of the latter half of the eighteenth century is the history of the most rapid growth and, on the whole, the most powerful representation of Unitarianism in England. For more than forty years had Nathaniel Lardner now been labouring in defence of the evidences of the Christian religion, and was still pouring forth the treasures of his vast learning on that subject. Lardner, however, was not so zealous a politician as he was a

---

* Adam Taylor's History of the General Baptists, ii. 133, 143. Life of Dan Taylor, by Adam Taylor.

scholar. He belonged now, at about eighty years of age, to a past generation. Next in repute stood Dr. Joseph Priestley, who was as distinguished for his philosophical attainments, his bold, and, to himself, perilous advocacy of liberty, as for his love of truth, his simplicity of character, and his purity of life. The theological works of Priestley are an armoury of the most advanced Unitarian doctrine, but to whatever extent he offended the great majority of his countrymen by the extremeness of his views, he could not offend them by his manner of argument. No more candid or gentlemanly controversialist ever defended an unpopular cause, and no man less deserved the disgraceful treatment which he received from his countrymen. His name is inseparably connected with one of the most melancholy periods of English history, when, as will have to be told, he stood most prominent amongst a noble band, in defiance of the arbitrary political and the unjust ecclesiastical government of England.

Almost equally eminent in science and politics was Dr. Richard Price, lecturer of the Old Jewry, Jewry Street, pastor of the church at Newington Green, and afterwards of Hackney. As a mathematician, Dr. Price had few equals; as a political writer on the side of liberty, no man equalled him in vigour. He was one of the class who are the natural product of an age of arbitrary power. Possessed of a keen sense of justice and right, and of an undaunted courage, he expressed his thoughts on the political situation of his time with an energy and indignation which would have brought a fatal revenge on a less eminent man. He was the leader, in the metropolis, of those Dissenters who upheld the rights of the American Colonies in the War of Independence, and of those who, in the first period of its history, most actively sympathized with the French revolutionists.

In the same period Dr. Andrew Kippis, the successor of Calamy and Say, preached to the Presbyterian Church at Westminster. Kippis was not eminent as a preacher; but in literature and in ecclesiastical politics he held a distinguished position. He was best known by his contemporaries in these two capacities; now, his celebrity is confined, for the most part, to his literary labours. As a writer in the "Gentleman's Magazine" and the "Monthly Review;" as the editor, for many years of the last-named periodical, and as the editor of the "Biographia Britannica," Dr. Kippis rendered an unusual service. Standing at the head of two fountains of literature, he did what no man before him had done, —gave a just proportion to Dissenting politics, history, and biography. His activity on behalf of the civil rights of Dissenters was equal to his attachment to them. For forty years—until nearly the close of the century—no movement in connection with their common interests took place without its securing his open and undaunted support.

Another name which was never missed in any movement connected with the extension of religious freedom was that of Dr. Philip Furneaux, of the Presbyterian Church at Clapham. Dr. Furneaux was celebrated for his extensive and accurate memory, to which the preservation of Lord Mansfield's judgment in the City of London Sheriffs' case is due. He was the author of an admirable essay on Toleration, in which the principles of Dissent were argued on the broadest ground. He also, with Dr. Priestley, defended the Dissenters, with great vigour and ability, from the malicious and unworthy attack on their principles made by Justice Blackstone, in his " Commentaries on the Laws of England." Dr. Furneaux, towards the end of his life, entirely lost his reason. Dr. Samuel Chandler, of the Old Jewry, was of still greater eminence. In the contemporary histories of this period his name is to be found occupying a position similar to that which was formerly occupied by Calamy. He headed deputations, and more often apparently, than any other man, presided at public and private conferences. He was far, however, from being a merely ornamental member of the Presbyterian body. He was one of the first and ablest writers against the Deists, and the author of a " History of Persecution," in which the interference of human law with religious matters was assailed as being necessarily opposed to justice, as well as to liberty. On dissenting questions he was one of the most frequent and vigorous writers of his age. It appears, however, that Dr. Chandler would not have been unwilling, providing that the constitution of the Established Church were altered, to belong to that Church. He was, at one time, engaged with Archbishop Herring, Goold, Bishop of Norwich, and Sherlock, Bishop of Salisbury, in discussing terms of comprehension for Dissenters, in which he does not appear to have advanced very greatly, if at all, beyond the ground adopted by the later Puritans. As a writer on the Evidences of Religion, on Biblical Exegesis, and on

Religious Liberty, he had few equals,* and no man, for nearly fifty years, was more honoured by his generation.† His successor in the ministry at the Old Jewry, Dr. Thomas Amory, the editor of Chandler's works and the writer of his life, carried on the same work, but while Chandler was one of the few eminent Presbyterian ministers who were not either Arians or Socinians, Dr. Amory was inclined to Arianism. ‡

The defence of the public interests of Dissenters was undertaken, for the most part, by the Unitarians. Although the creed of this section of the Free Churches was still under the ban of law, that law had already become a dead letter. No one presumed to put it in operation. There were churches which openly declared themselves to be Unitarian. Presbyterian they still were in name, and in one characteristic of old Presbyterianism they were also Presbyterian in practice. They recognized no creeds, and no confessions of faith were adopted by them. But they had abandoned the doctrinal foundations of the later Puritans. Instead of Baxter and Howe, Samuel Clarke and Whiston were their favourite authors. But, in relation to the civil liberties of Dissenters, such men as Priestley and Price were far in advance of their ancestors. It is remarkable that the class of which these eminent men were the principal representatives, instead of suffering in numbers because of their conspicuous advocacy of their liberties, were, at this time, rapidly

---

* As an indication of Dr. Chandler's industry, it may be stated that the list of his writings in the new Catalogue of the British Museum Library, occupies seventeen pages. Some publications, of course, are duplicates.

† "Protestant Dissenters' Magazine," vol. 1. Wilson's "Dissenting Churches," ii. 360—385.

‡ "British Biography," art. "Amory."

increasing. Amongst the Congregationalists the only man who apparently took a very active interest in public questions was Caleb Fleming, and his doctrinal sympathies were with the Unitarians. The Baptists were somewhat better represented, but the body, as a whole, was not in a prosperous condition, and was largely occupied with the discussion of distinctive Baptist and Calvinistic doctrines. Two new sects had just made their appearance in England—the Sandemanians and the Swedenborgians; but, as yet, their influence on religious thought was only nominal. The Established Church, drugged by an indolent and luxurious spirit, was asleep, and, while it slept, Methodism on the one hand, and Unitarianism on the other, were gaining ground on every side.

It was owing, mainly, to the existence of the Unitarian element in the Church that a movement was commenced in the year 1771 for the abolition of subscription to the Articles by clergymen and other professional men. In that year Archdeacon Blackburne published "Proposals" suggesting that a petition to Parliament for relief should be drawn up, and a meeting was held for organizing a movement in its favour. Blackburne's proposals met with considerable approval, and on July 17th a meeting of the clergy was held at the Feathers' Tavern, and a form of petition, drawn up by Blackburne, adopted. The petitioners enlarged on the rights of reason and conscience, and maintained that each man had been constituted a judge for himself in searching the Scriptures, and what might or might not be proved thereby. Their subscriptions, they said, precluded them from exercising this right; they were a hindrance to the progress of religion, they discouraged inquiry, and they gave a handle to unbelievers to vilify the clergy by representing them as guilty of prevarication. The cases of the clergy and of professional men were separately stated, and both parties prayed earnestly for relief.* This petition was no sooner adopted than vigorous measures were taken to procure support for it. The most active person in this work was the Rev. Theophilus Lindsey, vicar of Catterick, afterwards one of the most eminent Unitarian ministers in London, who, in the following winter, travelled two thousand miles to obtain signatures. His success, however, was but small. Most of the clergymen he found to be indifferent, while from the Methodists he met nothing but opposition and repulse.† This body, indeed, used its utmost influence to prevent the prayer of the petition being granted. Lady Huntingdon, especially, exerted herself with all her characteristic activity against it. She procured counter petitions; she waited on members of the House of Commons, and she obtained from Lord North, then First Lord of the Treasury, and from Edmund Burke, a promise to oppose the bill.‡

The measure was introduced into the House of Commons on February 6th, A.D. 1772, by Sir William Meredith, who, in his opening speech, enlarged on the imperfection, absurdity, and unintelligibleness of the Articles, and stated that there was no clergyman who thoroughly believed them in a literal and grammatical sense, as he was required to do by the nature of his subscription. The most obvious line of argument against

---

* "Parliamentary History," xvii. 245.
† Belsham's "Memoirs of Lindsey," p. 49.
‡ "Memoirs of the Countess of Huntingdon," ii. 286.

the petitioners was immediately adopted by Sir Roger Newdigate, who asked, with what face persons, who had subscribed, who did not believe in what they had subscribed, and who were therefore devoid of common honesty, could come to the bar of that House? After several speeches had been delivered, Lord North rose and stated the views of the Government. The most effective part of his speech was that which exposed the confusion which would be likely to follow the adoption of the bill. The rector, he remarked, would be preaching one doctrine and his curate another; the morning lecturer would preach in favour of the Trinity, and the evening lecturer against it. Burke followed Lord North. References having been made to the Dissenters by one speaker, who had suggested the danger to the Church which might ensue if they, also, were to be relieved from subscription, "Let him recollect," said Burke, "along with the injuries, the services which Dissenters have done to our Church and to our State. If they have once destroyed, more than once they have saved them. This is but common justice, which they and all mankind have a right to." The ablest speech in favour of the bill was delivered, at the close of an eight hours' debate, by Sir George Savile, whose impassioned eloquence is reported to have produced an astonishing impression on the House. Sir George Savile derided the notion of confining the Church within the narrowest limits, and he had no fear of sectaries. "Sectaries," he cried; "had it not been for the sectaries, this cause had been tried at Rome. Some gentlemen," he added, " talk of raising barriers about the Church of God, and protecting His honour. Barriers about the Church of God, Sir? The Church of God can protect itself." The debate had a curious ending by Lord North, in reply to Sir William Meredith, denying that he had said that the Articles were conformable to Scripture. The bill was then thrown out by 217 to 71 votes.* The motion was renewed in the two following years, and defeated with equal decision. After the third defeat several clergymen left the Church, and openly joined the Unitarians.† Blackburne, however, the promoter of the movement, retained his preferments, openly saying that he could not afford to give up his means of living. The movement, from the beginning, had no chance whatever of success. The majority of the people cared nothing for it, and statesmen and bishops were far too conservative to pull down one of the oldest foundations of the Established Church. But the rejection of the bill did not secure any greater unity of thought than had hitherto been characteristic of the Church. The Articles were signed, and not believed, just as before. It does not seem to have occurred to the Government, or to the clerical opponents of the bill, that the scandals attending subscription might have been removed without removing subscription itself—that boys of sixteen years of age, and physicians, might, at least, have been exempted from confessing their belief in the Thirty-nine Articles. The clergy could not reasonably have expected exemption. Church Establishments and liberty of thought cannot co-exist; or, if they do, those in the Church who exercise that liberty will always expose themselves to a reasonable suspicion of their

* "Parliamentary History," xvii. 245, 296.
† Belsham's Memoirs of Lindsey."

intellectual, if not of their moral, dishonesty. One of the first objects of the Established Church in England, and one of the reasons of its foundation, was to limit the liberty of opinion respecting theological and ecclesiastical subjects, and to do so by two methods—first, by conferring pay and privilege on those who would come into the terms of the State; and, secondly, by punishing all who would not accept those terms. The petitioning clergy had both pay and privilege: it was hardly to be expected that they should have liberty as well.

In the gallery of the House of Commons, during the first debate of this question, there sat two Dissenting ministers—the Rev. Edward Pickard, of Carter's Lane Presbyterian Church, and Dr. Furneaux. These gentlemen heard several members suggest that the Dissenters might apply, with good prospect of success, for their relief from subscription. Amongst others, Lord North remarked that, had a similar application been made by them, he should have seen no reasonable objection to it; for, said the premier, "they desire no emoluments from the Church."* Pickard and Furneaux accordingly laid the matter before their brethren, and it was resolved by the General Body of Dissenting Ministers, and by the Committee of Deputies, that a Bill should be prepared and brought in. At this time the law, as defined by the Toleration Act, required all Dissenting ministers, tutors, and schoolmasters, to subscribe the doctrinal Articles. Those who did not were subject to fines, imprisonment, and banishment. It was impossible for Unitarians to do this, and they therefore braved the consequences of refusal. It was now proposed to sub-

* Belsham's "Memoirs of Lindsey," pp. 65, 66.

stitute for this subscription a declaration in the following words :—" That we believe the Holy Scriptures of the Old and New Testament to contain a revelation of the mind and will of God, and that we receive them as the rule of our faith and practice." No time was lost in forwarding this measure, for on the third of April, in 1772 the same year, the Bill, which was in charge of Sir Henry Hoghton and Edmund Burke, was under debate in the House of Commons. Although it gave great alarm to High Churchmen, and excited one member, Sir William Dolben, to characterize it as a " wicked " measure, it passed its first stage without a division, and on April 14th the second reading was carried by 70 votes to 9.* It reached the House of Lords in the next month, but was not debated until it was before the Committee of the House. Here it received the support of the most eminent men amongst the peers, Lord Chatham, Lord Camden, and Lord Mansfield, amongst the number. The weight of the Court and the Bench of Bishops was sufficient, however, to defeat it. Five bishops, headed by the Archbishop of York, spoke against it, and only one, Green, Bishop of Lincoln, in its favour. " Green! Green!" exclaimed the king, when he heard of this, " he shall never be translated."† The Bill was lost by 86 to 28 votes. It was on this occasion that, in reply to Drummond, Archbishop of York, the Earl of Chatham made a memorable defence of the Dissenters. The Archbishop had charged the Dissenting ministers with being men of a "close ambition." " This," exclaimed the statesman, " is judging unchari-

---

* " Parliamentary History," xvii. 431.
† Dyer's " Life of Robert Robinson," p. 78.

tably; and whoever brings such a charge, without evidence, defames. The Dissenting ministers are represented as men of close ambition: they are so, my lords; and their ambition is to keep close to the college of fishermen, not of cardinals; and to the doctrines of inspired apostles, not to the decrees of interested and aspiring bishops. They contend for a scriptural and spiritual worship; we have a Calvinistic creed, a Popish liturgy, and Arminian clergy. The Reformation has laid open the Scriptures to all; let not the bishops shut them again. Laws in support of ecclesiastical power are pleaded, which it would shock humanity to execute. It is said religious sects have done great mischief when they were not kept under restraints; but history affords no proof that sects have ever been mischievous when they were not oppressed and persecuted by the ruling Church."

Having nearly the whole weight of the popular branch of the legislature in their favour, the Dissenters were not dismayed by their treatment from the Lords. On March 2nd, A.D. 1773, the Bill was again brought in, carried on the second reading by 87 to 34 votes, and through Committee by 69 to 16 votes, and at the last stage by 65 to 14 votes. A new feature was introduced into the question this year, and threatened, at one time, to be fatal to it. Several Dissenters, including some in London, Liverpool, Bolton, Exeter, Dursley, and Wotton-under-Edge, petitioned against it, on the ground, amongst other reasons, that "if it should pass into law it would undermine the establishment of religion."* A meeting of Dissenting ministers was also held in London

* "Parliamentary History," xv. 786.

to oppose it, at which resolutions were passed protesting against the measure. It appears from these resolutions that fears were entertained of the growth of Popery and Unitarianism,* but how the former would be affected it is difficult to see, while the latter had obviously increased and was increasing in spite of all legal prohibitions to the contrary. These petitions, however, had no weight, nor did the second successful passage of the measure through the Commons at all affect the determination of the king and the bishops. It was again decisively rejected.

From the Lords the Dissenters had, as had been their habit, appealed to the people. An admirable opportunity had been given to them to re-affirm and defend the principle of religious liberty, and they took the utmost advantage of it. The Rev. Ebenezer Radcliffe, of Poor Jewry Lane, boldly attacked the bishops;† the Rev. Isaac Maudit, Kippis, Furneaux, Gibbons, Stennett, and Robert Robinson, laid down anew the rights of conscience. These were well-known men, and they were the customary standard-bearers of Dissent. But another name, destined to acquire an equal eminence, now appeared. This was that of the Rev. Joshua Toulmin, Presbyterian minister of Birmingham, who, in two "Letters on the late applications to Parliament of Protestant Dissenting Ministers," ably dealt with the whole question. Most of these publications breathed a stronger spirit of defiance of the bishops and clergy than had ever before been shown by Dissenting ministers.

* Ivimey, iv. 31, 32.

† "Two Letters addressed to the Right Reverend Prelates who a second time rejected the Dissenters Bill," A.D. 1773.

They indicate that since the Toleration Act had passed there had been a growth, not merely of opinion respecting the claims of the Church, but of determination to resist those claims. Radcliffe, while he protested that "the oratory of all the Dissenting ministers in this kingdom could not prevail upon one man to attempt so ridiculous a project as that of pulling down the hierarchy," protested, with equal force, that he looked upon the conduct of the hierarchy with pity, indignation, and contempt. "You have put," he said, "a negative upon the lawful exercise of our religion; but you cannot make the world believe that religion itself depends upon, or is connected with, the will of the magistrates; you have limited the freedom of the Gospel, but you have not destroyed Christianity. Do you expect we should comply with your requisitions?" "Do not confound your principles with those of the State, nor your cause with that of Christianity, for fear they should disown your alliance."* "Many Dissenting ministers," said Dr. Stennett, "cannot conscientiously subscribe the Articles, as they apprehend the civil magistrates' requiring subscription to explanatory articles of faith, to be an invasion upon the rights of conscience, and the sole authority of Christ as King in His Church." Kippis declared that the Dissenters now denied the right of any body of men, whether civil or ecclesiastical, to impose human tests, creeds, or articles, and that they protested against such an imposition as a violation of men's essential liberty to judge and act for themselves in matters of religion."† Maudit, also, frankly acknowledged the change

---

* Radcliffe's Letter, pp. 83, 96. † Kippis's " Vindication," p. 29.

which had taken place.* But no writer more clearly illustrated this change than Robert Robinson, who, with unparalleled vigour and vivacity, attacked the whole system of human authority in matters of belief and of human legislation for the Christian Church. " Let any impartial inquirer," he said, "take up the Holy Scriptures, and ask whither do all the contents of these ancient writings tend? History, prophecy, miracles, the ceremonies of the Old, and the reasonings of the New Testament; the legislation of Moses, and the mission of Jesus Christ, to what do they tend? What is their aim? The proper answer would be, their professed end is to give glory to God in the highest, and on earth peace, and benevolence amongst men. . . . Now, to be a Christian is neither more nor less than to concur with this design: so much of this, so much true religion, the rest is *vox prætereaque nihil.* . . . What are the proper means of obtaining this end? One sect of Christians proposes oaths, subscriptions to creeds, fines and imprisonments; another proceeds to execrations, corporal punishments, and death, in various frightful shapes, itself. The present petitioners, supposing these means contrary to the nature of things, contrary also to the means prescribed by the Founder of religion, propose the abolition of the present penal means, and the introduction of the original mode of tuition."† " Piety and plunder," he exclaimed, " religion and murder, the service of God and the slaughter of His image!" Three years after writing this, Robinson, in the " History and Mystery of Good

* Maudit's " Case of the Dissenting Ministers," p. 15.

† " Arcana ; or, the Triumphs of the late Petitioners to Parliament for Relief in the Matter of Subscription." Preface, A.D. 1774.

Friday," returned to the attack. Dealing with the hierarchy, he wrote—"The cool, disinterested part of mankind consider a hierarchy as they consider a standing military force in absolute monarchies, where the main principle of the constitution is that of governing by fear —an hierarchy is essentially necessary to the despotism of the prince; but in free states an hierarchy will always justly be an object of jealousy. Hierarchical powers have found many a state free, and reduced each to slavery; but there is no instance of their having brought an enslaved state into Christian liberty." He then proceeded to dwell upon the vices that disgraced the priesthood. They were six—ignorance, perjury, ambition, avarice, time-serving, and hypocrisy: "Perjury," he said, "if they subscribe upon oath their belief in propositions which they have either not examined, or do not believe." Avarice, "ten thousand times more tenacious of a fourpenny Easter offering than of all the Ten Commandments." "What said you," he inquired, addressing a clergyman, "to the Dissenting clergy, whom you flatter and soothe, and call brethren in Christ? Are they freed from oaths, and subscriptions, and penal laws? Christian liberty! thou favourite offspring of Heaven! thou firstborn of Christianity! I saw the wise and pious servants of God nourish thee in their houses, and cherish thee in their bosoms! I saw them lead thee into public view: all good men hailed thee! the generous British Commons caressed and praised thee, and led thee into an Upper House, and there—there thou didst expire in the holy lap of Spiritual Lords!"

Such attacks, renewed and reiterated, the bishops of this period could, of all men, least afford to have brought against them. Nor could the Church afford to have her foundations re-examined and her breastworks so ruthlessly assailed. Whether from fear of prolonging the controversy, therefore, or whether from a desire of engaging the Dissenters in measures for the relief of Roman Catholics, they suddenly and unexpectedly surrendered. Preaching, on January 30th, in the [year 1779, before the House of Lords, Ross, Bishop of Exeter, took occasion to express his earnest wish that toleration might be extended, and that Dissenters might have a legal security for the free exercise of their worship. Acting upon this hint, the old Bill, slightly modified, was again brought in, and passed both Houses with scarcely any opposition. The declaration, substituted by this Act* for the previous subscription to the Articles, required Dissenters, as a condition of exercising the office of minister or preacher, to assert their personal Christianity and Protestantism by their belief in the Scriptures. This was the first step in the direction of enlarged toleration for ninety years, and at the end of even this long period it could not be accomplished excepting by a compromise.

While the attention of Dissenters was thus engaged in securing an extension of their religious rights, the Evangelical party in the Established Church, combined with the Calvinistic Methodists, were absorbed in a controversy with John Wesley and some of his followers, on the relative merits of Calvinism and Arminianism. At the Methodist Conference of A.D. 1770, Wesley procured the passage of a special minute, declaratory of the opposition of the Conference to the distinctive doctrines

* 19 Geo. III., cap. 44.

www.ingramcontent.com/pod-product-compliance
Lightning Source LLC
Chambersburg PA
CBHW051851300426
44117CB00006B/355